MW00658164

Old Garrison House

NEW ENGLAND CAPTIVES CARRIED TO CANADA

Between 1677 and 1760
During the French and Indian Wars

VOLUME 1

By Emma Lewis Coleman

HERITAGE BOOKS
2004

HERITAGE BOOKS

AN IMPRINT OF HERITAGE BOOKS, INC.

A Facsimile Reprint
Published 2004 by
HERITAGE BOOKS, INC.
Publishing Division
65 East Main Street
Westminster, Maryland 21157-5026

— Publisher's Notice —
In reprints such as this, it is often not possible to remove blemishes from the original. We feel the contents of this book warrant its reissue despite these blemishes and hope you will agree and read it with pleasure.

International Standard Book Number: 1-55613-257-3

A. W. Elson & Co. Belmont, Mass.

C. Alice Baker

IN MEMORY OF

C. ALICE BAKER

PREFACE

THE first New Englanders "could till the soil and expect a harvest"; their children and grandchildren were every hour in jeopardy of death or of a merciless captivity.

This book concerns those who "captivated by the Indian Salvages" in the French and Indian wars were carried to Canada — the first in 1677, the last in 1760.

Of the captives of one war Cotton Mather wrote: "'Tis impossible that I should know all that happened; and it would be improper for me to write all that I know. And very little is the advantage of having a name standing upon record only among unhappy sufferers."

Unlike this illustrious writer, I name all I know, hoping there may be "advantage" to some.

In 1897 Miss C. Alice Baker printed privately a collection of papers entitled "True Stories of New England Captives Carried to Canada During the Old French and Indian Wars." She wrote in its preface: "As often as I have read in the annals of the early settlers of New England the pathetic words 'Carried captive to Canada whence they came not back' I have longed to know the fate of the captives."

To learn their fate she went several times to Canada, trying first to trace members of her own family, then the search grew wider, and we, for I always worked with her, copied from many a parish register the names[1] we knew and the names we guessed, for the phonetic spelling of the registrars — ignorant of the English language — made guessing imperative.

In this book their spelling has been kept, but frequently marks of punctuation have been added.

Miss Baker left some of this material unused. In memory of her work I have tried to do with it what she would have wished; joining as far as possible the Canadian and New England threads

[1] Non-Catholic records begin in 1766.

and extending it through the long period of French and Indian warfare.

Because her own volume is out of print, and because I wish to make my lists as complete as possible, I repeat in less detail the stories of those captives about whom she wrote, and for which writing Mr. Parkman said "We are all your debtors."

Much help has been given me during the long making of the book. I wish especially to thank the officers of the Massachusetts Historical Society, Mr. Ford, Mr. Tuttle and his assistants; and Mr. Edmonds and Miss Farnum of the Massachusetts Archives; from them I have asked most and received most.

To all whom I can name and to all others, as if named, I offer my grateful acknowledgments. To Mr. Fitzpatrick and Miss Spofford of the Manuscript Division of the Congressional Library and Mr. Parker of Dr. Jameson's staff; to the New Hampshire Historical Society; the New England Historic Genealogical Society; to Col. Charles E. Banks and Mr. C. T. Libby, authorities for Maine families; to Mr. George Francis Dow and Mr. Albert Matthews; to Prof. W. B. Munro of Harvard and Dr. T. A. Jenkins of Chicago University; to Mr. F. J. Audet and Miss Smillie of the Canadian Archives in Ottawa; and Mr. P. G. Roy and Mr. E. Z. Massicotte of the Districts of Quebec and Montreal; to the Hon. D. C. Scott of Ottawa and the Hon W. D. Lighthall of Montreal, to Mr. Lapalice of the Fabrique of Notre-Dame, Montreal; and to the nuns and priests who have courteously answered my letters.

E. L. C.

The Fenway 42
Boston

CONTENTS

ILLUSTRATIONS

"There is no peace to him that goeth out, nor to him that cometh in."

"We gat our bread with the price of our lives, because of the sword of the wilderness."

CHAPTER I

THE WARS — DEFENCE

THE real cause of contentions among men is the ambition to take what does not belong to them." In the seventeenth, as alas in the twentieth century, men killed each other for that ambition.

The beginning of hostilities between the French and English in North America was in 1613 — seven years before the Mayflower came. The end was the Peace of Paris in 1763. The beginning was in Acadia, so-called, at Somes Sound, Mount Desert, when Captain Argall cut down at Saint-Sauveur the cross which had been placed there by the little colony of Jesuits and courtiers who had been sent out by the pious Madame de Guercheville.

The last intercolonial war ended with the Cession of Canada. In all the wars captives, mostly women and children, were carried from New England to Canada.

The friendship between the Indians and whites, both French and English, was doubtless based upon trade. Both colonies were eager to buy furs. Each was jealous of the other and so the chief cause of our intercolonial trouble was commercial. This is shown by the reports sent to Versailles by the governors of Canada. They are always afraid that the English and Dutch "by means of the cheap bargains they can give[1] will become masters of all the peltries thereby destroying the industry upon which Canada subsists."[2]

[1] See Chapter III. [2] N. Y. Docs., IX, 405.

Philip's War. 1675-1678. Treaty of Falmouth, signed under "The Smoking Tree" near Long Creek between Portland and Scarborough.

It was in this, a strictly Indian war, that the first captives were carried to Canada. After the death of Philip his scattered followers sold their New England prisoners to the French. If the Indians had not profited by the ransoms paid for the group of Hatfield and Deerfield people there would have been less suffering in later wars. They boasted that if they were successful "Canada Indians" would follow them.

First Intercolonial War — King William's, 1688-1697. "The Decade of Sorrows." Peace of Ryswick.

"Canada Indians," however, did not "follow" for eleven years. Then the war between France and England was brought over to their colonies. The right of William and Mary to the English throne was disputed by Louis XIV, who upheld James II. Apparently some New Englanders were less concerned than he, for a bold pamphlet was printed in London in 1691 entitled: "The Humble Address of the Publicans of New England to which King you please with some Remarks Upon it." But as the "Publicans" were uncertain whom they were humbly addressing, so had been their King two years earlier when he sent Letters of Instruction "To Such as for the Time being take Care for preserving the Peace and Administering the Laws in Our Colony of the Massachusetts Bay in New England in America."

During this war many of our people travelled the long, sad road to Canada. Of the first summer's campaign Governor de Denonville reported that because "of the good understanding he has had through two Jesuits with the Indians who occupy the woods in the neighborhood of Boston,[3] and who are disposed to become Christians, he has been able . . . to seize, exclusive of Pemkuit, sixteen forts."[4] This sounds boastful! After the massacre

[3] New England. [4] N. Y. Docs., IX, 438.

at Dover, which was an Indian revenge, attacks were made by French soldiers and Mission Indians, usually led by French officers and often aided by priestly zeal, on Pemaquid, Salmon Falls and Casco Bay; then on York, Oyster River and Groton; while all the time there was frontier warfare between the Connecticut River on the western and the Kennebec on the eastern border.

In May, 1697, at a castle belonging to William III near the village of Ryswick, a treaty was signed and peace came slowly across the seas. Four years later the ambition of Louis XIV to keep the crown of Spain for his grandson plunged all western Europe into the "War of the Spanish Succession" which in the New World became:

The Second Intercolonial War — Queen Anne's or Governor Dudley's War, 1702-1713. Peace of Utrecht.

New England bore its stress. Her settlements were scattered, unprotected and easily reached; weaker than New York, who had powerful friends in the Indians of the Five Nations (the Iroquois), she often received cruel punishment in revenge for Indian attacks upon Canada. It is difficult to understand how a civilized people could identify themselves with savage warfare, especially a people who knew the horrors of torture and massacre as did those of New France; but we must remember that the French believed the Iroquois were instigated by the colonists of New York and that Frontenac counted us all one people, "so if Albany provokes Canada they count it just to fall upon Massachusetts or any other Eastern Plantation."[5] New France asserted that she did not wait to be attacked. It was her way to strike terror rather than to be disturbed herself, knowing well that the Abenakis at a trifling expense could "greatly inconvenience" New England. To realize her success we need only mention the "inconvenience" at Wells, Deerfield, Haverhill, and all the border raids of this war. Scarcely a village escaped.

[5] Sewall's Letter-Book, Vol. I, 114.

In 1713 the Treaty of Utrecht brought peace of a sort. But the treaty did not settle important questions for the Western Continent where always the great issue was that of domination — French or English. But perhaps the Indian allegiance was of more vital interest to the people of that generation. The Five Nations were called British subjects, but the Abenakis of northern New England, claimed by both powers, were by French policy left within the boundaries of Maine.

Three Years' War, or Governor Dummer's — Father Rale's — Lovewell's, 1722-1725/6. Treaty of Boston.

By all these names has this war been called. The quarrel was between the two provinces of Massachusetts and New Hampshire and the Eastern Indians, especially those of Norridgewock.

The French openly had no part in it for the two Crowns were at peace, but when in 1724 the Norridgewocks asked for help Louis XIV wrote that while it is not expedient that France appear in this war, yet it is proper that Sr. de Vaudreuil "do secretly encourage the other nations to assist the Abenakis" by telling them that the English intend to become masters of the whole continent and to enslave all the Indian nations.[6] In revenge for the attempt to capture Father Rale the Indians burned the village of Brunswick, and then Massachusetts declared war. People were killed and prisoners taken from the eastern settlements and from far-away Northfield. Norridgewock was burned and Father Rale killed, although orders had been given to spare his life. Three of the four officers in command of the little troop had been captives in earlier wars. They were Captains Harmon and Moulton and Lieutenant Bean or Bane.

There were fewer atrocities in this war. The priest's intervention may have prevented some, but the chief reason was Governor Shute's order that non-combatants be removed from exposed places.[7]

[6] N. Y. Docs., IX, 936. [7] One instance of compliance was at Kittery, where thirty-six houses were made "defencible" and all the families were ordered to "Lodge therein."

When M. de Vaudreuil was consulted about a peace he answered that it did not concern the French,[8] and the Mission Indians of his country refused the belts of peace because they "wished to continue to harass the English." Nevertheless, in the Council Chamber at Boston in December, 1725, Dummer's treaty — now in the State House — was signed by four eastern sagamores and Lieutenant-Governor Dummer, who had been acting since 1723, when Shute ran away to England. Were these the four Indians who were presented two years later with elegant clothing? "A Broad Cloth Coat Trim^{d} with Silver Lace" and three blankets similarly adorned; with ruffled shirts and "a hatt with gold lace?"[9]

Third Intercolonial War — King George's War — Shirley's or Five Years' War — Locally the Old French and Indian. In Europe the War of the Austrian Succession, 1744-1748. Peace of Aix-la-Chapelle.

Frederick of Prussia began it. The shot he fired in Silesia in 1741 was heard the whole world over. Almost all the European powers became involved, and ultimately fire and carnage were brought again to our border.

After Norridgewock was burned the savages went to Canada "in deplorable condition," assuring the governor that so long as there is an Abenaki in the world they will fight the English; and the governor assures Versailles that they will do it unless the English destroy their forts and cease their encroachments.[10] Nevertheless, during the next twenty years New England was not much disturbed, partly because French influence had been somewhat lessened and partly because of better trading-houses and fairer treatment under Dummer's direction.

Thirty-five separate bands of Indians, counting from six to thirty-six men, were sent out in the winter and spring of 1746. They were sent "in the direction of Orange," or "to strike a blow towards Boston." Much property was destroyed and some scalps,

[8] Que. Docs., III, 126. [9] Arch. 31, 156. [10] Que. Docs., III, 114.

but not many prisoners, were brought back, says the French report.[11]

The treaty said: "All things shall be restored," but Frederick kept Silesia. In August, 1748, Canada, learning that the war was over, notified the nations that they were to send no more war-parties to New England, and that they would not be paid for prisoners or scalps. But the Government feared that the domiciliated Abenakis might continue their hostilities, not having satisfied their revenge for the warriors they had lost.[12]

Fourth Intercolonial War. In Europe, The Seven Years' War; in the Colonies, The Last French and Indian War. 1755/6-1763. The Peace of Paris.

This, the sixth and last Indian war of the century, was almost continuous with that which preceded it for the treaty of Aix-la-Chapelle, which was ratified by the Indians at Falmouth, was little more than a truce. The boundaries between Canada and the British colonies were still undetermined.

War was declared against the Penobscots in 1755, England making her declaration against France the next year. The general cause was the alleged encroachments of the French upon the English frontiers. Nova Scotia, ceded to Great Britain in 1713, was still claimed by France. Fort St. Frederick (Crown Point) was being strengthened, and forts were building from the head of the St. Lawrence to the Mississippi River. But hostile acts did not wait upon hostile words, and we find in that smaller part of the drama which concerns our writing that New Englanders were carried to Canada as early as 1750. It was in 1760, after the war was over, that the last captives made "the doleful journey."

For the French and English in America the questions of a century and a half had been answered on the Heights of Abraham.

[11] Que. Docs., III, 272. [12] "Journal of Occurrences," N. Y. Docs., X, 174.

Defence

Preparedness was not unknown but it was limited; nor was it popular. Colonel Westbrook, writing in 1724, says: "The people generally preach up peace to themselves, if the Indians do not knock some in the head in Six or Seven days."[13]

During King Philip's War the Massachusetts Council, endeavoring to protect the "whole country of Esex & a great part of midlesex" from the inroads of the heathen, asked twenty towns to consider the building of a fence — not a real Chinese wall — but "a fence of stockades or stones (as the matter best suteth) to be made about eight foot high . . . which fence . . . is not in length above twelve miles; a good part whereof is allready don by large ponds that wil conveniently fal in the line."[14] The towns were not eager to comply, one of them (Marblehead) saying that as the Merrimac River was fordable in several places the benefit hoped for would "no wayes counter-ballance the vast charge."

Men had to be pressed into service; to avoid which one at least quoted Scripture, for "the Law of God is plaine that when a man hath taken a new wife, he shall not goo out to warr . . . but he shall be free at home one yeare." (Deuteronomy 24: 5). And the "Law of God" prevailed. Nathaniel Byfield did not go.[15]

In King William's War Maine was poorly prepared as is shown by a Report from York, which counts less than two hundred soldiers in all the garrisons from Casco to the Piscataqua,[16] and the supplies of ammunition, food and clothing were meagre.

In 1694 an Act was passed, which continued during Queen Anne's War, prohibiting the desertion of frontier towns; even though many of their inhabitants had been killed or captured. A man could change his residence only by permission of the governor and council under pain of forfeiting his lands. Forasmuch as considerable sums had been expended in the defence and preservation of the out-towns and frontiers, it was enacted that they — naming eleven from Wells to Deerfield, and in later years increasing the

[13] Arch. 51, 406. [14] Arch. 68, 174. [15] Arch. 68, 231a. [16] Arch. 36, 52.

number — should not be broken up, for if they were deserted without permission being given for "their drawing off," it would lessen the strength of the province and the enemy would be encouraged.

Since the General Court ordered the people to stay in their exposed homes of the border it had to supply defence, but the "considerable sums" provided little, and very little help came from England. A letter sent from the King's Council to Massachusetts[17] in August, 1701, says that the Council had several times laid before His Majesty "the Desires" that war supplies be sent to the colony and a hope is held out that "some small quantity" may be sent in the future; yet Stoughton is told that the General Court must exert itself vigorously for defence, and the New England people were blamed in this as in other matters; but the gentlemen signed themselves: "Your very loving Friends." Versailles took better care of its colony.

In King William's War the frontier of Massachusetts could "be traced by a line beginning at Falmouth and running along the towns of Scarborough, Saco, Wells, York, Amesbury, Haverhill, Andover, Dunstable, Chelmsford, Lancaster and Worcester." The New Hampshire towns lay a little out of the track of the marauders, while "the seven outlying towns on the Connecticut were in some sort, though imperfectly, covered by New York and the friendly Iroquois."[18]

"Some proposalls Refferring to ye Deffence of ye Frontiers" in 1698[19] show that the garrisons at many of these places were at that time increased in numbers from two to twenty-five, with two or three scouting parties for them all, and the "Court was to consider the raising of a war tax." Frontier towns, in his majesty's name, required all male persons capable of bearing arms to take their arms and ammunition "to ye meeting-house evary Saboth day and at all other publick meetings," and also into the meadows and places where they worked, but if a man shot off a gun except at an Indian

[17] Arch. 70, 535. [18] Palfrey's New England, IV, 30. [19] Arch. 70, 380.

or a wolf he must forfeit five shillings, which amount he must also pay if he refused his above "dewty."[20] Five shillings was the whole of the soldier's weekly wage, yet there may have been waste somewhere for Penhallow says: "The charge of war was so great that every Indian Massachusetts had killed or taken cost at least £1000."[21] But we must remember that this was "old tenor" of Massachusetts currency, and also that it was many of us, but few of the Indians, who were "killed or taken." Frequently the men were "disadvantaged" in defence and pursuit by their lack of snowshoes. In 1702 the House "desired" the Governor to provide "so many good Serviceable snowshoes as they shall think needful with as many Indian shoes to be Disperst & lodged in the frontier Towns . . . that they may be ready if occasion should be, for the service against the Enemy."[22] But alas! They were not always "ready." Our men were less skilful in their use than were the French and Indians. A French officer wrote that "Raquettes were required only for those in advance for they make a hard path for those who follow and for the sledges dragged by the dogs."

New Hampshire ordered every householder at his own charge to procure "one good pair of snowshoes and mogasheens," or to be liable to a fine. They were obliged to keep them in repair and when damaged to replace them.

In Queen Anne's and the Three Years' War Massachusetts supplied them, allowing money for repairs, but in 1725/6, the war ending before the expiration of the year for which they had been provided, it was resolved that "the said Snow Shooe Men be not entitled to the three shillings mentioned." This was surely an economical order.

In the next war Governor Shirley told the Eastern Indians, then supposedly friendly, that they who would not fight must make snowshoes.

Wooden forts, block houses and garrison-houses were places of defence and refuge, and the terms are more or less interchange-

[20] This order is quoted from Newbury. [21] "Indian Wars," 48. [22] Arch. 70, 616.

able, especially the last two. The wooden fort was usually a stockade fence ten or twelve feet high enclosing cabins to shelter the people in case of alarm, and furnished at the corners with what were called flankers, which were boxes of thick plank, large enough to hold two or more men.[23] The Oxford Dictionary defines the block house originally as "a detached fort which blocked the access to a landing, a narrow channel or some strategical point." In later use — as in New England — it was a building "of one or more storeys, constructed chiefly of timber loop-holed and embrasured for firing." One of the largest was Vaughan's at Scarborough. In it during Queen Anne's war eleven families lived together seven years, "the war without made peace within" wrote the local historian.

Garrison-houses, so-called, sheltered the scattered soldiers of the garrison if there were any; but they were primarily places of refuge for the people. As the villages were open, few having the protection of a stockade, it was necessary to use those houses that were best situated or adapted for defence in times of peril. Throughout New England, to the latest time of Indian warfare, this was the common means of defence. Sometimes they had an overhanging story; not as was often said, "to shoot at savages," or "to pour boiling water upon their heads," but because it was the pretty fashion of the day. Bourne, writing of garrison-houses in Maine,[24] quotes these reasons and adds that the occupants could more easily extinguish fire if the enemy tried to burn the house, but he had never heard of boiling water being used.

If a garrison-house were to be built, permission must be asked, and the owner must consult the military commander and the chief person of the town. If a house already built were to be fortified for this purpose it was done at the town's charge.[25] In perilous times "All persons with their families" were commanded "to abide at the particular garrisons allowed by his Excellency whereto they

[23] Parkman's "Half-Century of Conflict," II, 230. [24] Maine Hist. Coll., VII, 113.
[25] Arch. 70, 339.

are orderly assigned in the towns respectively where they dwell, by the military commanding officer and the selectmen," and if any failed he was fined. This especial order was given in 1707, but it was the custom; the crowded, uncomfortable custom during the early wars. In March, 1691/2, in the eight garrisons of Groton there were living ninety-one men with their families.[26]

That preparations in 1711 were better than during King William's war is shown by "A List of the Frontier Garrisons" made in November of that year.[27] Wells had ten; York, twenty-one; Haverhill, twenty-five; Newichawannuck, sixteen; Dunstable, seven; Groton, eighteen; Lancaster, twenty-seven; and Marlborough, nineteen.

[26] Butler's Groton, 91. [27] Arch. 71, 871-6.

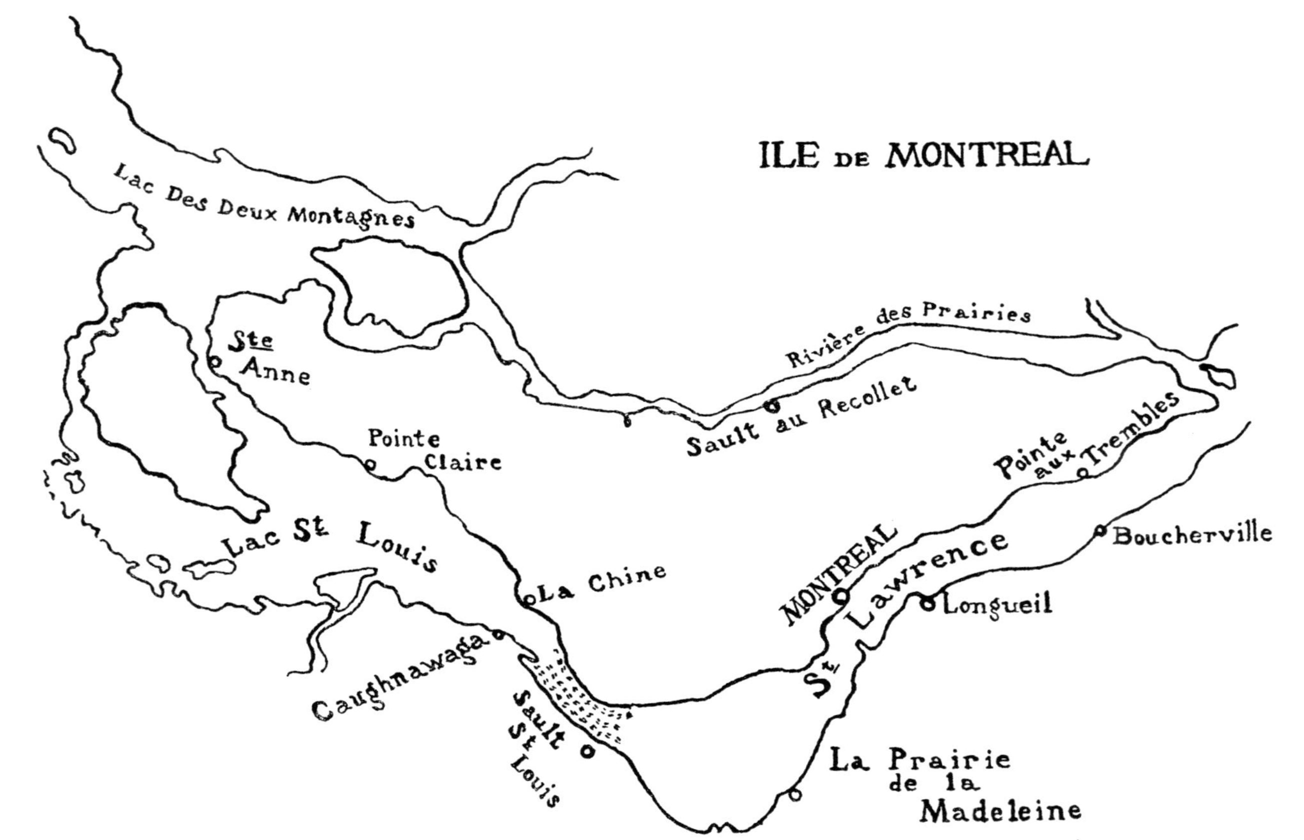
ILE DE MONTREAL
Lac Des Deux Montagnes
Rivière des Prairies
Ste Anne
Pointe Claire
Sault au Recollet
Pointe aux Trembles
Lac St Louis
La Chine
MONTREAL
St Lawrence
Boucherville
Longueil
Caughnawaga
Sault St Louis
La Prairie de la Madeleine

CHAPTER II

Missions and Missionaries[1]

In Canada — On Maine Rivers

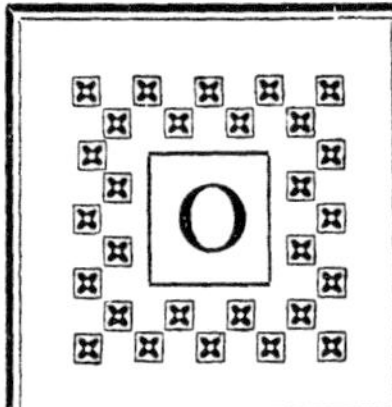

OUR Indian enemies in the Intercolonial Wars were almost without exception from the Missions. From those established on the rivers of Maine by priests going to Indian villages and from those in Canada, near Montreal, Three Rivers and Quebec; to which Indians from New England and New York had been urged to emigrate. And back to their mission-homes they carried our people, where today many of their kin are living. Because of this connection between the Missions and our captives their story may be told here.

For the beginning we must turn back to 1535 when Jacques Cartier, seeking always the passage to Cathay, sailed up the Great River of Canada. At the point where his course was barred by rapids he found an Indian town called Hochelaga. Greeted by "one of the principal lords of the said city" he gave to him "two hatchets, two knives and a crucifix, the last of which the Indian was invited to kiss." These were gifts many times repeated in Canadian history. He called the hill behind the town Mont Réal because of its beautiful outlook and from it island and city have both been named Montreal.

It was not to seek a passage to India, nor to build a New France,

[1] Among the authorities quoted are: The Lives of Marguerite Bourgeoys, Jeanne Mance, Maisonneuve, Laval, Saint-Vallier and Rale. Charlevoix (La Nouvelle-France), Parkman (histories and manuscripts). The histories of "Le Sault-au-Recollet," "Saint-François-du-Lac," "St. Lawrence and Franklin Counties," Maurault's "Abenakis" and Casgrain's "Missions," "The Redeemed Captive," Quebec and New York Documents and private letters.

nor yet to trade in furs that many Frenchmen followed Cartier across the sea. Religion urged them onward to strengthen the Church by converting the heathen of the New World.[2]

Champlain came sixty-eight years after Cartier and found Hochelaga deserted. He saw that *here* was a beautiful site for a settlement, and here, in 1642, was made an extraordinary one — conceived in mysticism and executed by religious zeal. No human agency was acknowledged, although Champlain's "Narrative" which described the place had been printed before the miracle happened. It was at his home in La Flèche, Anjou, that a very pious man, Jérôme Le Royer de la Dauversière, heard a voice commanding him to consecrate himself, his wife and their six children to the Holy Family; to found a hospital, or Hôtel-Dieu at Montreal — a place wholly unknown to him — and to establish a new order of nuns in honor of St. Joseph to conduct that hospital. On the same day, at Paris, a young priest, Jean Jacques Olier, heard a voice commanding *him* to form a Society of priests and to establish them at Montreal. The two, strangers until then, met in the Château of Meudon, and "as soon as they saw each other, one in the garb of a priest, the other wearing the sword of a gentleman, they called each other by name," and knew each other's secret thoughts and hopes.

To complete the mystic number of three they proposed to add a third community "to teach the Faith to the children, white and red." Then and there Montreal was founded. But this place of the miracle was a wilderness, and to supply patients, congregation and pupils it must be peopled.

A society was formed in Paris to provide money. The Island of Montreal was bought and a plan made to send out forty men to build a house for the priests and two convents for the nuns who were to be nurses and teachers.

When it was time to embark Olier had not founded his Semi-

[2] John Calvin had made many Protestant converts in France.

nary of priests and the Jesuits of Quebec were asked to take spiritual charge. Of course teachers were not needed, but there might be sickness, and for that the miracle did not fail. Jeanne Mance heard *her* divine call and hurrying to La Rochelle she met Dauversière, as by chance, at the church door and they knew each other, as Dauversière and Olier had done before.

The leader of the company which sailed from La Rochelle was that "devout and valiant gentleman," Paul de Chomedey, Sieur de Maisonneuve.

They approached Montreal in May, 1642, singing all together a hymn of praise. Parkman asks: "Is this true history or a romance of Christian chivalry" and answers: "It is both."

Later in Paris the settlement was consecrated to the Holy Family and was called Ville-Marie-de-Montréal, a sacred town, built for the honor of Christ, St. Joseph and the Virgin, typified by three persons on earth: the founders of the Seminary, Hôtel-Dieu and thc School.

The first act of the colony was one of piety if not of discretion, for even before the lands were tilled they built their hospital and Jeanne Mance lived in it, waiting for patients; while in France Dauversière was preparing the "daughters of St. Joseph" to nurse them.

The little group had been almost annihilated by the Iroquois when in 1653 M. de Maisonneuve went back to Paris for more men and more money. He went also to Troyes, where his sister was Superior of the Congregation nuns. These Sisters were eager for the Canadian mission, but cloistered women were not fitted for the work.

Connected with the convent, working outside, and of course without having taken vows, was a very gentle and devout woman, Marguerite Bourgeoys; not a mystic, yet destined to be the third in the sacred number and to found in New France the Order of the *Congrégation de Notre-Dame*, for which high purpose she crossed the ocean with Maisonneuve.

The Sulpitian priests sent out by M. Olier from his Seminary in Paris were called in Canada, as are their successors, "The Gentlemen of the Seminary."

The great Seigniory of the Island of Montreal and its adjacent places was later (1764) transferred to them from the Seminary of Paris and makes them one of the richest Societies in America.

Part of the building which they, in 1657, constructed out of Laurentian stone brought by glaciers from the farther north, is still standing. In it were kept until recently the registers of Notre-Dame parish in which were written baptismal, marriage and burial records of many of our captives, some of whom had been lost to their New England kin until found there.

Marguerite Bourgeoys' Sisterhood, consecrated to the Virgin, love to remember that her work began in a stable. In it cattle had been housed and doves flew in and out of the cote above.[3] It was beside the Hôtel-Dieu, the two Communities being close friends.[4]

The Sisters taught little boys and girls; all there were to teach! In the first fifteen years of the colony sixty children were born and one survived. She was their first pupil and stayed with them until she married.

The first Indian given to their care was a baby, neglected by its mother, who sold it for a string of beads. This little Iroquois baby — the first to be baptized — was named Marie des Neiges (Mary of the snow). Maisonneuve was her godfather. The annals say she died a holy death at the age of six![5]

Marguerite Bourgeoys came to the New World without the fraction of a farthing. For her personal use she brought one little bundle under her arm. Only that, "her blind confidence in God"

[3] School opened 1657.

[4] A sister of the Congregation, great-granddaughter of a captive from Kittery, Maine, and a very dear friend of ours, wrote: "We have had the most intimate relations with the hospital nuns. For two hundred years we have been neighbors — the walls of their enclosure touching ours. Many, many times we have from our two balconies sung hymns together.

[5] In 1685 forty Indian pupils had quitted their blankets. Two Iroquois women became nuns.

and a little image of the Virgin, a miraculous image, which gave her fellow-passengers a daily supply of wheat and caused the empty wine-barrel to give a full supply for the three months of the passage.

The Mother-House of her Order on Saint-Jean-Baptiste Street was begun with a capital of forty sous. In the very many buildings today there are over forty thousand pupils and more than three thousand Sisters to look after them.

It is interesting to note that Sister Bourgeoys established, too, the first school of domestic science in America. It was called "La Providence" and there the Sisters instructed some twenty older girls — New England captives among them — "in all the work of their sex, in order that they might earn their living."

The Mission of the Mountain

The Gentlemen of the Seminary, not making many converts when they went to Indian villages, determined to bring the Indians to the town, and they established — just outside it — the Mission of the Mountain.

The wigwams of the Iroquois and Hurons, some of them already converts, surrounded the palisade which enclosed a chapel and some huts of bark. In one of these huts lived the two Sisters sent by Marguerite Bourgeoys to teach little Indian girls and later little captive English girls.

When in 1669 some hospital nuns came out from France the parish priest took them through forest and marsh out to the Mission, and the Indians, to celebrate their coming, made a feast. The Sisters found the food very strange, but they tasted it out of consideration for the savages, and did their best to show their gratitude. The "strange food" was corn on the cob, pumpkins cooked in the ashes, and sagamite, a kind of gruel, made of coarse hominy.

Sixteen years later there were eighteen or twenty nuns at the Hôtel-Dieu. Saint-Vallier says they were "virtuous and could not be poorer." He wonders that they and their single building have not long before perished. That they *have* not is due to divine Providence; that they *may* not the King should increase their allowance.

At the Mountain the priests taught the Indian boys, who, when baptized, assisted in the celebration of mass. It was reported to the Government at Versailles that at all the Missions the youth were "brought up *à la Française*, except in the matter of their food and dress, which it is necessary to make them retain in order that they be not effeminate and that they may be . . . less impeded whilst hunting, which constitutes their wealth and ours."[6] They were also taught to be tailors, shoemakers, masons and farmers, thus antedating our Indian schools. The girls were taught to speak French, to read, write and recite their creed. They were taught also to spin, knit and make lace by special teachers sent from France, which was made possible by the gifts of Louis XIV, who was much gratified by this work of the Sisters. He sent repeated instructions about civilizing the Indians and giving their children to the Sisters, urging that the French population of Quebec mingle with the savages.

The Superior of the Sulpitians in Paris, when writing to the Superior at Montreal, said: "If you could introduce skirts for the women and drawers for the children and make them follow the *mode*, you would make yourself famous, for I think . . . nothing would have greater effect." This was accomplished, but it was not a lasting fashion.

The intendant (de Meulles) did not approve. Writing to Versailles in 1682 he suggested that the girls should be instructed to work with their hands "in place of being instructed at the Ursuline Convent, where they only learn how to pray and to speak French, all of which they soon forget, and when they have once been married to some Indian, they hardly ever pray and never speak French."[7]

A drunken Indian set fire to the wooden buildings within the

[6] N. Y. Docs., IX, 150. [7] Can. Arch., Report 1885, p. XL.

palisade, which in New France, as in New England, was called a fort, "*Le Fort de la Montagne*" and sometimes "*Le Fort des Sauvages.*" In 1698 the buildings were replaced in stone at the expense of M. de Belmont, Superior of the Sulpitians. Adjoining was "*Le Fort des Messieurs,*" surrounded by a wall, flanked by four stone towers, two of which still stand at the entrance of the great Seminary built upon the site of the fort. These towers, built in 1694, were set apart by the priests for the nuns and their pupils; they lived in that at the right; in the other was the school and the bakery. Standing beside them we can imagine that some of our own little captives may have here looked upon the sweet face of Marguerite Bourgeoys. She lived until 1700.

Sault-au-Recollet

The Mission of the Mountain, built near Montreal as a defence against the Pagan Iroquois, was too near the white man's brandy, so in 1696 the fathers transferred it to the other side of the Mountain, leaving for a time the Sisters and some Indians behind.

The new station was at the Sault-au-Recollet on the Rivière-des-Prairies. The river was not so called because of its physical features, but in memory of a sailor of Saint-Malo who followed Champlain up the river, taking this route to avoid the rapids beyond Montreal. The name of *Sault-au-Recollet* recalls the tragic fate of the first martyr of Canada, Father Nicolas Viel, who, descending from the Huron country, was here, where the current is swiftest, thrown from a canoe by his vicious Indian companions.

The church of the new mission resembled the Santa Casa of Loreto in Italy,[8] and was called Notre-Dame de la Nouvelle-Lorette.

[8] According to the legend this "Holy House" was the one in Nazareth in which the Virgin was born and lived. Its destruction being threatened by the Turks in 1291 it was lifted by angels and carried through the air to Dalmatia. Afterwards they bore it across the Adriatic and after more moves finally fixed it at Loreto. It is built of stone, 28 x 12½ x13 ft. Within is a small image of the Virgin and child in black cedar of Lebanon and covered with jewels. It is said to have been made by Luke, but its workmanship suggests the fifteenth century.

One of the nuns in charge of the school, which was established here in 1701, was Soeur Marie-des-Anges (Mary Sayward of York), chosen perhaps because of her English speech. Many captives were brought to the Sault-au-Recollet, and here as at other villages their captors were often cruel. The Government deplored the acts of cruelty, but it was impossible to check them without clashing with these important allies.

Here, as elsewhere, captives were sometimes forced to run the gauntlet, which is thus described by La Hontan: "As soon as a war-party approached their village, they uttered as many death cries as they had lost men, and at the distance of a musket-shot, they began the funeral chant and repeated it as many times as they had killed enemies. Then the boys between twelve and sixteen, armed with sticks, formed in two lines to strike the naked backs of the prisoners when the warriors made their entrance."

Lac-des-Deux-Montagnes (Oka). The Lake of Two Mountains[9]

As the first post had been too near civilization and brandy, so was the second, and to prevent greater demoralization it was again moved; this time, in 1721, to the Lake of Two Mountains, the place where the course of the Ottawa River, checked by two points of a mountain, widens into a beautiful lake.

Here was better hunting and fishing, and here was a good place for the hundred and fifty warriors of the mission to attack hostile Indians as they came down the river.

As a reminder of that defence there is even now a cannon on the most exposed point of the Mission.

The majority of the Indians were Iroquois from divers villages, but there were also Hurons and Algonquins, who had formerly been their prisoners of war. And to the new site were brought also the Indians from the Mission at Sainte-Anne-Bout-de-l'Ile, and some Nipissings from the Ile-aux-Tourtes, which was at the foot of the lake.

[9] Now the oldest in Canada. Its modern name — Oka — is for Post Office convenience.

And here came the Sisters with their pupils of many nations: Iroquois, Huron, Algonquin and English. They lived and had their classes in a bark hut, the fire in the middle with its smoke issuing from a hole in the roof. In the comfortable stone convent in which the Sisters now live we heard another gentle Marie-des-Anges teach her little Indian pupils their catechism.

Caughnawaga

Another mission to receive many of our captives was that of Saint-François Xavier, now at Caughnawaga.

Before the Gentlemen of the Seminary established their Mission of the Mountain seven Onneiouts (Oneidas — one a woman), had come eastward, and Père Raffeix, Jesuit, offered them land at La Prairie de la Madeleine if they would tarry and be made Christians — one was already a convert. They did tarry and were sent to the Huron Mission at Lorette to be instructed, for the Father there knew their language.

In 1668 Mgr. de Laval baptized them in Quebec, and although asked by the Hurons to stay at Lorette they chose to accept the Jesuits' offer and this important mission was founded.

It grew rapidly; five wigwams of the first year grew to twenty in the second.[10] To it came Indians of the Five Nations of New York. The word Iroquois included them all, as did often the term Maquas, which specifically belonged to the Mohawks or Agniers. The other four were Oneidas, Onondagas, Cayugas and Senecas. After the Tuscaroras came north and joined the league it became that of "The Six Nations." The majority of those who came were Mohawks and their dialect still is used. This has always been the principal gathering-place for the Iroquois; and to their grand councils came sometimes deputies from other tribes.

The Kahnawakerons, as they called themselves, were divided into seven clans: The Wolves, Big Wolves (or inhabitants of the

[10] For it two square leagues were given to the Jesuits in 1680, and they controlled it until 1783 when it became the charge of the secular clergy.

crags, that being the literal translation of the Indian word), Bears, Little Turtles, Big Turtles, Larks, and The Ancient Bears. (The seventh name was sometimes Calumets).

The children belonged to the mother's clan. If the father were a bear and she a wolf the children were wolves.

Each clan chose a *grand chef* and two sub-chiefs to serve for a long period.

The Government now requires them to choose "counsellors" every year, thereby approaching the white man's methods. Because of the continued intercourse between these converted Mohawks and their New York kin, Albany was often able to warn Massachusetts of intended attacks.

But La Prairie was very dry, not good for Indian corn, and was too good for brandy, so the Mission was moved. For these and other reasons it was moved four times along the river.

From 1696 to 1715 — the period of their most disastrous war-parties against New England — the village was at Sault Saint-Louis (St. Louis rapids) and the Indians were described as belonging to the Sault. "*Au Sault*" the Frenchman would say, and "Oso," the New Englander spelled it.

A garrison of French soldiers was kept at the Mission as a guard against their pagan Indian enemy. Three Jesuit priests controlled the village. From it the men went out to hunt, fish and fight, while the women cultivated the fields, selling their surplus in Montreal. As lived the Indians, so must have lived their captives.

Since 1716 the Mission has been fixed at Caughnawàga, which is higher up the river, opposite La Chine. La Chine, so named in derision of La Salle's expectation of finding China.[11]

From its beginning in 1667 its Iroquois name has been Kahnawake *(au rapide)*, changed by poor English spelling into Caughnawaga.

A great many of its inhabitants are descendants of captives, both red and white. The Latin registers name many Indians "taken

[11] Before 1670 it was called Côte de St. Sulpice.

Caughnawaga

in war" and many whites "formerly baptized by the English."

Unfortunately family names are not given, and unfortunately, too, the records are incomplete, but there must be more New England blood here than in any other place in Canada and more lost captives.

A careful student of the records, the Rev. J. Guillaume L. Forbes, once a priest of the Mission and now Bishop of Joliette, says there is not in Caughnawaga a single family of pure Indian blood. There are many named Tarbell, Rice, Williams, Jacobs, Hill, Stacey, etc. To Father Forbes' study and courtesy we are much indebted.

St. Regis

In connection with Caughnawaga should be mentioned the Mission at St. Regis on the New York border.

In 1752 thirty families from Caughnawaga, with some Mohawks from New York, established themselves under the direction of their missionary a little higher up the river. Peter Karekohe, son of a captive Tarbell of Groton was their chief.

Six years later they moved further up the St. Lawrence to the mouth of the St. Regis River where the King gave them the land. They called the place *Akwesasne:* "Where the partridge beats her wings."

As long as Mrs. Sigourney's poem is read so long will the St. Regis bell be remembered. Somebody calls it "a direct and consistent legend." "Direct," perhaps, but surely not consistent, for at the time of this legendary incident there was no St. Regis and there was no bell! Such as it is the story concerns Deerfield and the Mission at Sault Saint-Louis.

The following is the legend as told by an old Indian of the tribe and written out in 1837 by Père Marcoux, with a few parentheses from Hough's History.[12]

The missionary wanted a bell; told his people it was as necessary to the belfry as a priest to the church. They collected furs and

12 "Hist. of St. Lawrence and Franklin Counties," N. Y.

shipped them off to Havre, ordering a bell. It was put on the *Grand Monarque*, which was captured and taken to Salem; the bell was sold for the church in Deerfield.

The old Indian said that their missionary, passing near Deerfield, recognized the bell by its sound. Returning, he told this to his Indians, and with the eloquence of a Peter the Hermit described its miserable condition, retained in purgatory in the hands of heretics. They answered: "We will go and get it." So they took advantage of the first chance to fight and joined Hertel de Rouville at Chambly. It is said that Père Nicolas was with them.

Returning to Canada, the roads being bad, the Indians hid the bell in the snow until the following spring. Now, continues the story, whether the bell which calls the Indians of Caughnawaga to prayer at morning and at night is the original or whether that one has been melted and recast is a difference of opinion.

But verily there can be *no* opinion for when Deerfield was raided in 1704 there was no church-bell to be carried away. The first was hung in 1729.

In the Caughnawaga belfry are two bells: one, large and heavy, was in 1832 given by King William IV to some Indians of the Mission who had been taken to England by a M. de Lorimier. His ancestor, by the way, commanded the small French garrison at Sault Saint-Louis in 1704, and took for wife a captive of forgotten name.

The other bell, of about eight hundred pounds weight, is believed to be that of the legend. The maker's name has been obliterated, which is supposed to have been done by the Deerfield people.

Mr. Sheldon, historian of Deerfield, after the most careful search could not find that the story was known there before 1824. He believed it was first heard in St. Regis the previous year.

The Missions near Quebec and the Abenakis of Maine

Sillery

Older than the Missions of the Mountain and Caughnawaga were those near Quebec, and it was to them that most of the eastern captives were taken.

Oldest of all was Sillery, about four miles from Quebec on the strand between the river and the wooded hills.

It was founded by Noël Brulart, *Commandeur de Sillery*, in 1637, before the sacred city of Ville-Marie was conceived. Brulart had been a very great gentleman at the Court of France; turning to a religious life he sold all his princely possessions and devoted his fortune to good works in France and to the conversion of American savages.

The Sillery mission "may be called the Mother of all the Christianity of the New World because the Algonquins and Montagnais being converted here inspired other nations to hear the word of Jesus Christ," but the Algonquins proved unworthy and the mission was almost deserted when, in 1677, there came to it some Abenakis from Maine.

These eastern Indians — their name Wobanaki means "those whose country is near the sun-rising" — were first taught by a Jesuit who came to the Kennebec region seven or eight years before the Pilgrims came to Plymouth. He "found them," says Charlevoix, "a tractable people, who seemed to be not far from the Kingdom of God."

No immediate result followed this first Christian teaching in Maine. Frequently the Kennebec Indians went as far north as Quebec on their hunting-parties and some, who visited their Sillery friends, became Christians. They in their turn made converts in their own villages and then they asked for a missionary.

Charlevoix says that in granting this request there was, besides the religious motive, the strong desire of Canada to keep these people as friends; for they would be dangerous as enemies.

In August, 1646, Father Gabriel Druillettes was sent to them. He was the first European to make the long and difficult land-journey from the St. Lawrence River to the Kennebec. The Indians adopted him into their tribe, accepting him as the Ambassador of Christ.

It was he who came to Boston in 1650 and 1651 to answer a request from our colonies for free trade, and to secure assistance for the Abenakis against the Iroquois; Canada making the trade concession dependent upon the consent of Massachusetts to fight.[13] Had his errand been other than political he could not have entered the colony for Massachusetts prohibited the coming of a Jesuit, who, says Parkman, was "next to the Devil and an Anglican bishop most abhorred."[14]

Massachusetts followed the lead of England in excluding all "Papistical and Jesuitical intruders."

Probably the first mass said in New England was in Father Druillette's chamber, to which his considerate host — Major-General Edward Gibbons — had given him the key.

He says that the Boston people were very kind to him. Governor Bradford in Plymouth,[15] whom he visited on a Friday, gave him "a dinner of fish." He went to see "Mr. Heliot" who, he wrote in his diary, treated him with respect and affection and invited him to pass the winter with him. This was on or near Christmas. Picture the two men, the black-gowned priest and the Puritan parson, conversing perhaps in Latin and surrounded by Eliot's Indian pupils. Because of the failure of the priest's errand — Boston being unwilling to help the Abenakis — the Indians were irritated, their hatred for the English increased, and their alliance with the French strengthened.

[13] Acting upon the suggestion of John Winthrop New England proposed in 1647 a perpetual alliance with Canada. It was based upon trade, and was to be independent of any rupture between the two Crowns. It was unfortunate that Governor d'Aillebout should have made his condition.

[14] Jesuits in N. A., 326.

[15] Plymouth had jurisdiction over the region from which he came.

So useful was the alliance that opinions differed about asking the Indians to leave their villages to come to Canada. Perhaps they would be a better defence if left in Maine.

The Kennebec Mission was temporarily abandoned, but later in the century flourishing missions were established there and on the Penobscot River. The remnant of the latter is at Old Town, served today in their church of Saint Anne by a French Canadian priest.

Saint-François-de-Sales — Saint-François-du-Lac — Bécancour

About 1680 there began a large emigration of Abenakis to Canada. They asked for land to plant their corn.

Plainly Sillery was not large enough to take care of so many and a new mission, Saint-François-de-Sales, was established at the falls of the Chaudière. This is the river which, with the Kennebec, made the most direct route from Maine.

In a few months the new village was larger than that at Sillery. The priests — Jacques and Vincent Bigot — used often to send their converts to Maine to invite their compatriots to join them. The pictures they made of Canadian security, contrasted with the dangers of their own villages, subject to attack from the English, largely increased the emigration. Soon a few savages pushed up the St. Lawrence to its widening at Lake St. Peter. Selecting a site they told the Seigneur that they would like to stay there. They were vexed and possibly could not understand him when he explained *his* rights to the land. However, as the story goes, when he gave them all the milk they wanted they went away satisfied, which would prove that they were gentle savages! This Seigneur was M. Crevier.[16]

After two or three moves the village, Saint Francis of the Lake, was fixed on the most beautiful site of the St. Francis River, about five miles from its mouth and a hundred and twenty miles from Quebec.

16 Later captured and tortured by the Iroquois.

In the first year of the new century Canada made with the Iroquois a peace which endured, a peace made possible because of the laws enacted in New York and Massachusetts which forbade "Jesuits and Popish priests" to remain in the colonies; the English believing that they incited the New York tribes to attack them. Religious sympathies inclined the Iroquois to the French.

Never did an English colony see a picture like that of the September day in Montreal when after the signing of the treaty thirteen hundred Indians sang a *Te Deum* and then made holiday.

But Governor de Vaudreuil, fearing that the fair promise might not be kept, determined to make more sure by using the immigrating Abenakis, always inimical to the Iroquois, as a bulwark.

Tradition says that Father Bigot was sent westward that year with fifteen hundred of these Indians. Taking them from the Chandière Mission he left some at Bécancour, and more went on to Saint Francis of the Lake where still dwell their few descendants in whose blood is mingled that of some of their New England captives.

Of the Abenaki emigrations the Governor wrote to Versailles:[17] "We have placed them in the centre of the Colony in order to be prepared for service when required. Although this establishment will cost a good deal, we hope the Colony will derive a great advantage from it, both in a commercial and military point of view."

Their historian, the Abbé Maurault, counts their coming as "A special Providence of God, to protect the little colony of Canada whom He wished to save." He asserts again and again that the colony could not have endured without their support; as their own priest, Père Aubéry, had said before. The missionary claimed that his Indians alone were carrying on the Three Years' War, and that war was necessary in the best interest of religion and of the State. Without it the King's dominion on the south side of the St. Lawrence would be greatly endangered.[18] These Indians, more

[17] N. Y. Docs., IX, 762. [18] Can. Arch., Report, 1904.

than any others, hated the English, and many, very many captives were taken to their village.

In 1704 the Rev. John Williams saw there "several poor children, who had been taken from the eastward the summer before, a sight very affecting, they being in habit very like Indians and in manners very much symbolizing with them." We cannot trace many St. Francis captives because the records were destroyed when Major Rogers burned the church.

This was in the autumn of 1759, at the end of the last Indian war. The story reads backward. Now it was Englishmen who marched far across the country — a three weeks' journey from Ticonderoga — to carry vengeance to the Indian village and who used the Indians' own methods to destroy. The white men hid themselves near the place. In the evening their leader, with Lieutenant Turner and Ensign Avery, disguised as Indians, spied out the land during a grand Indian dance. This which Maurault calls "*un grand bal*" was to celebrate the return of some warriors from "an English excursion." "About break of day, when all things were silent and secure," the rangers, about a hundred and forty, surprised and killed the people and burned the village, sparing three houses which contained corn.

At seven o'clock all was over. Two hundred Indians had been killed. The priest, Rev. F. Virot, was spared and twenty women and children were held, fifteen of whom were released, for Rogers kept only five boys and girls.[19] Three English prisoners were rescued, but we find only one name, that of Lieutenant Kennedy, and the Indians thought his rescue was the object of the expedition.

Hideous as was the massacre the parallel ends there. The return of the Englishmen was disastrous. For them there were no triumphant shoutings; no "*grand bal*" on arrival.

Rogers' orders from General Amherst were: "to attack the enemy's settlement . . . in such a manner as shall most effectually

19 Two of the girls died of smallpox at Albany; one lad he sent to school to learn English — was this Sabatis Gill, Mrs. Johnson's friend?

disgrace & injure the enemy . . . Remember the barbarities committed by the enemy's Indian scoundrels on every occasion . . . Take your revenge; but remember that although the villains have promiscuously murdered women & children of all ages, it is my order that no women or children should be hurt."[20] In the partial darkness of the attack many women and children were killed. Perhaps the six or seven hundred scalps of English victims hanging in the air as adornments of the village enraged their fellow-countrymen beyond the possibility of remembering their chief's orders! The rangers brought back none of the booty the Indians had gathered in New England, but they did take some of the church treasure, including the silver image which the Canons of Chartres gave to the Mission in 1701. Because of their hunger and exposure on the return journey the men had to abandon this loot, and tradition says they buried it in the White Mountains, which has brought forth many legends and much search but no silver.

Lorette

Another Canadian Mission to which our captives were carried was at Lorette. When the Hurons, who were sometimes called "the nobles among the tribes," were driven out of their country by the Iroquois in 1650 a missionary brought some of them — terror-stricken as they were — to Quebec. After many vicissitudes they were fixed in a seigniory which belonged to the Jesuits a few miles north of the town. With them were some Sillery Indians. In 1697, lured by hopes of more abundant game they moved to the plateau above the rapids of Saint-Ambroise on the Saint-Charles River and here they dwell at "*Jeune* or Indian Lorette," while their former home is known as "*Ancienne* Lorette." Indians from *Jeune* Lorette were in the war-parties.

The very beautiful silver ornaments and vessels of the seventeenth century, which are in the church, were gifts from France, and the priests' vestments and embroideries that adorn the altar

[20] Rogers' Memoir in "Life of Stark" (and Rogers' "Letter from Amherst," 5 Nov., 1759).

were made by Madame de Maintenon and ladies of the Court of Louis XIV.

The Abbé Maurault in his "History of the Abenakis" asks why they, being such good Christians, were cruel to the English? Why had they not learned to pardon their enemies? He answers: that they fought to defend their faith. They knew that the only aim of the Puritans was to drive Catholicism from America. Their campaigns were veritable crusades. After prayer their ardor and intrepidity in beginning the combat astonished their commanders. The missionary would remind them of Saint-Louis, as he fought against the infidels of Palestine, and exhorted them to be as brave as their king; but the Abbé, writing fifty or more years ago, adds that their cruelty seems today "somewhat revolting."

It all depends upon the point of view. Protestant or Catholic — Catholic or Protestant. To us of New England the picture of these Christian Indians who burnt our villages and stole our women and children has *always* been "revolting," but to the Bishop of Quebec, Monseigneur de Saint-Vallier, the picture was different. He says that the Mission Indians of the Mountain and of Sault Saint-Louis lived as in a cloister: "Almost always some one is praying in the chapel, and after they have spoken to God in prayer with a charming simplicity, they sing hymns of praise while at work and when together they talk about holy things." To the zealous priest this is what they were. We do not recognize them. It all depends upon the point of view!

Missionaries

No one can doubt the devotion of the missionaries. Bancroft says of an earlier period that the whole strength of the colony lay in them. They travelled from Nova Scotia to Lake Superior; from Hudson Bay to the mouth of the Mississippi. To every tribe, however fierce, the Black Gown was known. The Recollets were first to come; then the Jesuits began their remarkable work which was that of conversion rather than of civilization.

It is true, as the Abbé Casgrain says, that with the exception of Eliot, Protestant ministers did not go out to preach. "How, indeed, could they," he asks, "go out with their families to live in the repugnant manner of the savage?" Even Eliot, the exception, used to carry to Natick food prepared by his careful wife, and Lord Bellomont wrote: "Without a Fort, tis next to impossible to prevail with the ministers to live among the Indians, who are so nasty as never to wash their hands, or the utensils they dress their victuals with. Their food is (some of it) loathsome to the last degree."[21]

The Abbé accuses Protestant writers of lessening the merit of the Catholic missionary, reproaching him with having mingled patriotism with his religion, and asks if when he ascends the altar he becomes a man without a country? He claims that the Mission Indians were humanized and "practised fewer horrors in war" because of the influence of the mission priests. We of New England might ask how there could have been greater horrors, and also if it be patriotism to incite savages to burn homes, to capture and murder women and children? That some missionaries did this we have positive proof in letters sent to and from Versailles which have been printed in volumes of the Quebec and New York Documents. Indeed some priests were blamed for *not* being militant. In 1694 the Minister at Versailles informs the Bishop of Quebec "that complaints had been made that Fathers Baudoin and Petit in Acadie were friendly to the English and even refused to confess those who fought against them."[22]

M. Robert Gay

One of the most militant priests was M. Robert Gay. He must have known and baptized many of our captives. For thirty-seven years he was with the Indians at the Mission of the Mountains and at their two later posts. They called him their "apostle and commander." Leading his flock against the heathen Indians he urged them to battle and to prayer with equal enthusiasm; telling them

21 N. Y. Docs., IV, 717. 22 Parkman's manuscripts.

that the Virgin was their leader and exhorting them not to tarnish the glory of their King — at whose name all Europe trembled — by a cowardice unworthy the name of Frenchmen![23] His Indians gave him the pretty name of *Taiorhensere* — the day is breaking.

Pères Jacques and Vincent Bigot

M. Gay was not concerned in the New England expeditions. Those who were and who were most hated in New England were Fathers Jacques and Vincent Bigot at St. Francis and at the Kennebec villages; the Abbé Thury of the Penobscot, and at a later period Father Rale at Norridgewock.

Of the militant priest of St. Francis, the historian of the place[24] says: "Father Bigot was all his life in Canada an emissary of the French Government, exciting his Indians to go out against New England. He believed he had accomplished a sacred duty when these savages, under his inspiration, committed atrocities which threw terror into the English colonies."

Casgrain — author of "The Sulpitians and Priests of Foreign Missions in Acadie" — says that Mr. Parkman belies his own character when he calls Fathers Thury and Vincent Bigot "apostles of carnage." Every statement herein made relating to the militancy of these missionaries is quoted from French archives or writers.

The Abbé Thury

The Rev. Louis Pierre Thury, taking orders in 1677 as a priest in the foreign missions, was sent from Quebec to Acadia — the Seminary having long been eager to establish a mission.

Escaping from Port Royal when it was taken by Phips he went to Panawamske (Indian Old Town) on the Penobscot, and until his death in 1699 he went out with his warriors. He was at Pemaquid, York and Oyster River. His services were much appreciated by Versailles, "especially his success in bringing the savages to begin again the war against the English, with whom they had made a peace." The minister writing to him in April, 1695, says

23 "Le Sault-au-Recollet," 156. 24 "*Hist. du Saint-François-du-Lac.*" B. Sulte.

it is hoped that he will "continue to *messager* (stroke down) his Indians with the same application," never letting them forget His Majesty's affection nor the help he will send them. He is besought to keep up their religious interests, while preventing all intercourse with the English.[25]

Six months later the agent for Acadie, M. Tibierge, wrote that: "The savages have great confidence in M. de Thury. . . . He is very necessary . . . for their services of the King and the good of the nation, and if it is desirable to make use of these savages for any considerable enterprise no one could be found who could better persuade them to do what is wished than he."[26] For his good work the Bishop of Quebec was directed to give him the largest portion of the fifteen hundred livres bestowed by His Majesty upon the priests of Acadia.[27] Typical of his "good work" is this exhortation to his Children: "How long will you suffer your lands to be violated by the encroaching heretics? By the religion I have taught you, by the liberty you love, I exhort you to resist them . . . This land belonged to your fathers long before these wicked men came over the great water, and are you ready to leave the bones of your ancestors that the cattle of heretics may eat grass on their graves." — And to prevent it the priest and his "Children" set forth!

Sébastien Rale or Rasles[28]

Father Rale, a Jesuit of the four vows, the fourth being to accept any mission to which he might be ordered, was the priest most hated in New England. "The estimates of his character are as diverse as the Romish and Protestant faiths can make them." He is "a saint and hero" or "a bloody incendiary," blamed for "most of the mischiefs that were done to us, by preaching up the doctrine of meriting salvation by the destruction of hereticks."[29]

Sent in 1696 to reëstablish Père Druillete's Mission he brought together some two hundred Indians with whom he founded, on a

25 Que. Docs., II, 174. 26 Que. Docs., II, 185. 27 B. P. Poore Coll., IV, 333.
28 He used both spellings. 29 Penhallow.

beautiful bend of the Kennebec River, the village still called Norridgewock, a corruption of Narantsouak, "Indian Old Point."

He lived simply, building his house with his own hands. He disliked the Indians' meat and dried fish and ate only their pounded corn; his "one luxary" being a little sugar made from the maple.

He hunted and fished with his Indians, always erecting a chapel of bark that he might say a daily mass, carrying in his "little chest" the sacred vessels. In letters sent to his kin in France[30] he describes his life and says that "the Indians are well aware of the advantages to be derived from trading with the English, but they fear to find themselves without a missionary and in danger of being plunged into their former heathenism."

Colonel Hilton destroyed his first church in 1705 when the Indians were absent. The second, built, says Hutchinson, by New England carpenters, was adorned with paintings made by the priest and described by him as of sufficient elegance to be esteemed in Europe. He dressed his choir of forty in cassock and surplice; crowds of Indians came long distances to see or join in the processions. There was always "a blaze of light" for the church for the country gave him wax. "Three bushels of bayberry makes almost four pounds of wax," he says, and by adding the same amount of fat — beef, mutton or elk — fine tapers are made. Forty-eight pounds will make two hundred, more than a foot long. (The recent revival of this home-industry makes this of interest).

At the time of Westbrook's surprise, when the priest's papers were seized, he had not even time to get his snowshoes. He says: "I had barely time to swallow the consecrated wafers, to crowd the sacred vessels into a little chest and to save myself in the woods," but somebody had time to fasten upon the church door a message to the Englishmen which, translated, was printed the next November (1722) in the New England Courant:

"Englishmen, I that am of Norridgewock have some tho'ts that

30 *"Lettres Edifiantes,"* Mass. Hist. Soc. Coll., Ser. 2, Vol. IV.

thou wilt come and burn our Church and our Father's House, for to revenge thy self without Cause: For the Houses I have burnt of thine 'twas thou that didst force me to it. Why didst thou build them upon my Land without my Consent? I have not burnt anything yet but what was upon my Land. Thou mayst burn it because thou knowest I am not there, such is thy Generosity; for if I were there, assuredly thou shouldest not burn it, altho' thou shouldest come with the Number of many Hundred Men. It is ill built, because you English don't Work well. It is not finish'd although five or six Englishmen wrought there during the Space of Four Years, and the Undertaker (who is a Grand Cheat) has been paid in Advance for to finish it. I tell thee nevertheless, That if thou dost burn it, out of Revenge, upon my Land, thou mayst depend upon it, I will revenge myself, and that upon thy Land, in such a manner which shall be more sensible and more disadvantageous to thee. For one of thy Meeting Houses or Temples is of more value without Comparison than our Church; and I shall not be satisfied to burn One or Two, but many. I know where they are, and the Effect will make thee know I shall be as good as my Word. This shall absolutely be done sooner or later, for the War does but just begin. But if thou wouldest know when it will Finish, I tell thee that it will not have an End but with the world. If thou canst not be driven out before I die, our Children and nephews shall continue it till that Time, without they be able to enjoy it peaceably. This is what I say to thee, who am of Norridgewock, in the name of all The Nations."

And so Colonel Westbrook could not bring back the priest, but he did bring his "strong box," which is owned by the Maine Historical Society. In this was the manuscript of his Abenaki dictionary, now in the library of Harvard College.[31] In it he wrote: "I have been among the Indians a year, and begin to put in the form of a dictionary the words I am learning." Other papers, found in the box, or copies of them, are in our archives; one

[31] Printed in 1833.

undated letter,[32] describing English cowardice, tells how he shewed himself during an attack made by his Indians (at Georgetown) and how the English dared do nothing to him, "although," he says, "they knew that the Governour had set my Head at a thousand Livres Sterling.[33] I shall not part with it, nevertheless, for all the Sterling money in England."

Remembering the law passed in 1700, which prohibited the coming of Jesuits into New England and New York, our General Court resolved in July, 1720, that because "it is derogatory to his Majesty's Honour & very injurious to this Province that Mounsr Ralle, a French Jesuit & Missionary should in Defiance of the Law, Reside in any part of this Province, Wch we are informed he now does as an Incendiary among the Indians of Norridgewock, therefore a Reward of £100 was to be allowed to any Person who shall bring Rale to Boston and Render him to Justice," and the next year the reward was doubled for any English or Indian person who would "take & Convoy to Boston Ralle or any other French Priest or Jesuit that may be found in this Province it being Contrary to a Good & Wholesome Law of this Province for any such person to reside their."

His Superior urged him to flee; he answered: "God has intrusted to me this flock; I will share its fate, too happy if I may be a sacrifice for its sake," which happiness was his in 1724,[34] although French Catholics and English Protestants do not agree that his death was "a sacrifice."

Parkman bids us remember in "considering the ascription of martyrdom . . . that he did not die because he was an apostle of the faith, but because he was the active agent of the Canadian government," and Palfrey[35] says: "If he obeyed his conscience, not the less if his conscience dictated brutal butchery, humanity required its instructions to be silenced."

When Vaudreuil accused Dummer of the "murder" he an-

[32] Arch. 52, 15. [33] £1000 Mass. currency then equalled £360 Sterling.

[34] See Chapter XVII. [35] "Hist. N. E.," IV, 438.

swered in January, 1724: "If after all, such an Incendiary has happen'd to be slain in the heat of Action among our open & declared Enemies, Surely no one can be blamed therefor but himself nor can any safeguard from you or any other in such proceedings justify him: And I think I have much greater cause to complain that Mr Willard, the Minister of Rutland (who never had been guilty of the Facts chargeable upon Mr. Ralle) who applied himself solely to the Preaching of the Gospel was by the Indians you sent to attack that Town, assaulted, Slain & scalpt & his Scalp carried in Triumph to Quebec."[36] Colonel Harmon made a solemn oath that Rale was "slain in fight, making actual resistance, at the same time attempting to kill an English captive in his hands."[37]

The Courant of August 24 announced the return of Colonel Harmon with twenty-eight scalps. One was Father Rale's and another was Bomazeen's. The soldiers had met this cruel Indian as they were marching towards Norridgewock. They killed his daughter and captured his wife. He, with his sons, escaped, but returning, the soldiers found and killed him at Taconnet Falls, now Winslow.

Harmon began the attack at Norridgewock with a few men, who were greeted with defiant shoutings, but when more soldiers appeared the terrified Indians took to the river and were slaughtered.

Father Rale and an Indian named Mang fought from their houses, declaring that they would neither take nor give quarter. They killed "a Friend Indian" and wounded two soldiers. The Courant writer continues: "The Priest's Flag is brought to Town, on which is pourtray'd five Crosses, one at each Corner and one in the middle surrounded with four Bows and Arrows, which he us'd to hoist as a Help to Devotion and Courage, when he granted them Absolution before any considerable Expedition, which by the Confession of Mang just before he was kill'd they were then pre-

[36] Arch. 52, 106.

[37] Letter from Dummer to Lords of Trade, Brit. Col. Papers, March, 1725.

paring for and were to be join'd by 200 men from Penobscot in a few days."[38]

Sewall wrote: "There is great Shouting and Triumph. The Lord help us to rejoice with Trembling." (Sewall often trembled where Indians were concerned, for he, as other of our Puritan ancestors, believed they might be descendants of the ten lost tribes of Israel).

The Rev. Hugh Adams, once of Oyster River, and later of Arrowsick, counted Rale's death an answer to prayer. In his notebook he wrote: "My Imprecation & Particular Faith against Sebastian Rale, The French Popish Jesuite." He relates how the Jesuit had an "Arthritick Tumour Inflamation and Acute Pain in his Shoulder the cure whereof in 3 days almost I was an Instrument to Accomplish Gratis; if possible thereby to gain him to Amity towards our English settlers at the Eastern Parts, so Adjacent to his said Settlement."[39] Gaining no "Amity," but continued hostility, the parson prayed three years for his destruction.

Louis, the King, was very angry about the priest's death and wrote to Vaudreuil that he was too fond of him to delay danger in compensating the Indians for his loss. He directed the Governor to take the necessary measures for their compensation and to send letters to the Abenakis with fifteen blankets and forty pounds of tobacco for each village, but he must first consult the Superior of the Jesuits at Quebec.[40]

A hundred years after the missionary's death Protestants and Catholics united in placing a monument over his grave (23 August, 1833). If we remember that the mission-priest promoted strife, let us not forget that the Puritan minister hated Quakers, and also, following the lead of Old England, minister and people persecuted so-called witches, thereby furnishing what the Rev. Abiel Holmes calls "an affecting proof of the imbecility of the human mind."

It was an intolerant age. The last words of the Protestant

38 A doubtful "Confession?" 39 MS. in Mass. Hist. Soc. 40 Que. Docs., III, 124.

biographer of Father Rale are: "So far as the patient toils of the missionary and love for the darkened soul of the Indian are concerned, we may place the names of Eliot and Rale in a fellowship, which they indeed would both have rejected, but which we may regard as hallowed and true."[41]

Père Meriel — not a Mission Priest

M. Henri-Antoine de Meriel of Meulan was the priest most closely associated with the captives. For over twenty years (1690-1713) he served in Montreal as chaplain of the Hôtel-Dieu; director and confessor of the pupils of the Sisters of the Congregation; and as priest of the parish of Notre-Dame. In all these offices he ministered to our people, and his interest followed them after their redemption.

To his knowledge of English, a rare accomplishment then in Canada, we owe the exact records of the registers. Because of his careful detail we can identify many, and sometimes supply a link missing to the New England genealogist. His exquisite handwriting is a joy to the searcher.

He made many converts. His Majesty was "informed that M. Meriel . . . has spent his fortune on the conversion of the English of the colony, and that he is so impoverished as to be unable to continue the good work." Before His Majesty could answer this appeal Father Meriel died.[42]

Père Cuoq — a later Mission-Priest

It would be ungrateful not to mention the mission-priest of the nineteenth century who was very helpful in our puzzling work. M. Jean-André Cuoq, Sulpitian, born in France, was sent on his arrival in Canada to the Lake of Two Mountains, where for more than fifty years he ministered to the Iroquois, Algonquins, and Nipissings, the tribes whose homes stretch along the *côte* on either side of the church and convent.

41 "Life of Rale," 333, Rev. Convers Francis.

42 In connection with Père Meriel, see Adelaide Silver of Haverhill.

A notice printed after his death says that his name will be remembered by his Indians and in the world of *savants.* By the first because he was their father and friend; by the second because of his admirable study of Indian languages.

His Iroquois name was "the fixed star," and the Algonquins called him "The beautiful double leaf." To help our search he made careful studies of the mission registers and personally gave us the satisfaction of meeting some descendants of captives.

CHAPTER III

CONCERNING INDIANS

Names — Adoption — Religion and Trade; Gifts — Rum and Brandy — Scalp Money — Visits to Boston — Visits to Court, French and English — The Protestant Effort — The Land.

INDNESS shown to an Indian was remembered as long as an injury, and lives were sometimes spared because of acts of humanity which had been shown to individual Indians or their kindred. Belknap[1] tells a story of Simon, a Christian Tarratine, who was guilty of many atrocities in Philip's War and who plundered the house of a man on Sturgeon Creek, but spared his life because the man had been kind to Simon's grandmother.

John Williams wrote:[2] "God made the heathen so to pity our children that though they had several wounded persons of their own to carry upon their shoulders for thirty miles before they came to the river, yet they carried our children incapable of travelling, in their arms and upon their shoulders."

Almost never does one read of an insult offered a woman captive by an eastern or northern Indian. This wonderful forbearance was probably the result of a superstition. Schoolcraft says the Indian thought women possessed some mysterious influence, and being always afraid of crossing his luck he thought it a bad sign if a woman crossed his path.

Whether or no Schoolcraft is right, from the testimony of women captives as well as from writers of the period we may be sure that "No English woman was ever known to have any violence

[1] History of New Hampshire. [2] Redeemed Captive, 14.

offered unto her Chastity by any" of the "Bruitish Salvages,"[3] and that "not the least liberty was ever taken with French women, even when they were prisoners."[4] Mrs. Johnson wrote that "Modesty has ever been a characteristic of every savage tribe — a truth which my whole family will corroborate."

Niles[5] gives the exception: It was as late as 1756, when perhaps the Indians' kindly superstition had weakened. Giving neither name nor place he says that "an ancient man" who had been a preacher at the east was murdered; his wife and daughter captured. The wife was grossly insulted by her Indian master, it being, says the writer, "the only instance of the kind that I ever met with under all the other abuses that poor captivated women have found among the Indians when under their command." But in this later period when Indians of the northwest were in the French army gross cruelties were practiced. They were brute-like even to cannibalism.

As has been said elsewhere the French at first believed that to civilize the savages it was necessary to bring them into contact with themselves, but they learned that the Indians did not become French while the Frenchmen who lived in the open often became savage. Many whites were Indianized — few Indians were civilized. It was not uncommon for prisoners, both French and English, to be unwilling to return to civilization when opportunity offered.[6]

Names

It is difficult to trace our captives who became Indians in manner and in name.

When recording a baptism the priest, ignorant of the language, could easily blunder. Indeed both English and savage names might be Gallicized; for example, Dicker became Dicaire; Rising,

[3] Cotton Mather. [4] Charlevoix. [5] Mass. Hist. Soc. Col., IV, 5, 410.

[6] Competent authorities tell us that in all the relations, peaceful and hostile, between Indians and Europeans, the proportion of whites barbarized to Indians civilized is as a hundred to one. Eds. Sewall's Diary, II. 375 note.

Raizenne; and Arosen (the squirrel) was changed to Roussin. Casco Bay was Kaskebé and Cape Porpoise, Kirparpes, which is only less bewildering than our Sadrohelly made from Sault-au-Recollet! Another difficulty is the fact that an Indian had sometimes two or even three names, and any one of them may have been used in the register, as happened to Eunice Williams; and an individual may appear under a simple soubriquet, as does Abigail Nims, who was called Elizabeth Kana8k8a (the slave). Family names are not transmitted from father to son. They use a different method. The father, naming his son, ordinarily selects the name of an ancestor, as does the mother for her daughter; and it is difficult, says Père Cuoq, from whose letters the above is quoted, to understand the meanings of many old names as they are recorded for they are of dialects now forgotten. The most intelligent Indians when questioned answer: "We don't understand, the word is too old."

Nor, wrote Père Forbes of Caughnawaga, are they "particular about one name or another. In the same family some go by the name of Williams, some by the name of Foster and so on."

Here are some forms of Iroquois Christian names: Louis is Rowi; Thomas is Atonwa; Jacques, Sak; Pierre, Tier; Jean Baptiste is Sawatis and Battis; Joseph, Sore; François Xavier becomes Saksarie or Onasateken; Nicholas is Nikora, and Ignace, Eunias.

At an early date the converts refused to be called by their original names, wrote Père Bigot, so much did they respect those of their baptism. All the women wished to be Marie so two names had to be given to each. Men and women of distinction acted as sponsors in baptism for Indian, as for English converts, showing their great interest in both.

A certain Peter Anthony, carried to France by some Jesuits, was baptized as early as 1508. His godfather was the Prince de Guimené.[7]

[7] Shea quotes this from Eusebius.

On the Canadian records we find names of the highest. Frontenac, himself the godchild of royalty — Louis XIII having been his sponsor — frequently accepted the responsibility in the New World.

Adoption

The Indians have a very special ceremony in giving the name to the individual adopted. Probably the ceremonial is the same now that it was during the intercolonial wars. The council is seated and the subject accepted; probably because of his courage, gratitude or as a captive of the tribe. He is introduced to the chiefs and members of the family into which he is to be received and is greeted with cries of approbation and friendship. The new name is solemnly proclaimed by the chief. M. l'Abbé Mainville says "the name always makes a picture." One can clearly see a characteristic or useful trait of the individual or of some aim to be attained.[8]

After a captive had been adopted into a village release was difficult, if not impossible. He could not be sold, but an exchange — white for red — might be made. The Indians of Sault Saint-Louis agreed to give up certain prisoners for some Panis, men or women.

They kept their captive children very closely. In the "Redeemed Captive" is the story of a father who, with the permission of his master, travelled on foot fifty miles to see his children at the Macqua fort (at Sault Saint-Louis) and was not allowed to speak to them nor to stay there.[9]

Religion and Trade — Gifts

Religion and trade, as friendship and trade, went hand in hand. In 1690 M. de Denonville, writing to the Minister at Versailles, says: "While the interest in the Gospel would not cause us to keep missionaries in all the Indian villages: Iroquois, Abenakis and others, the prosperity of our trade obliges us to keep them always

[8] "Hist. Sault-au-Recollet," 192. [9] Edi. 1853, p. 56.

there, because it is the missionaries only who can keep the Indians in our interest."[10] A few years later when Schuyler and Dellius were sent from Albany to Canada the Superior of the Jesuits and the secular clergy visited them at Quebec and said they were going to send their missionaries back to the New York tribes. Schuyler advised them to spare themselves the trouble for the Five Nations belonged to the diocese of the Bishop of London, which greatly surprised the clergy for they said they were paid twenty-four thousand livres annually for that mission.

There were always jealousies of trade, the French and English both being suspicious of the other's bargains. Here are some of their differences in 1689. At Albany the Indian pays two beavers for a gun, which in Montreal would cost him five; for eight pounds of powder he gives one beaver instead of four and for each of the following articles: "a Blanket of red Cloth, a White Blanket, Four Shirts and Six pairs of Stockings" he gives in Albany one beaver and in Montreal two. Tobacco and "other small wares" are supplied at the same ruinous rates, and alas! the English for one beaver give six quarts of "Rum, or Spirits . . . distilled from the Sugar Cane imported from the West Indies," while the French have no fixed rate for brandy, but "never give as much as a quart for a beaver."

But if Albany gave better bargains, Canada gave finer presents. In the earliest days guns were given to her converts in order, says the missionary,[11] to draw others to the true faith, for it seemed "that our Lord wishes to make use of this method in order that Christianity may become acceptable in this country."

Perhaps the English did not "make use of this method" so early. In 1676 a Penobscot chief asked what they were expected to do after they had eaten their corn and needed ammunition for their winter hunting, so entirely had they discarded the bow for the gun. He asked if they were to starve or to leave their country and go over to the French?

10 Que. Docs., II, 2. 11 Père Vimont, Jesuit at Montreal in 1643.

The French King sent gifts every year. In 1694 M. de Villebon, Governor of Acadia, asks the minister for "Two months Provisions . . . for the Indians estimated at 200 men." He wants 2000 lbs. of Flour, Molasses and Butter "to flavor their Sagamite," and 10 barrels of Brandy without which 'twill be impossible to prevail on them to act efficiently; and in the "Memorandum of Presents" for these Indians "which His Majesty grants them in order to wage war against the English," we find:

"2000 lb of Powder
40 barrels of bullets
10 barrels of Swan shot
400 lbs of Brazilian Tobacco
200 Tomahawks, of which Mr de Bonaventure will furnish the pattern.
60 selected guns like those of this year
200 Mulaix shirts averaging 30s each
8 lbs of fine Vermilion
200 tufts of white feathers to be given the Indians in order to designate them during the night, in case of attack, and which will cost at most only six @ 7c; to be selected in Paris by M. de Bonaventure."[12]

After the peace of Ryswick Villebon said they could dispense with the usual gifts, sending them only to the chiefs, who were to receive twelve hats trimmed with feathers of different colors, twelve shirts with lace, and arms of the best quality.

In 1700, the year that Jesuits and priests were forbidden to enter New York, the sachems at a conference with Governor Bellomont agreed to send away any priests that might come to their villages, but refused to deliver them to the English.

When the governor complains that some of their people have emigrated to Canada they answer: The Governor of Canada "feeds them when they are hungry and cloaths them when they are naked; for it is the French custome to cloath all those that are baptiz'd . . .

[12] N. Y. Docs., V, 577.

This wee presume is a great inducement to our people to turn papists. Wee doubt if our brother Corlaer would put the King of England to that charge."[13]

It is not surprising that the Indians were perplexed. In 1701 the spokesman of the Iroquois, addressing the Governors of New York and Canada, said: "You both tell us to be Christians, you both make us madd, we know not what side to choose, but I will speak no more of praying or Christianity . . . because you are both to dear with your goods; . . . Now we are come to this conclusion those that sells their goods cheapest, whether English or French of these will we have a minister. You both have made us drunk with all your noise of praying; we must first come to ourselves."[14]

Wiser and less self-interested was that high chief in the Red River region who at a later date, when rival missions were near, said to the priest: "You tell us there is but one religion that can save us, and that you have got it . . . the Protestant minister tells us that he has got it. Now which of you white men am I to believe?" After a pause, a long smoking and talking with his people, he said: "I will tell you the resolution I and my people have come to . . . when you both agree and travel the same road, we will travel with you; till then we will adhere to our own religion: we think it the best."[15]

In 1702 the Indians complained that they could neither buy nor sell so well at Albany as in Canada and that the New York "weights are too heavy when you weigh the Bares and other skins with all, and we are oftentimes not fairly dealt with by ye Trade." The best way to retrieve our Indians is to "lett ye Goods be cheaper and then there is no doubt but they will return very speedily, and as soon as ye goods are cheaper here, then we will consult about having ministers in our Castles, to instruct us in ye Christian faith for then we can afford to buy a good honest Coat to go to Church

13 N. Y. Docs., IV, 730. 14 N. Y. Docs., IV, 893, 920.

15 "The Red Man and the White Man in N. A." Geo. E. Ellis.

withall, which we cannot now, for it would be scandalous to come to Church with a Bear Skin on our backs."[16]

New York complained that the Five Nations expected gifts as a regular tribute and asked that a thousand pounds be spent annually. The lists of offerings are less picturesque than those of Canada. Some of those "recommended" in 1694 seem especially extravagant. "24 Coats of blew Cloath, which cost in England about 9£ a peece the said Coats to be laced with St Martin's lace and brass buttons find'g set forth; 24 Hats of ab^{t} 4£ a p^{ce} in England laced about." The same number of "Shirts of Ordinary Linnen" of "Necke-cloathes," "Shoes and Buckles" and "Pairs of Ordinary red Stockings," a "Barrell of Pipes, 6 Pound of Vermillion and "50 Brass Kettles of two, three & four pound a p^{ce}, thin beaten and light to Carry when they go a hunting, or to war;" — and if the war continue arms and ammunition should be added.[17]

To some "farr Indians" (the upper nations of the Great Lakes), Lord Cornbury sent among other gifts: "Jewells that they wear in their noses and eares and some toys for their children viz. 3 Doz. Tobacco Tongs, 16 Fanns 36 looking Glasses."

Massachusetts in a less lavish way sent presents to the Eastern Indians.

Rum and Brandy

The story of the Englishman's rum is little less hideous than that of the Frenchman's brandy. Indeed one writer asserts that the magistrates and people of Massachusetts were partly responsible for Philip's war because of their laws concerning Indians and spirituous liquors; the magistrates strictly enforcing the laws against the savages, which the people, for lucre, enticed them to break, or as he puts it: "The imprudent zeal in the Magistrates of Boston to Christianize the heathen before they were civilized." In 1686 Denonville of Canada berated Dongan of New York for supplying rum to the Indians and asked if he thinks religion will make any progress while New York merchants furnish the liquor

[16] N. Y. Docs., IV, 987. [17] N. Y. Docs., IV, 126.

which "converts the Savages into Demons and their Cabins into counter parts . . . of Hell"? To which Dongan, the Catholic governor, replied: "Certainly our Rum doth as little hurt as your Brandy and in the opinion of Christianity is much more wholesome; however to keep the Indians temperate and sober is a very good and Christian performance, but to prohibit them all strong liquors seems a little hard and very turkish."[18] Three years later the King directs Denonville to make no change in the brandy trade. If it should be stopped in Canada the English would get all the benefit.

In 1716 Captain Moody at Casco is ordered to furnish the Indians "with some small matter of bread and liquor as in his prudence & discretion he shall judge convenient;" and rum, pipes and tobacco were supplied.[19] However prudent and discreet Moody may have been he seems to have doubted the discretion of others, for in 1718 he states that all the disorders which happen amongst the Indians were occasioned by strong drink that is sold to them by coasters, which he desires may be prevented. At the same time Mr. Baxter, who is about to return as missionary if he can have "a Liberty from his Ch. at Medfield," recommended "as a very necessary thing for the more easy Preselyting the Indians that the Sloops going Eastward be prevented selling Rum to the Indians."[20]

About the same time Governor Shute in a letter to Father Rale deplores the consequence of such supply, which is "destructive to Soul and Body," assuring him that the government has nothing more at heart than to prevent the Indians having any rum sent to them, and he will "take it kindly" if the priest can suggest some method to stop it.

But the generous supply continued. In 1751 Squalook of the Penobscots wrote to Phips that the French governor threatened them because of their friendship for the English, but he assures him that they will not be frightened: "We live on our own

18 N. Y. Docs., III, 462-3. 19 Coun. Rec., 6, 492.

20 The two letters were read in Council, June 27.

Rights," he says, "what god has given us & where we live, we'll die by it." But he is not satisfied with his English friends as is shown by this postscript: "Brother, once more we don't like a great deale of Rum it hinders our Praires, we buy too much of it, it hurts our Souls it is not you but we that doe it, one Kegg & one bottle is Enough for one man and the women must have none . . . I expect your answer to this."[21]

Scalp Money

Both New France and New England offered scalp money in varying amounts, according to times of greater or less danger. Canada paid her Indians for English scalps and prisoners, while New England, so far as found, offered money for Indian scalps only. The one exception found was in 1747 when such reward was offered for *enemy* scalps "as a retaliation for killing men, women and children." The beginning in Canada seems to have been in 1690, and it caused a great increase of cruelty in the savage wars.[22]

The profits of a ransom might induce the Indian to save his captive's life, but when death was equally lucrative, more sure and less troublesome he chose to kill.

Many Acts of Reward were passed by Massachusetts. To quote that of 1696: "For better Encouragement to prosecute the French and Indian Enemy" the General Court offered "fifty pounds p head for every Indian man and 25£ p head for any Indian woman or Child, male or Female, under the age of fourteen years taken or brought in Prisoner, the Scalps of all Indians slain to be produced."[23]

In 1703 the prize was forty pounds for each scalp of an Indian enemy above ten years of age, and any volunteer who maintained himself free from the Province charge, and who might bring in a live Indian enemy under ten could "have the benefit of the sale thereof, as the law Directs, together with all other Plunder."

This infamous bill was to be in force one year and volunteers

[21] Arch. 32, 199. [22] Sullivan's "District of Maine," 251. [23] Arch. 73, 278.

from New Hampshire were to have four-fifths of the same "encouragements."[24]

Later in the war money was paid only for Indians old enough to bear arms.

During King William's war the King of France informs Frontenac that it is impossible to meet the great expense of twenty crowns for every male prisoner; of ten for every woman and a like sum for every person killed; that other means must be found to incite those who are disinclined to fight.[25]

It is easy to understand that the French treasury was much more severely taxed than that of Massachusetts.

In 1748 Mr. Doolittle of Northfield wrote: "It is a rare thing we can obtain an Indian Scalp, let us do what Spoil we will upon them; so careful are they to carry off and conceal their Dead," to prove which he continued: "At Fort Massachusetts, where it is probable near sixty have been killed, never have been found more than three Scalps" showing that "our Men will not venture out . . . on any Scalping Act whatsoever."[26] This statement seems to be modified by Goold[27] who says scalps were so remunerative that private companies were formed to profit thereby. Lovewell's was one of these. The reward for scalps at his time was one hundred pounds, but "the difference between the currency and sterling was then two and a half for one."[28]

Groups of individuals furnished support and received profit from this industry. In the diary of a Falmouth minister is this entry: "June 18, 1757 I receive 165 pounds 3 — 3 . . . my part of scalp money." So let us not forget when we count the priest over zealous in urging his flock to get English scalps that a New England parson had a financial interest in those of his enemies!

The New Hampshire Gazette of June 17 noted the arrival at Falmouth of a schooner, "which had been out on the Scalping Account," bringing two captured canoes, each with a pole bearing

24 Arch. 71, 664. 25 Que. Docs., II, 123. 26 "Hist. Northfield," 380.

27 "Portland in the Past," 190. 28 Farmer's Belknap's "History of New Hampshire."

a scalp, and probably having more "as they design'd to decoy the Enemy on board and went well arm'd for the Purpose." Perhaps these were some by which the parson profited. It's not a pleasant story, but in an earlier June issue of the Portsmouth paper one reads of the twenty fishermen who were killed by Indians near Damariscotta.

In this year the Canadian Government curtailed its bounties; shown by a bit of news quoted in the Boston Gazette[29] from the Halifax Gazette. The boatswain's mate of the snow, *Prince of Wales*—named Petit—had been taken and released and he heard how: "Some Indians had lately bro't in a Number of Scalps, for which they had received the Bounty; a Short Time after, they were found out to be French scalps (suppos'd some of the Neutrals formerly so called); whereupon the Governor and Admiral immediately order'd the Bounty on Scalps to be taken off, and only to be paid for such as were bro't in alive, and also ordered that whatever Indian should for the future presume to bring in any Scalp, should be severely punished which, if true, may be the Means of saving many an Englishman's Life."

Visits to Boston

Both French and English courted alliance with the savages. If the French had better luck let us not forget that the English tried for it. Our archives contain accounts of many a conference with the Indians of Maine and those of the Five Nations. Gyles and Bane were the usual interpreters when the Eastern Indians waited upon the Governor of Massachusetts and made to him their speeches, laying down before him their packs of beaver which they called their "letters."

Both French and English tried to profit by the existing enmity between the tribes of New England and New York, but when Massachusetts sought help from the Five Nations her only gain was in playing the part of benefactor.

[29] Nov. 7, 1757.

In 1722, when in trouble with the Penobscots, she sent word to the Nations that if some of their chiefs would like to visit Boston it would "be Acceptable to the Gov^{mt}."

Col. John Schuyler came with the visitors and Joseph Kellogg was their interpreter. They were offered rewards for scalps, if only they would go out and get them. Perhaps they were less eager to fight because one of the chiefs died, but Boston gave him a grand funeral. "Last week one of the Chiefs of the Mohawks lately come to town dyed at the Royal Exchange Tavern in King-Street, and was magnificently interred on Friday night last. A drawn Sword lay on the coffin, and the Pall was supported by six Captains of the militia. The Gentlemen of the Council followed next the corps, and then the Justices of the Town and the commission Officers of the Militia. At last followed four Indians, the two hindmost (whom the government had appointed to attend him in his sickness) with each a pappoos at her back."[30] Before they left in November six chiefs dined at the Green Dragon with the Honourable House of Representatives. They conferred with the General Assembly, expressed their Abhorrence of the Rebellion of the Eastern Indians and their gratitude for the presents received, especially the guns and ammunition. Then they rode away on the horses supplied.[31]

More came the next year with "sham proposals of alliance against the Eastern Indians." The newspapers show their reluctance, for although they agreed after several conferences to take up the hatchet they would wait until His Majesty had been informed and they had learned his pleasure.

Upon arriving they had been taken to the "large House in the Common, late belonging to Mr. Francis Wainwright."[32] Meanwhile they provided something of a circus for the townsfolk, who entertained them "with the sight of a Gun which has but one Barrel and one Lock, it was discharged of Eleven Bullets suc-

[30] N. E. Courant, 22 October, 1722. [31] N. E. Courant, November 26, 1722.

[32] Corner Tremont Street and Temple Place.

cessively in about Two Minutes . . . it was loaded but once for the Eleven Shot, and each of them went thro' a double Door at about Fifty Yards distance."[33] "The said Delegates" on their part "had an Ox given to them on Friday last, which they kill'd with Bow and Arrows and in the Evening a Fire was made in the Common and a Kettle hung over it, in which part of the said Ox was boil'd; where they Danced after their own manner in presence of some of our principal Gentlemen and also Thousands of Spectators."[34] Six of them did go to see Indians of the Eastward, but they quickly returned and the rest went home to deny at Albany what they had promised at Boston. It was hinted that the Dutch, jealous of New England, might have had a finger in it.

Some bills of expense for Indian visitors during the next decade are bad enough to quote. For a feast at the Castle the province paid not only for pipes, tobacco and great quantities of meat, rum, wine, beer and cider, but for what naturally followed in the breakage of dishes, windows, tables, chairs and general destruction. Pipes must have been smashed in the same generous manner for forty-eight dozen were supplied in nineteen days!

In 1736, when nine Penobscot chiefs came for a conference, there are similar charges: Six pounds of meat was furnished for each daily; rum, wine, breakage, and "candles all night" were paid for as was the cost for "showing them the rope-dancers" and for "washing forty-nine of their greasy shirts."[35]

Visits to Court (French and English)

To impress the Indian and to interest the European, groups of natives were taken across the ocean. Mme. de Caylies[36] in her memoirs speaks of "two young savages from America, who were presented at Court and loaded with gifts, among which were munitions to be given to those Christian Indians, who had lost theirs." These two youths were a source of anxiety to the government.

[33] It was made by Mr. John Pimm in Anne Street near the Draw-Bridge.

[34] The New England Courant and The News-Letter, September, 1723.

[35] Arch. 29, 317. [36] Quoted in the Parkman Manuscripts.

The minister at Versailles wrote to the Governor of Acadia (Villebon) that His Majesty did not think it safe to send the two children of the chiefs of Kenebequi and Pentagouët by a certain frigate — this in February, 1693 — so he was keeping them for a better opportunity, and he instructed the governor to send gifts and inform their fathers of this delay.[37] The two young Indians were probably over feasted at Versailles, where they spent another month, for they fell sick on the way to La Rochelle, whence they were to embark, and greater was the anxiety at Versailles.

One of them was the son of Madocawando. (Mr. B. P. Poore thinks that a certain page of hieroglyphics — copied in the Parkman manuscripts — may be part of a letter written by him). When he arrived in Quebec he was told that his father had behaved badly in his absence and because of the good treatment he had received in France it was his duty to bring his parent to the fighting point. This he could not do, however, because certain hostages held by the English were kin to Madocawando.

In 1696 more Indians, both friendly and hostile — the latter being prisoners of war, friends of the English — were taken to France that both allied and enemy Indians might be impressed by the splendors of the Court and the strength of the King's armies, and he, for their benefit, marshalled before them the army of Flanders. They were instructed that the armies of England were inferior.

In 1705 Vaudreuil sent to Paris Assacambuit, "who," says Penhallow, "was, of all the Indians that were ever known since King Philip never any appeared so cruel and inhumane . . . and being introduced before the King, lifted up his hand in a most vile and arrogant manner, saying this hand of mine has slain 150 of your majesty's Enemies within the territories of New England, which bold and impudent speech was so pleasing to that bloody monarch that he forthwith knighted him and ordered 8 livres a day to be pay^{d} him . . . besides Captains pay."[38] By all this he was so

[37] Que. Docs., II, 106. [38] "Indian Wars," p. 49 of MS. in Congressional Library.

exalted on his return that he drove his people to exasperation and was forced by them "to fly his country and never returned after."

In Queen Anne's war things were going badly. The colonists, waiting for an English army to reinforce their own, and eager to again attack Port Royal, had grown weary. Following the French lead, and hoping to arouse the Queen to action, Col. Peter Schuyler of Albany persuaded some chiefs of the Five Nations to go with him to England.

There were months of delay in Boston; the savages must be diverted so the Governor "was pleased to allow them to go into the frontiers to passe Some time in Hunting," and as an earnest of greater glory to come Colonel Hobby's regiment was mustered for their benefit. In February, 1709/10, the House of Representatives, knowing that Schuyler was about to embark "with four of our good friends the Maquas with Designs of generall Service for these Her Maj[esties] Provinces" voted him "30£ towards furnishing his Table & Conveniences for the said Maquas in their Voyage."

We have pictures of their London days in Smith's "History of New York" (he quoting Oldmixon), and in other books. Steele tells us that: "They were placed in a handsome apartment at an upholsterer's in King-Street, Covent-gardens." Wherever they went mobs followed, for their arrival "made a great Bruit thro' the whole Kingdom . . . The Court was at that Time in Mourning for the Death of the Prince of Denmark; these American Kings were therefore dressed in black under Clothes, after the English Manner, but instead of a Blanket, they had each a Scarlet-in-grain Cloth Mantle edged with Gold, thrown over all their other Garments. This Dress was directed by the Dressers of the Playhouse, and given by the Queen, who was advised to make a Shew of them. A more than ordinary Solemnity attended the audience they had of her Majesty. Sir Charles Cotterel conducted them in two Coaches to St. James's and the Lord Chamberlain introduced them into the royal Presence."

This was April nineteenth, 1710. They told the Queen that they had taken the long voyage, which none of their predecessors could be prevailed upon to undertake, . . . to tell her those things which they thought necessary for the Good of her and for them, her allies, on the other side of the water. They continued: "We mightily rejoiced when we heard our great Queen was going to send an army to reduce Canada, and in token of our Friendship, we hung up the Kettle and took up the Hatchet." Then, they told her, because she had been prevented in her design, they were made sorrowful and feared the French would think they were unable to make war against them. "The Reduction of Canada is of great Weight to our free Hunting, so that if our great Queen should not be mindful of us, we must with our Families forsake our Country . . . or stand neuter either of which will be much against our Inclinations." The address, read by Major Pidgeon, was doubtless "made for them and not by them."

"The 4 Indian Kings' speech, translated into verse, with their effigies taken from life" was published in London, and the effigies have been several times reproduced.[39] They were made, probably, from the portraits painted by royal order and hung, says the Spectator, in the British Museum.

After their return they sent from Boston a letter to the Archbishop of Canterbury reminding him of his and the Society's (for propagation) kind promise of providing missionaries with a chapel and house, and the Archbishop, addressing "My most worthy Lords," answers that he has not been forgetful of the Business and that when "the fort and Chappell & missionary house are fitt" two good men will be sent, for which purpose money has been deposited. He signed the letter "y^r affectionate lrd Canterbury."[40]

The Protestant Effort

Few, if any, converts were made in the early years in New England. A contemporaneous writer accounts for it by the difficulty

39 In Wilson's "Mem. Hist. of N. Y.," II; "Nar. & Crit. Hist. of Am.," V, 106, and "Am. Mag.," 1878. 40 Manuscript letter, Cong. Lib.

of the Indian language, but he naively adds that the whites easily acquire enough facility for trade, but not to make themselves understood about "things spiritual."[41] The Massachusetts charter, however, demanded that the people should "be soe religiously, peacablie and civilly governed as their good life and orderlie conversac̄on maie wynn and incite the natives of country to the knowledg and obedience of the onlie true God and Savior of mankinde, and the Christian fayth, which in our royall intenc̄on and the adventurers free profession is the principall ende of this plantac̄on," and in 1629 Gov. Cradock reminds Endicott that the main end is "to bring the Indians to the knowledge of the Gospel." But the example of godly living and "orderly conversation" did not suffice, and to counteract the efforts of the Jesuits, Parliament in 1649 established "A Society for propagating the Gospel among the natives of New England." That Society died at the Revolution, but Charles II incorporated another for "New England and parts adjacent," which still exists as "The New England Company." The remittances to New England were cut off in 1779, but missions in Canada still receive its help.

It was under the first Society that Eliot worked. Its object was conversion by "visits, schools and sermons." Visits were difficult; even Eliot's were usually short. The minister could not live among the Indians as could the priest.[42]

In 1700 the General Court named a committee "to consider methods to obviate the Industry of the french Missionaries in Debauching the five Nations."[43] Perhaps the gift of a hundred pounds was one method employed, for in August John Schuyler reported that he had divided that amount between the "Cagnawogs" in Canada and the nations. With the money he bought stroud blankets, brass kettles, fine shirts and "Caggs for Rhum." The next year Massachusetts considered her nearer neighbors, believing that the Frenchmen had "debauched 'em from their former obedience to the King," and instigated them to murder, so it was

[41] The Planter's Plea. [42] See p. 32. [43] Arch. 30, 456a.

resolved that: "Three able Learned Orthodox ministers" should be sent speedily to the Eastern Indians and those of Merrimac River,[44] and the Corporation for Propagating the Gospel was asked to pay their salaries.[45]

The bewildered savages raised no question about the "Orthodoxy" of these "able" men, but a little later Father Rale gave his opinion of the "Learning" of one of them, being very contemptuous of the Latin of the Rev. Joseph Baxter, but Governor Shute told the critical priest that the main qualification of a missionary to the barbarous Indian was "not to be an exact scholar as to Latin, but to bring them from darkness to the light of the gospel,"[46] and in this Mr. Baxter seems to have been pleased with his success.

He wrote 31 August, 1717: "I preached at Brunswick and several Indians came to hear me; Capt. Gyles interpreted to them ye Heads of ye Sermons, and they seemed well pleased therewithall."[47] That his opinion was justified seems to be proved by a petition to the Great Governor at Boston, dated Fort George, Brunswick, Oct. 3, 1717:

"We, Indian Chiefs Belonging to Pagipcut River, whose names are under Riten, Desiear y^t^ Mr. Baxter may Be at Pagipcut whear thier is an Intarpreater, for he is a Very good man . . . and we Desiear ye Great Governor & Councill would order a small Praying house to be built near the ffort for the English & U^r^ [underwritten?] to meet in one Sabath Days." John Gyles Interpreter.

Signed with the marks of Sabatis and two more.[48]

For three months' service Mr. Baxter was paid thirty-seven and a half pounds. But the greatest effort for conversions was by the writing of sermons or tracts. One high-sounding title is typical of many: "The Day-Breaking if not the Sun-Rising of the Gos-

44 Before Philip's War the Praying Indians were about four thousand, and President Mather wrote in 1687 that there were six regular churches of baptized Indians, eighteen assemblies of catechumen, twenty-four Indian preachers and four English ministers who preached in Indian tongue.

45 Arch. 30, 461. 46 Arch. 51, 306. 47 His Journal is in Gen. Reg., 21, 45-60.

48 Arch. 31, 94.

pell with the Indians in New-England." This, written by Eliot, was printed in England in 1647. "Eliot's Catechism" was the first book printed in the Indian language. That was made at Cambridge, Massachusetts, in 1653, and the first bible printed here in *any* language was that which "the apostle" translated for his Indians; the two Testaments appearing in 1661 and 1663. The literal translation of the title is: "The Whole Holy His-Bible God, both Old Testament and also New Testament. This turned by the servant-of-Christ, who is called John Eliot." Its preface commends it to Prince Charles the Second.

"James Printer," an Indian journeyman, worked with Samuel Green on the second edition; he being the only man "able to compose the sheets and correct the press with understanding."

Among the other attractive books which our good apostle translated for his aborigines are: Baxter's "Call to the unconverted" and Shepard's "Sincere Convert," the "Indian Primer" and "Indian Grammar Begun," "Dialogues" and a metrical version of the Psalms.

The following instance shows the difference in Catholic and Protestant methods. A priest would go through fire and water to baptize a child and so save it from perdition. Chaplain Hinsdale, at Fort Dummer, although doubtless believing as strongly in the efficacy of baptism, showed his bigotry and lack of sympathy while he waited to write a long letter to "His Excellency Jonath^{n} Belcher Esq ed^{t} the other Honour^{ble} Commissioners for Propagating The Gospel Among The Heathen," telling the gentlemen how he had delayed a baptism that he might first instruct the relatives of the child in the principles of religion. He said "They Seamed to be well pleased & satisfied," but the mother had gone into the woods to the Hunt contrary to his Expectations! But Hinsdale chose to lose the child rather than break the Covenant.

In New York there was complaint that ministers were too lazy to learn the Indian language and it was recommended, but not accomplished, that five or six English youths, who well understood grammar, be sent to the tribes to learn their language, customs and manners.[49] On the other hand when the sachems were asked to send their children to New York to learn to read and write they said: "Wee answer that wee are not masters or disposers of them; that is a matter that relates to our wives, who are the sole disposers of their children while they are under age." Governor Fletcher was able to keep a bright lad in his family until he had learned to speak English and Dutch, then "his Mother came down and inticed him away to kindle his father's fire and build up his house."

Schools

The charter of Harvard College states that one of its objects shall be "the Education of the English and Indian youth of this country in Knowledge and Godliness," but of the latter "Caleb Cheeshahteaumuck Indus" stands alone on the catalogue of its graduates. He, the son of a sachem of Holmes's Hole, now Vineyard Haven, was of the class of 1665 and soon died of tuberculosis.

Other young Indians were members of the college for longer or shorter periods, but in 1698, not being of great use, "the old Brick College com̄only called the Indian Colledge[50] is pulled down to the ground, being sold to Mr. Willis the builder of Mr. Stoughton's Colledge."[51]

Thirty-four years later at a conference at Falmouth Governor Belcher said to the chiefs: "If you are willing to send your Children to Boston they shall be brought up to Learning at the College that so they may officiate as Fathers among you, and teach you the true Religion and this Education shall cost you nothing." He assured them that the better they know the English the more will they love them. Before they "knew the French religion" they thought the Pagan a very good one, and they ought not to be

49 N. Y. Docs., IV, 184.

50 Mather described it as strong and substantial, not very capacious, but big enough to accommodate twenty scholars with convenient lodgings and studies.

51 Sewall's "Diary," I, 480.

averse to looking into another, for they might find the English better than the French.[52]

The offer for free education was evidently not accepted for Mr. Matthews[53] says that so far as he is aware Benjamin Larnel was the only Indian student at Harvard after 1700. He, of the class of 1716, died before graduation.

The School at Stockbridge was begun in 1734 with about twenty boys of the Housatonic tribe. Mr. John Sergeant, a tutor of Yale, was its head. The boys studied in winter and scattered in summer. Two years later Mr. I. Hollis, nephew of Thomas, Harvard's benefactor, sent money to educate twelve boys "in letters and husbandry";[54] and Samuel Holden of London offered to educate some girls. This was more difficult because the girls, placed in white families, were homesick. Work for them continued, however, for a writer in the "Boston Post Boy" of Sept. 3, 1739, says that he saw at Stockbridge "several young women sewing cloth, making shirts etc." Probably there was a hiatus because in 1751 the Secretary of the Society for Propagation, Mr. Jasper Maudit of London, made known to their commissioners in New England[55] that "by way of tryal for this year" the Company in their zeal desired that some girls, not exceeding ten, should be educated there by Mrs. Sergeant or some other proper person and allowances were made for the cost.

A letter written by Dr. Benjamin Colman in 1743 shows his point of view. He says: "The matter is of absorbing interest," and that they, the people, were "not left at liberty either as men or Christians, for there cannot be a propaganda of religion among any people without an equal regard for both sexes; not only because females are alike precious souls, . . . but because the care of the souls of children" lies chiefly with the mothers for the first seven or eight years.

Moor's Charity School, Dartmouth College—the most noted

52 Report of Conference in pamphlet, Mass. Hist. Soc.

53 Trans. Col. Soc., 17, 274. 54 See Martin Kellogg. 55 Arch. 32, 156.

of the schools — was that begun at Lebanon, Connecticut, in 1750 by the Rev. Eleazer Wheelock. His small parish demanded but about half his time; the other half he gave to the education of Indian youth, of whom he wished to make missionaries to their own people.

Joshua Moor, a farmer, later gave to Dr. Wheelock a house and two acres of land in Lebanon, and in his honor the name of "Moor's Charity School" was given.

Among those interested was Whitefield, who presented a bell, for "Indian children are inclined to ramble & it is difficult to get them together."

Among the first lads sent to Lebanon were two from the Delawares; one, eleven; the other fourteen years old. One of them soon died; the other, four years later, "could read Virgil, Tully and the Greek testament very handsomely." He was sent to Princeton College, but disgraced himself and finally ran away.

A pew in the parish church was set aside for the boys in 1755 and six years later they "gave the Indian girls liberty to sit in the hired seat on the woman's side below." These pews must have been crowded, but Mr. Wheelock found "that of forty Indian youths that had been under his care twenty returned to the vices of savage life."

Samson Occom, a Mohegan of Connecticut, was the most famous graduate. In 1765 he, quite in the modern fashion, was sent out to solicit funds, and so successful was he in England and Scotland that the school was enlarged and removed to Hanover, New Hampshire, in 1770, thereby bringing it nearer the Indians.

Now called a college it was named for the Earl of Dartmouth. It was a kind of Normal School where not only Indian boys and girls might be trained, but white lads could be fitted to be missionaries.

The collected funds were used separately; the English gifts being used for the white pupils and the Edinburgh Society holding those from Scotland for the use of the Indians.[56]

[56] The librarian of the College tells me that Indians who now come there, receive a certain financial aid from the Moor fund, but there have been only three or four to use it during the past twenty-five years.

In 1772 the Rev. Sylvanus Ripley and Lieutenant Taylor[57] went to Caughnawaga to induce some boys to join the school. A council of chiefs was called and they "to a man" agreed to send some children against the zealous remonstrance of their priest. Nine were chosen, two being Hurons from Lorette, who had already set forth to seek an education, and who "appeared to be endowed with a greatness of mind and a thirst for learning which is uncommon."

Mr. Wheelock found the younger boys from Caughnawaga as sensible of kindnesses as English children commonly are. They showed too "that they had been under Government in the Families to which they belong."

Among the first boys chosen — for others went afterward from this and other Canadian villages — were three who were children or grandchildren of captives. A Tarbell (Groton), Stacy (from near Saratoga) and a grandson of Eunice Williams, who being sick with measles at this time was to go later. He never did, for as Mr. Wheelock wrote:[58] "Through the influence of the Priest and the aged Grandmother, the Boy . . . was like still to be detained." Another descendant, however, Eleazer, the fake dauphin, was a pupil of the school in 1807.

In 1774 when messengers again went forth from Hanover seeking pupils they took four little boys from St. Francis. "Fine, sprightly Lads . . . and they all have a good share of English blood in their Veins."[59]

The Land

The land question is too big to touch, but is it not always answered by the ever-old and ever-true word of the Prophet: "The place is too strait for me, give room that I may dwell?"[60] This is the word of civilized man to the savage. In New England there *was* room. A terrible plague had made it. Room for more men than England could spare.

[57] See Chapter XVIII. [58] "Continuation of the Narrative of the Indians' Charity School."

[59] See Samuel Gill, Salisbury. [60] Quoted in this connection by Dr. Geo. E. Ellis.

Governor Cradock instructed Endecott: "If any of the salvages pretend right of inheritance to all or any part of the lands granted in our patent, endeavor to purchase their tytle, that we may avoid the least scruple of intrusion." The first colonists asserted that in no single instance did they take land without the consent and compensation of the owners. But who were the owners? Not the sachems who marked their totems on the deeds. They did not know what they were doing. The land was owned in common, and often it had been gained by conquest. Any Indian had the right to use what belonged to his nation. It had been their fathers; they held it in trust for their sons. It was impossible for an Indian to understand how an individual could own the soil. He possessed only the right to hunt and fish, and to occupy the land with others.

Acts were passed to protect the Indians. In 1633 it was (generously!) decreed that they had a just right to such lands as they possessed and improved. No individual could buy without leave or license from the government.

In 1701 all deeds which had been obtained from Indians after 1633 without that license were declared void; and if any such were made after the date of this act, the purchaser, at discretion of the Court, could be fined an amount not exceeding double the value of the land — in Connecticut it was twenty pounds for every acre — and imprisonment not exceeding six months.

CHAPTER IV

Redemptions, Ransoms and Naturalization

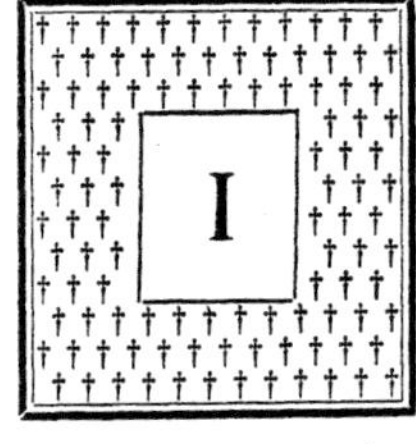N March, 1676, the Governor of Massachusetts sent a messenger to "The Indian Sagamores and people that are in warre against us," offering to redeem the captives, who are mostly women or children, either for payment "in goods or wompom" or by exchange of prisoners. The messengers carried "paper, pen and Incke" that an answer might be written if any among them could write.[1]

The next year Maxus[2] and others sent this letter addressed to "Loving English frinds, I have sent Mrs hamans to you to tell you that we have bin carefull of our prisnors this is 3 times we have sent to you & have all ways mised of you gouorneur of boston wee would first know your mind you send [illegible] for piese you allways broke the pese. Hince I intret you to send vs a Answer of this leter by mr garner or mr oliver if they be not at home send mr wesell but send non of them that have bin here alredy we think that them men that you sent before were minded to Chet vs mrs hamans & the Rest of the prisners can tell that wee have drove Away all the damrellscogin engins [Androscoggin Indians] from vs for thay will fight and we are not willing of their Company we are willing to trad with you as we have don formerly wee pray you send vs such things as we want powder cloth tobarco liker cornbread and send the captives that you toke at pimaquid gouorneur of boston we do vnderstand that Squando is minded to Chet you he is mind to get as many prisnors as he Can & so bring them

[1] Arch. 68, 193.

[2] A Tarratine living east of the Piscataqua, that being the Nipmuck name for the Abenakis.

to you & so make you belive that it is kenebeck men that have don all this spoul [spoil]."[3]

In later years it was well understood among "Canada Indians" that white captives had a money value. Nevertheless it was the general policy of Massachusetts not to ransom her people; thereby setting a price on women and children. To raise the funds to redeem the first Canadian captives — those carried from Hatfield and Deerfield in 1677 — required the effort of forty-six towns.[4]

Many of our people were kept in Indian villages in the Maine woods and frequent exchanges of prisoners were made there. Capt. John Alden[5] was sent down the coast several times on this errand.

After an agreement had been made at York in November, 1690, "by some Gentlemen Commissionated by the Governor & Council with John Hawkins, an Indian Enemy Captain, in behalfe of the Eastern Sagamores," Alden took some Indians from Portsmouth and went to Sagadahock where he received ten English captives and a promise that the rest should be brought to Storer's Garrison in Wells on May first. The President of the province went then to meet the chiefs, but, as Mr. Palfrey says, "the favorable season for their inroads having returned, the savages had changed their minds."

[3] Arch. 30, 241, Indexed "Letter from Moxus and other Indians concerning their desire to live in peace with the English — by Mrs. Hamond, July 1, 1677."

[4] See Chapter V.

[5] John Alden, "the tall man of Boston," son of John of Plymouth, was captain of the sloop in the colony service, "to provide provisions and clothes for the force at Falmouth and parts adjacent." The service was not without danger. His predecessor in command, with some of his men, had been killed by pirates. Alden himself, with his son and Messrs. Nelson and Tyng, were once taken by a French frigate, but the Aldens were soon released. A greater peril came to him in the accusation of witchcraft, made in May, 1692, when he was seventy years old, by some "wenches playing their juggling tricks," in which connection he dared to use "sea language." After fifteen weeks in Boston jail he escaped to Duxbury where he stayed in hiding till the delusion passed.

The following bill of charges gives dates of other redemptions by Captain Alden.

"Ordered by Govern^{r} Bradstreet and Council to goe to Sagatahock in the Sloope Mary to buy ye Captives

£10:00:00

For the hire of my vessell on the same Service for Captives to Casco Bay & Penobscott in March and Aprill 1692[6]

£18:00:00

Ordered by Govern^{r} Phips in Aprill & May 1694 to Penobscott thrice to Kenebeck and there to stay for ye Captives Charges of vessell men & provisions

74:12:10

£102:12:10."[7]

1691 — Nov. 23 — Ten captives were redeemed at Sagadahock, "Among them Mrs. Hull whom they were unwilling to part with, she being a ready good writer, they had employed her in the place of a secretary." She had been captured 22 Aug., 1690, when "travelling betwixt York & Kittery" says Pike. Her husband, Phinehas, escaped.

1690. *An Exchange at Quebec.*

Phips and Frontenac exchanged prisoners in 1690. Monseignat reported this very satisfactory, as they gave only women and children, with the single exception of Captain Davis, while they received adult men fit for service.[8]

He hopes the Admiral (Phips) will be badly received in Boston where the people are masters, for they will be irritated by his failure, which has cost so much in men and money.[9]

6 For his Instructions see "York," Chapter IX. 7 Arch. 71, 249.

8 M. Myrand in his "*Phips devant Québec*" contradicts this on the authority of Juchereau-de-Saint-Ignace, Superior of the Hôtel-Dieu.

9 Que. Docs., II, 23.

Immediately after the massacre at York came this order from the Governor and Council: "It having pleased the holy and Righteous God in his Sovereign pleasure at several times to suffer many of their ma^ties Liege People to fall into the hands of barbarous and merciless Enemies, and to be led away captive by them out of their own Land; whose misery and sufferings bespeake pity and Succour. Its therefore Recomended unto the several Ministers throughout this Colony in their respective congregations to Excite their people to put on bowells of compassion and Christian Charity towards their Bretheren and neighbours who are in such distress in the Enemies hands and to contribute towards their Redemption."[10] The money collected was to be distributed by Samuel Sewall, Esq., and Capt. Jeremiah Dummer.

1695. *Matthew Carey.*

In this year "a cartel or accord" for the exchange of prisoners having been made between the two Crowns the brigantine *Tryal* was allowed to go up the St. Lawrence as far as Tadousac, carrying Matthew Carey[11] to exchange all prisoners. Governor Stoughton wrote to Frontenac "No one of your nation is detained here as prisoner. Those who have ever been brought have had entire liberty to dispose of themselves at their own will, and to receive the profit of their labor as long as they lived here. They have seized the opportunity to go to Europe or other countries as they have chosen with the advantages of receiving good wages for services rendered on their voyage until reaching home."[12] He said also that he had great difficulty in making some return. "They rather choosing (if so they might) to continue here than to be dismist."[13]

It should be remembered that the French prisoners held by Massachusetts were mostly from Acadia — Nova Scotia and New Brunswick — and the high seas. Canada was too remote for retaliation, but Acadia was brought near by the many fishermen New England sent to her waters. Carey brought so few prisoners

[10] Arch. 37, 299. [11] Carey's Instructions have been printed in Gen. Reg., 24.

[12] Que. Docs., II, 184. [13] Arch. 2, 535.

(Frontenac says only two women and three children, thereby ignoring the Port Royal soldiers) that it was doubted if all had been sent, and the French Governor contrasted the spirit of the English with his own noble behavior for he had sent many English prisoners into France that they might go to Old England and thence to New. Others he had allowed to return by way of Orange and Manhattan; and he had also with much trouble and expense redeemed from the Indians as many as possible and placed them among the French, where they had been treated more kindly than if they were of the same nation. Continuing this letter of October 10, 1695, he has heard with sorrow of great cruelties practised by "the Gent of Boston, Manatte and Orange," of their sending some French prisoners to the Barbadoes and Virginia and that instead of redeeming prisoners from the Savages, whom they use to make war against the French, they constantly urge them to burn the prisoners "& to treat them with such cruelties as would cause horrour in a man that bears the name of a Christian." You must "find out means to hinder the continuance of this business, to which I should give the name of fury, because that however I am naturally inclined to lenity & humanity, I shall find my selfe in fine necessitated to suffer our Indians to dispose of the English prisonrs as they shall see good wch they would doe & would follow the Inclination that they have to Cruelty, wch I have allwayes hitherto opposed."

On the other hand Carey made "Proposalls . . . in the Beehalfe of Christyan Subjects taken by fforce of Armes." He asks for an agreement between the three Governours of Massachusetts, New York and Canada — that they shall by command or "Persswation" forbid such cruel practices as "cutting Scalping or Burning," and to encourage any Christian who might buy, barter, truck or in any way redeem any person from the Indians, that the said person shall receive the full value and also be paid for any further trouble or expense. If the captive be capable of labor, he shall work out his ransom, or if the ransom be produced he shall be free to return to his own habitation.[14]

In our archives[15] are the following lists. With few exceptions the captives can be identified. There are errors in the hometowns, as in all the lists.

November, 1695.

"Nams of English Captives Redeemed from Qubek by math^{w} Cary in octb^{r} / 95

Capt. Josf Hamand		of Piscadawa
Jno Key Senr		Do
Jno Key Junr		Do
Jam^{s} Rose		Cascow
Edwd Jones		n^{o} west
Hen^{y} Simpson		York
Jno Read		Samanfals
Jam^{s} Alexand^{r}		Cascow
Thos Drew		Groton
Jesp^{r} Swarton	boy	Cascow
Mrs Mar^{tt} Stilson		Pemequid
Mrs Mary Plasted		York
Hitobl Goodin		Kittrey
Eliz^{h} Tozer		Do
Sarrah ffargisson		Do
Abeg^{ll} ffargisson		Do
Mary Tibs		York
Johana Swarton		Do
Eliz^{h} Smart		oyster River
Cisia Brakett		Do
Magd^{n} Addams		York
Mary Cooper		Do

Nam^{s} of thos Remaining Still in hands of the french at Canada

Sam^{ll} york	of Cascow
Sam^{ll} Senter	Do

14 Cary's Seven Propositions. Arch. 2, 532. 15 A 38, 1-4.

Abig^{ll} Willey		oys^{r} River	
Judy Willey		Do	
Eliz^{h} Willey		Do	
Grysell Ottis		Cachicha	
Christen ottis		Do	
Abig^{ll} Key		Kittery	
Mercey Addams		Do	
Jos Perkins	boy	Dover	
Abig^{ll} Cursinwhitt		Do	
Steph^{h} ottis		Do	
Lidey Langly		Do	gerl
Mary Swarton		Cascow	Do
Jam^{s} Stiltson	boy	Pemequid	
Jno ottis	Do	Dover	
Abig^{ll} Brakett		Do	
Jno Stephins	boy	pemquid	
Rose ottis	gerll	Cichicha	
Jno Antony	boy	Do	
obada Pribble	Do	Do	
Eliz^{bh} Squir		Dover	
Mary Stilson	gerll	pemquit	
Kath^{n} Stephens	Do		
Jno Persons	Boy	Dover	
Sara Davis	Cascow	gerll	
Roland yong	boy	Dover	
Robt Clark	Do	York	
Rich Persons	boy	Dover	
Mary Sayard	gerll	Do	
Ester Swayard		Do	
Richd Short	boy	Do	
Char^{les} Trafton		York	boy
Jno Shiply	boy	oy^{r} River	
Sara Whitt	gerll	Do	
Sam^{ll} Rand	boy	Do	

Hana Dongan		
Mary Astin	gerll	York
Thos Baker	boy	Cascow
Geo Gray	Do	Do
Rich^{d} nason	Do	
Jos^{h} Michell"		

In October, 1698, Major Converse and Colonel Alden were instructed by the Council[16] "to endeavor Speech with some of the Sachems." They demanded that all prisoners should be returned and the missionaries at Penobscot, Norridgewock and Androscoggin be removed. The Indians answered that the good missionaries must not be driven away, but the white captives should be free to go or to stay with their Indian friends as they chose. In the meantime Frontenac had told the Indians he could no longer support them in their war, advising them to give up their captives; and of these "as many as were able to travel above an hundred miles in this terrible season of the year from their headquarters down to the sea-side" were brought to the Englishmen with promises "of the rest as early in the spring as there could be any travelling."[17]

Later in the year Converse and Colonel Phillips, of the Council carried in the *Province Galley* (Cyprian Southack, commanding) prisoners for exchange. At Pejepscot they made with the Indian delegates such a treaty, says Palfrey,[18] "as they had been accustomed to make, and as soon as they dared, to violate."

Among the prisoners carried from Boston was Bombazeen of Norridgewock, a most "ferocious sagamore."[19] This was much against the will of the people, but it was thought best to make no exceptions.

The "Petticion To Governor Stoten," sent soon after Ryswick, does little credit to the spelling of Bombazeen's amanuensis: "It Is humbely to Aquaint yor Exellance y^{t} I have been thes four

[16] See York, Chapter IX. [17] Magnalia, II, 642. [18] Vol. IV, 158.

[19] See Oyster River and Groton, Chapter X.

years now in Prisone w[t] out any hearing, and now since yr is a publick peace Amongst all nations I doe not desire any thing as to my self Contrare to ye law of ye land, but as to y[t] wch Consists w[t] nature for ye liberty wch all men desires is desireabl.

May it yrfor pleas yor Excelance yt I may have ye liberty to be Called befor you w[t] and interpetare and I will give you y[t] satisfactione y[t] is dew from a subject to his Maties and Government wch is Earnestly desired by yo[r] poor Petticoner etc."[20]

1698/9. *January. Brought by the Province Galley.*

Two frigates, the *Newport* and *Sorling*, had been used to protect New England vessels from privateers, but they could not enter shoal water and the General Court built and equipped a small vessel of ten guns which was known as the *Province Galley.* John Phillips, its commander, was Cotton Mather's father-in-law, and on the "24 d. 10 m. 1698/9," Mather wrote in his diary:[21] "And my *Father-in-Law*, being by order of the General Assembly this Week sail'd unto the East-ward on a difficult Work in a dangerous Time, to fetch home our *Captives* in the Hands of the Indians and see what is to bee done about a Peace with the Salvages, I thought my Duty to carry the Concern of his Voyage with Special *Supplications* before the Lord," and to do that, he spent "the Day in a secret FAST." The result of the voyage is shown by a paper endorsed Colonel Phillips' Journal.[22] "A list of captives brought home in the Province Galley and of them that are yet in the Indians hands ye 24 Jannery 1698/9.

Cascoe Bay ye 17 Jannery 1698/9

Mary ffarbankes	of Lancaster
Mary Glasser	of Lancaster
Susanna Wood	of Haverhill
Daniell Lade	of Haverhill
Hannah Bradley	of Haverhill
Elizabeth Egerly	of oyster River

20 Arch. 30, 437. 21 Vol. I, 282. 22 Arch. 70, 398.

John Derry	of Ditto
Susanna Egerly	of Ditto
Sam[ll] Hutchings	of Spruce Crick taken in may Last.
Bethia Paine	of Yorke
Mahitable Parker	of Yorke
Dorothy Millberry	of Yorke
Elizabeth Barnes	of Sandy Beach
John Houlding	of Grotten
Tamazin Rouce	of Grotten
Mary Hatter(?)	of Kettery

The names of the Captives yett in the Indians hands.

Steven Houlding	of Grotten
Steven Houlding Junior	of ditto
Sarath Braginton	of Yorcke
Mary Parker	of Yorcke
Abiall Masterson	of Yorcke gon to Penacooke
Juda Emmerson	of oyster River
Joseph Egerly	of oyester River
Petter Denbow	of oyester River
Amie Nell	of Newichawanick
Ephriam Ropper	of Lancaster
Hannah Rugg	of Lancaster gon to Allbanie[?]
Joseph Bean	of Yorck a young man
Mary Sanders	of Billerica
Benj Hutchings	of Spruce Crick
Mary Emmerson	of Haverhill gon to Penacook
Elizbeath Sanders	of Pemaquid
Jane Higgaman	of ditto

An Eastard Boy his name is Robart cannot speak one word of English he att the fort cald Narrockeome-gog

Daniell Bradley of Haverhill

Carried to Canada a: 7 yrs ould

Jon[a] Hutchings of Spruce Crick

14 yeares ould Carried to Canada the Last octob[r]

Sam[ll] Gill of Salsbery Caried to Cannada

Nick ffrost drowned

Able Morton drowned"

1698. *Schuyler* and *Dellius.*

We have seen how the captives were brought home from Maine. After Ryswick, the Earl of Bellomont (Governor of New York and Massachusetts) sent Col. Peter Schuyler and "the Dutch Dominie" to secure the release of those in Canada.[23] They were instructed to demean themselves with great respect unto Count Frontenacque, and "by all means to avoid giving him any distaste."[24] They went to Montreal, Three Rivers and Quebec and reported that all the English, male and female, in the convents and among the townspeople were brought before them, "all of whom (except two or three) unanimously refused to return." They demanded the children under fourteen, who were reluctantly given to them. But even of these "Some still remained who hid themselves."[25] However, twenty-five came back with them, the only known New Englanders being Martin Smith and the three Beldings.

1705. *Capt. John Livingstone, Ensign John Sheldon* and *John Wells.*

After the Deerfield massacre letters were sent to Canada — in April and August — concerning the captives. As no answers had come there was some doubt if the messengers had received safe

[23] They carried to Frontenac the first news of the Peace.

[24] N. Y. Docs., IV, 340. [25] N. Y. Docs., IV, 350.

conduct from Albany; therefore when John Sheldon and John Wells asked permission to go to seek their kindred the Council advised their going, under the guidance of two French prisoners, "by water to Casco and thence by the direct course through the Country to Quebeck." The Frenchmen were "used to that Rhode," and were willing to undertake the journey and safe return of the messengers "at the peril of having their near relations here exposed." But after that "setting" of the Council the Governor "discoursed" with Capt. John Livingstone, who happened to be in town. He had been several times to Canada and was well acquainted with "the way thither from the upper Towns . . . which he accounted to be more safe than to Travail through the Eastern Country" and he would go without any Frenchmen at a cost of one hundred pounds and expenses, so the Governor, because of greater safety and certainty of the way, as well as of lower cost, advised that "the inconveniencies that might happen" from the Frenchmen's going be avoided and that Livingstone be engaged.[26]

They went by the Bay Path to Hatfield, over Hoosac Mountain to Orange, and by the lakes and Richelieu River to the St. Lawrence. The letter they carried informed Vaudreuil that Massachusetts had about a hundred and fifty French prisoners, and that in the spring, as soon as a list of the English prisoners was sent, Dudley would send the Frenchmen to Penobscot, they being mostly from Port Royal. In case his messengers should be by severe winter weather unable to return seasonably, he proposed that an Indian be sent to Casco Bay to appoint the time and place of the exchange. Instead of an Indian Vaudreuil sent Samuel Hill, with two Frenchmen, to guide him "through the woods."

They reached Portsmouth in May. Hill was a paroled captive from Wells. The list he brought showed one hundred and seventeen New Englanders held by the French and seventy by the Indians, but of all these Livingstone and Sheldon, who soon fol-

[26] Coun. Rec., 128; Dec. 13 and 19, 1704.

lowed, brought home only four or five. John Wells's mother had died. Sheldon brought his daughter, his son's wife, Esther Williams and two more, says Mr. Sheldon in his Deerfield History. The pious pastor of Deerfield said that "God's time of deliverance was not yet come." That he was, however, grateful for his friend's efforts is shown by his letter to Mrs. Livingstone dated "Quebec 21 Apr. 1705: I should be guilty of ingratitude if I should forget to offer you my thanks for your denyal of yourself the desirable companionship of your beloved consort for the sake of poor captives . . . There are hundreds here that are obliged to yourself. I hope to have the honor of kissing your hand & of a personal acknowledgment of your compassionateness herein."[27]

Eight soldiers escorted the commissioners and captives. With them was le Sieur de Courtemanche, who was sent by the Governor, to "make himself acquainted with the country" and to demand the release of Captain Baptiste as conditional to a general exchange. "Capt. Baptiste" was Jean Baptiste Guyon, a notorious pilot, useful to both Governments, loyal to neither. His release was frequently made a condition.[28]

When Courtemanche went home he said he had been very kindly treated in Boston, and in return he "entertained nobly" Stephen Williams and his father. Sewall notes that "Capt. Courtemaruh" (so print his editors) "din'd in the Hall" at Commencement, probably going to Cambridge by water as did Sewall.

On that very day in July Dudley wrote a letter to tell Vaudreuil he was sending the gentleman home by sea because he was ill!

1705. *Captain Vetch* and *William Dudley.*

The illness of the Sieur de Courtemanche was doubted. Perhaps it was feigned that he might be sent home by water, thereby making a cover for trade with the enemy in which shipowner, captain and Dudley himself were suspected of having an interest.

27 "Winthrop Papers." Mrs. Livingstone was Mary, daughter of Fitz John Winthrop.

28 See Rev. John Williams, Deerfield.

He was in John Borland's boat, Vetch commanding, and with him was the governor's youngest son, a youth of seventeen, and Samuel Hill, the paroled captive from Wells, whose French companions were sent overland. This was young William's first journey. Twenty years later he was one of Dummer's three commissioners.

The commissary was ordered to carry "A Hoggshead of good wine to the Governor there," and Courtemanche the promise that Baptiste should be released if Vaudreuil would sign certain articles. Dudley made this promise in spite of a vigorous remonstrance against the release by leading "Merchants, Traders and Sailers." They describe him as "A pretended ffrenchman Whose former Piracies Murder's and Villanies have been Notorious," and they "dread his Capacity of further Mischief." Dudley was sly about it. He wrote: "that as for Baptiste I think le Sieur de Courtemanche has learned so much that is infamous . . . that you will agree that he is a rascal, who does not deserve that you should want him back, and perhaps you will think is not worth my Keeping. This is why I am resolved to send him back."

But again negotiations failed and Vetch returned in November with only eleven captives, for which Borland was allowed £22. They were "the Meanest," said Dudley's enemies,[29] "leaving the Principal of the Captives behind" that they might have a Pretense to go again in "their Treacherous Design of Trading."

Three of the mean ones were Deerfield youths, Stephen and Samuel Williams and Jonathan Hoyt.

In 1705 Vaudreuil rejected the treaty Dudley sent. In the draft of one returned by him was an article that the two Governments return all prisoners without regard to number and do everything possible to "withdraw" those in the hands of Indians.[30]

Vaudreuil was accused of intentional delay and then, saying that the time fixed had passed, he allowed "several small parties of our Indians to recommence hostilities in his [Dudley's] government in order to force him to declare himself."[31]

[29] "Deplorable State of New England." [30] N. Y. Docs., IX, 772, October.

[31] N. Y. Docs., IX, 776. Vaudreuil to Pontchartrain, Apr., 1706.

1706. *John Sheldon* again.

In December, 1705, "as an exemplary act of generosity" Dudley returned some Port Royal prisoners — thereby avoiding the cost of their subsistence during the winter — but he kept Baptiste!

To secure the reward for generosity "John Sheldon was impressed by his Excellency to goe to Cannada to Treat about ye English Captivities." He left Deerfield with John Wells and Joseph Bradley of Haverhill late in January and reached Quebec early in March.

Vaudreuil was not satisfied, but he released some, who sailed away from Quebec early in June in the *Marie*, Capt. Thomas More, with orders to the Governor of Acadia to keep them in Port Royal until "all the French prisoners without distinction" should be returned there; but they were not very long detained as is shown by the News-Letter which says: "On Thursday 1 August arrived a Flag of Truce Back from Canada with Mr. Sheldon, the Messenger whom His Excellency sent to the Governour of Quebec for the Exchange of Prisoners who has brought with him 45."

Mr. Williams, whose opinions are always biased, says of these captives: "Such were sent away, who were judged ungainable [to popery] and most of the younger sort still kept."[32]

Much may be read in the items of what Mr. Sheldon "Expended upon ye Countrys account in Canada for himself and ye Captives in Generall:

	livres sous
by Taylors work in making clothes	17-
To m^r^ Dulenot paid for cloath for cloathing, for stockins shoes a shirt and a hat and a pair of gloves and a neck cloath	106-11
for a Coriall To goe to See ye captives att ye mohawk fort	12-
For a Cannoe and men To goe from Quebec To viset mr. williams	6-
more paid To m^r^ La Count my land lord at Quebec	38

[32] "Redeemed Captive," p. 83, edi. 1853.

more payd To ye Barbour for me and my men and for blooding 21
more paid for washing 8
more paid to my land lord att Montreal 77-06
more paid for my 2nd viset of ye captives at ye mohawk fort 4-08
more what i laied out for the captives when I came away from canady and one the salers 42-10
[There were expenses for Wells and Bradley his companions and]
Delivered To mr Jno Williams 200-
Layd out for my daughter mary for her nesesary cloathing 59-
more for my darter 15-
more for ye captives for Two Blankets 17."[33]

Besides this, on August 8 is a charge of £35 for Mr. Sheldon and £20 for each of his companions.[34]

Many Deerfield captives were on the *Marie*. Mr. Williams, because he might "neither be Permitted to Return" nor to see his people before they left, sent a "Pastoral Letter" to be read on the voyage, and Cotton Mather, that others might "share with them in the Benefit" printed it in his tract, now of the rarest, "Good Fetched out of Evil." He called Mr. Williams "that Suffering and Shining Servant of God . . . who is held still in his Captivity and with-held by the French Papists from Opportunities to make his Personal Addresses to the Rest of the Captives for their Establishment in our Holy Religion."

In the Letter Mr. Williams said: "I would Bless God who is opening a Door of Return for you: and if God be your Front guard and Rereward it shall yet go well with you." He asks them to pray for those left behind, and bids them not to "think to go shares or partners with God in His Glory," nor that they will have done their duty in asking in the Congregation for thanks to be

[33] Arch. 71, 239. [34] Arch. 71, 237.

given to God for their redemption, and he tells them that "Thanksliving is the best Thanksgiving."

1706. *Samuel Appleton.*

The French prisoners, who had been scattered among the towns, were brought together at Cambridge, and two men were sent overland with letters to Vaudreuil that he might collect the English prisoners. (Samuel Hill helped in this work, travelling at his own expense from Quebec to Montreal; although somewhere it is said that Vaudreuil sent him to arrange the exchange because Canada, like Massachusetts, found the expense of keeping the captives too great).

Samuel Appleton of Ipswich, one of the Council, was appointed commissioner, and on August 30, 1706, under a flag of truce he sailed on the brigantine *Hope*, Rowse commanding, for which the owners were paid thirty pounds a month. With it was the *Marie* and another, on which were the Frenchmen bound for Port Royal. The *Province Galley* convoyed them ten leagues beyond Cape Ann.

In November fifty-seven New Englanders landed in Boston. The worthy pastor of Deerfield coming in exchange for the unworthy pirate, "Captain Battis."

The Boston News-Letter, announcing the arrival on November 20, says they left Canada on October 29. "These were all that could then be got ready, and the rest are expected in the Spring. The French say that the Indians who made a Descent on our Frontiers this Summer, finding them so Lined with men, they were constrained to throw away their Arms Blankets &c. for the more speedy flight and returned again without so much as a flap to cover their nakedness." The General Court paid twenty shillings "to each of the Captives, this day, Return'd from Canada."

Among Mr. Appleton's charges were one hundred and fifty-five livres for the redemption of three captives and £2, 13s., 6d. for five bibles sent to the captives by Governor Dudley.

Mr. Appleton's tavern bill suggests a much more generous fare than that of John Sheldon.

1707/8. *John Sheldon's third Journey.*

Edmund Rice, Nathaniel Brooks and Edward Allen were his companions. Rice and Brooks both had children in captivity.

In January of this year the Governor told his Council that Vaudreuil proposed an exchange of prisoners — there were about ninety English persons in Canada — and he thought it would be well to have "a person Leger at Quebec to put the affair forward," suggesting that "Mr. John Sheldon . . . might be employed with suitable Retinue . . . if the season will permit."[35]

And from Versailles there was sent a letter, dated 30 June, 1707, to Vaudreuil assuming that all English prisoners, except Catholics, had been returned; and that of course he has given Dudley the reasons for their staying. If any others have stayed they must be carefully watched to be sure they are not spies, and if Dudley should demand these not to make trouble by holding them.[36]

But there was excitement in Canada. Rumors were many. New England was said to threaten an invasion and our friends were under constant surveillance.

Peter Schuyler wrote that two spies had come into Albany who said "they see Deaken Shelden at mont Royall, who walk'd y[e] streets, but they were told he was deteined & had not y[e] liberty to goe home."[37]

In the summer, escorted by Chambly de Rouville with a few soldiers, they came down the lake in canoes. In Albany their escort was kept in prison that they might not gather too much information; then, all together, they were sent down to Lord Cornbury at New York, and a newspaper announced on September first that "Capt John Sheldon returned from Canada last night with seven captives." From New York they went by water to "Seabrook;" after which the charges are those of the road.

[35] Coun. Rec., Jan. 14, 1707. [36] Poore MSS., 5, 353; and Que. Docs., II, 473.
[37] Arch. 2, 444.

His "Disbursements" from mid-April to mid-September, £58, 16s., 8d., include the following: The barber was paid for trimming, they were all furnished with shoes and tobacco. There was a deerskin also for shoes and a bottle of brandy "for the voyage." Most significant was six livres paid "To an Indian to guide us into the way when bewildered." Significant, too, of the times was that a portion of his payment of fifty pounds for services was "thirteen pounds, twelve shillings by a Muletto." He redeemed a mulatto captive taken at Exeter; let us hope it was not he! He received besides three hundred acres of land.

The Roll of 1710/11.

After the surrender of Port Royal (Annapolis) in October, 1710, the French and English commanders sent a representative "through the forest" to Vaudreuil in Quebec. This was Major John Livingstone.

In the Public Record Office, London, is: "A Journall of ye Travails of Major John Livingstone from Annapolis Royall in Novia Scotia to Quebeck in Canada, from thence to Albany and soe to Boston, begun Oct. 15, and ended Feb. 23, 1710/11."[38] The Boston News-Letter (February 19-26) announces his arrival on Friday, the twenty-third, and gives details of the journey.[39] From the "Journall" and the News-Letter the following is taken. It is the only story found of a journey through the Maine wilderness, and it is the story of greatest hardship and peril.

He went to "St. Casteens Harbour," and anchored; whence he sent messengers "to get Indians to forward him on his Journey, but none would go." So he "went to St. Casteen's House where he met with very civil and friendly entertainment, and the 26th departed thence in Company with St. Casteen and three French Men which he hired and his Servant." At the Island of Lett they met thirty-five canoes from Penobscot "with about 100 Indian Men, besides Squaws and Children," and with them "a Jesuitt

[38] Printed in Calendar of State Papers, Colonial Papers, 1710/11, 371-386.

[39] The only known copy — and that somewhat mutilated — is in the Boston Athenaeum. In an earlier issue (No. 342) copies of the letters sent by Nicholson and Vetch are printed.

Pier La Shas" [Père La Chasse] and "two English Men Prisoners which they had taken at Winter Harbour about the 15th Currant." One of the said prisoners escaped while hunting on an island with his master, taking "a Burch Cannoo & his Gun and left his Master on the Island, who afterwards coming to the place where Major Livingstone &c. were with the Indians made an uprore, insomuch that they designed to murder Major Livingstone; one of the Indians took him by the Throat and with his Hatchet was going to give him the fatal blow, but Monsieur Casteen interposed" saying that he was "an ambassadour," and the Indians answered that the "English had killed some of their Penobscot men they sent as Ambassadours at Casco," and, wrote Livingstone, "as they had the oppertunity they would kill me, but by Casteens perswasions they desisted for the present."

This was not the only time that Castine saved his life. On November first, he says, the weather was so terrible and his fear of the Indians so great, that he was "forced to lett out all my kegs of rum for fear of ye event, if they should gett that in their hands; and we suffered much after in our journey for want of it." And this was all before the hardest part of the journey began. The day after they left the Island of Lett the major's "Cannoo Overset," an Indian was drowned and Livingstone lost his gun and all he had. A few days later (Nov. 9) "coming amongst abundance of Ice which cut their Cannoos to pieces, made them Travel the rest of the way by Land through a horrid desert place, being forced to head Rivers, Lakes and sometimes knee deep in Snows . . . wading through deep and dangerous Rivers, and for 19 days never see the Sun, the Weather was so stormy and Cloudy with excessive Fogs, the Trees so prodigious thick, that sometimes they could hardly get passage through, they being mostly Spruce and Cedar, and the way under foot very rocky and hardly passable at last their Provisions was wholly spent that for six days together they had not one morsel to eat but what they could scratch out of the ground or of the trees until December the 6th."

Approaching Quebec: "Castine sent an express to ye Governor Generall to acquaint him of our arrivall, who immediately sent mouns. L'favour and two canoes with some wine and brandy to present us, which was very acceptable to us, soe we proceeded on our journey to Quebeck where we arrived about sun sett."

The next day, "in ye Governour's slay," Livingstone paid a visit to the Intendant, who handsomely received him "and soe did all ye Gentlemen in town." He "took up 1000 livers french money to buy" himself and servant clothes, for he says "I had not so much as a shirt for to wear; that I had on I had worne 44 days, my clothing all lost when ye canoe oversett, Severall English prisoners came to visit me at my lodging whom I supplyed with money." He immediately asked for the release of Eunice Williams[40] and that the gentlemen who are to return with him be sent for. They arrived December 24 and their "names are M. Romvelle and Depeiu" [Rouville and Depuis].

He wrote: "Dec. 25 I had many English prisoners and others to wish me Merry Christmass wh. cost me much money amongst them," and "Jan. 1st. This being our New Years Day ye English prisoners came to see me, and wish me a merry new year. I knew their meaning and gave them money."

On the tenth they left Quebec. "At Ponat of Tranbell" [Pointe-aux-Trembles], where they lodged, they saw English prisoners, "one Whiting was one of them."[41]

His servant grew sick and had to be left in the hospital at Three Rivers and it was near there at "St. Franceway" that the party divided to meet at Chambly.

Vaudreuil tells Pontchartrain that he sent the two Frenchmen "in order to obtain information . . . and to make them acquainted with the Country & the most favorable routes to send parties thither."[42]

On January eighteenth they met "at Monsieur Artells [Hertel], at Shamblee," where several French gentlemen came from Mon-

40 See Eunice Williams, Deerfield. 41 See Dunstable. 42 N. Y. Docs., IX, 854.

treal to see them, and on "the 21st they parted from Sham'blee and brought with them three Birch Cannoos being 13 in number [eight French, four Indians and the Major], they had all things necessary for their Journey; they carried their Cannoo's 75 miles by Land through the Woods and on the Ice and then 60 miles by Water in crossing the Lake, where they left them, and on February 3d they arrived at Albany and the 23d at Boston."

The next day Major Livingstone calls to help settle the French Gentlemen in their quarters — the George Tavern on the corner of what was later Dock Square and Elm Street — and to assure them the Governor, who assigned the House, "will take care that they be not imposed on by excessive rates for their expenses," and that the Sheriff will attend them to the Town House where the Governor will see them in Council.[43]

Dudley says that the French gentlemen "shewed themselves good men." (Deerfield and Haverhill might have dissented).

They, having agreed to return all prisoners in June, departed on March 17 with a letter to Vaudreuil and a list of one hundred and thirteen New England names.

They had, too, a letter to Colonel Schuyler in which Dudley thanks him for his "Kind Discreation in sending them the Round Way (by Rehoboth and New London] that they might not know our Albany Road," and Dudley sent them back by the same route, rejoicing that no news from England had arrived during their stay.[44]

Vaudreuil answered on June 16.[45] It would give him pleasure to accept the articles signed by Dudley and his two messengers, but the conditions are impossible; to give up all the prisoners, men, women and children, in exchange for those held only by Dudley would be unfair. Moreover, he says: "I have news that you are fitting out an expedition to come to this country and it's useless to propose an exchange now nor would it be prudent to send back your prisoners who, by the great liberty we have always given

[43] Coun. Rec., 24 Feb., 1710. [44] Arch. 71, 765.
[45] Arch. Pub. du Canada. Cor. Gen., Serie F., Vol. 32, pp. 119-123.

them, know as much about our country as we ourselves." He does, however, send back "Johnson harmon," who promises to return if "le Sr de beaumeny" is not sent in exchange[46] and with him *"le valet du Sr major l'Evington."* He sends also messages about Esther Wheelwright and Mary Silver.[47] The reasons for this clemency are disclosed in a letter sent four months later to Versailles.[48] Having heard that Colonel Nicholson had gone to England to bring back a fleet to attack Canada and, desiring information, he makes this a pretext to send spying messengers to Orange with Harmon and *le valet*, but his three Frenchmen have been held in Orange and he has heard nothing of his paroled prisoner.

"Roll of English Prisoners in the hands of the French & Indians at Canada Given to Mr. Vaudruille's messengers."[49]

Name	Place	Name	Place
James Houey (for Hovey) Malden		Timothy Rice	Marlboro
		Adonijah Rice	
Benj^{a} Mussey	Cambridge	Silas Rice	
Zech^{a} Tarbal	Groton	Elisha Ward	
John Tarbal		Mary Sergeant	Wooster
Sarah Tarbal		Matthias Sergeant	
Matt Farnsworth		John Sergeant	
Lydia Longley		Thomas Sergeant	
Elisha Sarle	Northampton	Mary Sergeant Jr.	
Abraham Haseltine	Bradford	James Sergeant	
Benj^{a} Savery		Samuel Benythen	Saco
Jonathan Kimball		Samuel Stevens	Pemaq^{d}
Zecha Shed	Bilrica	Elizabeth Wallis	Perpuduck
Hannah Dunkin		Josiah Lovett	
Samuel Whiteing		Edward Cole	Black point
Daniel Rogers		Mary Cole	
Sarah Levistone		——— Williams the ministers Daughter	Deerfield
Marcy Rogers			

[46] See Johnson Harmon, York. [47] See Wells and Haverhill. [48] N. Y. Docs., IX, 857.

[49] Copied as deciphered. Some names of places and persons are known to be errors.

Zechª Davis	
Joshua Davis	Casco
Grace Davis	
Mary Davis	
Johnson Herman	
Charles Trafton	
Hannah Heard	
Mary Sawyerd	
Herster Saywerd	
Mary Osten	
Wm. Moore	York
Jabeth Simpson	
Obediah Preble	
Benjª Preble	
Abiall Bragdon	
Marcy Parsons	
Joseph Molten	
Joseph Fry	
James Frethy	
Abigail Key	
Aabigail Coursin	Kittery
William Hutchins	
Patience Hammons	
Aaron Littlefield	
Ruth Littlefield	
Mary Storer	
Rachell Storer	
Precilla Storer	
Robert Islington	Wells
Hannah Parsons	
Titus Jones negro	
Joseph Cloyes	
Thomas Russell	
Hester Wheelwright	
Thomas Dean	

Benjamin Dudy	
Rachel Dudy	Cape porpus
Sarah Dudy	
——— Jourdain	
——— Jourdain	
Elizabeth Webber	Casco
Nathan Webber	
——— Webber	
——— Slew	
William Tayler	
Andrew Gillman	
Samuel Stevens	
John Wedgwood	
Joshua Hilton	
Sarah Dolhoofs	Exeter
Margaret Dolhoofs	
Mary Dolhoofs	
John Dolhoofs	
Benjª Dendy	
Rachel Dendy	
Phillip Huntone	Kingstowne
Jacob Gillman	
Mary Silver	Haverhill
James Huckins	
Thomas Huckins	
Mary Huckins	
Joseph Watson	
Joseph Thomas	
Azariah Jenkins	Oyster River
Remembrance Rand	
Sarah Davis	
Nathan'l Tibbetts	
Lydia Drew	
Elizabeth Lum̄ox	
John Ricor	Cochick

——— Sergeant	Saco	——— Cole	Saco
——— Sergeant		——— Cole	
William Lucas		——— Cole	
Samuel Benighting			

Besides the Garrison taken from St. Johns at NewfoundLand and Such others whose names I could not come at

Signed J. Dudley"

1712. *Lieutenant Samuel Williams.*

In June Vaudreuil proposed an exchange. Several men were eager for this Canadian service, but Williams was "pitcht upon" because he had "the Frentch tongue." With him were three more Deerfield men: Jonathan Wells, John Nims and Eleazer Warner. (Mr. Sheldon mentions also Sergt. Thomas Taylor). The French prisoners were to be brought to Deerfield, but some refused to come and there was delay. It is interesting to know that one or two, even if of doubtful reputation, made this choice when so many of ours preferred to stay with the Indians or the French.

The reasons given for or by the Frenchmen was that one had changed his religion and the other having "an Affection for the people and Countery" would go only to see his people and to return. (He was La ffever and one of similar name was a spy!)

Dudley had written three years before that he had sent to Port Royal all the French who were in Massachusetts "Except two or three men who have voluntarily of their own choice Embraced the true Christian Religion without any Swasion or constraint and Desired to Stay here."[50] Williams carried few Frenchmen. Indeed Partridge saw only two when he went up from Hatfield.

On September 24 the young lieutenant delivered to the Council a letter from Vaudreuil; he having returned "with nine English Prisoners several of whom also attended," and a few days later he was allowed £35, 6s. for his services from July 7 to October 7 — thirteen weeks at thirty shillings a week.[51] Of the nine, the names only of Barrett and Sanford have been found. That some

[50] Arch. 2, 620. [51] Coun. Rec., V, 608.

belonged to New Hampshire is shown in the Council Records,[52] which relates that Samuel Ashley and Daniel Bagg are paid £15, 19s., 9d.; that being nine-fifteenths of "the foot of their accompt . . . for subsisting, Horse hire & conducting of nine Englishmen prisoners brought from Canada to Albany, from thence to Boston; five of 'em belonging to this Province And that a letter be written to Goverm^t of New Hampshire to pay 'em of three of them belong to that Province." This is dated 2 July, 1713.

Wells and Nims received eleven pounds and ten shillings and Warner thirteen.

Samuel Williams died in June, 1713. Thirty years later his half-brother Elijah, aged one when the service was rendered, profited from it by receiving at half-price the twenty-five hundred acres for which he asked.

1713-1714. *Rev. John Williams* and *Maj. John Stoddard.*

After the peace of Utrecht these two men, who were under the same roof on the night of the Deerfield massacre, were sent "to attend Mons Vaudreuil in Order to the Return of the English Prisoners there." With them as interpreter went Martin Kellogg and Capt. Thomas Baker with Eleazer — or Ebenezer — Warner and Jonathan Smith. The major was allowed seven shillings a day, the clergyman five, interpreter three, while "the able men" who attended had only two shillings. Money for their "outset" was provided in similar proportion.[53] They left Northampton on horseback in mid-November and were detained ten weeks at Albany by "very soft weather." Hendrick, a Mohawk chief, guided them northward. From Chambly to Montreal they travelled in *carrioles*, the Canadian sleighs.

Stoddard's Journal [54] names the thousand and two obstacles put in their way. Governor de Vaudreuil tells them that all the captives shall have "free liberty to return" and that those who would go shall have his blessing. Was he perhaps a little weary of New

[52] Vol. VI, 60. [53] Prov. Laws 9, 318, under date of 30 Oct., 1713.

[54] Gen. Reg., V, 21-42.

England importunity? And later he said he didn't care how few stayed, the fewer the better. When the commissioners complain that "some priests . . . go from house to house to solicit our people to tarry" Vaudreuil answers that he could "as easily alter the course of the waters as prevent the priests' endeavors." They visited some English nuns who . . . were well pleased with their present circumstances. They were told that those prisoners whom the King, "after divers objections," had naturalized could not, of course, return. The commissioners contended that this was contrary to the Articles of Peace, and Vaudreuil agreed that "Naturality" was "a fraud and deceit."

At Montreal Mr. Williams made his supreme effort and sorrowful failure — the release of Eunice. She was still a minor, though already a wife.

He is forbidden to have any religious conversation with the English in Montreal, and complaints having been made that he is abroad after eight o'clock in the evening for that purpose, the Intendant threatens to confine him in his chamber for, he said, "the priests tell me you undo in a moment all they have done in seven years." A great compliment to Mr. Williams.

Captain Baker, carrying three captives, was sent back to Massachusetts for further instructions. The Council Records show that he left "Mont Real" on the second and was in Boston on the twenty-seventh of April.

Capt. Cyprian Southack is "directed forthwith to look out for a suitable Ship of about one hundred and fifty tons to be sent to fetch home the English prisoners," and "a letter was digested to Mr. Vaudreuille," in answer to that brought by Baker, whose account "for expenses for subsisting himself and English captives from Canada to Boston & Horse hire" is allowed. The "Proclamation for inquiry after French Prisoners" is ordered to be again printed, and the Brigantine *Leopard*, Perkins, master, with Capt. Southack aboard, is made ready to sail in May.

On Tuesday, September 21, she returned with the commissioners and twenty-seven captives. The council ordered: "That Mr Treasurer take care to have the Prisoners brought ashoar & provide some victuals for their refreshment in order to their appearg before the Board in the afternoon."

Twenty shillings was given to every captive for present relief.

Did some of them stay at the old Greyhound Tavern in Roxbury on what is now Washington Street, opposite Vernon? Mary Smith was paid in January 1714/15 fifteen shillings for entertainment and Posts for captives from Canada.[55]

Stoddard's and Williams' charges and expenses for themselves and attendants were 592£, 15s., 7d.[56] But the letter sent back by Baker had not been sufficiently "digested." The disappointed agents were resentful because Vaudreuil had not given them the promised list of captives; that he had not brought them all together in Quebec, nor had one-half been asked whether or no they wished to return.

The Governor's story differs. He says that Major Stoder and Jean Williams were given "*une grande liberté;*" that the prisoners *were* told that all who wished could return, and that there might be no suspicion of restraint — acting upon His Majesty's command — he sent out "a Proclamation" on August 14 "to be read, published and posted at Quebec, Montreal and Three Rivers and sent to all the *côtes et Seigneuries* in the country," that no English person, man, woman or child, may be ignorant that a boat is waiting to take home all the prisoners and that "carriage and food will be furnished."[57]

Seven years later when Shute was demanding the return of New Englanders, Vaudreuil again declared that all who would return had gone with Captain Cyprien in 1714. Some having embraced our religion, he said, chose to remain, but it was by their own free will, a proof being that several of them asked permission to visit

[55] Coun. Rec., VI, 306. [56] Arch. 81, 868. [57] Que. Docs., III, 4.

their relatives and he put no difficulties in their way, and of all who went, not one failed to return![58]

It was Captain Baker who had the triumph of this commission. He brought back a bride, Christine (Otis) Le Beau.

Judd in his "History of Hadley" say that "Messengers were sent from Hampshire County to Canada by way of Albany five times and from Boston to Quebec by water twice from 1705 to 1713." All these have been noted, but it would be tiresome to recount all the stories of redemption. Schuyler said of his own efforts that "to Dilate thereon would be prolix." This was in 1713 when he brought the letter about Eunice Williams and nine captives to Albany, whence "five of 'em" came to Boston and three to New Hampshire.

John Craft, 1714.

John Craft of Hadley and Hatfield is named in the "Craft Family" as a messenger to Canada. He was son of Thomas and Abigail (Dickinson) and had for a stepfather Samuel Crowfoot, whose little son Daniel was "still absent" in 1714. Did John go and fail to find his little stepbrother?

Although Stoddard does not mention him, he was leaving Canada at the same time, coming back by land. He wrote in his diary: "Aug. y. 28th 1714, This day we took our jurney from Quebec for new england," and having crossed from Otter Creek to the Connecticut valley he is on September 26 at "ye great meddo."

Claudius Petitpas, 1720.

His was an individual service for which Massachusetts offered her best reward. "In Consideration of the tender Regard the Petitioner hath shewn to sundry English Captives in the late Indian War, not only in relieving & succouring them when in great Want, but purchasing them from the Indian Enemy at his own Cost & Charge & setting them at Liberty; as is certified by divers

[58] Que. Docs., III, 64.

Persons of good Repute" it was resolved that one hundred pounds be paid to him, and "That one of his Sons be fitted for & brought up at Harvard College for the Space of four Years at the Charge of the Governm^{t}, And that Mr President Leveret be desired to take the Charge of his Education."[59] The man was an Acadian who had taken his oath of allegiance to Great Britain in 1695. Married to a Micmac squaw, he was a valuable friend and interpreter. It is interesting to note that no Petitpas was at Harvard, but a letter sent from Quebec to Versailles in 1722[60] tells us that Barthelémy, son of Claudius, was in Boston three years, it being the intention of the government to make a clergyman of him that he might bring the Micmacs to the English allegiance and religion; but M. de Saint-Ovide[61] found a way to get the young man out of the hands of the English and entice him to Quebec, where they wanted to make him a priest, but he preferred to be a pilot and for safer keeping he was sent to France to learn his lesson of navigation.[62]

As a pilot he was again in Boston, but then he was in Boston prison. In 1747 Governor Shirley justified this because his father "a faithfull subject . . . had received marks of favour . . . and consequently his son had no right to throw off his allegiance & go into the french King's service, so that," Shirley continues, "I had an undoubted right to detain him, however his death must end any dispute about him."[63] Drake[64] calling him the Indian interpreter (he had been officially appointed by France in 1732), says that all ransoms for him were refused and they "finally put him to death," but of this no proof has been found. From the Council Records we know that he was pilot of the *Vigilant*, which was captured in May, 1745, and was imprisoned as "a dangerous person."

59 Prov. Laws, IX, 676, dated 30 June.

60 Vaudreuil and Bégon to Council of the Marine N. Y., Docs. IX, 912.

61 Gov. of Ile Royale. 62 Can. Arch., 1904, 34. 63 Que. Docs., III, 379.

64 French and Indian Wars, p. 43.

1722, *June.*

Another instance of individual service and rescue was planned by "Christian Newton & Margarett Blinn" who prayed "that as they have fitted out a Sloop to go in Search after their Husband and Children taken by the Indians this Court would be pleased to lend them some of the Province Arms for their Defence."[65] The "husband" was James Blin, captain and ship-owner, who had married Margaret Dennison of Milton. The "children" were Hibbert Newton and his son Tommy, "not quite four years old." Christian Newton was widow of Thomas, who had been Attorney-General of the province. It was ordered that thirty men with an officer and ammunition be put upon the sloop which was to go to Passamaquoddy, and if they could not recover the persons who had been "so unjustly and forcibly seiz'd upon, to make Reprisal of the like Number of Indians."[66]

This was sent up for Concurrence but failed to pass; the reason being that the captivity was short as shown by the declaration of Arthur Savage, Esq.,[67] and the Journal of Hibbert Newton (June 11-16). Savage, with a few other passengers, was on Captain Blin's Sloop *Ipswich* sailing from Annapolis for Boston. At Passamaquoddy they landed for water when the "husband and children" were seized. Newton's Journal details their escape.[68]

1725. *Col. Samuel Thaxter* and *Col. William Dudley* from Massachusetts, *Mr. Theodore Atkinson* from New Hampshire, and *Samuel Jordan* as interpreter.

After the death of Rale these three gentlemen were sent to demand that Canada should cease her meddling and to ask for the return of the captives.

From Atkinson's diary[69] we learn how very difficult was their journey. They left Boston on Wednesday, January 20. At Albany Col. John Schuyler joined them to seek his niece Mary,

65 House Journal, 1722, p. 51. 66 Prov. Laws, X, 186. 67 Coun. Rec., VII, 361.

68 Nova Scotia Papers, Gay MSS. Mass. Hist. Soc.

69 Printed by the New Hampshire Society of Colonial Wars.

whom he took away from the Ursuline Convent at Three Rivers. The diarist writes of the extreme cold, beyond any ever felt before; of snow and ice; and then of travelling over "wavering ice" so "rotten" that they fell in; of giving up the ice and water-way "to travell thro mountainous Desert for 200 miles" — an exaggeration of distance rather than of fatigue, probably.

In a wigwam on the Chambly River he saw an Indian who was at the taking of Mr. Hanson's family,[70] but from him they got no news.

Arriving at Chambly Fort in March they awaited the Governor's permission to proceed. At Longueuil they were entertained at "Mr. Laplashs."[71] Reaching Montreal they delivered Dummer's letter, which the French called "only a vague answer" to Vaudreuil's complaints of the attack upon Norridgewock and the killing of Rale.

The Englishmen asked that Vaudreuil cease to supply the Abenakis with arms and food, which was contrary to the Peace of Utrecht, and he answered that his offerings were the annual gifts of the King. If the Indians used them in making war the English must blame themselves for having taken the Indians' lands.

Gov. John Wentworth instructed Atkinson to tell the Canadian that he esteemed his conduct "not only unneighborly, but an open breach of the Treaty of Utrecht."

Messrs. Thaxter and Dudley sent a letter to Lieutenant-Governor Dummer on March 26 saying: "This is the first opportunity we have, and this obtained by Secrecy and great Difficulty by one cagnawaga indian only, which is to inform your Honour & ye Government that all the eastern indians were gone before we arrived." They tell him that the Design of the Indians was at first to hunt, then to fall on the frontier and suggest that the frontier be strengthened "particulary on merrymack & Connecticutt."

Captain Jordan had been to St. Francis and Bécancour where he saw a few Indians and many squaws who all told him the In-

[70] Taken from Dover in June, 1724, redeemed in the summer of 1725.
[71] Lestage, husband of Esther Sayward of York.

dians wanted peace and urged the commissioners to tarry until the Indians returned.

When they asked Vaudreuil about the prisoners they had the usual answer; those with the Indians were beyond French control; others could be ransomed for the price paid to the Indians. It was, however, frequently asserted that the French asked from the English much larger ransoms than they had paid to the Indians.

Penhallow, whose history was published in 1726, says of the captives now redeemed that although the demands were exorbitant sixteen were ransomed and bargains were made for ten more, but not one of the twenty-six names is known unless the Governor's "utmost Indeavours," of which Atkinson wrote, released "Mrs. Rollings." Atkinson wrote also of Captain Jordan's bringing back captives from St. Francis, but never a word about his sister, Mary Ann (Arabella) Jordan, whom he must have seen at Three Rivers, or of any other. Vaudreuil offered to bring Indians from St. Francis and Bécancour to make terms, but the commissioners explained that that was not their errand. "Why, then, did they take the trouble to come," he asked, and they told him, seemingly begging the question, that "if he would not cause the Indians to go to Boston or piscataqua . . . [to make peace] he must be looked on by God and man as the instigator of the warr, which they could prove by his own and other letters."[72]

Abenakis from the two villages did come for an interview, but the French Governor saw them first because he knew, as he told Versailles, "that nothing was more opposed to his Majesty's interests than peace between the Abenakis and English;" therefore he suggested to the Indians that it was not enough to demand the demolition of the forts and restitution of their lands and prisoners, but they should ask also for indemnities for the death of their priest, burning of their church, etc.[73] But if complaints were

[72] See Father Rale, Chapter II. [73] N. Y. Docs., IX, 948.

made of French diplomacy, that of New England was not sleeping.

Atkinson wrote: "12 [april] Monday about noon above 15 of the Enemy arrived at Mount royall . . . 13, gave ye mohawk Privatly a Belt for to Speak to the Enemy & there wants."

The commissioners said that the Governor was "intirely Governed by Père La Chasse, the chief of the Jesuits," he being the interpreter at the interview,[74] at which much was said, and the gentlemen promised to tell it all in Boston. Nothing was done and, says Mr. Parkman, "the war went on as before."

Vaudreuil's despatch to Versailles dated August 7[75] says that the Englishmen took their departure two days after the Abenaki interview; the chiefs having spoken with such "haughtiness & firmness . . . that they separated with dispositions very adverse to peace."

The Governor thought he could not avoid defraying their expenses during their sojourn in Montreal out of the king's funds because of what had been done in Boston when he sent officers there three years before.

While in Montreal Atkinson not only visited Esther (Sayward) de Lestages, but he saw Mary (Storer) Gaultier, who lived "Grandly."[76]

He wrote of quiet "Sabath Days" and says that on the Saturday preceding Palm Sunday "the Preast forbid our Landlady to Dress flesh." On April 20 "Put Down the river in our Conoe about 30 miles & Campt Early for that some of our Company was yet behind . . . about Sun down Mad^{m} L Stage over tooke us." Hostile Indians were seen before they reached Chambly, but on the "23^{d} Mr. Leguuil[77] overtook us, who brot an order from the

[74] In 1699 Cadillac addressing the Conte de Maurepas accused the Jesuits of being unwilling to teach the Indians to speak French, that they — the Jesuits — might serve as interpreters.

[75] N. Y. Docs., IX, 949.

[76] The editor of the Journal thinks the Storer captive was Priscilla, but the description better belongs to Mary's family.

[77] Priscilla Storer's husband.

Governor for a Guard of 6 men" and the Indians disappeared.

From Chambly they made quick time, arriving in Albany in seven days. The captives were sent ahead on foot[78] while the commissioners waited for their horses to be brought from Westfield to Albany. The poor beasts were almost unfit to travel; "Look nothing but the Image of Death, but there was no relief in the case," wrote the diarist.

Jordan's, indeed, had disappeared by death or otherwise, but when he petitioned for payment the thrifty Court voted that the thirty pounds he claimed "be paid & Returned again into the Treasury if the Horse shall be afterwards found."[79]

The captives followed "the Great Road" and the "Bay Path." Bills for their entertainment all along the way may be found in the Archives.

The commissioners reached Boston in the afternoon of May thirteenth and the next day Atkinson "Set out from Boston & rid to Ipswich about 12 at night." He, second of the name of the Newcastle-Portsmouth family, was paid £130 for his services,[80] with a later payment of £118, 14s., 7d. Massachusetts paid to Thaxter and Dudley £233, 9s., 9d., deducting from their general account twenty-two pounds due from John Wells, who evidently was of the party.

1727/8. *Joseph Kellogg.*

In January it was voted to send "a fit . . . Messenger . . . with suitable Attendants to the Number of seven English, & one or two Indians to Pilot them from the County of Hampshire, the nearest way to St François near Canada River" to demand the British subjects and to have leave to "search & Speak with all the said Captives . . . & to inform themselves upon what Terms they may be obtained in order to return."[81] Williamson, without giving his authority, adds: "to encourage them in their mission sev-

[78] Jon^a^ How of Marlborough was paid £1, 8s., 10d., for entertaining the commissioners and "sundry English captives that came with them."

[79] House Journal, 1725. [80] N. H. Coun. Rec., IV, 215. [81] Prov. Laws, XI, 271.

eral Indian captives the property of individuals, were ransomed at the public expense and despatched in company with the agents."[82] Joseph Kellogg, chosen as "the fit Person," was to be paid fifty pounds "to enable him handsomely to equip himself to appear at Canada," and a hundred pounds was given him to clothe and provision his men, all of which was to be repaid out of their wages. Nothing is found of the results except that "Gideon Prat was paid £17, 2s., 8d. for Expense and Horse Hire in bringing four English Captives, redeemed by Capt. Joseph Kellogg, from Springfield to Boston," in June, 1728,[83] and the various accounts allowed by the Court in the same month. To Lydius in Montreal £413 for money supplied for purchasing prisoners, etc. (2480 Liveres & 7½ Sols). To Schuyler, for "Money, Bisket, Tobacco" &c. and wages for himself and company.[84]

1747. *August. By the Vierge-de-Grace.*

Many of the captives of the Third Intercolonial War were more truly prisoners of war. Others taken by the Abenakis of St. Francis and Bécancour were bought by Frenchmen at Three Rivers and were sold again (at better prices) to the King, after which they were kept in the Quebec prison.[85] Many died there.

In June, 1747, the Governor of Massachusetts required all persons who had French prisoners who were not married or had not taken the oaths to His Majesty to give in their names to the sheriffs, and the sheriffs on their side were to make diligent search. As a result, says the News-Letter, a "Flagg of Truce" (Capt. Jeffry Bedgood commanding, for which he was paid £8, 12s., 2d.), sailed with sixty or seventy French prisoners to exchange for ours.

Beds for the prisoners to be brought from Quebec were provided out of the stores for the Expedition against Canada. "Blankets or Rugs for them all" were to be purchased; all to be returned to the Commissary General;[86] and back to Boston on the

82 "Hist. Maine," II, 155. 83 Court Records, XIV, 66. 84 Prov. Laws, XI, 331-2.
85 Que. Docs., III, 273. 86 House Journal, 28 July, 1747.

packet *Vierge-de-Grace* (often changed into Verd le Grace), Captain Larregni commanding, came the redeemed English people.

Through the neglect of the commander at Castle William (Fort Independence) the ship came up into the harbor, and the Council, when asked if it should not be ordered below, "thought better to let her stay on account of any knowledge the officers may get of the Channel."

The anonymous English diarist of the Quebec prison, later quoted,[87] wrote on July 25, "4 P. M. marched us to the wharf to embark" and on "16 Aug . . . At 11 Came to an Anchor off the Long Wharff at Boston; and at about 1 in the afternoon Landed at Boston Gloria Deo."

The News-Letter of Thursday, Aug. 20,[88] says: "Last Lords Day arrived here in 21 Days from Quebec the Ship *Verd d' Grace* as a Flagg of Truce, with 171 Persons who had been at divers Times taken by the French and Indian Enemy." Then follow the names of "Many taken on the sea" and of those "Taken by the Salvages." Of the latter, those said to be of New England are here given. The majority of those taken on the sea may be found in a later chapter.

Taken April 24, 1746, by M. Der Virville [Boucher de Niverville.] John Spafford of No. 4.

Taken by Monsieur Ramsey Jan. 30, 1746-7,[89] George Chavolony [a Greek], Master of Boston, and in the list of the "Post-Boy" is also Anthony Woodbury; Wm. Jarmaine [Jermin] of Plymouth, Ensign; Capt. Elisha Doane of Cape Cod, John Crocker Master and James Crocker of Newbury; Lieut. George Gerrish of Boston; Joseph Griffin, James Dillaway, Ichabod Young of this Province, John Ward and Jonathan Gage of Plymouth this Province, Wm. Rogers, Capt. Doane, Matthew Fowler, James Buckford, Walter Powers, and John Emmit of

87 MS. in Cong. Lib. 88 Mass. Hist. Soc. and Am. Ant. Soc.

89 Jean-Baptiste Nicolas Roch de Ranezay, then military commander in Acadie.

this Province, James Gordon of Captain Doane's Company, Moses Ward of New-Hampshire, John Hadley of Casco-bay.

Taken by —— Robert Adams, Benja. Milton and George Trask of this Province.

Taken by the Salvages May 29, 1746, Isaac Parker and Stephen Farnsworth of No. 4; David, Benjamin and Thomas Woodwell and Caleb Burbank of New-Hampshire; James and Samuel Anderson of Sheepscut; Timothy Brown [Massachusetts] and Robert Muffet of Ashuelot; John Beamount of Northfield; Obadiah Sartwell of No. 4; Isaac Tylor of Tisbury; June 1st John Richards [New-Hampshire].

Taken at Fort Massachusetts by the French, August 20, 1746. John Norton, Minister; John Hawks, Lieut; Joseph Scott, David Warren, John, Mary, Elihu and Simeon Smead; Ebenezer and Moses Scott; John Perry and Stephen Scott.

Taken by the Salvages, Aug. 10, 1746. Alexander Roberts of New-Hampshire; Daniel How of Northfield; Benja. Tainter of Westboro'; Richard Stubbs of Casco-bay; Jonathan Williams [Williamson] of Wiscasset. Oct. 20th John McNish [McNear] of Sheepscut. Feb. 22d 1746, 7 John March, [Biddeford] Benja. Mayhew and Benja. Cox of this Province; John Larmond of Damariscotty. Apr. 15, 1747 Wm. and Joseph Knights of Casco bay. Samuel Sayers of Rhode Island was taken at Saratoga.

Among those who died during their Captivity and Imprisonment were John Bradshaw, Matthew Loring, Samuel Stacy & Jonath Dunham of this Province, John Pitman of Marblehead, John Jordan of Rehoboth, [Antonio, a Portuguese Boston] John Dill of Nantasket, Joseph Denning and Francis Andrews of this Province; Nehemiah How of No. 2, Jacob Reed, Edward Cloutman and Widow Briant of Gorham Town; Samuel Burbank & Mary Woodwell of New-Hampshire; Timothy Cummings of Georges, Wm. Nason of Casco-bay, Robert David

Roberts of Dartmouth; [Robert Roberts, dead, Falmouth], Samuel Goodman, Jonathan Bridgman, Nathan Ames, Phinehas Forbush, Amos Pratt, Mary Smead, John Smead jun. Daniel Smead, Captivity Smead, Samuel Lovett, Jacob Shepherd, Nathaniel Hitchcock, Miriam Scott, Moses Scott, Rebecca Perry, all taken at Fort Massachusetts; Pike Gordon of Biddeford; William Bagley, Jacob Bagley and Samuel Evans of Newbury; Hezekiah Huntington and Lemuel Martin of Connecticut; —— Johnes of this Province; Robert Williams of Falmouth.[90]

Among those "turn'd over to the French" are: Daniel Larey [Mallaley and John Curren of Boston.]

"Tis said there are about 100 more English Prisoners remaining in divers Parts of Canada, and 10 were left sick at Quebec."

Several had to be carried to the hospital in Boston. The soldiers were boarded at the Work-House from Sabbath Day to fryday 21 August at the rate of forty shillings per week.[91] Massachusetts paid the wages of the soldiers and gave to every prisoner, whether of New or Old England, of her own or other provinces, five pounds, old tenour.

The names of the captive-passengers were printed also in the "Boston Gazette or Weekly Journal" of 18 August, copies of which are in the Boston Public Library and American Antiquarian Society in Worcester; and in the "Boston Weekly Post-Boy" of 27 August, of which the only known copy is in the library of the Massachusetts Historical Society.

From these the bracketed names in the News-Letter list have been taken. Other names of New England are: Ambrose Ryan or Lyon of Cape Ann taken 29 June 1745; Samuel Deverix Boston belonging to the late Capt. Donahew; From the sloop Albany 19 July 1746, Anthony Newgent, Zechary Hubbard, Boston.

The following are printed only in the Gazette: Wm. Topham,

90 Pote says of Portsmouth, England. 91 Arch. 72, 752.

Wm. Allen, —— Boyd, Wm. Bright, all of Boston; and taken by French and Indians at St. John's as of Boston are: Bennet, Kings Naun and Gorham, and taken at places unnamed are John Smith, Boston; Zeph. Pinkham, David Bunker, James Gardner, Joseph and Mordica Job, John Scitturee, Wm. Brewer, Wm. Ransdell, Jos. Dankid, John Godfrey, all of Nantucket; Jesse Crow and James Chase, Cape-Cod, Isaac, Robert and Peter Martin, New London, Jos. Lamire, James Thompson, Wm. Brewer, Massachusetts. In a letter dated September, 1747, Shirley mentioned Ensigns Laurence and Newton of his own regiment.[92]

It was not until 1749 that Massachusetts sent a bill of £174, 8s., 5d. to New Hampshire for her share in the costs of the *Vierge-de-Grace.* The papers having been destroyed by fire in the Custom House at Boston, new accounts were sought in Canada. Six passengers only are named — many more came — and of these one name, Caleb Wade, does not appear elsewhere.

Perhaps the Schooner *Success* came in company with the larger vessel; on it were the following passengers:

Capt. Drake	Matthew Tobin
James Dunlap	John Gale
Antip[s] Gilman	Wm M'Dugle June 8th
Joseph Paul	Solomon Smith
Rubin Stevens	Mich[l] Johnson Cap Nichols
Edward Webber	Jonathan Barker
William Bell	Benj. Glazier
James Clemment	

1747/8. *Sergeant John Hawks,* with two "attendants," *Lieut. Matthew Clesson* and *John Taylor.*

This journey was of a private sort. Raimbault arranged it as an exchange for himself. The governor's passport dated Dec. 14, 1747, says it is "to redeem one Samuel Allen" and requires his Majesty's subjects "to suffer Hawks with Mons. Pierre Raim-

[92] Que. Docs., III, 389.

beaut (a French gentleman lately captivated by the English, & has liberty from me to return home) to pass from this province to Canada without let or molestation." . . . Raimbault[93] had agreed to get two English prisoners in exchange for himself, although he had no authority to make the promise.

They went by way of Number Four, where the Frenchman heard that the garrison lacked snowshoes, which information he later used, and continued by way of Otter Creek to the Lake.

Arriving on March ninth at Montreal Raimbault was given up and Samuel Allen, Hawks's nephew, was demanded. The French Report says: "We have the three Englishmen well treated and closely watched. They ask to take back with them two prisoners, men of family, who are here."[94] Hawks and his companions went to Quebec, leaving Raimbault at his father's house, which was on the fief of Simblin, a portion of the Seigniories of Verchères and Contrecoeur.[95]

Nathan Blake was the second prisoner asked for, but the Indians were loath to give up so useful a man; and only after much discussion did they yield, which story disagrees with that in Hale's "Annals."

Returning from Quebec the messengers were entertained by a banquet and ball at Simblin. The redeemed cadet joined them and was ordered to conduct them from Montreal to the frontier. Hawks says:[96] "At a Crotch of the river where is their Common Road from Crown point to No. 4 & other places: they had Informed us that there were but 12 Indians out on our frontiers, and when we had come to this path, they found the signs of them returned with one Captive; our Guard told us there was no Dainger & that they need not come to No. 4 as they proposed, provided these Indians were not Returned, and that they would bid us fare-

93 See Chapter XVIII. 94 Que. Docs., III, 403.

95 This came to Pierre-Marie-Joseph's father, through his wife, a daughter of Marie Jeanne Jarret de Verchères. The family name is written Raimbault de Simblin and R. de St. Blin.

96 A fragment of his Journal is in Arch. A 38, 90, and is also printed in "Hist. Deerfield."

well by Black River, but They had not been gone many minutes before Mr. Rainbout turning Back, Hallowed to us to make haste away from that place, and not to go in the Common Road."

Hawks reached Fort Dummer April 29 where, he says, "we refreshed our Selves, Set out on our Raft for Northfield, where we Lodged," and the next day "Set out for Deerfield on Horses accompanyed by many of our friends from Northfield. Half way from Deerfield we met Col° Williams with near 20 of our friends from Deerfield."

A word might be written of Raimbault. In a Canadian Report of 1747-8 it is said that "the gentlemen cadets are more difficult to restrain than to stimulate." Among them were "Three young Messrs Blein, grandsons of M. Raimbeau, Lieut. General of Montreal." Pierre was one of the three.

This time he had been sent out with forty savages. The story of his supposed death had been told in Canada.[97] It said he had sent his men to slaughter some cattle and was alone by the roadside guarding their plunder when twenty of the enemy's cavalry came along and mortally wounded him. When his Indians came back he had only time "to recount the causes of his death."

The story, as told locally,[98] shows that "the enemy's cavalry" were some horsemen returning to Northfield from Ashuelot. They saw the racing cattle; they saw and shot the Frenchman, who "saluted Alexander[99] handsomely but grew faint." Then, believing that he was dying and that their shots would bring his friends, they left him and hurried on their way. His Indians found and carried him to the river's bank and there they, fearing pursuit, also left him to die. But he didn't die; he revived and after days of wandering, living upon nuts and cranberries, he came to Northfield. The first man he saw chanced to be one of "the cavalry" — Captain Alexander — who took him to Mr. Doolittle, parson and surgeon, to be cured. And when cured he was sent to Boston

97 N. Y. Docs., X, 143. 98 "Doolittle's Narrative," Hist. of Northfield, 377.

99 Captain Ebenezer of Northfield.

where, says Mr. Drake, "Rainbow made quite a sensation, being much noticed by the ladies." The commission, which gave him authority to go out and kill, was written on a scrap of paper which is now in the Massachusetts Historical Society. As literally translated: "It is ordered to the sieur Raimbau^{t} Cadet in The Troops to go at the Head of indians to the Borders [Côtes] of the Government of Orange to make war on our enemies of whatever nation they may be armed as warriors charging him to prevent as much as he may be able the savages from using their customary violence against the prisoners they take.

Montreal 27, 7th 1747 Boisberthelot."

He, the governor of Montreal, was Jean-Maurice-Josué de Boisberthelot de Beaujours. He came to Canada in 1688 and was in her service until 1748.

The News-Letter of May 5, 1748, says: An Express from the westward informs that Seargeant Hawks, who was sent to Canada last winter with Reinboe reported: "That upon the said Reinboe's relating to the French People at Mon Real the kind Usage he met with from the English . . . they treated him, Hawks, and two men that went with him with much Civility and told him they would show the English Prisoners more Respect for the future."

Nevertheless, the last word of Doolittle's "Narrative" is that since the Frenchman's return to Canada he "had been out with the Indians and done much Mischief on our Frontiers."

1748. *October* 6.

Boston Harbour: "An Account of sundry English Prisoners brought in from Louisbourg . . . in a schooner *Britannicus* where were Transported there from Canada."[100] Some of these were:

Capt. John Brett of Boston, taken in a vessel; Maloy Arthur, of Piscatiqua, a passenger; Boyce Cooper, taken at Capt. Bradbury's fort by Indians of Georges; Robert Buntin taken at Sun Cook by the Indians 18 days to Montreal; Andrew, son of

[100] Arch. 73, 204.

Robert; Reuben Pitcher, tak. at Geo: Fort Bradbury of Barnsteber; Dan Lewis, tak at D^{o} of Georges; Presbury Wolling tak at D^{o} of Sandwich; Noake Leach, at Pleasant point, of Bridgewater; Wm Kent tak. at Pemmiquid of Pemmiquid; Job Avery, tak. at Sheepscat or Sheepscut; Job Felbrook, tak. at George Town; Sam Malloon, of Piscotaque and Sam Pain of Braintree, also taken at George Town; Benj^{a} Lake, Ebenezer Clough and Abraham Petingill all of North Yarmouth and there taken; Peter Bovay of Deerfield from Ft. Massachusetts; Jno Henderson of Lancaster, taken at No. 4; From Ft. Dummer, Daniel Farmer of Groton; Wm Blanchard of Dunstable; Benj^{a} Osgood of Bilrica; Mark Perkins of Concord; Matthew Wyman of Lancaster; Daniel Sergent of Fort Dummer; John Dunlap at Canterhook, N. York of Westburrough; Moses Washburn of Wrentham, taken at Brunswick; Tim^{o} Cave taken at Harry Mcdow of Sowhagan; Jason Badcock of Pacuicgog, there captured; Wm. Davison of Boston, taken at Menis as was Rob. Vickery of Dighton.

1749. *Capt. Phineas Stevens.*

This year Messrs. Chandler and Heath were named as agents to seek the captives left behind. Fine preparations were ordered. There was to be "a Surgeon with a Box of Medicines, an Interpreter, a Pilot & two Servants . . . & further that it might be decent & convenient for some suitable Person to proceed as Chaplain." But the gentlemen declined to serve and Capt. Phineas Stevens, who had been named as pilot, was sent with Governor Shirley's letter. His son Enos[101] was then in Canada, so he must have been a willing messenger. The boy, however, was redeemed before his father started.

The News-Letter asked the people to send to the Secretary's office the names of their friends in Canada, with the time and place of capture and the French captives, if there were any in the Province, were given liberty to return.

101 See Chapter XVIII.

Stevens was ordered to be frugal and expeditious. He seems to have been both.[102] He left Number Four September 26, arrived in Montreal in about a month, and "humbly submits" his Journal[103] to the Governor and Council in mid-December.

He seems to have had neither surgeon nor chaplain, but he tarried at Hadley for the finishing of clothes he had making there, and, too, for the pleasure of meeting his son, with whom he spent a Sunday.

He took with him an ensign, John Burke, of his own company. At Albany he engaged four Caughnawaga Mohawks to conduct them and carry their "baggage" up the Hudson, lodging at Dutch houses in their slow progress. At Fort Saint-Jean on the Chambly River he was detained until the Commandant could receive orders allowing him to proceed, but "having a convenient opportunity by a cart going to Lapperary" [La Prairie Madeleine] the condition was waived. The ferryman took him across and the Governor invited him to supper, but as he had no special orders for the Governor-General he was not allowed to go to Quebec; a messenger being sent with Shirley's letter. During the week of waiting he was "entertained very well." Although forbidden to converse with any Indian under pain of imprisonment he made it his "constant business to inquire after prisoners," but heard of only three from his parts: Daniel Eaton, Jonathan Door, and "daughter to the widow Forster" of Casco Bay.

Immediately after the messenger got back he was ordered to leave Montreal, taking with him only one Dutch captive. An officer and five soldiers escorted them to Crown Point.

Stevens had been instructed if the Governor of Canada could not engage for the peaceable behavior of the Indians to make an independent treaty with the Caughnawagas, and from Colonel Lydius' trading house, at the "Great Carrying-place on the Hudson" he sent back a belt and invited their chiefs to come to Boston.

102 His Instructions are in our Archives 70, 558. 103 N. H. Hist. Soc. Coll., 5, 199.

1751. *January*. *Phineas Stevens* again. With him his cousin, *William Heywood*, and *James Farnsworth.*

In October, 1750, Secretary Willard wrote to tell Stevens he was to carry a letter to Canada demanding "the Restoration of the English prisoners lately taken in the Eastern parts with other matters of importance."[104] He is "to set out without delay lest the season for passing by water sh^d^ escape." He answers from N° 4 saying: "I am disposed to go as soon as possible, but winter time being so near and the affair so unexpected It will Require Sum time to prepare myself for such a feteagueing Journey." And adding that the season is so far advanced that the benefit of going by water was uncertain he waits for an answer while "fixing" himself. The French had told him that it was unsafe to cross the lake upon the ice before the last of January, therefore he ventures to propose a delay. He fears also if he should go at this season that he should have to stay too long, "which will be very Disagreeable to the French."

He left New England in January and had a very difficult journey.

The letter which he carried and La Jonquière's answer are mentioned in the story of the Swan Island captives. Arriving in Montreal March third he seems to have quickly done his business. The Governor agreed to give up all the captives who had been bought of the Indians, even though their ransoms were not immediately paid; not one was to be withheld. At the end of March the little party was in Deerfield; whence Heywood[105] went to Number Four while Stevens, with one or two captives (we know only of Timothy Whidden), returned to Boston. The News-Letter of April fourth says that he had arrived from Quebec.

Because of La Jonquière's promise to send the captives soon the Secretary of the Province was directed to write to their relatives telling them that they are coming to Crown Point and that provision must be made for the ransoms.

[104] Arch. 53, 553. [105] Saunderson writes of a diary kept by Heywood.

1752. *Stevens* and *Wheelwright.*

At a Council held at Harvard College[106] in April, 1752, the Lieutenant-Governor (Spencer Bennett Phips) was "advised" to appoint "Capt. Phineas Stevens & Mr Nataniel Wheelwright to negotiate the affair of Redeeming the Captives in Canada," according to a vote of the General Court. They were to proceed with dispatches as soon as the season would permit. The treasurer was to pay ninety pounds towards their expenses.[107]

Among the Force manuscripts in the Congressional Library is Stevens' "Journal of his Travels." He set out from No. 4 with his son Samuel for Deerfield on April 27. At Hatfield Wheelwright joined them, and Heywood again "entered the service for Canada." At Fort Massachusetts he gave the soldiers a present of a dollar. At Albany, Lord's Day (10 May), the sermon was "exceedingly dry." After two Stockbridge Indians came to guide them he, his son and cousin set northward followed the next day by Wheelwright. In eleven days they were at St. John's Fort, Chambly, from which place, on June sixth, carts carried their baggage, and horses themselves to Montreal.

Two days later "Mr. Wheelwright went to Connewago with a number of French gentlemen," and Stevens "visited French's sister." (French was probably Thomas, of Deerfield. Three sisters were left behind when Thomas was redeemed. Which did he visit, Freedom Daveluy, Martha Mesnard or Abigail the Indian? They all lived near Montreal.)

On June 16 Wheelwright with Mr. Deplace, the high sheriff, set off for Quebec. In July both commissioners went before the Governor about Solomon Mitchell and another captive and "upon their refusing to go home the Governor would not give them up."

Longueuil was the acting-governor, the Marquis de la Jonquière having died. Under date of July 25[108] he wrote to Phips that although all the English prisoners held by the French had

106 Meetings were held in different places. 107 Coun. Rec., Vol. 12.

108 Arch. 5, 548.

been returned in 1750 by "Mr. Stouder,"[109] and returned without ransom, having been well treated, yet he had received Stevens and "Weerliwright" with pleasure.

The only English captives were those held by the Indians, who were accountable to no one. "Indeed it would be a wonderful thing *(une nouveauté merveilleuse)*" he says, "one that the French would never dare imagine if the savages of the colony should recognize any other law than their own passion or caprice."

Since the war some captives "from sentiments of humanity" had been bought by Frenchmen, and the two New Englanders were given liberty to see and ransom them.

Wheelwright sought those in the region of Three Rivers and Quebec, while Stevens stayed in the Government of Montreal.

Their official report[110] — of the same date as Longueuil's letter and signed by him and Maddox, the interpreter — contains the names of all the captives about whom they had any information, saying that these were all they could find.

Those known to be of New England may be found in the following pages. Of the others, three were of New York, one of Pennsylvania, and Timothy Mackerty of an unknown place.

Berney Gradey wished to stay in Quebec. Rachel Quackenbush (N. Y.) and Elizabeth Skinner also preferred Canada. Samuel Freeman, an Indian, and a negro named Williams were considered slaves and held as such. Thomas Neal preferred Montreal, and Saras Davids, adopted by the Iroquois of Sault Saint-Louis, did not wish to leave them.

Another document connected with this mission is the report of the conference at Montreal with some Abenakis of St. Francis and Iroquois from Sault Saint-Louis and the Lake of Two Mountains, in presence of Longueuil.[111] An Abenaki began: "Brother, We shall talk to you as if we were speaking to your Governour

[109] Lieut. Benj. Stoddard of New York.

[110] Arch. 5, 542.

[111] Printed in Que. Docs., III, 509, and N. Y. Docs., X, 252, and in the Appendix of "True Stories."

in Boston. We hear on all sides that this Governour and the *Bastonnais* say the Abenakis are bad people. It is in vain that you charge us with bad hearts; it is always you, our brothers, who have attacked us; you have a sweet tongue, but a heart of gall. I admit, that when you begin it we can defend ourselves." He says that his fathers were willing to tolerate the English on the coast as far as Sawakwato (Sagadahock?) and under no pretext must they pass that boundary. "The lands we possess have been given us by the Master of Life; we hold them only from him." The Iroquois told Ati8aneto that he had spoken with spirit and promised to help to defend the lands; and Stevens promised faithfully to report their point of view to his Governor.

Of the return journey we know little. William Heywood and seven prisoners lodged at Fort Massachusetts on the way.

1753. *Noble* and *Mitchell.*

Among the captives left behind were some children of these two men, and in the summer after Stevens and Wheelwright returned they, Lazarus Noble and Benjamin Mitchell, were allowed to hire an interpreter to seek them.

Van Schaack, of Albany, had brought back Noble and part of his family two years before, so he was the man they chose; he had been once a prisoner and was delivered to Stoddard in 1750. Although courteously received by the Governor of Montreal they were the very next day ordered to leave Canada under pain of imprisonment.[112] This so enraged Governor Shirley, now returned from England, that he sent a letter to Duquesne (Oct. 22, 1753) demanding these children and all other prisoners.

Major Nathaniel Wheelwright was "the suitable person" who carried it. Duquesne apologized, saying that Van Schaack was "a suspected Character, who, besides began to behave in so insolent a manner that I determined to cause him to depart immediately rather than to be forced to put him into Prison."[113] If "sus-

112 Arch. 5, 554; Letter from the Gov. of Mass. to Gov. of Can., partly quoted under Noble and Mitchell captivities.

113 Arch. 5, 558.

pected," he was also alert, for in their few hours of liberty "Mr. Mitchell and the Interpreter both saw Mitchell's son, and the Interpreter acquainted Noble that he saw his daughter."[114]

1753. *Major Nathaniel Wheelwright.*

It was on the twenty-ninth of November that Wheelwright with his servant and Mr. Lydius reached Montreal. The officer who had accompanied them from Fort St. Frederick took him immediately to "the General Monsieur le Marquis Duquesne" who asked his business; asked it, perhaps, because some doubts had existed about his last visit; explained by "a Monsieur St. Luc la Come, an officer much in favour with Duquesne" and a particular friend of Wheelwright.

There had been suspicions that the person who passed for his "Domestick" on his last visit was an engineer who made plans of Montreal and Quebec, but the major cleared himself. In the letter quoted,[115] which he wrote to Governor Shirley the day after his arrival, he said that Governor Duquesne "very genteely told me as I wasn't a Stranger I could go & repose myself & procure Lodgings where I pleased." He was given liberty to see Solomon Mitchell, and M. Saint-Ange de Charly was ordered to give up Fanny Noble. How M. St. Ange had deceived Wheelwright about Fanny on his former visit may be read elsewhere. His greatest difficulties concerned this child. The chiefs of the two Indian villages near Three Rivers asked its Governor, Rigaud de Vaudreuil, to forbid the Englishmen to come to their villages, saying that they could not be responsible for the acts of their young men; and while promising to do everything that he could to secure the child the Governor advised him to stay away.

Wheelwright believed these threats to be "a made Story by Mr St Ange, but the Governour's letter proved the contrary."

He learned from an interpreter at Quebec that the two English children with the St. Francis Indians had gone a-hunting; their squaw-owners refusing to part with them either by exchange or

[114] Arch. 8, 280. [115] Arch. 54, 263-266.

A.W. Elson & Co. Belmont, Mass.

for money, but the squaw who had Noble's child, "being necessitated, would part with it for money." How he failed to get it "for money" on his return to Three Rivers is told in Fanny Noble's story. He appealed to the Governor, who confessed his helplessness, proving it by telling him of a recent Council when a sachem said: "Who are you? You are General of Canada and I am King of my Village," and Wheelwright complains in his Journal of the Frenchman's lack of force.

Leaving Montreal for Quebec and home, he had with him his servant, the boy Solomon Mitchell, and an officer with seven soldiers "to conduct the batteau;" making on his way a last effort to rescue Fanny Noble.

In late June he sailed from Quebec for Louisburg with Solomon, Freeman, an Indian of Saratoga whom he had rescued from slavery, two soldiers, and three Scotch girls; "all the prisoners that I could at present obtain their Liberty."

At Louisburg he reëmbarked. On 21 August, 1754, he wrote: "This day arrived in York River & next day went to Wells, where I spent 2 or 3 days very agreeably with my Relatives & Freinds." And they must have been interested to hear of Mother Esther, the Ursuline, carried away half a century before.

The End.

In December, 1754, a motion was made that Captain Stevens be sent again to Canada if New Hampshire would share the cost, but a few weeks later the committee which had been appointed reported that it was not "Convenient at this time for the Court to Employ any Person in Purchasing Captives" because "the Indians by Means of such Purchases had been encouraged to continue their Depredations."[116]

Seven years later (June, 1761) the committee which had been appointed "to Project some Method for the redemption of Persons . . . in the Hands of the French & Indians" reported: "That since it has pleased Heaven to subject Cannada with its

[116] Arch. 6, 180.

Dependancies to the Obedience of the Brittish Government & thereby a Door is now opened for the more easy recovery of such as have been heretofore detained from their Freinds & Relatives by the French & Indians, There be two Suitable Persons Appointed to proceed to Cannada." But "after further consideration the House determined not to proceed on this affair."[117] Was it perhaps because Samuel Harnden had already been empowered to seek some of the captives?[118]

Ransoms

Although it was contrary to the general policy of the English to pay the Indians for the release of their victims, and although we find now and again statements like this: "Read and non-concurred: As a Matter of dangerous Consequence, for this Government to give allowance to the Ransoming of Captives from the Indians,"[119] yet ransoms were constantly paid, and Belknap says because of this the French received enough to "pay the whole charges of their predatory excursions besides reaping a handsome profit themselves."

In the later wars, when ransoms were larger, it was said that redemptions brought more evil than good, for by paying or even offering extravagant ransom the Indians were encouraged and tempted to take more prisoners, thereby prolonging their "diabolical kidnapping mode of warfare."

Individual stories somtimes show how ransoms were paid. Often the captive had to work out his own, as did Ethan Allen.

The commandant at Sault Saint-Louis wrote to the Governor-General in 1750 that the man belonging to Delisle changed his mind because he has embraced our religion. His father is dead and "by the laws of his country whoever has been ransomed, if obliged to borrow the money, is bound to service until he have repaid by his labor the sum he cost; that he prefers being a slave with the Indians than in his country where there is no religion."[120]

117 Arch. 79, 758. 118 See Chapter XX.

119 House Journal, July 25, 1715. 120 N. Y. Docs., X, 215.

And he who was with Ononragueti's nieces said the same when told that he was free to go: "No, he hated too strongly the English nation where he was almost a slave to give up his religion & liberty." Perhaps the nieces misunderstood his words, but he stayed.

And so because they had become Catholics or Indians or both, or because it might be difficult to raise their ransom-money, they stayed, and staying they became citizens of New France.

Naturalization

In October, 1698, Frontenac wrote to Versailles: "The first news we had of peace in Europe came to us last winter by some Englishmen [121] who for love of their kin, who were prisoners of war here, came to Montreal over the snow as soon as they knew of this peace." And it was confirmed even before the ships came from France by other English messengers sent by Governor Bellomont. These brought French prisoners for exchange, and Frontenac says that he surrendered all the English except those "who have established themselves and have embraced the Catholic religion, who beseech you, as do we, to grant them *Lettres de Naturalité* that they may be known as French." Children under twelve will not be allowed to remain, notwithstanding their desire, because it is represented to us that they cannot clearly understand the religious motive.[122] Many children under twelve, however, *did* remain, some, of course, being with the Indians.

The next year the King signifies that he is willing to grant the requests of these English Catholics who have, for religion's sake, refused to return to New England, and he asks for their names.[123] They were, of course, only those who had been ransomed by the French. That was the best thing that could happen, for then the captive might hope for exchange or release, which was impossible if he had been adopted into an Indian family, for he was then no longer a prisoner but one of themselves.

121 Mr Abraham Schuyler, Mr Vroman, and Mr Jean Rosie, a Frenchman, were sent from Albany "to advertise the Govr of Montreall" of the peace.

122 Que. Docs., II, 309. 123 Que. Docs., II, 327.

Not all captives with the Indians were held by adoption, but it sometimes happened, if given the choice, that the captive preferred the wild life. As has been said it is far easier to Indianize than to civilize. Children grew up with the Indians and knew no other life. It was the same with French children held by savages. When in 1697/8 certain French prisoners, some of whom had been ten years in captivity, were given up by the Iroquois the chiefs explained that they would bring all "except the little children, who are become almost Iroquois."

And some New Englanders chose to remain, not as Indians with the Indians, but as Catholics with the French. Some took husbands and wives, and a few took the veil.

A modern writer says of those who married that they were "enchanted to remain, having had the precious advantage of allying themselves with our best families." Another, writing of converts, says: "Indeed she and her sister were greatly tried at the time of their captivity. But it was the way God judged more proper to lead her to a religion which they thought afterwards to be the only one able to lead men to eternal happiness (and for them to a suitable establishment)."

In the following pages many stories are told of the unwillingness of our captives to return.

Among the many obstacles that Stoddard and Williams found in 1714 was this spirit of unwillingness. Stoddard says: "We went to Cagnawaga, to visit the natives and the prisoners with them, which we found rather worse than the Indians."[124]

No records have been found of "Letters" at this period, but to relieve the Colony's treasury the King sent money for the converts.

Beauharnois, the Intendant, writing to Pontchartrain, the colonial minister, on November 11, 1702, says that as the "Clergyman, who has charge of the poor English Catholic men and women," who were taken at Boston and who prefer to live here because of their "love for the religion" has sent to him the list of their names.

124 Gen. Reg., 5, 34.

He (Beauharnois) has "caused to be apportioned among them, according to the annexed return, the sum of 2000 livres that the King has had the goodness to grant them and the Bishop of Quebec's proctor will pay what is due to each."[125]

A copy of the "annexed return" is in the Parkman manuscripts.[126] In it we find the new home-towns of the "Boston people."

"List of the English men and women who are in New France, to whom His Majesty grants the sum of two thousand livres, which has been distributed among them as follows:

At Quebec

Agathe Clark 80
Magdeleine Flisson 70 (Stilson?)
Gabrielle Villis 60 (Willis)
Magdelaine Villis 60
Marie Magdeleine Villis 60
Marie Catherine 70
Rose Ottys 30
Lidivine Standers 30
Claude Thomas 30
Marie Louise 30

At Montreal

Abel Bear 60
Magdeleine Warren 70
Marie Sayer 90
Anne Herd 30
Jean Stilson 30
Guillaume James 30
Jean Thomas 50
Louise Trasson 30 (Louis Trafton?)
George Gré 60 (Gray)
Paul Ottys 30
Louise Braquette 30

125 Que. Docs., II, 396, and N. Y. Docs., IX, 741.

126 Mass. Hist. Soc.

Marie Joseph Sayer 50
Catherine Dankeen 60 (Duncan)
Elizabeth Flashing 30
Marie Anne 50
Jean la ha 60 (La Haye)

At Three Rivers

Marguerite Key 300
Louise Corsonoüit 60

At La Prairie

Marie Louise Christancien 60

At St. François

Marie Ursule Mistrete 30 (Mercy Adams)
Richard Naason 30

At Longueil

Andre Fret 30 (André Fry?)

At Island St. Lawrence

Pierre called Perrot 30

At Beaupré

Jean Baptiste 30

At St. Anne

Jean Willem 30
Guillaume Brak 30

Cape Tourmente

Jean Baptiste Ottys 30
Jean Bap. de Mahathe 60."

It is signed Beauharnois and a note says that Etienne Le Vallet, Canon of the Cathedral of Quebec, made great exertions to convert the prisoners.

The care of prisoners became a burden, and in 1704 Vaudreuil wrote to Versailles repeating Frontenac's request. He says: "A large number of English prisoners whom we are obliged to clothe and feed, some being persons of consideration, whom we have bought from the Indians give us great expense," and he hopes His Majesty will make the concession for which they beg.[127]

That a formal application was made two years later is shown by a ragged scrap of discolored paper which a book-lover of Quebec treasured for its signatures of Vaudreuil and Raudot. It has the names of Louis Marie Strafton, Pierre Augustin Litrefield, Christine Otesse, Elizabet Price, Elizabeth Casse, Mathias Claude Farnet, Madeline Ouarem, Thomas Hust, Marie Françoise French, and Thérèse Steben.

In the month of May, 1710, Louis, fourteenth of his name, gave at Versailles in the grandest manner his gracious permission to these[128] and other boys and girls, men and women, to live and die in New France or elsewhere in his possessions.[129]

"Louis, by the grace of God, King of France and Navarre, to all present and to come, greeting: Our well beloved . . . Jean laha, Irishman living in Mont-royal, married to an Englishwoman and having three children.

Richard Naasson of N. E. living in Sainct francois m. to a French woman, children.
Jean baptiste otis, N. E. at Coste de beaupré, French w. and children.
Paul otis, established at villemarie
Phylippe Montase*
André fray (Fry)
Guillaume Tailor, at villemarie
Mathias Claude farmont (Farnsworth)
Gabriel Jourdan,* Quebecq
Joseph hastings of the coste of Beaupré
Joseph Kalogg
Thomas hust

127 Parkman MSS. 128 Trafton's name is omitted.

129 The names which follow have been copied from the *Lettres de Naturalité* in the Canadian Archives, omitting those known to belong outside of New England. An asterisk means unidentified. The names are printed as written, but abbreviations are used and repetitions avoided.

Pierre augustin Littlefiere
Jean Carter
Louis Price
Michel Searls
Nicolas hutchins
Joseph Stoüer
Anthoine Nicolas hust
Louis Philippes Sergen
Richard . . . formerly living with sieur de linquetot major of three rivers
Jean baptiste . . . at beaupré near Quebecq, French w. children
Jacques Charles Stebbens
——— Coal
Joseph hins (Haynes) at cap Sainct ignace
Another Joseph hins, his brother, at coste de beaupré
André—living with Guillaume Lemieux at Bellechasse
Benjamin Mussy
henry Stroton*
Jean Ricard of the seminary at Quebecq
Magd[ne] Warin m. to Philippe Robitaille, cooper of villemarie, by whom she has four children
Marie Swarten m. to Jean laha, Irishman of the island of Montreal, having three children
Margueritte Renéé Kay, m. to a sergt. named Chevalier
Marie françoise Stozer (Storer) m. to Jean Berger, painter of villemarie
anne herd, m. to Sebastien Cholet, called laviolette, weaver of villemarie
Christine otis, brought with her mother to Canada m. to Louis le Beau, carpenter of villemarie
Elisabith Priser, m. to Jean fourneau of villemarie, having two children
Marguerite Stebbens, m. to Jean des noyons, sergeant, with children

Marie Anne* m.
Magd^ne Stilson m. to one named Chevalier, wigmaker — of Quebeq, having children — (so says the Letter, but elsewhere he is J. Bapt. Cardinet, called Chevalier chirurgien).
Marie Ursulle Mistrot (Mery Adams) m. to Charles Brisebois of sainct françois
Marie Stevens, m. to Pasquet, l. near Quebecq, several children
Marie Magdelaine willis m. to vildaigre *garde-port* at Quebecq
Rose otis m.
Marie Jeanne Gefferis wid. of Thomas hust
Marie Louise Pitman, wid of Estienne willis of Quebecq
Marie Joseph Sayer
Catherine Donkin
Marie Stozer
Louise Therese Stebbens
Louise Gabrielle Brakett
Marie francoise Ferns (French)
Marie pricille Stozer
Marie Elisabeth Waber
Margueritte Tarbel
Marthe frins
Elisabeth hust
Marie Louise Kembell
Magdelaine allyn*
Marie Charlotte Brojon*
Elisabeth Cos (Corse)
helenne Davis
Marie françoise hammon
anne hust (Hurst)
Marie Brook
Magdelaine Cout* (Cutt?)
Marie Elisabeth Lamax
Marie Drody;* all professing the catholic, apostolic and roman religion, have shown us that they have been established sev-

eral years in New France and desiring to end their days as our subjects, they have very humbly supplicated us to grant these Letters which facilitate in every way possible their residence in the "country of Canada and new france," they yielding obedience to us.

The above named are to have "all the rights, privileges and immunities enjoyed by our born subjects, as well as the same rights to hold and dispose of property, real and personal," but: — "They cannot leave the country without our express and written permission, nor can they either transmit information nor be employed as go-betweens with foreigners on pain of forfeiting these rights."

Given at Versailles May, 1710.

Signed & "sealed with the great seal with green wax on ribbons of red and green silk."

And at Ramboüillet in June of the year 1713, and of his reign the seventy-first, Louis signed and sealed another Letter, in form similar to the first, and granting privileges to forty more new subjects, wrongly grouped as natives of Old and New England, with two from Ireland. Some are soldiers taken with Major Lloyd at Fort St. John, Newfoundland. The names are:

Jean otis — Is it Jean-Baptiste of the earlier Letter?
Jean arnauld (Fort St. John)
jean Willet
Edoüard flechier (m. to Stephen Willis's widow.)
Edoüard Clements
Guillaume White
Jacques Pillsbury
Richard Taylor
Thomas Jeffereys
Thomas stillet
Jean Scothow
Richard Pearse

Christophe Wood
Jacques Hovey
Charles steuard
Charles taylor
Jacques Leigten (a Piscataqua name)
Isaac Ruff
Charles davis (Fort St. John)
Guillaume Wilding
Robert Dixon
Jean denis
Thomas schoulden
Jean Banistor
Charles Menning
Marie Hocman,[130] Widow of höar
Marie anne Drew.

The above were all in the jurisdiction of Quebec; those that follow, of Montreal, and excepting the last four said (wrongly) to be of Old England.

Joseph Greenhill
Guillaume Perrins (probably Perkins)
Thomas Buraff
jean Reed
joseph Robert
Daniel maddox (Newfoundland)
jeanne Wardaway (Ordway) and as of New England are:
Daniel fisk
Simon Lucas
Victor Thomas Dian
Catharine Parsons

130 Probably Oakman.

CHAPTER V

Hatfield and Deerfield

September 19, 1677

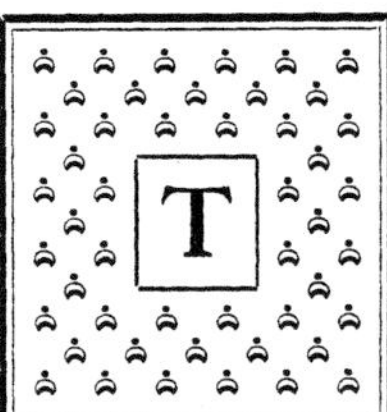

HE first captives who made "the doleful journey" were taken from Hatfield and Deerfield at the end of Philip's War. Hubbard, writing in that very year, said that the people of Hatfield "were a little too secure and too ready to say the bitterness of Death was past, because they had neither seen nor heard of any Enemy in those Parts for half a year before,"[1] but on this September morning at about eleven o'clock, when most of the men were in the meadows, some River Indians fell suddenly upon the place, attacking a group of men who were framing a house outside the palisade.

"River Indians" was an indefinite term, believed here to describe those of the Hudson and Housatonic Rivers who had fled to the French.[2]

Some of their families had previously lived in a friendly way near Hatfield. Now they came back to carry off their old neighbors that they might sell them to the French. Of about thirty persons killed, wounded and captured, twenty-five were women

[1] "Indian Wars," II, 239.

[2] Twenty years later, in Dec., 1696, Governor Fletcher of New York told some sachems of the River Indians that recent murders in New England were said to have been committed by their people, and the Governor of New England asked him to command them not to hunt that way. He advised them not to do it because fifty pounds a head had been offered for every strange Indian. In parting he said: "I give you this Kegg of Rum to comfort your hearts this cold weather, so I bid you adieu." N. Y. Docs., IV, 208.

and children. Seventeen of them they carried away. There was Obadiah Dickinson and his child; Benjamin Waite's wife, Martha, with three little girls; Mary, wife of Samuel Foote, with two young children; two children of John Coleman, whose wife and baby were killed; Hannah Jennings, wife of Stephen, with two of her children named Gillett; Samuel Kellogg, Abigail Allis and Abigail Bartholomew — one father, three mothers and thirteen children, all under six years of age except Samuel Kellogg, he was eight!

This proportion of adults and children was common in Indian warfare for the weaker captives could more easily be held for ransom.

At Deerfield, "between sunset and dark" of the same day, the few brave men who — driven away in 1675 — had come back to rebuild their homes were surprised and hurried into the woods on East Mountain where the Hatfield people had been left. They were Quentin Stockwell, whose "Narrative" was first published by Dr. Increase Mather in 1684, Benoni Stebbins and John Root, "Old Sergeant John Plympton" and little Samuel Russell, the eight year old child of Philip. He found his playmates among the Hatfield children and was told that his mother and brother had been killed that morning.

The next day the party travelled northward, and about thirty miles beyond Northfield encamped for three weeks. Some eighty Indian women and children from Wachusett joined them; they being part of the emigration of Massachusetts Indians to Canada.

For two weeks the distracted people of Hatfield knew nothing of their friends; then Benoni Stebbins, having escaped, brought them tidings. He said that the Indians had "been encouradged that they should have eight pounds apiece" for their captives, and that the French Indians intended "to come with them the next time . . . if they had sucses this time."

Benjamin Waite and Stephen Jennings went out into the wilderness to seek their wives and children. Picture them, and think of their courage. After long delay, aided by a friendly Indian, they reached Lake George; thence in an old patched canoe, guided by a chart drawn on a bit of bark, they went alone into an unknown world. Probably they were the first New Englanders to cross Lake Champlain.

From Chambly, "a small village of ten houses," they travelled toward Sorel, finding Jenning's wife in "a lodging of Indians." She told them "how hard it was with the Rest." At Sorel were five more; "two of which the Indians had pawned to Frenchmen for Drink; the Remainder of them were in the Woods."[3] Stockwell, helpless with frozen feet and hands, was in "the Captain's house," having been bought of his captors for twenty-one beavers, or "their worth."

Waite and Jennings hurried on to Quebec where, helped by the governor, they ransomed their friends.

In May, escorted by French soldiers to Albany, came back almost as many as went away. Plympton, after many weary days, had been burned "in the Indians cruel manner." Samuel Russell, too, and Mary Foote had been killed, but Canada Waite and Captivity Jennings had been born.

For nine long months nothing had been heard in Hatfield, and now came letters, and in all the pages that follow none more pathetic will be found. Stockwell wrote from Albany.

"May 22, 1678

Loving wife, having now opportunity to remember my kind love to the and our child and the rest of our freinds, though wee met with greate afflictions and troubles since I see thee last, yet now here is opportunity of joy & thanksgiving to God that wee are now pretty well and in an hopefull way to see the faces of one another before we take our finall farewell of this present world; likewise God hath raised up freinds amongst our enemies, and

[3] Hubbard's "Indian Wars," II, 244.

there is but 3 of us dead of all those who were taken away . . . so I conclude being in hast & rest

Your most affectionate husband
till death makes separation
Quintin Stockwell"

And Waite wrote:

"From Albany May 23, 1678

To my loving freinds & kindred at hatfield these few lines are to let you understand that we are arrived at Albany now with the Captives, and we now stand in need of assistance wth my charges for it is very greate and heavy and there fore any that hath any love to our condition let it moove them to come & help us in this straight. There is 3 of ye captives that are Murdered . . . all the rest are alive and well with mee now at Albany. [He names them, with no special mention of the new-born, only "Hannah Gennings with 3 children," and "my wife and four children."] There is 2 or 3 french Embassadors Coming to go to Boston. [This sentence was erased in the copy, perhaps they were not allowed to go to Boston.] I pray you hasten the matter for it requireth greate hast, stay not for ye Sabath nor shoeing of horses. we shall Endeavor to meet you at Canterhook it may at houseatonock we must come very softly because of our wives and children. I pray you hasten them, stay not night nor day, for ye matter requireth great hast. bring provisions with you for us.

Your loving kinsman
Benjamin Waite

At Albany, written from myne owne hand as I have bin affected to yours, all that were fatherless, be affected to me now & hasten ye matter and stay not and ease me of my charges You shall not need to be affraid of any Enemys."

"We must come very softly" says the tender father, but "very roughly" seems to say the little tattered red shoe which Sarah Coleman, aged four, wore on the journey.[4] Hatfield "stayed

[4] It is now in Memorial Hall, Deerfield.

not." Help was sent westward and copies of the letters eastward to the minister of Medfield, who again copied and sent them on to the governor.[5] He had already appointed a day of fasting, and to the congregations he sent this message dated "30 May 1678 Having Intelligence that Benjamin Waite being at Albany wth the Captives on the 23^d^ Instant and that their sufferings are great & their cry for reliefe is loud, which comes so timely before the day Appointed for publick fasting and humilliation on the 6th Day of ye next Month; Judging it Suitable for such a day's service when we are Imploring mercy of God, to be manifesting bowells of mercy to those in necessity wee Judge these delivered Captives to be objects of such Bowells, knowing that the labor travaile, hazard & charge of the undertakers Benjamin Wayte & his Associate have been great, who went forth with the Countenance of Authority. Therefore wee doe recommend their Case with the Captives for releife, to the pious charity of the Reverend Elders ministers & Congregations of the Severalle Townes in this Jurisdiction that . . . they manifest their Charity . . .by thereupon contributing to the releife of those the forementioned persons. And the Teaching Officers and ministers . . . are desired to . . . stir up the people of all degrees thereunto according to God and for their better quickning to this worke wee doe herewith emitt a Copie of Benjamin Waytes letter to be read publickly either before or upon the day."[6]

It is probable that Waite's letter stirred the people more than the governor's. Forty-six towns contributed three hundred and forty-four pounds, three shillings and six pence; Boston leading, Portsmouth, Charlestown and Cambridge following. The Isles of Shoals gave more than Salem,[7] and of this almost three hundred pounds was sent to Canada as ransom-money.

Three years later Obadiah Dickinson asked for individual help "because he had expended abt. £11 in his country's service" and had "been through many difficulties & straits" by reason of his

[5] See Arch. 60, 205. [6] Arch. 69, 206. [7] Arch. 69, 206a.

captivity, and because the destruction of his habitation had caused him to remove to the other Colony (viz. Coniticot), but it was "not consented to."

An account of the disaster, written probably by Maj. Gen. Daniel Gookin, between May and September, 1678, is printed in the Genealogical Register.[8] He says in part: "Only last Michelmas a party of French Indians that heretofore were belonging to o^r^ neighborhood being furnished and sent out by the Earle ffountracke Governor at Quebecke (as o^r^ messenger sent thither last winter give us evident proof) I say that party being not above 27 persons, fell at unawares upon the village at Hatfield near Hadley, slew some persons . . . captivated about 23 persons . . . and carried them all to ye French territorys. Two men . . . whose wives and children were carried captive did obtain l^rs^ and a pass from o^r^ Govr and Council to goe into the French Country to seek for their wives and ye rest of ye captives. The history of their travells, interruptions from the English at albany and at ye Moquas Country by ye underhand dealing of the two French Jesuits and their servants that live there, whom o^r^ men saw, together with y^e^ many hazards . . . and vicissitudes of Providence that befell them would take up a large sheet to recite."

[8] Vol. 38, 381.

CHAPTER VI

At the Eastward—Dover (Cocheco)

1689—1696—1706—1723—1724—1725[1]

OTTON MATHER wrote in his grand manner that "while those parts of New England which had the *glory* of Evangelical churches in them, for a defence to be *created* upon, were thus tempestuated by a terrible war, there were other parts lying in the northeast of New England, of a less evangelical temper, which felt a furious euroclydon also beating upon them."[2]

Except for a fringe of settlements the northeast was occupied by Indians who were largely dominated by French missionaries.

There had been no open hostilities before 1675, but the Indians then had become uneasy. They accused the English of disturbing their hunting-grounds and fisheries and of refusing in return to sell them firearms; "Whereas the French were free and cheerful to supply them with whatever they needed."

Firearms and fire-water were what the savages most coveted. The early traders and fishermen along the Maine coast supplied these in small quantities, but with the exception of Morton at Merry-Mount the English colonists of Massachusetts had denied them. King James, at the request of the Council for New England, had in 1622 forbidden the trade.

Some Indians, exasperated by rough and lawless border settlers,

1 The later captivities may be found in Chapter XVII.

2 Magnalia; Bk. VII.

had already been persuaded by missionaries to migrate. Canada protected them and their tomahawks were at her service.

The lawless acts caused perhaps by the lack of Mather's "evangelical temper" may have justified the "euroclydon" which followed, although Mather failed to described them.

As the ground of the quarrel between the Eastern Indians and "those who lived about Pemaquid and Kennibeck" Hubbard[3] names an injury of a high nature which, he says, brought the first Indian war of these parts.

In the winter 1675/6 Maj. William Waldern issued a warrant to seize any Indians Eastward who had been guilty of harm to the English in that region. Under that warrant seventeen persons, men, women and children from "about Cape Sables," although they "never had been in the least Manner guilty of any Injury," were "perfidiously and wickedly" enticed aboard a vessel, carried away and sold as slaves.

Nor was this kidnapping the only enormity of the English, although Mr. Drake says "the Historians of the Time have barely given us but an apologetical glimpse of them."

It is true that William Waldern and two or three more men were committed to prison, and the master of the vessel was accused of man-stealing, "being Instigated by the Divill" to take the Indians "away to ffyall[4] & there sold them."

Waldern, not having been present, was acquitted and the punishment of the others was slight.

The Sagamore and his squaw were soon redeemed by order of Governor Leverett through the efforts of Bernard Trott. Nothing is said of the fate of the others.

Trott sent his servant to Fayal and bore all the expense of redemption and travel. Again and again he petitioned for reimbursement. At the end of one appeal, beautifully written, he adds in his own poor writing "for ye Lords sake I begg y^r^ Excell^y^

[3] Indian Wars, II, 136. [4] Fayal, Azores Islands.

petty & Compassion one me;"[5] but at his death, thirty-two years after the event, the last instalment had not been paid.

Naturally the Indians were not wholly appeased by Governor Leverett's benevolent deed, nor by the attempted punishment for the crime.

And alas! as has been said, many other Indians were sold into slavery. John Eliot in 1675 made a fine appeal against "the terror of selling away such Indians unto the Islands for ppetual slaves," and reminded the law-makers that "the designe of christ in these last dayes is not to extirpate natives, but to gospelize y^m^."[6]

The news of Philip's uprising reached York twenty days after its outbreak. Raids were made along-shore from the Piscataqua to the Kennebec. In the following winter Massachusetts troops were ordered out to subdue the Indians, but the snow was deep and lacking snowshoes the soldiers accomplished nothing.

The Indians, pinched with the hunger and cold of a hard winter, promised to be quiet and to give up their captives without ransom. This promise, made first to Maj. Richard Waldron, was signed in July, 1676, by whites and sagamores as a "Treaty of Peace" at Cocheco.

The death of Philip, a cause of rejoicing in the southern colonies, was calamitous to those at the eastward, for many of his followers, joining the eastern tribes, incited them to break their treaty.

To prove their own good faith the Penacooks, with some of their Abenaki neighbors, and alas! many "strange Indians" — Philip's men, who probably hoped to be overlooked in this friendly company — came to Dover, but the government wishing to secure the refugees determined to take *all* that "Were met about Major Walderne's dwelling," and by a strategem in September, 1676, four hundred Indians were seized. Three hundred of them being friendly were set free. The others, doubtless guilty and to be feared, were taken to Boston; a few to be hanged and more to be sold into slavery. The tribes considered this an atro-

[5] Arch. 31, 4. [6] Arch. 30, 173.

cious and treacherous deed and held Waldron and Frost responsible.

Belknap, who based his account on the most authentic traditions, thought Waldron was the victim of circumstances, but the Rev. John Williams was told by a priest that the Indians were justified "in what they did against us,[7] rehearsing some things done by Major Waldron above 30 years ago," and the Abbé Casgrain, writing recently, says that the Abenakis "swore a mortal hatred to the English" from the day of this treachery.

Because they did not forget, on the twenty-eighth of June, thirteen years later, they attacked the town. Then they cruelly tortured and killed Waldron, but they allowed Frost to live eight years longer. Of his murder the town clerk of Kittery wrote only: "deceased on Saboth day, July 4, 1697."

Joseph Storer, writing from Wells a few days later to "Brother Hill," says:

"It hath pleased god to take a way; Major Frost, the Indens waylad him Last Sabbath day as he was cominge whom from meeting at night; and killed him and John Heards wife and Denes Downing . . . it is a Great Loss to the whole Province; and Espesely to his famyley . . . mistress Frost is very full of sory; and all her Children."[8]

The attack upon Dover might have been averted had the previous day been of fair weather.

The Council of Massachusetts sent from Boston on June twenty-seventh a letter of warning, but a furious wind delayed the messenger's crossing of the Merrimac River at Newbury and he reached Cocheco a few hours after the place was reduced to ashes.

It was addressed to

"Major Richard Wald . . .
Mr Peter Coffin
or Either of them

[7] Meaning the massacre at Deerfield in 1703/4.

[8] Gen. Reg., III, 165.

At Cocheco
These with all possible
Speed"

Alas! That the wind was of greater speed.

In our Archives[9] is a copy of the letter which says that the Governor "having this day received a Letter from Chelmsford that some Indians are come into them, who report that there is a gathering of some Indians in or about Penecooke with designe of mischiefe to the English, amongst the said Indians is one Hawkins [son of Wannalancet and grandson of the great Passaconaway] is said to be a principle designer and that they have a particular design against yor Selfe and mr Peter Coffin." The letter which was sent is owned by the Waldron family, and it was from that Dr. Quint made the copy which was printed in the Dover Inquirer of January, 1880.[10] Dr. Quint considered Major Richard "the boldest and ablest man Dover held for a generation." Peter Coffin they did not kill, having no particular enmity to him, but they pillaged his house and scrambled for the contents of his money-bag which he scattered among them.

Friday, June 28, 1689.

Of this day the Rev. John Pike[11] wrote in his Journal: "The eastern Indns joyning with those of Pennicook . . . suddenly seized on Cocheco about break of day, wn all things were silent & secure Killed 23 persons . . . Carried Captive 29."

In the town were five garrison-houses. To each of them on this summer evening there came two squaws, asking for a night's shelter; only one refused its hospitality. While the people slept the doors were opened and the signal given.

[9] Vol. 107, 144. [10] It is also in N. H. Prov. Papers, II, 148.

[11] Son of Maj. Robert Pike, and until his death the settled minister of Dover. He removed to Portsmouth after the massacre and was chaplain at Ft. Pemaquid from 1692 to 1695. In his Journal he wrote down the "Observable Providences" beginning "Anno: Dom. 1682" and continued until 1709. The Journal was printed in the Proceedings of the Mass. Hist. Soc., 1875.

In our Archives[12] is the following letter written shortly after the Dover massacre.

"To bee Communicated
To the Inhabitance
of the Province of Maine
& all others Concerned

Falmouth 17 Sept: 89 3 [illeg] Yesterday ye Indians came in sight and made signs to ye Dutch privateer for a fflie, yy sent yr boat to ym, and after some discourse yy promised to bring Major Waldens daughter & her child to exchange for ye Indian captive; accordingly yy came and some few hours since yy received ye woman and her child and delivered ye Indian to ym. ye woman declares yt ye Indians are in Number upwards of two hundred and fiftie all on palmers Isle; besides ym on ye Isle yy have other forces near; ye Indians told ye woman yt since yy came into our Bay yy have some of them beene under everie of our Garrisons and know wt wee are, in Number and all our circumstances; yy resolve forthwith to set upon this Towne which yy reckon as yr owne alreadie, and then to pursue their design in taking and ruining ye whole Province. yy deride and scoff at us after a strange manner, yy say yy are much encouraged by some Gentlemen in Boston for ye managing ye warr against us wc makes ym go on wth undaunted courage. this is a Ralation of what: presents at ye fort from yr

Affectionate freind

Silvanus Davis."

List of Captives

1689.[13] Church, John, erroneously called Joseph Chase. He escaped, says Dr. Quint, before the party reached Winnepesaukee. Was killed by Indians six years later.

Evans, John

Gerrish, Sarah

[12] Arch. 107, 333. [13] Less than half the names are known.

Hanson, Mrs. Elizabeth (Sen.)
Heard. "a young woman of Cocheco" liberated by Captain Church in 1690, not identified.
Lee or Leigh, Esther (Waldron)
Her child.
Otis, Grizel, w. of Richard
Margaret
Rose
John
Stephen
Nathaniel
1692. Heard, Anne (See York)
1696. Ricker, Judith
Tucker, John
Otis, Wife of Nicholas, Jr.
1706. Ricker, "Little Son" of Maturin. (Noah? Jean François)
Ricor, John, on Roll of 1710/11.
1705. Tibbetts, Nathaniel

The following may be found in Chapter XVII.
Ham, Tamsen
Ann
Hanson, Mrs. Elizabeth
Sarah
Elizabeth
Ebenezer or Daniel
"Mary Ann Frossway"
Downes, Ebenezer
Evans, Benjamin, Jr.

The following "remaining still" in 1695 may have been victims of the 1689 massacre.

"Jo[s] Perkins boy" was doubtless son of Nathaniel of Dover Neck and grandson of Jeremy Tibbetts.

Eliz[bh] Squir may have been wife or daughter of Bernard Squire, who owned land at Little Bay.

Jno Antony boy has not been found nor Abig[ll] Cursinwhitt. On the 1710/11 list she is Aabigail Coursin. Probably a foreign name, anglicized in Dover; she may have been the daughter of Cornelius Carson, who was then living there.

We may be quite sure she was baptized in Canada, for as Louise Corsonoüit, living at Three Rivers, she received sixty livres of the king's money as we learn from a Parkman manuscript.

Evans, John.

His was probably not a Canadian captivity. He may have been son of Robert, an early inhabitant of Cocheco, who was killed in 1689.

John Gyles in his "Narrative" calls Evans "My most intimate and dear companion, a young man taken from Quochecho," and says that in 1692 (the third year of Gyles' captivity) "John Evans went into the country and the Indians imposed a heavy burden on him, while he was extremely weak from long fasting;" and as he was crossing "a place of ice, which was very hollow, he broke through . . . and cut his knee very much." He went on until overcome by wind and cold when "he sat or fell down, and all the Indians passed by him. Some of them went back the next day after him or his pack, and found him, with a dog in his arms, both frozen to death."

Gerrish, Sarah, daughter of Capt. John and Elizabeth (Waldron).

She was, according to the narrative "as communicated" by Mr. Pike: "A very beautiful and ingenious damsel, about seven years of age, and happened to be lodging at the garrison of Major Waldron, her affectionate grandfather. The savages made her dress for a march, but led her away with no more than one stockin upon her." Her first master "sold her to a fellow that was a more harsh and mad sort of *dragon*, and he carried her away to Canada. A long and a sad journey she had of it . . . in the midst of a dreadful winter."[14]

Taken to Quebec she was bought from the Indians, and sent by Mme. de Champigny, wife of the intendant, to the nuns of the Hôtel-Dieu. Their historian describes her as of such rare intelligence, noble bearing and exquisite tenderness that she became the idol of the Community.[15] She spoke "equally well English, French and the language of the savages." Under the influence of the Sisters she became an ardent Catholic, and at eight was admitted to her first Communion.

In the exchange of prisoners of 1690, for Sieur Trouvé, a missionary who had been taken by Phips from Port Royal, and who was now brought back as interpreter, there was given a "Girl of nine or ten years of age . . . somewhat good-looking." This was Sarah Gerrish. Madame the *Intendante* was so sorry to part with her that she consented only for the public good.[16]

When the child was told that she was to return to New England she burst into tears and could not tear herself from the embraces of the nuns, promising them to keep always her Catholic faith.

Casgrain adds that she wore a little crucifix on her neck which one of her brothers, who was in the "*armement*,"[17] wished to take away from her, but she cleverly hid it under her arm-pit.

A year after her return she wrote to the Reverend Mother and sent her "a gold piece which is," the annalist adds, "a mark of distinction among the English." The child assured her friend of her loyalty.

On July 29, 1697, her parents lost their "desirable daughter." Mr. Pike wrote: "Mrs. Sarah Gerrish died of the fever and bleeding."

Although this was seven years after she returned to her Protes-

14 "Magnalia," II, 592. 15 *"Hist. de l'Hôtel-Dieu," par l'Abbé Casgrain.*

16 N. Y. Docs., IX, 489.

17 Neither a Gerrish nor Waldron was in Phips's army, but one may have been of the crew.

tant home the Catholic historian wrote: "God doubtless called her to Himself before contact with heresy should destroy the precious germs planted in her soul."

HANSON, MRS. ELIZABETH, wife of Tobias.

Pike names "old widow Handson" among those killed. She was Mary, the widow of Thomas.

Elizabeth was her daughter-in-law. She was taken and her fate is unknown.

Tobias, in 1693, was "killed by the Indians, as he travelled the path near the west corner of Thomas Downs his field."

For the captivity of the John Hanson family (1724) see "Three Years' War."

LEIGH OR LEE, MRS. ESTHER (Walderne — Waldron); b. Dec. 1, 1660.

Her father was Major Richard. Her husband, Abraham Lee "chymist." He was killed.

Three months after the massacre[18] Captain Church found her "on board of a Dutch vessel" near Peaks Island, at the mouth of Casco Bay; she having just been ransomed, and to him she gave useful information.[19] Lee was Esther's second husband, the first having been Henry Elkins. After her release she took Richard Jose for a third and died in the island of Jersey.[20] Captain Davis in the letter before quoted tells us that "Major Waldens daughter & her child" were delivered. Nowhere else has mention been made of one.

OTIS. (Otheys, Oteys, Otesse, Autes, Hautesse, Hotesse, Rozotty, Thys and other variants).

The Family of Richard.

18 See Silvanus Davis Letter.

19 Drake's "Church's Indian Wars," 1675 to 1704, p. 163.

20 Gen. Reg., VII, 255.

Nearest to Waldron's garrison-house was that of Richard Otis, blacksmith. It sheltered a large family of his children and grandchildren.

Savage says that no other family in New England could match this in three generations for measure of calamity in war.

Richard Otis, an old man, was killed. His wife, the third he had married, was the mother of two little children. Hannah, aged two, they killed, the younger they carried away with her mother as they did Rose, John, Stephen and Nathaniel. Others of the family, among whom were three daughters of Richard,[21] were rescued by the pursuing party near the present town of Conway.

Probably Richard's wife and young child were soon ransomed by some kindly French person.

Grizel, wife of Richard, daughter of James Warren and Margaret ——, was baptized in Montreal.

"On Saturday, 9th May, the day before Whitsunday, 1693,[22] was solemnly baptized an English woman formerly named Madame Kresek, who was born at Barwic[23] in New England Feb. 24th (old style or 6 March new style) of the year 1662, of the marriage of Jacques Waren, Scotch Protestant and of Marguerite, Irish Catholic, and married to the deceased Richard Otheys, Inhabitant of Douvres, in New England, having been captured the 28th June of the year 1689[24] (of which remains only one little girl, aged four years, having been born 15 March 1689) named in baptism Christine, having been captured the 28th June old style (or 8 July new style) 1689, living in the service of Monsieur de Maricour. She was named Marie-Madeleine. Her godfather was Monsieur Jaques Le Ber, Merchant. Her godmother, Dame

21 Experience, Judith and Rose, Gen. Reg., V, 181.

22 In the Register dates are written.

23 Berwick.

24 Here is plainly an omission, the registrar being ignorant.

Marie-Madeleine Dupont wife of Monsieur le moine *Ecuyer* Sieur de Maricour, *Capitaine de détachement de la Marine.*

[signed] Le Ber
Fran: Dollier de Casson, Gr. vic.
M. M. Dupont. E. Guyotte Curé."

Four months later Marie-Madeleine Hotesse was confirmed, and soon she took a new husband and had a new family.

"In the year of grace, 1693, on October 15th after the betrothal and one publication of the banns, made at high Mass on the 11th day of the said month and year, between Philipe Robitaille, son of Jean Robitaille and of Martine Cormon, his father and mother, of the Parish of Biencour in Artois,[25] and Marie Madeleine oüaren, widow of deceased Richard Otheys, inhabitant of Douvres in New England, both of this parish, Monsieur Dollier grand vicar [illeg] having dispensed with the other two, and no impediment having been shown, M. Meriel, priest, with the consent of me, undersigned curé of the parish of Ville-marie, married them according to the rites prescribed by the Holy Church, in presence of Charles Le Moyne, *Ecuyer* Sieur de Maricour *capitaine reformé dans les troupes de la marine,* who are present with Dame Marie Madeleine Dupont his wife, with Monsieur Jaques Le Ber Merchant, with Mr forestier and several other friends."

In the contract signed the day before the future husband consented to take the little Marguerite as his own child.

M. Tanguay gives the following names of the Robitaille children.

Philippe (1695), Jacques (1697), Jean (1699), Georges (1701), and Marguerite (1703).

In May, 1710, citizenship is granted to "Magdne Warin, Englishwoman married to Philippe Robitaille, cooper, established at Ville-Marie by whom she has four children."

Of the king's distribution she had seventy livres.

In the "Redeemed Captive" she is called "Madam Grizalem."

25 Diocese of Boulogne.

She seems to have befriended her fellow-captives and to have aided Father Meriel in his ministrations among them. In the will of her father, dated Dec. 9, 1700, is written "I doe give unto my daughter Grizel five shillings." Her mother, who made her will in 1712, did not mention her.

Here is the record of her burial in Montreal: "The 27th October, 1750 was buried by me, undersigned, in the cemetery near the church, the body of Madeleine philippe dite robitaille aged about eighty-nine years, deceased the Day before widow of the late philippe robitaille her husband, in presence of messieurs Beauzèle and Benausse." They signed, as did Gay, priest. She had been bed-ridden nine or ten years.

Margaret (Christine) *Otis*, b. 15 March, 1689.[26]

A captive when three months old, baptized, renamed and probably educated by the nuns, she became at eighteen the second wife of Louis Le Beau.

"On 14th June 1707, after one publishing of the banns, and dispensing with the other two by permission from M. François Vachon de Belmont, Grand Vicar of Monseigneur, the Bishop of Quebec, I, undersigned Priest, officiating as curate of the Parish of Ville-Marie, having obtained the mutual consent of Louis Le Bau, aged twenty-nine years, son of Jean Le Bau and of Etiennette Loré, inhabitant of the Parish of Boucherville in this Diocese, of the one part, and of Christinne Otesse, aged eighteen years, daughter of the late Richard hautesse and Marie-Madeleine la garenne of the town of Douvre in old England[27] now living in this parish, of the other part, having married them according to the rites of our Holy Mother Church, in presence of the said Jean Bau, father of the bridegroom and of the said Estiennette Loré, his mother, of Jean Baptiste Bau, brother of the said bridegroom, of the Sieur Dominique Thaumur, master surgeon, of Philippe

26 The story of her romantic life may be found in Miss Baker's "True Stories."

27 An error.

Robitail Master Cooper, Stepfather of the said Bride. The said Jean Beau and Robitail have declared they do not know how to sign, inquiry as to this having been made according to law."

In May, 1710, naturalization is granted to "Christine Otes, English woman brought with her mother to Canada, married to Louis le Beau, carpenter, established at Ville-Marie." Louis died in February, 1713.

Their children were Louis, bap. 20 Nov., 1708, bur. 25 Jan., 1709; Marie-Anne Christine, bap. 14 June, 1710, m. 20 Feb., 1726, Pierre Trefflé, merchant of Montreal; she died at Quebec in December, 1726, as did her little baby. Marie-Madeleine, bap. 20 May, 1712.

Tanguay gives to Christine another child (Louis) but she, in a legal paper of her widowhood, names only two little girls.

The year after her husband died there came to Canada as interpreter for Stoddard and Williams Capt. Thomas Baker,[28] and his charms drew the young widow back to New England.

The State, the Church and her mother opposed her going. Stoddard tells us about it in his Journal.[29] The intendant ordered her husband's goods sold and "the money put into the hands of a keeper." Stoddard, acting for her, asked that it be distributed, Christine being in need, but he was told that the king commanded if any persons were absolutely set to leave the country their money should be kept from them and that she, being a prisoner of a former war, could not profit by the terms of the Peace of Utrecht.

The Church threatened to keep her children, and the governor said her daughter should be put with the Ursulines. Stoddard, with New England spirit, answered that Mme. Le Beau could put her child where she pleased, "and so long as it was well cared for, no Prince could with justice, forcibly take it away."

Her mother told her there were no bake-shops in New England and that she did not know how to make bread, but State, Church and mother could not keep her. Her lover triumphed, and with

[28] See Chapter IV. [29] Gen. Reg., V, 26.

the governor's grudging assent Christine, "prisoner of a former war," sailed away leaving her children behind.

In the Archives of Montreal is an Act of the notary Le Pallieur — a "*Donation par Christine Hotesse à P. Robitaille,*" dated 9 June, 1714. From it we learn that Christine, being about to depart for the Country of "Peskadaoué" her home, never to return to New France, as she believes, and taking with her, her daughter, Magdelaine Lebeau (who was two years old), but finding it impossible to take her other daughter, Marie Anne Lebeau (aged four), she leaves her in the care of Sieur Philippes Robitaille and of greseul Magdelaine Warrin, her stepfather and her mother, begging them to bring up the child as if she were their own. For this care and in consideration, not only of this but of other obligations, she of her free will cedes to Marie anne beau, not only all rights in the land and house situated on Rue Saint-francois, according to the agreement made between her and the late Lebeau, but of all other property she may have in the country, without exception, even that which would come to her daughter Magdelaine in case of her death; and in case of the death of Marie Anne Lebeau it should belong to the said Sr. Robitaille and the said Warin his wife, but if she, the donor, should return to this country with her daughter Magdelaine, or either one of them should come, then they should enter into their rights, without holding the said Robitaille and his wife to render account for any former income.

Monsieur and Madame said they could not sign, but "Christinne otes" wrote her name.

Gov. de Vaudreuil, however, would not allow the little Magdelaine to go to New England, so with or without justice the child was taken from its mother.

Agatha, daughter of Louis Lebeau by his first marriage, now the wife of Jos. Laporte of Boucherville, brought a suit against Mme. Robitaille (widow) to recover the house on rue Saint-François. This was about 1740, when probably both daughters of

Christine had died, but it did not become hers until after Mme. Robitaille's death.

"Margaret Otis" with Patience Hammond was "entertained" in Boston by Joanna Perry, who was paid therefor in the following January.[30]

Thomas Baker did not take his betrothed to the Piscataqua country, but to his own home in Brookfield, and there, was made a grant of land, "upland and meadow," to "Margarett Otice, alias Le Bue, one that was a prisoner in Canada and lately come from thence, provided she returns not to live in Canada, but tarries in this province and marries to Captain Thomas Baker." She tarried and married.

Again she was baptized, Parson Stoddard giving back to her the name of Margaret, and on June 5, 1716, was recorded at Northampton the birth of "Christian Baker, daughter to Thomas and Margaret." Other children were baptized in Brookfield.

Once her half-brother Philippe Robitaille came to visit her. Christine longed for her children. In March, 1721/2, Thomas and Christian addressed a Memorial to the General Court showing that "the said Christian from her natural affection to her Children in Captivity at Canada [taking their father's estate, they were not captives] and in hopes of Recovering them, Design to Undertake a Journey thither, That She is Encouraged to hope she may be Useful to perswade many others, in the Hands of the French & Indians to return to their Countrey, and Religion & praying a Suitable allowance for her Support in this affair."[31] The Council allowed her twenty pounds. The Governor sent a letter to Vaudreuil by Thomas, "Provided he will accompany his Wife to Canada as an express from this Government for a sum not exceeding twenty pounds."[32]

They, and Joseph Kellogg with them, went in April, and on

30 Coun. Rec., VI. Joanna, widow of Michael, continued his business of book-selling at the shop under the "west end of the Town House."

31 House Journal. 32 Council Records, 7, 350.

July 7 Baker was paid thirty pounds and Kellogg a larger sum for having carried the letter.[33] But Christine came back without her children, to whom she was, of course, a stranger.

Did this visit inspire the letter sent to her in 1729 signed "Seguenot of the Seminary at Ville-Marie: you know me very well"? D. Henchman at his Corner Shop in Corn hill printed it: "A Letter from a Romish Priest in Canada to One who was taken in Infancy etc. With an Answer thereto By a Person to whom it was Communicated." The "Person" was Governor Burnett.

The priest addresses Christina as his "Spiritual Daughter," she having "had the happiness of making one of the holy Family of Jesus, Maria, Joseph, Joachim and Anne, whereof I had the honour to be the Director, and that you, as well as Madame Robitail . . . were of the Number of about Two Hundred Women of the best fashion of Ville Marie . . . who then made up the mystical Body of that holy Association."[34] He begs her to abjure her Apostasy, and tells her if she and her husband will return she shall not want Bread. He offers her husband land, or work if he has a Trade; and he describes the Happy and Christian death of her married daughter in Quebec where she had lived with her husband "peaceably and to the edification of all the town."

Christine's husband sold their Brookfield possessions — for which he was not fully paid — and about three years later, in 1735, the family moved to Dover.

Christine, in June of that year, relates to the Court of Massachusetts that she "Suffer'd many hardships" in her twenty-five years of captivity and "that she took a Journey to Canada with her husband" to redeem her children, "and was there Instrumental In bringing back Divers Captives etc." The Court "sensible" of her good offices, gave her five hundred acres in York County. The same year she petitioned New Hampshire for leave to keep a

[33] House Journal.

[34] Père Chaumonot, Jesuit, established the *Confrérie de la Ste. Famille,* which spread throughout Canada.

"Public House for Entertainment of Travellers etc.," being reduced to very low circumstances by the chances of fortune, having a large family (six children) and her husband "past his Labour." She recites her past difficulties, but affirms that she hath this Comfort: "That she is alsoo returned into the Bossum of the Protestant church."

Apparently five hundred acres was not enough. In March, 1736/7, she asked for more, fearing that her several children may become burdensome. That petition was laid over to the next session.

Christine died Feb. 23, 1773, twenty years later than her husband, leaving a large posterity and having lived "in good reputation, being a pattern of industry, prudence and economy."[35] She was buried in Pine Hill Cemetery, Dover.

Rose Otis. Françoise Rozotty.

Françoise Rozotty of Canada was surely Rose Otis of New England, but who was Rose Otis? In Canada in 1702 "Rose Otis living in the region of Quebec" (and already married) was given thirty livres of the king's money. In 1710 she was naturalized. Here is her marriage record which shows that she had been baptized and named Françoise Rose.

"On the 29th October 1696, by us, undersigned Priest, Curé of Beauport after the required publication of banns and betrothal with all the ceremonies of the church, no impediment being shown, celebrated the marriage between Jean Poitevin, son of Jean and Magdeléné Guillaudeau of the parish of Charlebourg, of one part and Françoise Rozotty, English girl, living since her childhood in this parish, where she was brought from Boston, her native country, by the savages. Present at this marriage the said Jean Poitevin Father, Jacques Parent, Pierre Morel, Maurice Derry all living in the said Beauport except the said Derry of Charlebourg. They have all, with the bride and bridegroom, de-

[35] N. H. Gazette, Portsmouth, 5 March, 1773.

clared they could not sign this register inquiry having been made according to the law.

E. Boullard Priest."

M. Tanguay gives this list of her children:

Marie Madeleine, bap. 1679, at Charlesbourg.
Jean, 1699, m. at Quebec 1728, M. A. Bourget.
Françoise Josette, 1702, m. Louis Bourget.
Anne, 1704, m. 1730 François Jouet, d. 1737.
Charles, 1705.
Madeleine, 1708.
M. Madeleine, 1710.
Michel, 1712.
M. Thérèse, 1715, m. Didier Degré.
Pierre-François, 1717.

Rose died 7 July, 1729, and two years later Jean Poitevin, sometimes called Laviolette, took another wife. But who was Rose Otis? Probably a granddaughter of Richard of Dover. She has been called his daughter, but did he have two named Rose? One married John Pinkham in New England. She may have been fathered by Richard, his son, who was also a blacksmith, and who died intestate before 1701, but Susannah (Hussey, dau. of John of Hampton) his wife was too young (b. 1667) to have been her mother. Perhaps Rose was the child of an earlier marriage.

Susanna was made administrator of the estate of Richard, Sr., in 1704, "there being several children of the said Richard Otis the sonn [eldest] now liveing of whome the said Susanna Otis is appointed by me as their Guardian And the said Richard Otis the sonn dying possessed of the Estate (in lands)."[36] One of the five children was Rose.

Susanna married John Varney who, about to die, named the five Otis children in his will, giving to Nickles "land he had by his

36 State Papers, 31, 537. Probate.

wife" and to "herDafter Ros otis" he gave "five Pounds of Laful money . . . that her Grandfather Give to her mother."[37] This suggests for Rose a grandfather Hussey. Then did Richard (2d) have two named Rose, the first being Rozotty of Beauport?

JOHN OTIS—a puzzle.

"Jn° ottis (boy) Dover" is on the list of those remaining in 1695. Nowhere else in New England has the writer found his name.

In Canada, in 1702, Jean Baptiste Ottys, living at Cape Tourmente, was given thirty livres of the king's money; so the boy of Dover had before this been taken into the Catholic Church.

Married in 1703, he is called "son of the late Richard and the surviving Anna." This seems to indicate Susanna, widow of Richard (2d). John was not one of the five for whom she was made guardian.[38]

In 1710 "Jean baptiste otis of new england, living on the Coste de beaupré, Married to a french woman and having some children" is naturalized, as is "Jean otis" in 1713. Were there two? Or is it an error and are both "Jn° ottis (boy) Dover"?

From "*La Famille Otis*," written by M. Gérard Malchelosse, a descendant of Jean-Baptiste, we quote the following story.

The account-books of the Seminary of Quebec show that Jean-Baptiste was working for them in July, 1702, at the "Little Farm" in Saint-Joachim, that being the place where the pupils spent their vacations.

In November, 1703, he and Cécile Poulin signed their marriage contract (made according to the Custom of Paris) before Etienne Jacob, notary of Beaupré. Cécile, too, was employed at the Little Farm. She, born in 1676, was daughter of the late Jean and Louise (Paré), who was living in the parish of Saint-Joachim. And now, at the house of another Jean Poulin, in the presence of several relatives and friends, the future wife brings

[37] As above p. 489. [38] See Rose Otis.

one hundred livres given to her by the Gentlemen of the Seminary and also what is due from her father's estate. The future husband endows his bride with three hundred livres and the conditions common to contracts are written out in detail.[39]

Cécile died 27 April, 1731. Her only child, M. Josephte, b. in 1704, had three husbands and died before 1759.

Jean-Baptiste took a new wife 9 Feb., 1733. She, a widow, M. Françoise Gagné, became the mother of six children: Germain (1733), m. Françoise Fortin, one Jean-Baptiste, b. and d. in 1735, and a second b. the next year, lived to carry on the Canadian line; twins came and soon died, and Prisques (1739), who died when he was six. Tanguay says that Jean-Baptiste was so much esteemed that almost every one in the parish came to this child's funeral.

The Canadian genealogist gives more or less traditionary details of the life of his ancestor. He says he was son of Richard the blacksmith (both Richards were blacksmiths) and Anna Shuah. She, the second wife of Richard I, is not known to have had any children and certainly was not living in 1703. He calls him the brother of Rozotty and a guest at her wedding. Brother, perhaps; but his name is not among her witnesses — as shown by a certified copy. He says the captive was brought to Canada by way of the Chaudière, that he was hideously tortured, ("ears cut off and nails pulled out") and in that condition was given to an old squaw at the Côte de Beaupré. She was good to him, and later he was given to the Gentlemen of the Seminary where we find him in 1702. They gave him "land on the *Grande Ferme* at Saint-Joachim. Jasmin was often added to his name in their account-books and the place is still called '*le coteau Jasmin*.'" He was sometimes "*Otice dit Jasmin*," sometimes "*Jasmin l'Anglois*," as was his son. In 1732, the year after Cécile died, he went to Baie-Saint-Paul as overseer of the Gentlemen's farms and domains.

[39] See Joseph Fry, Kittery.

There he was given more land. The house in which he lived was kept by the family until 1900.

For forty-eight years he rendered "good and loyal service" to his employers; then in 1750 he gave up the position, was made church-warden and given an annual payment of thirty minots of grain, which the Gentlemen gave him faithfully until his death in 1760, "for they rightly had great confidence in his integrity" says his great grandson.

STEPHEN OTIS (Joseph-Marie).

Son of Stephen and Mary, daughter of William Pitman of Oyster River.

Stephen, Sr., was killed; Mary's fate is not known.

Stephen, renamed Joseph-Marie, was living in Quebec when in 1710 he conveyed property to his brother Paul. This is all that is definitely known of him.

M. Gérard Malchelosse, author of "*La Famille Otis*," is quite sure that he and his brother Paul were baptized at the Mission of Saint-François de Sales, and from certain notes given him by Mgr. David Gosselin[40] he is sure that Joseph-Marie lived at Lorette. He gives him Marie Weber for a wife, but she was married to his brother Paul. Tanguay married him to Louise Harel (time and place omitted). With her he witnessed Paul's third marriage in 1728.

M. Malchelosse hesitates to trace Stephen's line from 1712 to 1796, but thinks it probable that his descendants are still living in Lorette.

Tradition gives him several children, of whom two were sons, Jean-Jacques and Jean-Baptiste. The latter left male descendants who were Joseph (b. 1752) and Zacharie, whose wife was a chief's daughter, and who, himself, became one among the Hurons of Lorette.

40 Collected by the abbé Charles Beaumont concerning families of Charlesbourg, of which Lorette was once a part.

NATHANIEL OTIS (Paul).

Son of Stephen and Mary (Pitman).

When he received his baptismal name is not known, but in 1701 "Paul" was an "habitant." On April 11 the Gentlemen of the Seminary granted him land in the Coste St Laurent, the parish north of Montreal, joining that of the Sault-au-Recollet. In 1702 he was living in that parish and signed a contract as carpenter to build a shed, which contract was signed at the home of Pierre Robillard on François Xavier Street, near Notre-Dame church.

In 1706 he asked for citizenship, which was granted in 1710; he was said to be established in Montreal. He was in Quebec in 1710 when Stephen made the transfer of land, and when, on the 31 October, was signed the marriage contract between Paul Hotes and Elizabeth Wabert. "Paul, Englishman, son of Joseph [Did he not know his father's name?] living in the village of quequiker about ten leagues from Boston & of Marie pitteman, his wife, Major of 27 years, and Marie Elisabeth Wabert, minor of 19 years, daughter of Michel Wabert, inhabitant of Kepen [Cape Ann] about 10 or 12 leagues from Boston and of ébrard Calais his wife,[41] also for her and In her name were present Sieur Nicolas Pinaud, Citizen And Merchant of Quebec & of damoiselle Louise Donais, his wife, who having Brought her up for about 8 years, when they bought her from the Abenaki Indians, who had taken her prisoner. They, in the presence & with the consent of Messire C. de Ramezay" and other French persons, "of gabrielle pitteman, aunt of the future Bride, [This should be aunt of bridegroom. Gabrielle was Abigail (Pitman) Willis and Marie Wellis was her daughter, now married to a second husband.] of the sieur

[41] Michael Weber m. in 1686 at Falmouth, Deborah, dau. of Nathan Bedford of Scarboro. After Bedford's death his widow (Deborah's mother) m. Richard Calley which explains the name Calais or Calair given by her daughter, "Marie Elizabeth." The local historian says that Michael Weber's wife, with six children by her side, was barbarously killed at Purpooduck in 1703. Evidently one daughter, M. Elizabeth above, was spared and probably the Nathan (a family name) of the 1710/11 list, as of Casco, with a nameless Weber, were also of the Michael family. The people of Purpooduck were generally from Cape Ann.

pierre Perrot de Rézy and of Marie Wellis his wife cousin german of the future bridegroom," and of several others. A Louise Kimball was one.

On the 3^{d} of 9bre after two publications of the banns Paul Hotes son of Joseph of Kekiker, and Marie Elisabeth Waber daughter of Michael of Kepin and Ebrard Calair were married by J. P. Pacquet, curé of Quebec, in the presence of Nicolas Pinaud and others; several of whom signed. Paul said he could not, which is not to be understood for he had signed contracts and his signature varied little. Three days after the wedding Nicholas Pinaud, by an act of the notary Chambalon, gave the bride eight hundred livres.

In 1712, as a shoemaker, Paul receives a concession on the rue Saint-Denis (now St. Vincent Street). In this paper he is not called English, but the signature is his. The next year more land on a level with rue Saint-Paul is sold to him and to "M. Eliz. Waber." In 1724, when another purchase is made, he is styled cooper.

Paul received thirty livres of the king's money.

In Montreal are the following baptismal records of their children; the variations of spelling are interesting.

On Wednesday 20 Jan. 1712 was baptized by me the undersigned Priest, Paul Nicolas Otes, born the preceding day son of Paul Otes, Master Shoemaker, of this city, and of his wife, Marie Elizabeth Webber. The godfather was Monsieur Maitre Jaques Alexis de Fleury Deschambault, Ecuyer, Councilor of the King and his Lieutenant-General at the seat of the Provost of Monréal. The godmother, Catharine de Ramezay, daughter of Messire Claude de Ramezay, Knight of the order of Saint Louis and Governor of the island of Monréal and adjacent places, who have signed with me

paul hotesse — Deschambault

Meriel — Catherine de Ramezay."

Paul-Nicolas m. Marie-Madeleine Truteau and had several children.

And then came:

Aug. 11, 1713, Ignace Laurent, son of Paul hotesse, cooper of this town, and of Marie Elizabeth Webber. He was bur. 9 Oct., 1713.

Dec. 11, 1714, Marie Louise, dau. of Paul hautesse and of Marie Elizabeth Wabert; bur. Jan., 1715.

Apr. 14, 1716, Louis, son of Paul hotesse and of Marie Elizabeth Waber. He m. 20 Oct., 1749, M. Françoise Martineau.

Sept. 20, 1717, Marie-Catharine, dau. of Paul Otes and Marie Elizabet Ouader. She m. I, 8 Feb., 1740, Louis Pouget; II, 9 Jan., 1748, Laurent Bertrand.

Sept. 8, 1718, Joseph, son of Paul hotesse, Englishman, and Elizabet 8aber;[42] bur. 15 Nov., 1718.

Sept. 10, 1719, philippe Marie, son of paul hotesse and Elizabet Ouabert. Philippe Robitaille was godfather; bur. 9 Dec., 1719.

Poor Marie Elizabeth dies about 9 Sept., 1721, and very soon at Montreal, on "Oct. 20, 1721, after one publication of the Banns, Mr. de Belmont dispensing with the other two, finding no impediment, I, the undersigned priest, performing the duties of curate in this parish, having received the mutual consent of paul hotesse, son of Estienne hotesse and of Marie pitmenne of the parish of douvres, of new england; of one part and of Magdeleine toupin, aged twenty-seven years daughter of Jean Baptiste toupin and Marie Magdalen Mesevay of the parish of pointe aux trembles of Quebec, married them in presence of Philippe Robitaille, of Jean Baptiste dagueil[43] of Laurent Trudeau, of Nicolas Boudet. All have signed except philippe Robitaille who declared that he could not."

A child, Marie Magdeleine was born in August, 1722, and two months later the mother and baby died.

After six years Paul took a third wife. He signed the contract

[42] See Appendix for Indian symbol. [43] Husband of Priscilla Storer.

of 19 Sept., 1728, "Hotesse" (but between the lines was written "Authesse"), "widower of Madeleine Dussaud (Toupin dit Dussaud)." His bride was M. Anne Caron, widow of Jacques Paré and daughter of Vital and Marie Perthius of Lachine. Philippe Robitaille, Etienne Lecompte, the bride's father, and several members of her family were present.

On the marriage record Paul is about forty-six years old.

His sons, Paul and Louis; Grizel Warren's husband or son, Philippe Robitaille; and J. Bapt. d'aguille, Priscilla Storer's husband, witnessed the third, as they had the second marriage.

And in this record as in that of his first marriage Paul's parents are misnamed. Here they are "Joseph and Louis Harel," the priest, J. P. M. Du Lescoat, mistaking the brother's for the father's name.

There can be no doubt of the identity of the bridegroom for he is the widower of Madeleine Toupin.

Two children were born of this marriage, Marie Joseph, bap. 26 June, 1729, m. Gabriel Desfours, and Madeleine Amable, bap. 5 Oct., 1730, m. Michel Lefebre at Châteaugay in 1750 and lived at Ste.-Anne-Bout-de l'Isle.

On "Dec. 26, 1730, was buried in the cemetery beside the church[44] the body of Paul hotesse, master cooper of this town, Englishman, aged about forty-six years, died on Christmas eve, the 24th of this month. The witnesses were M. Doinet, priest, and simon bedeau, who have signed."

In the inventory of his estate, dated 31 Oct., 1735, Robitaille was made guardian of the children of his first marriage; and the next year Anne Caron, his widow, took her third husband.

The following letter was written by Paul to his sister Mary Varney:

"Montreal May 1st, 1725

My Most Dear Sister:

I would not let slip so fair an opportunity of writing to you as

[44] Notre-Dame, Montreal.

that of Mons'r leguille[45] without assuring you of my love and to lett you know the Joy that I have had in receiving of your news by one of those Gentlemen that is come here, who says he is one of yo, neighbours. [Mr. Theodore Atkinson reached Montreal in April of this year] I was in hopes of having ye pleasure to go to see you, butt my affairs will not admit of it, for you know my Dear Sister, those Journeyes are not made without great Cost; but the great distance that there is between us dont hinder me of having the same Tenderness for you, as if I was near your dear person. I am allways in hopes of having the consolation of seeing you before I Dye. What Joy will it be to see a Dear Sister I never saw . . . Permission is not easyly obtained to go such a Journey. I pray you, Dear Sister, if you do me the Honour of writing to me, to lett me know all the News that concerns me relating to all our relations; my Dear Sister I've a favor to ask of you which is ye gift of a Seal, that at least every time I write to you, you may know by the seal that it is yo'r dear Brother that writes to you My Grandmother [Grizel Warren Otis Robitaille] Salutes you as also my little children who . . . their dear uncle and their dear aunt . . .

Signed Paul Oatis."

The editor says that Paul's handwriting has improved since he signed the lease in 1714 or else the letter was written by another. It is the only instance found of Oatis as a Canadian spelling.[46]

When Ebenezer and Mary took possession of "The hill" or Otis estate they, to strengthen the title, secured quitclaim deeds from Stephen and Nathaniel of their portions of their father's estate.

"Stephen Otis of Kebeck in Canada" conveys on Oct. 1, 1710, to "Nathaniel (sirnamed Paul) Otis of Mount Royall," his right and title in N. E. "to houses, lands and other goods whatsoever," he owning "as a good perfict and absolute estate of inheritance in fee simple," and signs "Joseph-Marie Autes." Four years later

45 Priscilla Storer's husband, Paul's friend. He came to New England with the three commissioners, Mary Storer and Esther Sayward.

46 Gen. Reg., V, 186.

"Nathaniel (sirnamed Paul)" Otis releases to Ebenezer Varney this land with "all sorts of buildings," which release is signed Paul Hotesse and Marie Elizabeth Hottesse.[47]

1696. RICKER. Riccor—Ricor—Ricard. JUDITH (probably not a Canadian captivity).
NOAH.
JOHN—?
TUCKER, JOHN.
OTIS, NICHOLAS, JR.'S, WIFE.

Pike wrote: July 26, 96, "Being sacrament day. An Ambush of Indians layd between Capt. Ger: field, & Tobias Hansons Orchard, shot upon the poor peo: returning from Meeting;" killed and wounded several persons and "took John Tucker Nic: Otices w: & Judith Riccor."

Belknap says "they were taken to Penobscot and soon found their way home." Miss Baker, without giving her authority, says that Judith was taken to Canada. She was at home on April 14, 1699, when she was married to Thomas Horne. She was dau. of George and Eleanor (Evans), b. Feb. 1, 1680/1.

1706. *Noah,* the "little son."

Again quoting Pike's Journal: "Jun 4, 1706 George Riccor & Maturin Riccor of Cocheco were slain by the Indians. G. was killed Running up the lane near the Garrison.[48] Mat was killed in his field & his little son was carried away."

They lived in that part of Dover that was Somersworth and is now Rollingsford.

Do we not find Noah, the "little son" in Quebec the next year? Family authorities name the child Noah, the Church now names him Jean François Ricard, giving back the original family name; Ricker being a corruption of Ricard of Jersey, whence they are said to have come to New England.

47 Gen. Reg., V, 185. 48 Heard's.

"On 11 June 1707 was baptized by me, priest of the Seminary of Quebec, Jean François Ricard, aged fourteen, native of New England, of a place near Dover named Quihecga.[49] He having asked now for the sacrament of baptism, which he had not before received as was learned by inquiry.

His godfather was Louis Deschamps *Equier officier dans les troupes de la marine.* godmother Geneviève Macar, wife of Monsieur Dologny *de L'ordre militaire de St. Louis, Colonel des troupes dans ce pays*, who have signed

G. Macart dologny

L. Deschamps.

Pocquet priest."

It has been said that he became a priest, but his name is not found among the parish priests of Canada. "Jean Ricard, living at the Seminary of Quebec" was naturalized in 1710. On the Roll of 1710/11 is the name of "John Ricor Cochick." Is not this another Ricker? Plainly a John of Dover, for Jean-François of New France, once Noah of New England, would not be masquerading under a new baptismal name in a Puritanical home-list. The only John found who might fit is a brother of Judith, son of George and Eleanor, who at this time was twenty-eight years old and is not known to have been a captive.

1705, *November* 4.
TIBBETS, NATHANIEL.

Son of Jeremy of Dover Neck and Mary Canney.

The Tibbets permanent home was on the upper end of Dover Neck. Penhallow says Nathaniel was taken alone at Dover. Pike wrote: "Nov. 4, 1705, Sab. Nath. Tibbets of Oyster River was carried away by the Indians abo^t^ sun-set." Belknap's date is 2 August, 1706. He was still a prisoner in 1710/11. Before 1717 he was still absent, and probably known to be dead, for his wife Elizabeth had married Francis Pittman.

Was Mary Tibs, redeemed by Cary and said to be of York, a Tibbets?

[49] Cochecho.

CHAPTER VII

The Assault on Pemaquid

5 August, 1689

HE first English settlement in Maine was made by the unhappy Popham colonists who came in 1607 in *The Mary and John* and *The Gift of God*. The next year, when they went home, they had a new ship, the pinnace *Virginia* (of about thirty tons), the first built in the ship-building State of Maine! And as they sailed eastward they might have spoken the little squadron which was bringing westward the French colonists who were to found Quebec and later to dispute with the English the sovereignty of the land.

Pemaquid,[1] on the borderland, was always a point of dispute. There was here a small village, and near the mouth of the river on its eastern bank was Fort Charles, built by Andros in 1677. News of war between France and England reached Canada in July, 1689, after the Dover disaster. Could it have reached Père Thury at his Mission on the Penobscot before he set forth to attack Pemaquid? With his own people were some from Sillery, says Champigny,[2] in all about one hundred Indians, and perhaps a few Frenchmen.

Père Thury wrote[3] that most of his warriors confessed before leaving their village and promised to fight in the open if occasion

[1] Several derivations of the name have been given. Mr. W. B. Cabot, the most careful student of Indian place-names, is pretty sure that it means "high ground lying across one's natural line of travel." Another, giving pemi, oil; and quidden, a ship, explains a local industry, for in 1605 Captain Weymouth found here some Indian whalemen at work, and here in 1614 Capt. John Smith "fished for whale."

[2] Que. Docs., I, 468. [3] Que. Docs., I, 478.

offered. Their women and children also confessed, that they might "raise purer hands to heaven while their husbands and fathers were combating the heretics," and they recited, too, a perpetual rosary in their Penobscot chapel, relieving each other from dawn to nightfall.

The Indians, "having come very near the village, prayed together, after which they tucked up their shirts and threw themselves upon the houses in their fashion, breaking down the doors, taking and killing all whom they found." The next day Lieutenant Weems, the commander, surrendered the fort; "basely yielded it up to the Indians and French" wrote Mr. Pike.[4]

The savages swore that no harm should follow — and to Weems none did. "Fear nothing" said they, "we pray, we will keep our promise."

Thury says that they did not insult a woman nor drink any of the rum found in the fort, which he considered their greatest triumph, nor did they torture any, "but killed immediately those whom they wished to kill," even though they had promised to spare! As they began with prayer, so did they now thank God for their victory, and so elated were they, that one of the chiefs told the priest that "If we had 200 Frenchmen with us, somewhat acquainted with the country, we would go as far as Baston."

Weems and his fourteen soldiers were sent to Boston.

About fifty[5] men, women and children were carried to the Penobscot village, and some of them afterwards to Canada.

Captives

Gyles, Family of Thomas
- His wife and
- James
- John
- Mary
- Margaret

[4] Both French and English accounts say that he surrendered under promise of life and of liberty to himself and followers.

[5] Niles says thirty or forty.

Hegeman, (Higiman)
Dennis
Grace (Darling)
Joseph?
Jane
Sanders, Elizabeth
Stephens, Katharine
John, boy
Samuel
Stilson, Family of James
Mrs. Margaret (Gould)
Margaret
James
Mary

GYLES, THE FAMILY OF THOMAS.
HIS WIFE and
JAMES, b. abt. 1675; JOHN, abt. 1678;
MARY, abt. 1682; MARGARET, abt. 1685.

In the early morning the savages seized a man who was going from the fort to New Harbor, about two miles eastward. To save his own neck he told them that Weems had few men in the fort; that Thomas Gyles, whom the chronicler called "the principal inhabitant," had gone with fourteen men to one of his farms some three miles up the river, and the other men were "scattered abroad about their occasions." Consequently the Indians separated into two parties.

The "Memoirs" of John Gyles, written for his family "at the request of his second consort," were published in 1736. From them we learn that his father, Thomas, was living at Merrymeeting Bay in 1674 when he left to seek his English inheritance; his father having died.

While he was in England the Eastern Indians drove the settlers from that region, and when he came back he took up land at

Pemaquid. Being a magistrate, and a strict Sabbatarian he had many difficulties with the lawless people. On the day of the attack he took three sons up the river. The eldest, Thomas, Jr., alone escaped; he had gone "with some of their people to a field of English hay." The younger boys were with their father, when suddenly thirty or forty Indians sprang upon them. Distant firing had been heard before.

Mr. Gyles was shot; the boys unhurt, ran but were soon brought back to their dying father who asked to be allowed to pray with his children. John wrote: "He parted with a cheerful voice, but looked very pale by reason of his great loss of blood." After they parted the Indians led the father aside and killed him.

Old Moxus blamed the "strange Indians" for the shooting and expressed sorrow.

The boys later saw their mother and little sisters who had been taken from the fort, but soon they were all scattered. The mother and girls were redeemed and lived in Boston, Mrs. Gyles dying not long after her return.

Mary married Andrew Ham in 1710 and nine years later John Brewer.

Margaret became the wife of Jonas Weber, a sawyer, of Boston in 1717.

James escaped, was recaptured, tortured and burnt at Penobscot Fort in 1692.

John was sooner or later taken by his master, a Maliseet, to Meductic — now Lower Woodstock — in New Brunswick, where he lived through six cruel years. Then there was trouble; he was claimed by his first master and by the widowed squaw of his second, and his death was offered as a solution, but "honest Father Simon"[6] advised selling him to the French.

Gyles' account of his three years with "Monsieur and Madame" is picturesque. They called him "*le petit anglais.*"

Monsieur was in France in 1696 when Colonel Hawthorne

[6] Père Simon, a Recollet, "is a very honorable man, who does not mix himself up with anything outside his religious duties," Que. Docs., II, 187.

came up the St. John River to attack Fort Naxouat. Madame knowing that John could "serve or disserve" her promised him his freedom if he would be loyal to her interests, and he answered — as he wrote in 1736 — "Madame, it is contrary to the nature of the English to requite evil for good."

The lady had nailed on the door of the house a request that the English officer spare their property, adding that they had shown kindness to the English captives as they were "capacitated," having bought and freed two and promising that the one now held should go whenever opportunity and his own desire offered. Then she, with John and the rest of her people, left the place and went up a branch of the river for safety.

The honorable "general" spared house, barn, cattle and poultry, "except one or two" which he took for his own use, and consequently John was treated with civility and gratitude.

They let him go home when peace came, but Monsieur gave him nothing, only offering to pay his passage-money, which the master of the sloop refused. When he arrived in Boston, June 19, 1698, a youth came on board who asked him many questions, and finally told him that he was his little brother who escaped into the fort when Pemaquid was attacked. "He told me," says John, "that my elder brother . . . and our two little sisters were alive, but our mother had been dead some years. Then we went on shore and saw our elder brother."

John immediately applied for government service and was of very great use as an interpreter. When not in service he tried to get some "schooling."

In 1703, at Salisbury, he married Ruth True. In 1722, at Roxbury, Hannah Heath became his wife; and at Roxbury he died in 1755. Gyles was generally acceptable to the Indians. At the end of a long conference at Falmouth in the summer of 1726 they said to Lieutenant-Governor Dummer:

"We Observe that Capt. Gyles is Weakly and Sickly and if he should be Removed by Death We Desire that somebody else might be sent down to St. Georges to take care of the Trade . . . We think Capt. Gyles behaves very well in the Place this we mention sideways as it were."[7]

A little later these Indians complain that their young men are allowed too much rum and that "sour meal and damnified tobacco" was sold at the trading-house, but for this Gyles was not held responsible. In the appendix of his "Narrative" printed in Drake's "Tragedies of the Wilderness" is a list of his many appointments.

HIGIMAN (Hegeman).

DENNIS.
GRACE (Darling) his wife.
JOSEPH, perhaps.[8]
JANE?

Dennis Hegeman was of Pemaquid in 1687.

Grace, his wife, was probably daughter of John Darling of Pemaquid or Monhegan.

She, testifying in Boston on May 31, 1695,[9] Bomazeen being present, recites her tale of woe.

She said there were two or three hundred attacking Indians, but no Frenchmen. Her master was "one Eskeon, a Canadian Indian." Taken to the Penobscots she was "very hardly treated by them, both in respect of Provisions & Cloathing, having nothing but a torn blanket to cover me during the winter Season and oftentimes cruelly beaten," and continuing: "After I had been with the Indians three years, they carried me to Quebeck and sold me for Forty Crowns unto the French there, who treated me well, gave me my liberty and I had the King's allowance of Provisions and also a Room provided for me and liberty to work for my selfe. I continued there two years and a halfe," during which time a child was born.

[7] Arch. 29, 246.

[8] Col. Charles E. Banks thinks that a Joseph may have been captured and that he died before the other Joseph was baptized in Canada.

[9] Arch. 8, 36.

With three Frenchmen she was taken to St. Johns where she stayed three weeks; thence to Port Royal where she spent the winter, and in May, 1695, she was brought to Boston by Abraham Boudroit of Port Royal "who" wrote M. de Villebon, "goes to and from Boston by Count de Frontenac's and my advice."[10] She says that several Eastern Indians, among whom were Bomazeen, his son Moxis, and the son of Madokawando, brought in prisoners and scalps, receiving, as the French told her, for each scalp twenty French crowns from the Intendant, and for the prisoners as much as they could agree for with the purchasers. When she left Quebec, Sept. 4, 1694, Bomazeen, who had brought in ten scalps and two prisoners, was there.

Let us hope that Mrs. Grace had the solace of her husband's companionship during her whole captivity, but the following record and signature alone show that he was taken.

Joseph.

"The 5th March 1693 was baptized by me François Dupré curé de Québec, Joseph born yesterday, son of denys egman Englishman and gres dalain, his wife, the godfather was le sieur François pachiot, the godmother Louise douaire wife of the sieur Pino who have signed.

Denys Hegman.

Louise Douaire
pachoss
François Dupré."

Jane.

Was she their child? Jane Higgaman was "yett in the Indians Hands in 1698/9."

Sanders, Elizabeth.

She, of Pemaquid, was "in the Indians Hands in 1698/9." We find William Sanders in Pemaquid in 1672 and a John in 1687.

Stephens, Katharine.

Is the "Marie Françoise" of the following record in the Quebec

[10] N. Y. Docs., IX, 574.

register with "*angloise*" written in the margin "Kath^{n} Stephens gerll, pemquid" or is it the record of a lost captive?

"August 1st, 1697 after the publication of the three banns of marriage made the first on the 25th, second the 26th and third the 28th of July of the above year between Jacques pacquet son of maurice pacquet and of françoise forgette, his father and mother of this parish and bishopric of one part and of marie françoise, daughter of nestyus and of marie meray, also her father and mother of this parish and bishopric of the other part, and having found no impediment I, francois Dupré curé of Quebec have married them and given the nuptial blessing according to the form prescribed by our holy mother church in presence of meurice pacquet, father of the bridegroom and rené pacquet uncle and francois and louis pacquet also brothers, and Jean paradis brother-in-law and J. du breuil who has signed, the others named above have declared they did not know how to sign, as well as the bridegroom and bride."

From the marriage contract we learn that the strange names of her parents, so-called, are those of her Indian captors — her parents by adoption. The contract signed July 28 says that Jacques was a minor about twenty-two or twenty-three years old.

Nicolas Pinault, merchant-citizen, acted for Marie francoise Nestinues, native of New England of the place called abscadois (a line was drawn through sc), a minor, about nineteen years, having said that she does not remember the baptismal names of her late father and mother, nor even the surname of her mother who died in her infancy, and having been taken prisoner about ten years ago by the Indians our allies, from whom she was bought, and is now in the service of the said pierre pinault.

Tanguay says she had fourteen children, but names only four, all of whom married.

In Quebec are the following:

Pierre, b. 1698, m. Angélique Bourg, d. 1766.

Maurice, b. 1699, m. Thérèse Drapeau. In this record the mother is called Marie Stiv, in the margin is Nestyus.

François, b. 1710, m. Géneviève ——, d. 1784.
Jean-Baptiste, b. 1712, m. 1, M. M. Buisson; 2, M. F. Bélanger.

In this the mother is Marie estivs, which is the nearest found like Tanguay's "Marie Françoise Stevens surnamed Nestyus."

But as "Marie Stevens English woman" married to Pasquet, living near Quebec and having several children, she was naturalized in 1710. On June 6, 1741, Marie Françoise Nestius, wife of Jacques Paquet, was buried in Quebec, aged about sixty-four. Her husband died in 1764.

The marriage contract gives Katharine — if she it is — an approximate birth date of 1678 and a captivity beginning in 1687, an approximate date for the Pemaquid disaster. With her on the list of those remaining in 1695 is "Jn° Stephens boy;" and on Dudley's list of 1710 is "Samuel Stevens Pemaq^{d}." These three were probably children of Thomas who was in Pemaquid in 1685 and who later lived in Scituate and Boston.

1686, 1687 or 1688.

(Probable dates given by Mr. John Hassam and confirmed by Margaret (Stilson) Hilton).

Stilson, The Family of James.

He was killed. His wife and their children — perhaps four — were taken. Mrs. Stilson was Margaret, daughter of Alexander (or Sanders) Gould and Margaret (Brown).

In May, 1686, James, John, Margarett and Mary, children of Margarett Stilson, were baptized at Marblehead. Probably all were captured with their mother.

"Mrs. Marg^{tt} Stilson Pemequid" was redeemed in 1695.

"Mary Stilson gerll pemquid" and "Jam^{s} Stil^{t}son boy Pemquid" remained.

The local historian[11] says that three children made the family, James, Jr., Margaret, and one unnamed; that the boy and girl were "detained 6 years longer than their mother, and by what

11 Bristol and Bremen.

means they obtained their freedom is not known." He assumes that the name Mary, quoted above, should be Margaret, but we know that Mary was taken and always "remained" and that Margaret came back.

Mrs. Stilson was, with Hannah Swarton, a servant in the house of the intendant, and the two women had "many sweet, refreshing seasons of religious conversation and prayer," and together withstood all the efforts made for their conversion.[12] After redemption the widow Stilson married on March 30, 1696, at Marblehead, Thomas Pitman. She had a long life, dying in 1750 in her ninety-third year.

It is said that the first deed of conveyance of American soil was made in 1625 by Sagamores Samoset and Unnungoit to Margaret's grandfather, John Brown, who paid fifty beavers for an enormous tract in the Muscongus River region. Brown in 1660 gave to Alexander and Margaret Gould, Margaret Stilson's parents, an area eight miles square, and in what is now the town of Bristol at the head of New Harbor the Gould and Stilson families lived, and from here they were taken.

Margaret, b. abt. 1679.

The historian of "Bristol and Bremen"[13] prints the story of the capture as told by Margaret and repeated by her granddaughter, Hannah Teuxbury.

She says the Indians fired upon them when they were in a canoe on the Muscongus waters and killed her father. "Then they took a nursing baby [John?] from her mother's breast and burnt it on the fire, and carried s^{d} Margaret and her mother [apparently forgetting to mention James and Mary] into captivity, and sold them to the French in Canada, where she was detained 12 years, and then being released, she returned home."

This fixes 1687 as the date of capture because on June 2, 1699, she married Lt. William Hilton in Marblehead, and they seem to

12 Mrs. Swarton's "Narrative."

13 Page 244.

have gone back to the old Stilson home where they lived until driven off by Indians.

In 1717, perhaps to strengthen the family claim, Margaret Pitman of Marblehead, late widow of James Stilson, deeded the land to her son James Stilson, now of Piscataqua, and to Margaret and William Hilton, coaster of Manchester. Margaret "being returned from her captivity and servitude of twelve years in Canada," having married, and then she and her husband "as heirs to the gift of Brown, entered into possession of the whole eight mile tract, claiming half through the rights of her mother."

Hilton is also called coaster and fisherman of Marblehead, York and Muscongus. They had a large family. Four years after he died—about 1723—Margaret married John Allen of Manchester, where she died in 1763, aged eighty-four years.

Mary.

Perhaps she lived with her mother in the home of Mme. de Champigny for: "On Oct. 28, 1695 was baptized by me françois Dupré, priest, of Quebec marie magdelaine of New England daughter of Jacques and of Marguerite, the godfather was Jacque Charles bochard de champigny, ensign, and the godmother, dame marie magdelaine de chaspoux, wife of Monsieur Bochard de champigny intendant in all the country of new france — who have signed." It is interesting to note that Mary was baptized immediately after her mother's departure, and that Mme. de Champigny, who could not convert the mother, was godmother of the daughter.[14] On Oct. 31, 1702, Mary Stilson married Jean Baptiste Cardinet, called Chevalier, surgeon—it may be that he was surgeon-barber for elsewhere he is styled wig-maker—son of François and his wife, Anne Françoise Sabatier of St. André de Clery, diocese of Orléans, by François Dupré, priest of Quebec. Her brother James was one of the witnesses.

In Quebec are recorded the baptisms of sixteen children:

Jean-Baptiste, 1704, m. 1743, Marie Anne Gautron; d. 1786.

[14] Mrs. Stilson was redeemed in October.

Marie Magdeleine, 1706, d. 1760.
Marie, 1708, d. 1709.
Charles Guillaume, 1709, d. 1711.
M. Françoise, 1710, m. Jacques-François De Bouchel.
Geneviève, 1712.
M. Thérèse, b. & d. 1713.
Pierre, 1715.
M. Anne, 1716.
Jean François, 1717, d. 1733.
M. Anne Louise, 1718.
M. Claire, 1719, d. 1724.
Marguerite, 1720, d. 1749.
Jean Jacques Philippe, 1722, d. 1733.
M. Anne, 1724.
Renée Thérèse, 1727, d. 1729.

Cardinet died in 1737.

"Magd^ne Stilson Englishwoman married to one named Chevalier, wigmaker, established at Quebecq and having children," was naturalized in 1710. Magdeleine Flisson (Stilson?) received seventy livres in the king's distribution.

James Stilson, b. 1681 at Marblehead.

"On Oct. 4, 1705, after the publication of the three banns, no lawful impediment having been found, I, the undersigned Priest, by permission of Messire François Vachon de Belmont, *Grand Vicaire de Monseigneur l'Evêque de Québec*, after having obtained the mutual consent in words of those present, of Jaques Stilson, dit le Tilly, aged twenty-five or twenty-six years, son of the late Jaques Stilson, inhabitant of Marblehead, in New England and of his wife Marguerite —— of the one part, and of Anne Marguerite Odiorne, aged thirty years, daughter of Jean Odiorn and of Marie Johnson, Inhabitants of Newcastle, in the same New England, of the other part, have married them according to the rites of our Holy Mother Church in presence of Robert de (illegible) *Ecuyer* Sieur du Buisson, Keeper of the King's Store houses; of Sieur Tibierge, armorer of the King; of Jean Thomas, master ship carpenter; of Mr Michel le Pailleur Royal Notary and of Damoiselle Marguerite Bouat, wife of Sr Antoine Pascaud, Merchant; and of several others, friends of the bridal pair who have signed with me." (See Anne Odiorne Batson) "Mrs. Badston now Stilson" is mentioned in "The Redeemed Captive"[15] as being present at the death-bed of her cousin, Abigail Turbet, and of Esther Jones in the winter of 1705/6.

We have the baptism of only one child in Canada, Tues. 3 Aug., 1706, Marie-Anne Stilson, born yesterday, dau. of Jâques Stilson called du Tilly Englishman and of Anne Odiorne his wife also English. The godfather, Antoine Barrois, was clerk to M. Leber. The godmother, Marie Anne Lemaitre de la Moille. In New England she became Hannah and married 1, Thomas Mead; 2, Samuel Clark. After their redemption James and his wife Anne must have gone to the Odiorne home in New Castle for he was living there in 1738. The local historian says "little is known of him."

Three more children were born to them.

In a deed of 1710/11 he is called a fisherman of Portsmouth. He, with Hannah his wife, Margaret and William Hilton gave to their "loving father-in-law," yeoman of Marblehead, and their mother some of the land on the "Misconcus River."

[15] Edi. of 1853, pp. 61-62-82.

CHAPTER VIII

Salmon Falls, Casco Bay, Sandy Beach (Rye) and River St. John

PARKMAN says that Louis XIV "had done his best for Canada, and had got nothing for his pains but news of mishaps and troubles." In 1689 Callières, governor of Montreal and acting-governor of the colony, went to beg further help from His Majesty, and laid before him an alluring plan for the destruction of the nearest settlements of New England and the town of New York, whereby "the Iroquois, deprived of English arms, would be at the mercy of the French." But when he came back, accompanied by Frontenac, who in spite of his seventy years was again appointed governor, they learned that the *French* had been at the mercy of the Iroquois and knew that their great plan could not succeed. Still it was necessary to revive the spirits of the soldiers and people, to which end three war-parties were formed respectively at Montreal, Three Rivers and Quebec to strike at border settlements of New York, New Hampshire and Maine. The first to be ready went from Montreal to Corlaer (Schenectady). The Indians—less than half the command—were from the missions of *Sault Saint-Louis* and the Mountain.

Previously Frontenac, to encourage them and to prevent their becoming friendly with the English, had promised to pay ten crowns for every scalp brought in; now he changed the reward because there were all the time war-parties in the field and often scalps were produced about which nothing could be learned; consequently scalps were reduced in price, and for every prisoner brought from near Boston or Orange twenty crowns was promised and for others ten crowns.[1]

Corlaer was burned and they brought back prisoners and horses laden with spoils; "But ye Snow was so Extream Deep y^t^ it was impossible for any woman to march a mile. So y^t^ they took none but men[2] and boys that could march." So wrote Peter Schuyler on Feb. 15, 1689/90. After describing the brutalities committed, he adds, "But what Shall we Say, we must Lay our hands upon our mouth and be Silent. It is Gods will and Pleasure and we must Submit; it is but what our Sinns and Transgressions have Deserv'd."[3] John Pynchon, writing to the Council from Springfield in July, 1689, about the Dover massacre, the dangers at Northfield and the using of Maquas against the enemy, was less submissive. He believed that man's power availed but little, but said: "Let us take ye more heart to follow God wth o^r^ Prayers Night & day & never to give him rest til he hath made o^r^ jerusalem a Quiet habitation."[4] It had been voted three days before Pynchon wrote the above to engage the Mohawks (Maquas) to destroy the eastern hostile Indians, promising "for their Incouragement" eight pounds for every fighting man's head or scalp.[5]

Second War Party
Salmon Falls

Tuesday, March 18, 1689/90.

The second party left Three Rivers January 28 led by François Hertel, known in Canadian annals as "*Le Héros*." With him were his three eldest sons, twenty-five Frenchmen and as many Indians; "half one and half t'other" says Mather, "half Indianized French, and half Frenchified Indians." The Indian leader was Hopehood, who had once been a servant to some man in Boston.[6] After two months of hardship they reached the little village by the Piscataqua River on the night of March 27.

[1] Que. Docs., I, 579.
[2] One of whom was John Lahey, who married Mary Swarton of Casco.
[3] Arch. 35, 239. [4] Arch. 108, 178. [5] Arch. 107, 161.
[6] "Hist. of the Indian and French Wars," Niles.

A French prisoner examined at Portsmouth the next day stated "y^{t} their Designe was not against this place when they came forth, but principly against monsieur Tyng[7] & the place where he lived, but, he saith, the Indians who were their principle pilots did often vary in their opinions about w^{t} place to fall upon."[8]

Was this the French prisoner "who was so tenderly treated that he embraced & professed the Protestant religion" as says Cotton Mather? Even allowing for that gentleman's prejudice and accepting Abiel Holmes's criticism that he "believed more and discriminated less than becomes a writer of history," yet is it pleasant to read of a convert to Protestantism for the Canadian records teem with converts to Catholicism.

Lying hidden in the forest the enemy waited, then "Made their onset between break of day & Sunrise when most were a bed & no watch kept neither in fort nor house."[9] Houses were burned, inhabitants murdered and fifty-four captives taken, mostly women and children, few of whom we find.

Sewall, writing for the Council to the Governor of Connecticut on March 24, says: "On Tuesday . . . about 60, ½ French, ½ Indians fell upon Salmon Falls ab^{t} Break of day k. w'd & carried away seventy nine persons. We know not of above 2 Fr kill'd & 2 Indians & one French taken who says are in pay from ye French King & several other parties out. Name of ye Capt Monsr Artel Surpris'd our People, finding y^{m} without any watch, burnt many Houses."[10] Lawrence Hammond in his "Journal"[11] says: "Not one Indian was known to have been killed."

An exaggerated French account states that two thousand horned beasts perished in the stables!

Two Indian scouts brought news of the coming of the English from Piscataqua and Hertel hurried his retreat. He was overtaken at Wooster River where in the skirmish his son, Hertel de

[7] Capt. Edward Tyng lived at Casco, his brother Jonathan at Dunstable.

[8] Arch. 35, 325. [9] Letter from Portsmouth. Arch. 35, 326.

[10] Arch. 35, 362. [11] "Mass. Hist. Pro.," 14, 126.

la Frésnière, was wounded and Louis Crevier, his nephew, was killed. Sending part of his force with the prisoners to Quebec, and learning at an Indian village where he left his wounded son that le Sieur de Portneuf had not yet struck his blow, and was distant but two days' journey, he, with the rest of his men, joined the Quebec force near Casco Bay.

It was in this year, because of his forty years' service, that François Hertel applied for Letters of Nobility, but when Frontenac later asked that the fees be omitted because of the Hero's poor financial condition, Colbert, answering for the King in 1698, said if he were too poor to pay for the seals he was too poor to support the position and so denied him.

Captives

Barnard, Benjamin's wife
Goodwin, Thomas
    Mehitable (Plaisted)
Grant, Martha (Mills | Smith)
Smith, John
Hurtado (or Fortado), Elizabeth
Key, John
    John, Jr.
    James
    Abigail
Oicbac, Jean Baptiste—(?)
Read, John
    Mrs.
Rogers, Robert
Short, "Six or seven children of the family" of Clement
Tozier, Richard, Jr.
    Elizabeth (Wentworth | Sharp)

BARNARD, SARAH (Wentworth).

"Benjamin Barnard's wife of Salmon Falls" was rescued by

Captain Church at Fort Androscoggin in September, 1690.[12] Benjamin died at Watertown in 1694. He was of York Co. in 1685 and 1689 and owned land bordered by that of Richard Tozier. In 1705 Paul Wentworth, uncle of the two Barnard children, was made their guardian. This seems to show that Mrs. Sarah was daughter of Elder William and sister of Elizabeth (Wentworth) Tozier. In 1698/9 she married Samuel Winch of Framingham.[13]

GOODWIN, THOMAS.

Son of Daniel and Margaret (Spencer).

MEHITABLE, his wife, dau. of Lieut. Roger Plaisted and Olive (Coleman).

They were married in 1685, ten years after her father, commander of the little garrison, was killed. That was when Richard Tozier's house was attacked the second time, and when he was murdered. Lieutenant Plaisted with twenty soldiers went out to bring in the body of his friend and the ambushed Indians waiting for that "last Office of Love" fired upon them, killing the lieutenant and one son and mortally wounding another.

Thomas and Mehitable were separated after capture and each believed the other dead; indeed a local tradition says that "Hetty" took to herself a new husband in Canada and left him when she learned that Thomas was living. This seems doubtful, as no record of the marriage has been found. Mehitable's story has been printed in the Magnalia and elsewhere.

She had a cruel master who was disturbed by the wailing of her young baby. To quiet the child she would sit for hours in the snow far from the fire, but the Indian, impatient of her slow progress, snatched it from her arms and killed it.

Three years later, at Montreal, on "Monday, 11 May, 1693, there was solemnly baptized an English woman, called in her own country, Mehetabel and by the French, who captured her in war 18 March 1690, Esther, who, born at Barwic, in New England 30 April (old style or 19 May new style) 1670, of the marriage

[12] See Church's Wars. [13] "Wentworth Genealogy," I, 109-111.

of Roger Pleisted, Protestant, and of Olive Colman, of the same religion, and married to Thomas Gouden, also Protestant, living since nearly three years in the service of Mademoiselle de Nauguiere.[14] She was named Marie Esther, her godfather was Messire Hector de Calieres, Chevalier, Governor for the King in the Island of Monreal and adjacent places. The godmother Damoiselle Marguerite Renée Denis, widow of Monsieur La Nauguiere de la Perade, in his life Captain of the Guard of Monseigneur the Count of Frontenac, Governor general of New France. The baptism performed [an erasure] as well as the preceding by Messire Francois Dolie de Casson *Grand vicaire de Monseigneur L'Illustrissime et Reverendissime* Bishop of Quebec.

Chevalier de Callière
Marguerite renée denis
Fran. Dollier priest
E. Guyotte curé."

"Hitobl Goodin Kittrey" was redeemed by Cary in 1695.

Several children were born after her redemption. She was alive in 1740.

Her quaint, little handmade gravestone is in the old Fields burying ground in Berwick. Her descendants of the seventh generation live where she herself lived.

GRANT, MARTHA (Mills | Smith).

B. 18 June, 1653, dau. of Thomas Mills and Mary Wadleigh (who was the daughter of John of Saco and Wells). Martha was the widow of Christopher Grant; her first husband having been James Smith.

At Montreal "On Monday, 29 June 1693 was solemnly baptized *sous condition* an English woman named in her country, Marthe, whose name was kept in baptism, born in Sacio in New England 8 Jan. (old style or 18 new style) 1653 of the marriage of Thomas Mills, native of Excester in Old England and of Marie

[14] Written also de la Naudière.

Wadele native of Brestol near London and married to the late Jaques Smith, inhabitant of Barwic in New England, having been captured there the (illegible) March 1690 by Mr. Artel living for three years in the service of Monsieur Crevier at St. François. Her godfather was Monsieur Pierre Boucher *Ecuyer* Sieur de Boucherville *officier dans le detachment de la Marine.* Her godmother Dame Marie Boucher, widow of Monsieur de Varennes, Governor for the King at Three Rivers.

Martha mills
Boucherville Marie boucher
E. Guyotte curé"

Jean Crevier, in whose service Martha Mills Grant lived, was seigneur of Saint-François and father of the lieutenant who had been killed at Salmon Falls. In 1693 the seigneur was himself captured when harvesting his grain near the fort and was carried to New York by the Iroquois, who tortured him frightfully. Major Schuyler paid "£50 for his redemption from ye flames." He must have died in Albany soon after.[15] Martha Mills's first husband, James Smith, died in 1687. Her second, Christopher Grant, was either killed in the attack or died in captivity as administration of his estate was granted 24 February, 1689/90. In her baptismal record Martha is called the widow of Smith. As godmother of Samuel Sentar (1696) and of Jeanne Wannannemin (1698) she is the widow of Grant and signs as Martha Mills.

Mr. Stackpole says she was redeemed.

SMITH, JOHN.

Son of James and Martha (Mills).[16] At Montreal: "On Sunday 3 May 1693, was baptized a young English child aged seven years and nine months, as having been born the 26 July old style or 5 August N.S. 1685 at Barwic, town of New England of Jacques Smith and of Martha Mills his wife Protestants the child cap-

[15] N. Y. Docs., IV, 66, and "Hist. de Saint-François-du-Lac."

[16] James Smith's will names four children—John the last.

tured in war the 18 March 1690 and living in the service of Mr Dargenteuil, *Lieutenant du détachement de la marine.* He was named Jean Batiste by his godfather Mr Jean Batiste Daillibout, *Sieur des Musseaux,* Lieut. *du détachement de la marine.* The godmother was Damoiselle Felicité Le picard, wife of Mr Daillibout de Coulonges, the baptism was solemnly made by Messire Francois Dolie de Casson, *Grand Vicaire de Monseigneur l'Illustrissime et Reverendissime* Bishop of Quebec."

After his redemption John married Elizabeth ——, lived in Berwick and was the father of eleven children.

HURTADO (Fortado?), ELIZABETH.

Dau. of Antonio and Mary.

In "An Essay for the Recording of Illustrious Providences," the Rev. Increase Mather printed in 1684 "A Brief Narrative of sundry Apparitions of Satan unto and Assaults at sundry times and places upon the Person of Mary the Wife of Antonio Hortado, dwelling near the Salmon Falls: Taken from her own mouth Aug. 13, 1683." It was a merchant of Boston who took the "Narrative," passing it to Mr. Emerson, the schoolmaster, who gave it to the minister, Mr. Joshua Moodey, and he sent it to Mr. Mather.

The "occurrences" were like other witchcraft tales. Evil spirits were visible, and invisible hands tortured; and once when the said Mary and her Husband were "going in a Cannoo over the River they saw like the head of a man new-shorn and about two or three foot distant from each swimming over beyond the Canoo the tail of a white Cat . . . but no body appeared to joyn head and tail together." The sea serpent could have been no greater wonder!

And in this month and year their child, Elizabeth, was born. Carried away by the Indians she must have been ransomed, and when nine years old was taken into what probably had been the Church of her father, Antonio. Here is the baptism.

"This day 24 May, 1692 was baptized *Sous condition* a little girl born in Pescatoué in New England in August 1683, of the marriage of Antoine Hurtado of Fayol in Portugal[17] and of Marie Hart, native of York in New England, the girl taken the 18 March 1690 by Mr Artel and living now *à la Providence*[18] having had in her country the name of Elizabeth, received in this ceremony, the name of Louise. Her godfather was Francois Hardouin, clerk of Monsieur Le moine, Sieur de Maricour, Captain. The godmother De Louise Boideau, wife of Mr. Poitier, Merchant, formerly warden of this parish. The baptism solemnly made by Messire Francois Dollié de Casson Priest *Grand Vicaire de Monseigneur l'Illustrissime et Reverendissime* Bishop of Quebec.

signed fran dollier
francois ardouin E. Guyotte
curé."

Her name is not found again, and this name is questioned by Mr. C. T. Libby, authority for early Maine families. He is sure that her father was Antonio Fortado and her mother Mary Start, daughter of Edward of York.

In July, 1673, "Antonie Fortatoe and Mary Start" were accused together. In 1674 Mary Portadoe shared in Edward Start's estate.

KEY, JOHN, and children:
JOHN, JR.
JAMES.
ABIGAIL (Marguerite).

John and John, Jr., were redeemed by Cary in 1695. John, Jr., soon married Grizzel Grant.

James. Mather says he was a little boy — five years old — and because he cried for his father and mother was cruelly whipped and then killed by Hopehood.

Abigail.

At Three Rivers, "The 25 Aug. 1695, by me the undersigned

17 Hurtado may have come hither in a whaling ship, which then touched at the Western Islands in search of sperm whale.

18 Domestic School established by Marguerite Bourgeoys, see p. 16.

priest, was baptized, *sous condition* an English girl, converted to our religion, and about nineteen born of the marriage of Jean Quée and of Sara de Gearches.[19] She was named Margueritte Renée. The godfather was Monsieur Tonnancour, *Capitaine reformé* The godmother Madlle Bourdon

Signed: Tonnancour
Marguerite Seigneuret
A. Maudoux. Priest."

And at Montreal on "Tuesday 20 Oct. 1705, after one publication of the banns, Monsieur de Belmont, *Grand Vicaire de Monseigneur* the Bishop of Quebec, having granted a dispensation of the other two, and having found no impediment, I, the undersigned priest of the Seminary of Villemarie, empowered to act by the said *Grand Vicaire*, after having received the mutual consent by word of mouth of Charles Michel l'Huilier, sergeant in the company of Sabrevois, aged forty-two years, son of the late Michel l'huilier, Citizen of Paris, and of Anne Bourguignon his wife, native of the city and diocese of Paris, parish of Saint Nedaire of one part, and of Marguerite Renée Key, aged twenty-six years, daughter of Jean Key master-carpenter and of Sara Church, his wife, native of Piscatoué in New England of the other part, married them and gave them the nuptial benediction according to the rites of our Holy Mother Church in presence of Damoiselle Marguerite Seigneuret, wife of M. Bourdon, godmother of the bride, of Michel de Pailleur Royal Notary, Sieur Valerien de —— *Ecuyer* Sieur de Beaumont, sergeant in the company of Saint Ours" — and of several others. Marguerite signed, but the bridegroom could not write his name.

Perhaps her people did not know of her marriage. Her father gives to each of his three daughters £2, 10s. Two have different names, but she, in 1710, is called Abigail Kye. Her brother John named his daughter for her.

[19] Church.

"Margueritte Renée Kay, English woman, married to a Sergeant of the troops named Chevalier" was naturalized in 1710.

We have baptismal records of four children:

Marguerite, 1709, m. 1731 Henri Campeau.

Jean-Charles, 1711. In this the father is called "Charles L' huillier, dit Chevalier." He was absent. The godfather was "Sieur Batiste Dagueil," husband of Priscilla Storer of Wells. He m. 1, M. Jeanne Chevalier; 2, Angélique Larche.

Pierre, 1714.

François, 1716, m. 1752 Marguerite Gamelin.

Louis, 1721, m. 1754 Catherine Gareau.

OICBAC, JEAN BAPTISTE.

This must be a little boy of Salmon Falls of name like Wickby. At Three Rivers:

"The 8 September 1690 by me, priest undersigned curate of Three Rivers was baptized *soubs condition*, with the usual ceremonies Jean Baptiste Oicbac, an English child aged about three years and a half, made prisoner by the war-party from Three Rivers, commanded by Monsieur Hertel the year above written. The godfather was Messire Francois Duchesne *Ecuier oficier dans le troupe de la marine*, the godmother Madame Elizabeth Ratison de la Vallée, who said she could not sign.

A. Maudon, Priest."

REED, MRS.

"READ JN^{o} of Saman fals."

John Reed, Sr., was killed. Is not the "Mrs. Reed" of the following record in Braintree his wife? That is the family tradition. "Mrs. Reed, a captive taken at Casco Bay and carried to Canada was redeemed & came to Braintree and died 16 May 1691." John, Jr., the only son, was redeemed in 1695. He was married in Braintree. In 1714 he was living in Lyme, Connecticut.

ROGERS, ROBERT.

Robert Rogers, a corpulent man and unable to carry his heavy burden, threw it in the path, trying afterwards to hide. The Indians tracked him, tortured and burned him.[20]

SHORT, CHILDREN OF CLEMENT and FAITH (Munt of Boston).

Clement Short had an early grant in what is now South Berwick. Cotton Mather, not always reliable, says: "This honest man with his pious wife and three children were killed: and six or seven of their children were made prisoners. The most of which arrived safe to Canada . . . and the most of them were afterwards redeemed."[21]

Was "Richard Short boy, Dover," who remained in 1695 one of the six or seven? Mercy, known to be one, was redeemed by Phips in 1690 and later came into perhaps greater danger, as described by Cotton Mather in a paper he named "A Brand pluck'd out of the Burning."[22] It relates that "Mercy Short had been taken Captive by our cruel and Bloody Indians in the East who at the same time horribly Butchered her father, her Mother her Brother her Sister and others of her Kindred and then carried her and three surviving Brothers with two Sisters from Nieuchewannic unto Canada; after which our Fleet Returning from Quebec to Boston, brought them with other prisoners that were then Redeemed. But altho she had then already Born the Yoke in her youth Yett God Almighty saw it Good for her to Bear more of that Yoke, before seventeen years of her Life had Rolled away."

The poor girl, alone in Boston, became a servant, and in the Summer of 1692 she was "sent by her Mistress upon an Errand unto the prison and was asked by one of the Suspected Witches for a little Tobacco, and she affronted the Hag (t' was one Sarah Good since executed at Salem) by throwing an Handful of Shavings at her and saying That's Tobacco good enough for you Whereupon that Wretched Woman bestowed some ill words upon her

20 "Tragedies of the Wilderness," Drake. 21 Magnalia, II, 596.

22 The story was not printed, but Mather lent it to his friends. The manuscript was thought to have been lost until about 1870 when found among some Mather papers owned by the American Antiquarian Society, and it has since been printed by the American History Association in its "Original Narratives of Early American History."

and poor Mercy was taken with just such, or perhaps much worse Fits as those which held the Bewitched people then Tormented by Invisible Furies in the County of Essex."

Thirty-eight pages of manuscript describe her tortures by the devil. Mather and his friends kept "Three Successive Dayes of Prayer with Fasting on her behalf and then saw her Delivered" on New Year's Eve. For this, there was solemn Thanksgiving. But after seven weeks her Tormentors returned; her Miseries were renewed and his neighbors being weary, Mr. Mather Alone in his study fasted and prayed — and at last, she was "finally and forever delivered from the hands of evil Angels."

TOZER or TOZIER.

RICHARD, JR., b. abt. 1660, s. of Richard and Judith (Smith).

ELIZABETH, his wife, b. abt. 1653, according to her baptismal record, dau. of William and Elizabeth (Knight) Wentworth.

In September 1675, "Two cruel and barbarous Caitiffs" (Andrew of Saco and Hopehood of Kennebec) assaulted Richard Tozier's house[23] about a mile from Salmon Falls, wherein were fifteen women and children. A girl of eighteen discovered their approach, shut and stood against the door until the others escaped to the next house, which was better secured. The Indians chopped the door to pieces, knocked her down, leaving her for dead and pursued the rest. Two children who could not get over the fence were captured. The unknown heroine recovered.

In October the place was again attacked and posthaste a letter for help was sent to Dover; "Sirs: if ever you have any Love for us, and the Country now shew yourself with Men to help us . . . They that cannot fight let them pray."

Richard Tozier and one son were killed and the boy Richard, Jr., was captured, "but returned after some Months Restraint."[24]

[23] Sullivan calls it John Tozier's. [24] Hubbard's "Indian Wars."

Lieut. Roger Plaisted who was killed in the attempt to rescue his friend's body was one of the signers of the above letter.

Tradition gives two Canadian captivities to Richard and three to Elizabeth his wife. It is unlikely that he was carried so far away in 1675. We know that she was in 1690 and probably Richard, too, was in Canada. Elizabeth's father, William Wentworth, was the progenitor of all the distinguished men of the name in the country. He went from Exeter to Wells with the Rev. John Wheelwright, later returning to Dover. There, at the time of the attack, he was in Heard's garrison and awakened as the Indians were coming in "he pushed them out and falling back, pressed his feet against the gate and held it till the people were alarmed so that the women and children were saved."[25] Elizabeth was quickly converted and her baptismal record at Montreal gives much information.[26] "The same day September 8th 1693 was baptized *sous condition* and afterwards confirmed, an English woman of New England, named in her country Elizabeth which name was kept for her. This woman, born at Pescatoué about forty years since, of the marriage of Guillaume Wintworth Elder in the anglo-Calvinistic religion and of Elizabeth Kenaits, both native of old England and married first to Jaques Sharp, native of Kent in old England and second to Richard Tozer Protestant, was taken the 18th of March of the year 1690 by Monsieur Artel and has lived for two and a half years in the service of Monsieur Boucher, Seigneur of Boucherville. Her godfather was Monsieur Claude de Ramezay *Ecuyer* Governor of Trois Rivières. her godmother Damoiselle Jeanne Crevier wife of Monsieur Boucher

Signed:
De Ramezay
Jeanne Crevier
Elizabeth Tozer."

The record is indexed "Winterotchs." Nowhere else, so far as the writer has discovered, does James Sharp appear as Eliza-

[25] "Hist. Wells," 29. [26] See French record in Appendix.

beth's husband. In 1671, when she was of marriageable age, he was living in Great Island where one of her brothers lived. In 1699 she and her husband, Richard Tozier, conveyed land in York that was formerly in the possession of James Sharp,[27] and several years later testimony was given that James Sharp lived there — on the "north Side of the highway that leads from York Meeting House, towards the upper Part of the Town of York" — in 1674.[28] In the list of those confirmed on Sept. 8, 1693, is Isabella Tozier Wintworth and the Tozier was erased. The author of the "Wentworth Genealogy," quoting Tanguay, says "There can be no question that one wife of Elder William Wentworth was Elizabeth Kenny . . . the mother of this Elizabeth, the captive." And again: "There is a question whether Elizabeth Knight of Wells, Me., was one of the wives of Elder William Wentworth." The above record answers the questions; proving that Elizabeth Knight was the wife of Elder William and that she — and not Elizabeth Kenny — was the mother of our Elizabeth. Nothing definite is known of other captures or redemptions; all is traditional.

It is said that the Indians came once while she was boiling soap and she, throwing it upon them, caused their retreat. Again, dressed in man's clothes with gun in hand she acted as sentry while the men were in the fields.

Of her last capture the Genealogy[29] says that when Richard saw the Indians coming he told his wife she must do the best she could; he preferred death to another captivity. If she were taken he would redeem her if he lived. So covering himself with a feather bed he ran out of the back door to the frozen river. The ice was thin and he broke through. The Indians seeing the hole and the bed believed him drowned and did not follow.

They pillaged and burned the house, carrying off Elizabeth and all its inmates. Meantime Tozer was watching from the river's bank.

After this attack he built the blockhouse which stood until 1885.

[27] York Deeds, 6, 41. [28] York Deeds, 10, 164. [29] Vol. I, 150.

The Third War Party
Casco Bay or Falmouth

16-20 *May*, 1690.

Here was "a village called Falmouth and a wooden fort," which was Fort Loyal, built where now is the foot of India Street in Portland.[30]

Le Sieur de Portneuf, with Courtemanche second in command, left Quebec late in January with fifty Frenchmen and as many Abenakis from the St. Francis Mission. By visiting Abenaki villages in Maine he increased their number. Among them were certain leaders of Philip's war who had been imprisoned at the fort and released by Andros. Of course they knew the place well.[31] Saint-Castin, too, came with his Penobscot Indians, and all these with Hertel's men made a body of four or five hundred who were ready in May to attack what the French described as "A large fort well supplied with ammunition and eight cannon, with four other small forts near." Massachusetts had been too busy deposing Andros to remember her far-away settlements. In the fall of 1689, however, Captain Church was sent to the "poore Distressed province" and in checking the enemy, aided by information given by Mrs. Leigh,[32] it is believed that the State of Maine was saved to Massachusetts and the United States. Fort Loyal had been garrisoned during the winter of 1689-90, but most of the soldiers from this and other eastern posts were withdrawn before Phips sailed for Port Royal. Nevertheless, the people from the Kennebec and beyond, deprived of their own defence, had hurried to the fort. There had been "desperate need" among the soldiers who, the commissary writes, "enquire for Cloathing, Shoes & Blanketts, and if you (the Honored Governor and Council) think good . . . Sumthing Suitable to make Straw beds."

30 The authorities quoted are Willis, "History of Portland;" Hull, "Capture of Fort Loyal;" Goold, "Portland in the Past."

31 It is said that in 1690 there were 4,210 Indians between Boston and Canso. In 1726 the same territory was rated for 506. Winsor's "Nar. & Crit. Hist.," IV, 529.

32 See Dover, Chapter VI.

Let us hope they did not have to wait for these until 1703, but on July 28 of that year, in the House of Representatives, it was "ordered that there be Twenty Suitable Beds and Bolsters with a Blanket to each Bed, Procured at the Publick charge for the Lodging of the Souldiers at the Garrisons at Saco and Casco, there having been no Bedding hitherto Provided for that Occasion." It is comfortable to know that this order was "Read and agreed to." Among the needs of the garrison in 1689 was an hourglass; clocks of course were few, and in a letter to the governor the commander asks instructions concerning rum. He requests their "honors to Intemate to me what allowance of Rum the soldiers must have, as yet I have allowed them a pint among Six men for each day they are upon a march. They expect the same while they lie still, being tould by Some here present that the Country will allow it."[33]

A few days before Portneuf's attack Capt. Sylvanus Davis, who depended for defence mostly upon the settlers of the region, sent to Boston an urgent cry for help, he being "Greeved to see our poore nabors Destroyed and soe Littel care Taken amongst our folks to Indiver the discovery of the enemy," nevertheless he assures the governor that "wee will hassard our lives upon the place rather than Drawe of without orders naither have wee any desire to be drawed off."

No help was sent. They gave their lives. To meet Portneuf's large force Captain Davis had not more than seventy fighting men. Seeking refuge within the fort were some two hundred more of the inhabitants, old and young, weak and strong.

After Captain Davis's return from captivity he wrote a long account of this "bloody Design by the French and their Abettors," which was printed by the Massachusetts Historical Society.[34] Therein he says "The 16th of May, 1690 about dawning began our fight, the 20th at 3 o'clock afternoon, we were taken."

He, with seventy men and many women and children, surrendered on the promise of "good quarter" for all, "both wounded

[33] Arch. 35, 2. [34] Third Series, I, 101-112.

and sound," with liberty to march in safety to the next English town, which the French commander "did solemnly swear to perform;" but when they filed through the gate and laid down their arms they were seized by the Indians who murdered many and carried away the rest. When Captain Davis protested at the breach of faith he was told that they were all rebels against their King, James II, who was under the protection of the French King.

Destroying the fort and "All the houses within two leagues," not even waiting to bury the dead, the triumphant allies departed.

After two years, during which time no white man lived east of Wells, Captain Church stopped at deserted Casco and "buried the bones of the slain as they were bleaching upon the soil." Frontenac had ordered that no fort be attacked for fear of losing too many men, the object being to devastate the country. M. de Portneuf can hardly have been called rash; his losses being thus reported: "One Frenchman had his arm broken . . . by a cannon ball and an Indian was wounded in the thigh."[35] All the people of the region who had escaped went to Wells — to Storer's Garrison — where they were ordered by the Government to remain.

Captives

Few names are known. M. Ernest Myrand in "*Phips devant Québec*" says that seventy were taken, exclusive of women and children, but he names only four. We have:

Alexander, James

Brackett, Lieut. Anthony

Clark, The Family of Lieut. Thaddeus.

Tradition names wife and daughter Rebeckah. Local authorities give "Two Daughters," probably Elizabeth (Tyng) and Martha.

Isaac, his son.

Davis, Capt. Sylvanus

Morrell, Peter

Parker, William

35 Que. Docs., I, 498.

Ross, James
Swarton, Mrs. Hannah
Samuel
Mary (m. John Lahey)
John
Jasper
York, John
Samuel

As of Casco, remaining in 1695, are Sara Davis and Thos Baker, and on the Roll of 1710/11, Zacha, Joshua, Grace and Mary Davis; Two Jourdains; Elizabeth, Nathan and —— Webber; and —— Slew.

Of these, "Thomas Baker boy, Casco" may have been son of Thomas of Scarboro and Falmouth; the son was living in Taunton in 1721, when he sold land in Scarboro. Folsom in his Saco (p. 33) says that Thomas Baker was recaptured from the Indians in Sept., 1690. This implies an error of the 1695 list. The Davises may have been of Isaac's family who lived on the Purpooduck side of the harbor. Grace Tucker and Mary Davis witnessed a Davis deed in 1733, which implies two redemptions and one marriage.

The Webers were probably children of Michael of Purpooduck. See Marie Weber, married to Paul Otis. Leonard Slew may be found in "Along Shore."

Alexander, James.

"James Alexander, a Jersey man," was, with John Gyles, tortured at an Indian village on the St. John river.[36] Two families of Cape Sable Indians, who had lost friends by some English fishermen, came these many miles to avenge themselves on poor captives. They yelled and danced around their victims; tossed and threw them; held them by the hair and beat them — sometimes with an axe — and did this all day, compelling them also to

36 "Tragedies of the Wilderness," 84.

dance and sing, until at night they were thrown out exhausted. Gyles says it was the worst torture he had! Alexander, after a second torture, ran to the woods, but hunger drove him back to his tormentors. His fate is unknown.

BRACKETT, ANTHONY, 3^{d}.

B. 1699, s. of Anthony 2^{d} and Ann (Mitton).

Lieutenant Brackett was kept four months in the Maine woods until he escaped in September. He afterwards lived in Boston, dying there in 1716.

CLARK. Some of the FAMILY OF LIEUT. THADDEUS.

Possibly his wife, ELIZABETH (Mitton). ISAAC, his son, b. abt. 1666, d. 1768. "Two daughters." Rebeckah, a third daughter?

Thaddeus Clark came from Ireland. He married in 1663 the daughter of Michael Mitton, then eighteen years old. Her grandfather was George Cleeves, the first settler of Falmouth. Lieut. Thaddeus was killed, leading a brave sortie from the fort. "Two daughters" only are mentioned among those captured, but his son Isaac was certainly taken. The story of the capture of Mrs. Clark and the daughter named Rebeckah comes from Lieut. Isaac's granddaughter, Mrs. Beulah Patterson, as printed in Barry's "History of Framingham";[37] upon the authority of the Rev. Joseph Allen of Northborough. This states that her grandfather Isaac's "Mother and sister Rebeckah were carried to Canada, where the mother died.[38] Rebeckah was sold to the French, among whom she lived so contented that when money was sent for her ransom she refused to leave; sending word that the money sent was not sufficient to supply her table for a single day." This sounds more or less legendary. Another tale is that one of Isaac's sisters married an Indian and remained in the North.

[37] Page 208.

[38] An error, she died in Boston in 1736, aged ninety-two.

Isaac.

Barry says that Isaac had a thrilling career. He certainly had a long one. He escaped or was ransomed from his captivity and went to live in Marlborough, where he learned the carpenter's trade and where he married Sarah Stow. He was a captain in the Three Years' War and was of such vigor that on his hundredth birthday he rode a horse a long distance. "He lived seventy years with the wife of his youth. His offspring that descended from him was 251." Thus is it written on his tombstone.

"Two daughters"

Elizabeth and *Martha.*

These with Isaac are the only children named as heirs of Lieutenant Clark.

Elizabeth was the wife of Capt. Edward Tyng and the mother of four children.

Captain Tyng was commander of the fort until 1688 when he was appointed Governor of Annapolis by Phips, and it was on his way home that he too was captured.[39]

Martha, who married a Harvey and was a widow in Boston in 1719, was probably the second daughter. The "two daughters" were among the prisoners exchanged by Phips, and in that long "*Relation* of 1689/90 written by Monseignat and addressed probably to Mme. de Maintenon[40] they are described as having been very well born. He says, too, that: "The Count had ransomed them and had put them in a place to board."

DAVIS, CAPT. SYLVANUS.

He bought land at Damariscotta in 1659; barely escaped death at Arrowsick in 1676, and after the peace lived in Casco.

The complexity of his service is shown in a petition dated 22^{d}, 10th, 1690. Not only had he served his country until Casco fort was captured but he says: "I did offitiate in the place and duty of Chyrurgeon amongst the souldiers & sick men about Eleaven months

39 See "From the River St. John." 40 Que. Docs., I, 527.

time. Also I pformed the Duty of a Comesary for about four months time. & Also I maintained a Drum̄ and Drummer about thirteen months for the service of the fourt, & all the Marching fources that was sent to that place from time to time."[41]

Of his captivity, he wrote: After they had "cruelly murdered our women and children and especially the wounded men, the French kept myself and 3 or 4 more and carried us over land to Canada . . . about twenty four days we were marching . . . on land and water carrying our canoes with us . . . I must say they were kind to me in my travels . . . our provision was very short; Indian corns and acorns—hunger made it very good & God gave it strength to nourish. I arrived at Quebeck the 14th of June 1690, where I was civilly treated by the gentry and soon carried . . . before the governour the Earl of Frontenack."[42] He was lodged in the château.

It was the Indian custom not to give up their captives until the price of ransom was actually paid, but this time they consented to let M. de Portneuf keep Captain Davis and the two daughters of Lieutenant Clark during the journey on his solemn promise that later the governor would pay for their redemption. They relied not only upon this promise, but upon the knowledge that Frontenac would pay them well.[43] On October 15 Captain Davis was exchanged for the Sieur de Granville, an officer captured by Phips.

He afterwards lived in Nantasket and died in 1703. Davis told Frontenac that he grieved for his fellow-captives who had been half-starved and tortured on the journey; and the governor promised him that they "should be got out of the hands of the Indians." Probably this was why a majority of the eighteen captives who were delivered to Phips were from Casco.

Morrell, Peter.

He came to Falmouth about 1681 and lived on "the Neck" now India Street. After his return from captivity he joined his wife,

41 "Maine Hist. Coll.," II, 5, 174. 42 "Mass. Hist. Coll.," III, Ser. I, 101.

43 "*Sir William Phips devant Québec.*" E. Myrand.

Mary, and their children in Beverly where they subsequently lived.

Is this the man who generously gave his shirt to redeem Juda Emerson?

PARKER, WILLIAM.

Captain Davis, after his return, petitioned for compensation for his services as commander-in-chief and surgeon and asks "also compensation for Wm Parker who has been a soldier for ten months and was now in captivity."

ROSS, JAMES.

B. 1662, son of James and Ann (Lewis) of Falmouth. James was a shoemaker living at Back Cove, and in 1690 was one of Davis's soldiers.

He had been captured with his father's family in 1676, so this was his second captivity, from which he was redeemed by Cary in 1695. Among his fellow-captives he found his bride, Sarah Ferguson,[44] marrying her on December 19, immediately after their redemption. In June, 1696, he petitioned for his soldier's wage "having rec^d severall wounds in the body from the french & Indian Enemies wth whom he was many Months a captive."[45] Thirty years later he, "James Ross of Salem, Shewing" that by one of his "Several Wounds . . . his Collar Bone was Split and Cut off . . . that he Suffered much Pain & Trouble" during his captivity, "and was at last put to great Charge for his Redemption" prayed for "Some Allowance" from the Court. He received five pounds annually.

Sarah died before 1706, when James married Martha Darling of Salem, where he had lived since his return from captivity.

In 1734, when aged about seventy-two, he testified in Salem that "he lived at Falmouth in Casco Bay ever since he can remember anything till drove from thence in the First Indian Warr &

[44] See Kittery, Chapter XIII. [45] Arch. 70, 277.

then he removed thither again betwixt the First & Second Warr and lived there about Six Years until he was taken in the Second Warr," when he was taken in the Fort with Capt. Davis.

This contradicts the story of captivity in 1676. Surely he would have remembered that!

SWARTON, MRS. HANNAH OR JOANNA.

(Ebal on Canadian Record) wife of John, and their four children.

SAMUEL (1674).
MARY (1675).
JOHN (1677).
JASPER (1685).

(Spelled on Canadian records: Soarre, Shiard, Shaken, Soüarten, Sowarten, Schouarden, Souard).

John Swarton of Beverly received in 1687 a fifty acre grant in North Yarmouth. In his petition he said he had fought with Charles II in Flanders. Charles, when Prince of Wales, went to Jersey where he was proclaimed king and then went across the Channel to fight. Perhaps Swarton went with him. When in 1689 Captain Church made his "First Expedition Eastward" he saw "One Swarton, a Jersey man; . . . whose language he could hardly understand." The old Norman French of the Channel Islands would make his English difficult. During the attack a John Swarton, living near the fort, was killed and his wife and children were captured. Hannah Swarton's "Narrative" was first published in 1697 as an appendix to Cotton Mather's "Humiliations followed with Deliverances," and was later collected in the Magnalia.[46] In it is the same story of cold, hunger, cruelty and pious reflections. She says it lay heavy upon her spirit that they had left Beverly, where they had had the privilege of the public worship of God, to remove where there was no minister of the gospel, which they had done for "large accommodations in the

[46] The only perfect copy known of the original pamphlet was sold in 1916 for two thousand dollars; a second copy is in the Congressional Library.

world, thereby exposing their children to be bred ignorantly like Indians."

She describes her Indian mistress as "one that had been bred by the English at Blackpoint and now married to a Canada Indian and turned Papist," and the squaw would say "that had the English been as careful to instruct her in our religion as the *French* were to instruct her in their's, she might have been of our religion."

At Norridgewock the captives were separated and no English were left in Mrs. Swarton's company but one John York. Here she was told that her eldest son had been killed. She says that by her bleeding feet she could be tracked in the snow and she found it "Very tedious to travel." Arriving in mid-February near Quebec her master sent her to beg for food. On her second visit she stayed over night with a French woman. The next morning two men — one English — came to the house and advised her to go with them to Quebec, four miles away, telling her that she would be ransomed. The woman, too, advised her to go. The Englishman took her to the wife of the intendant who fed and clothed her and sent her to the hospital where she was "physicked and blooded and very courteously provided for." Her Indian master and his squaw came after her, but the lady bought her and she became her servant "And I must speak it to the honour of the French," she wrote, "they were exceeding kind to me at first even as kind as I could expect to find the English." Soon new trials came; snares were laid for her soul, which she describes at length. "The lady, my mistress, the nuns, the priests, the friars and the rest set upon me . . . to perswade me to turn Papist." Love, promises and entreaties first they used, then finding her obdurate, threats and hard usage. She was strengthened and consoled by conversations with Colonel Tyng and Mr. Alden, and especially with Margaret Stilson who was in the same house, but those conferences were shortly forbidden. In 1695 she, with her youngest son, Jasper, was redeemed, leaving Mary, whom she had not seen for two years, and John from whom she had parted the day after they were taken. Of him we have no trace.

Her last word is for her children: "I earnestly request the prayers of my Christian friends that the Lord will deliver them."

Swarton, Mary, and
Lahey, John.

Among the "Nam^s of thos Remaining" (1695) is that of "Mary Swarton Cascow gerl." In May, 1710, "Marie Swarton Englishwoman, married to Jean Laha, Irishman, established in Montreal and having three children," becomes a French citizen. Jean laha's name is first on the same list.

His abjuration is on the Montreal records: "On Monday, 19 March 1696, Jean Lahe born in 1670 at Tollo in Ireland of the marriage of Thomas Lahé, Catholic, and of Catharine Williams, Protestant, and baptized in his country in the Catholic religion & later having professed the Puritan religion until last year, when he was taken in the month of July among the Flemish of Corlar and living now in the service of M. le ber, Merchant, solemnly made abjuration of heresy into the hands of Mre Henri Antoine Meriel, Priest of the Seminary of Ville Marie, authorized to receive it by M. François Dolie priest, Grand Vicaire etc. And this in the presence of M. Yves Priat, priest of said Seminary of Ville Marie and of several others." (Signed by all herein named.)

"The 9th Sept. 1697, after the publication of 3 banns of marriage made the 29th August last, the 1st and 3^d of the present month and year as above between Jean lehait Irishman, son of Thomas lehait and of Catherine Guilloses, father and mother of the town of boston in hirlands of one part and of Marie Madeleine Souard, daughter of Jean Souard and Anne Ebal[47] of Selam, her father and mother of the other part, and having found no obstacle I, françois Dupré, curé de Québec have married and given them *la bénédiction nuptiale* according to the form pre-

47 Was not Anne Ebal daughter of Robert and Joanna Abel of Weymouth?

scribed by our mother the Holy Church in presence" of several French witnesses, all but one of whom signed.

The baptismal records of their eleven children testify to their friendships with New England captives.

1698, Jean François, b. and d.

1701, Madeleine, m. 1724 Pierre Couleau.

1702, Jean-Marguerite, then living at Côte Saint-Laurent, m. 1719, Pierre Normand.

1706, Marie-Anne, god-mother Christine Otis of Dover; m. 1729, Jacques Benoist, dit la guerre, at Saint-Laurent.

1708, Jean-François; Freedom French of Deerfield, god-mother.

1710, Jean Lahaye brought little twin babies to Notre-Dame; one to be buried, one to be baptized. Father Meriel wrote that the first had been baptized by the midwife. To the other, Mary Silver gave the name of Marie-Sylvie. She m. 1740, at Saint-Géneviève, J. F. Benoit.

1711, Marie-Joseph.

1713, Marie-Catherine.

1714, Joseph.

1715, Marie-Magdeleine.

1717, Claude-Jean-Baptiste.

With the Report sent to Versailles in September, 1714, concerning the return of English captives, the intendant sent a petition from Jean la Haye, who has lived for twenty-two years at the Côte de la Chine, Montreal. La Haye had been arrested with an Englishman named Jean Joublin for having counterfeited and used card-money of different denominations,[48] as did later Pendleton Fletcher of Saco. Joublin, being a prisoner of war, it was thought might be ignorant of the law in regard to counterfeit money.

The Report says that because Monsieur de la Haye has rendered the King and colony great service, criminal proceedings have been suspended until further notice, and out of consideration for the

48 See Appendix.

envoys [Messrs. Stoddard and Williams] of the Queen of England, who have demanded these two prisoners as being of their nation, the Sieurs de Vaudreuil and Bégon [governor and intendant] have promised to beg His Majesty to order their discharge without trial. The long imprisonment that they have already suffered, and which they must still endure until orders from His Majesty are received, is a severe punishment; it being certain that these counterfeit bills have simply been made and have never been in circulation. They are besides so badly made that no one could be deceived."[49]

York, John.
Samuel.

John was probably son of John and Ruth (Graves). John, Sr., was killed in the attack as John, Jr., was said to have been, but Mrs. Swarton wrote that when the captives were separated she and "one John York" were the only two at Norridgewock, and that they "were both, almost starv'd for want." Their masters told them if they "could not hold up" they would kill them. "And accordingly John York, growing weak by his wants, they killed him."

Samuel.

The carpenter of the following memorial may have been brother of John who was killed. His wife was Hannah and they lived in what is now Topsham. Their son Samuel testified in 1726 that their house was made a garrison where several other families were entertained until driven off by Indians. York Ledge and York Landing of Falmouth Foreside recall this family. Samuel, Sr., must have returned, as householder or soldier as shown by the "Memoriall of Samuel York, Carpenter addressed to his Excellency the Earle of Bellomont at Albany the 2^d^ of Septr 1700 sheweth: That I was taken prisoner in Casco Bay . . . in the moneth of May 1690 and carried to Canada where and in

[49] "Que. Docs., III, 6.

the hunting Indian countries I have lived ever since till the 29th day of this last July that I made my escape to come hither and during the last two years & half I was imployed in cutting masts for the use of the French King's Navy."

He gives the governor much information about the Western Indians; says that they and several bush-rangers who are with them are discontented and wish to come and trade with the English.[50] Before he returned to Casco Lord Bellomont sent him and others with a message to the Dowaganhas Indians, but they were stopped by "Indians of the Five Nations, who refused to accompany them and who told them (York and his friends) to return to Albany unless they meant to be knocked in the head by the French or their Indians."[51] Samuel York died in March, 1718.

Sandy Beach (Rye)

Captives

1691. Barnes, Elizabeth.
Brackett, Cisia.
Abigail.
Rand, son of Francis.

Barnes, Elizabeth. Was she perhaps granddaughter of Francis Rand? He died in 1689, leaving a daughter Mary Barnes. Elizabeth came home on the Province Galley in January, 1698/9.

The Brackett Family suffered much in the Indian wars.
Anthony, first of the name, immigrant of Portsmouth, or Sandy Beach, was killed there 28 September, 1691, as was his wife.
Anthony (2) and all his family were captured at Falmouth (1676).
Thomas, second son, was killed and all his family taken in 1676.
John, third son, was spared; his daughters captured 28 Sept., 1691.
Nathaniel Mitton and Thaddeus Clark, who were brothers-in-law

[50] N. Y. Docs., IV, 748. [51] N. Y. Docs., IV, 768.

of Anthony (2) and Thomas, were killed at Falmouth, 1690.

Thaddeus Clark sent the following letter "from Casco-bay 14.6.76" (Aug. 14, 1676) "ffor his honoured Mother, Mrs. Elizabeth Harvy, living in Boston." Mrs. Harvey's first husband was Michael Mitton; three of her daughters were the wives of Lieutenant Clark and of Anthony and Thomas Brackett.

Clark wrote: "The Lord of late hath renewed his witnesses against vs & hath dealt very bitterly with vs in that we are deprived of the Societie of our nearest friends by the breaking in of the adversarie against us: On Friday last in the morning your own Son with your two Sons in Law, Anthony & Thomas Bracket & their whole families were Killed & taken by the Indians, we Know not how, tis certainly known by us that Thomas is slain & his wife & children carried away captivaue, & of Anthony & his familie we have no tidings & therefore think that they might be captivated the night before because of the remoteness of their habitation from neighbourhood . . . Your dutifull Son

Thaddeus Clark"[52]

Anthony (2).

Anthony lived on Back Cove at Falmouth, where, on August 11, 1676, he, his wife (Ann Mitton), five little children and a negro servant were captured through the treachery of Simon, one of Philip's Indians, who had joined the Penacooks.

The savage may have had a glimmering memory of the kindness he had received at Brackett's, for the little children, all under ten years of age, were not killed, as children frequently were, that there might be no delay in the progress of the hurrying Indians.

Different stories are told of the family's escape after capture. Drake says that the Indians held them until November, then leaving them on the shore of Casco Bay the savages went to share in the plunder at Arrowsick, expecting to gather in their captives on their return, but they were not found.

52 "Portland in the Past," Goold, p. 114.

Mrs. Brackett had discovered some needles and thread in one of the deserted houses, and helped by her husband and servant she patched up an old leaky canoe in which all but her husband crossed the bay safely to Black Point. He, probably fearing to overburden the frail craft, escaped through the woods. From Black Point they went by boat to the grandfather's house at Sandy Beach. Anthony was killed in a skirmish in 1689. His son Seth was killed and Lieutenant Anthony captured at Casco Bay(1690).

Thomas.

He, married to Mary Mitton, lived on her father's homestead at Falmouth, now the Deering estate.

Thomas was killed on that same August day while working in a field near his home. His wife and their children, Joshua, Sarah, Mary and perhaps Samuel, were carried away. The young wife died during captivity or immediately after her release. The children, redeemed by Grandfather Brackett, lived with him at Sandy Beach.

John.

Youngest son, lived with his father. Sandy Beach was then within the town of New Castle. His day of suffering was Tuesday, Sept. 28, 1691.

The story of the attack as told by an ancient chronicler is as follows:[53] "The sons of Francis Rand went a fishing; the sons of ould Goodman Brackett were in the salt marsh and with no suspicion of danger. . . . Early in the afternoon a party of Indians came from the eastward in canoes, landed at Sandy Beach, left the garrison there unmolested and attacked the homes of the defenseless ones, killing and capturing twenty-one persons. Among the killed was Francis Rand. . . . When his sons came in from fishing they followed the Indians over to Brackett's, fired upon them and frightened them away. The sons[54] of Anthony Brackett who had the guns with them ran to the garrison at Odiorne's

[53] From "Brackett Genealogy." [54] Son John, grandson Joshua.

Point."[55] The next morning "their tracks were distinctly traced in the sand as were also the tracks of two women and one child."[56]

It is said that of the twenty-one victims not less than fifteen were slain, which leaves six to be accounted for. Do we trace four or only three?

BRACKETT.

KEZIAH.

ABIGAIL (Marie Louise).

Is "Gabrielle Louise" a third?

Of two daughters of John and Martha (Philbrick) we are sure. Keziah or "Cisia Brackett of Oyster River" was redeemed by Carey in 1695. She must have been a favorite grandchild. Anthony, Sr., making his will about two weeks before he was killed remembered all his grandchildren, but named only three. "Item: I give and bequeath unto my grandaughter Kasia bracket three cows to be payed at age of Eighteen or day of marridge." The family genealogist says there is "no further record concerning her," but let us hope that the legacy was paid for she lived to marry Joseph Maylem of Boston, and as his widow made her will in March, 1732, shortly before her death. She named no child and made her nephew, Anthony Brackett, her executor and principal legatee.[57]

Abigail.

"Abig[ll] Brakett of Dover" was still in the Indians' hands in 1695 when Cisia was redeemed. The Brackett Genealogy says she was carried to Canada where she married a Frenchman. Upon her father's death in 1727 she came back to New Hampshire to claim her share of his estate, part of which was seven acres of land. In the list of Portsmouth's taxpayers of 1727 is "Frenchman Brackett." The family historian adds that "nothing further is

55 The first house in New Hampshire was built on this point, which is a mile across the water from Hotel Wentworth.

56 Dow's "History of Hampton." 57 Suffolk Probate, 31, 317.

known of her, probably she returned to Canada." Some verses were made to celebrate her coming to claim her inheritance.

From Canadian records we learn a little more. In the list of pupils of the Ursuline Sisters from 1639 to 1700 are these names:

"Braquil (Breaky?) Gabrielle-Louise baptized in the convent.

Marie-Louise also baptized in the convent, (Pierre Roy)" that being the name of her husband.

It is bewildering to read of two; more bewildering to try to identify two! The New England record says two daughters were taken. We know of Keziah and Abigail. In Canada the English Abigail is often changed to Gabrielle. Of the names Marie, Gabrielle, Louise we have some changes, but only in the Ursuline list are two individuals distinctly named. There is but one record of baptism, of marriage and of burial; but one recipient of king's money, and of naturalization. This act of baptism is on the Register of Notre-Dame, Quebec:

"The 17th Dec. 1698 was baptized by me priest, curate of Quebec, in the holy church of the ursulines, gabrielle Louise, daughter of Jean Braquit and mafi [very short for Ma-rtha Phi-lbrick!] his wife of the country of England, sixteen years old, her godfather was the sr. Nicolas Pinaut, citizen merchant and her godmother was Louise Douaire, his wife, who have signed

Pinaut Louise Douaire F. Dupré."

(A duplicate record gives Gabrielle loussy, dau. of Jean braquet and meti his wife).

In 1702 "Louise Braquette" was given thirty livres of the king's money, her residence being Montreal — probably an error.

In 1710 "Louise Gabrielle Brakett" is naturalized.

In 1715 Marie-Louise marries. "In the year 1715, Dec. 16, we jean, bishop of Quebec, having received the mutual consent of marriage between pierre roi called leveille of the diocese and archbishopric of paris, parish of St. Sulpice, and Marie-Louise Braquil of peskadouet, new england, daughter of Jean Braquil and of mafie her father and mother, have given them the nuptial blessing with the ceremonies prescribed by the Holy Church, in presence of Jaques Racicot, veteran, and roland tessié witnesses, who have signed with them in the way that the interested parties who do not know how to sign have made their mark.

M. L.

Jacques Racicot Tessié

Jean, bishop of Quebec."

In 1717 a son, Guillaume, was born and died. Very likely other baptisms are recorded.

"In 1743, Dec. 3, was buried in the cemetery of this parish [Notre-Dame of Quebec] Marie-Louise Breakie, English woman, wife of Pierre Roi called Leveillé, deceased yesterday, aged 57 years. Poulin priest."

Is it not probable that all these records are of Abigail alone?

RAIN, JEAN-BAPTISTE.

May not this be one of the sons of Francis Rand? In this way his name might be spelled. If it were he, he had become a convert and had been renamed in baptism, and as an "Englisman, born in the Great Island near (devant) Piskatakoué, New England," he was buried at Montreal, Dec. 5, 1699.

FROM THE RIVER ST. JOHN

1691, *August.*

Nelson, John.

Tyng, Colonel Edward.

Alden, John, Jr.

These three men hardly belong in our captive list. They were more truly prisoners of war; yet they were of New England, they were captured and taken to Quebec and France, as were so many of less degree. It was in August. They were sailing toward Boston from Annapolis on Capt. John Alden's vessel. Villebon, on a French frigate just coming from France, learned that they were near and pounced upon them.

Captain Alden was released that he might carry a letter to "the Governor of Boston" which Villebon dated: "From the river St. John, 25 Aug. 1691."[58] In it he complains of Phip's breach of faith in failing to release the fifty-nine soldiers who had been taken with Meneval at Port Royal and demands that Alden's vessel be sent back immediately with the soldiers on board, Alden having promised it. As security, Villebon is holding "Colonel King" (always so written in the French correspondence) and "*le sieur Aldin fils.*" Mr. Nelson had already been sent to Quebec, having boldly promised that in exchange for himself Frontenac would return English prisoners. Either dates differ or winds were light for it is not until 19 October that Sewall writes: "This day news is brought of Capt. Aldens being taken by a French Frigot at St. John's. Mr. Nelson carried to Quebeck; Colonel Tyng and Mr. Jn° Alden jun^r kept Prisoners till Articles made for Capt. Aldens coming home are fulfill'd." He mentions also the loss of eighteen thousand pounds by Boston merchants! The French account[59] hopes that much benefit may be derived from the capture of Nelson, "a gentleman of merit and intelligence," who had been kind to French prisoners. Meneval had lived under his roof in Boston where he was given the freedom of the town, and to Nelson he owed his release.

But the Port Royal soldiers were not sent back and Colonel Tyng with young Alden was sent to Quebec. Tyng had been appointed governor of Annapolis (Port Royal) but the settlers were hostile and with the small force given him he had no influence, nor could he restrain the Indians, so he was returning to Boston on Alden's vessel. His wife, Elizabeth, daughter of Lieut. Thaddeus Clark, was already in Quebec, having been taken from Casco, and we must hope that she, like Hannah Swarton, was "consoled by his conversation." He was later carried to France where he died in prison before January, 1694.

John Alden, third of the name, called a merchant of Boston,

[58] Que. Docs., II, 69. [59] N. Y. Docs., IX, 527.

was also carried to France. Hannah Swarton mentions him too.

He was born in 1663, his mother was Elizabeth (Phillips | Averill).

Mr. John Nelson, gentleman and merchant, of Boston, was nephew and heir of Sir Thomas Temple, in whose right he claimed the proprietorship of Acadia under an old grant of Oliver Cromwell.[60] That was a large tract, for Acadia included Nova Scotia, New Brunswick and Maine to the Kennebec or the St. George's.

The Report, already quoted, said that in Canada he "may anticipate every civility that can be extended to a prisoner," but those "civilities" necessarily ceased when his loyalty to New England made him dangerous to New France.

Madockawando came to Quebec to deliver five English captives and to receive his reward from the Governor, and the reward disappointed him. Nelson, understanding his language, tried to ingratiate himself and his people with the disgruntled Indian, from whom he learned the French plans.

At the risk of his life he bribed two Frenchman to carrry the information to Massachusetts. Frontenac was to send Madockawando with two or three hundred Indians to the coast of Maine where two French ships would meet them and the combined forces were to attack the settlements from Pemaquid to the Piscataqua.

Nelson's letter, dated 26 August, 1692, is printed in Hutchinson's History.[61] He wrote:

"I promised to send my thoughts thereon to yourselves. Madocawando gave daily advice of all their results." To send this and more important information he said: "I have corrupted two Frenchmen . . . to be bearers of this letter, and also to be guides to two Dutchmen and two Englishmen, who promise to be with you in twenty-two days. I pray that they may be contented. I have furnished them with 13 French crowns which it is just should be allowed to my wife." The letter was duly delivered, and Massachusetts profited thereby, but alas! she tried to make further use

60 Parkman's "Frontenac," 357. 61 Vol. I, 378.

of the two deserters, concocting a plan to kidnap Castine. In that scheme the betrayers were betrayed and were shot (*la tête cassée*) at Mount Desert after they had disclosed Nelson's part in the plan.

Versailles instructed Quebec that as there were in New England no French prisoners of sufficient importance to exchange for these three gentlemen, excepting always the Port Royal soldiers, and as it would be easy for them to escape and also that the charge to keep them was heavy it would be well to send them all to France.[62]

It was on Jan. 28, 1693, that the Minister was notified of the arrival of Nelson. It was impossible to put him into one of the royal prisons, and as he had to be carefully guarded he was taken to the Château d'Angoulême and the keeper was told that because he was a dangerous person he must not be allowed to have communication with any one, especially the new converts.[63] For two years he was kept in this dungeon of the château.

A biographical note in the "New York Colonial Documents"[64] says that he was confined in a small hole without seeing any one "but a servant who brought his victuals to a grate." Then in contradiction it continues that a gentleman noticed this and spoke to him at the grate, offering his service. Through him Nelson sent a letter to Sir Purbeck Temple in England, after which a demand was made for his release. In January, 1694, a letter from Versailles informs Bégon in Canada that the King allows Nelson to go from the Château d'Angoulême (on parole) to England that he may bring about the exchange promised when he was taken; one of his merchant friends in La Rochelle giving a bond of fifteen thousand livres for his return if he failed to get this order from the King. Alas! he did fail and King William ordered him not to return to France. But to save his own honor and his friend's purse he did return and was put into the Bastile, there evidently being then more room in the royal prisons.

[62] Que. Docs., II, 80 and 86. [63] Que. Docs., II, 103. [64] Vol. IV, 206.

Versailles was told that the few Port Royal soldiers left in Boston had been returned somewhat against their will as they had married in New England. Others had either returned to France or been scattered throughout the country, and a message is sent to America to inquire if it be true.

And here is the last word in Nelson's own petition: "John Nelson to William Stoughton Lt Gov. of ye Province of Massachusetts Bay in New England

"Nov. 30, 1698, That whereas y^{r} Petition^{r} hath for neare Seauen years last past been a prissoner unto the french unto pretence of a reprisall for sundrie souldiers, which had been taken at Port Royall, by the Late s^{r} Wm Phipps, in ye Yeare 1690 & as they Alledged Contrarie unto ye Articles there made by him, Instead of returning them unto some of ye french Kings dominions they were here detained as prisoners, by reason of which, y^{r} P^{r}tioner and sundrie others of this province, have been great sufferers in france, soe that y^{r} P^{r}tioner for ye obtaining of his lybertie was Constrained to Comply with ye Demand of ye french Court, by ingageing the returne of ye said souldiers, in the space of eighteen months after ye Inlargem^{t} of y^{r} p^{r}tioner from his Confinem^{t}."

The Massachusetts authorities having agreed to this he says that his "Wife & freinds were at ye Labor & Expence of finding out such of ye said souldiers as yett remained, they being dispersed throughout ye Country, & by their great paines & Charge, did gather to geather sundrie of them," expecting them to be sent to Quebec "on ye account & for the behalfe of the Petitioner." But instead they were exchanged for an equal number of English prisoners, and because of this failure he had to surrender himself again a prisoner.

He adds that while he was a prisoner at the Eastward he "did buy & release from ye Indians seaven English Captives some of which would have been put to death according to theire Barbarous maner" if he had not interposed and redeemed them at his proper Charge.[65]

[65] Arch. 70, 389-90.

While in England he appeared before the Commissioners for Trade and the Plantations, and in answer to their request sent to them later a Memorial (24 Sept., 1696)[66] in which he says that having been for twenty-six years conversant with the French in Nova Scotia, Acadia and Canada he was in 1691 sent by the Governor and Council in New England "to setle and establish one Coll: Edward Tyng in the Command of Port Royal, a place that has been newly subjected to the Crown of England, in which enterprize I had the misfortune to be taken by the French."

After his return to New England the House of Representatives (22 Nov., 1698) gave him a Vote of Thanks for the valuable help given in this Memorial concerning the fisheries and boundaries.

With his petition, sent the same month, was an account, allowed and paid, of about twenty pounds for expenses incurred by "Wife and Freinds," and one hundred pounds was given to him in early December for "Getting the French Prisoners & Redeeming the Captives and other his Good Service for this his Maj[ties] Province."[67] The Nelson home was probably on the southeast side of Hanover Street, between Court and Elm Streets.

[66] N. Y. Docs., IV, 206.

[67] Prov. Laws, Vol. VII.

CHAPTER IX

The Attacks Upon York

1691/2 — 1693 — 1703 — 1705

25 *January*, 1691/2.

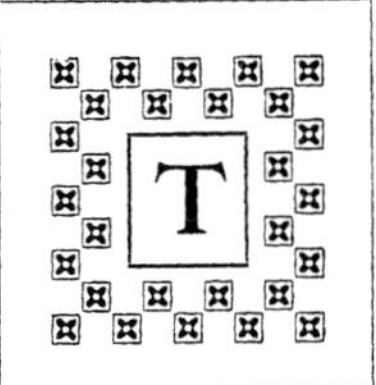

HE ABENAKIS were wavering in their allegiance. After the truce was signed by the Massachusetts commissioners and Sagamores in 1690 the French court and colony were both alarmed. The Governor of Acadia wrote in 1691 that if the Indians had made peace with the English after the fall of Port Royal, Canada might have been lost because of the ease of reaching Quebec in ten or twelve days from the river St. John and Pentegoet.[1] He adds that half New England supports itself by the cod-fisheries, and as the Indians prevent the fishermen from entering Acadian ports for water and shelter, the English will leave nothing undone to attract them.

So M. de Villebon was hurried off with supplies and gifts to hold the allegiance of the Indians; and the missionaries, of whom Père Thury was the most influential, were charged to make them break off the negotiations with "the Bostonnais."[2]

So well did they succeed that down the frozen Chaudière and Kennebec Rivers came Indians from the mission at Sillery to join those from the missions of Fathers Bigot and Thury who, with Thury himself, were waiting at the mouth of the Kennebec.

Between this river and the Piscataqua nothing was left but the villages of Wells, York, Kittery and Appledore. From the Kennebec the Indians travelled westward until they reached Agamenticus.

1 N. Y. Docs., IX, 506.

2 "*Les Sulpiciens et Les Prêtres des Missions-Etrangères en Acadie,*" Casgrain.

Parkman says the best account of the attack upon York is that sent to Versailles the following October by Champigny, the Intendant. A copy of his letter is among the Parkman manuscripts in the Massachusetts Historical Society, and from it part of what follows is quoted. It was based upon the report of a chief who was of the party and who says that toward the end of January a hundred and fifty Abenakis set out for a place called Iarc [York]. Within six miles of it they found tracks of two Englishmen which three of their people followed, "but they were of the day before." They encamped at the foot of the mountain and climbing it, saw the little town lying along the river banks and along the shore. In the town were perhaps three hundred persons living in about forty houses.

It was Sunday. The Indians were hungry and cold; snow was falling heavily, and a council was called to determine whether to attack or to wait for better weather. Hunger hurried the chiefs to immediate action. Their leader was Madokawando, sachem of the Penobscots.[3]

They separated into two bands and soon made themselves masters of a "fort" (garrison-house) and ten houses—evidently on the outskirts; then scattering "they laid waste everything for about a league and a half in less than two or three hours."

Champigny said that all the houses were burned, but this is disproved by other statements and by inventories made soon after the massacre.

Continuing, the Report says: "Our people spared the lives of a dozen little children[4] and three old women, whom they sent back to a near-by fort with a letter which one of the captives had been made to write." This brought threats to kill all the prisoners if certain conditions were not fulfilled, and boasts of the great compas-

[3] He had been friendly until badly treated by rough settlers who destroyed his people's corn and did other harm. His daughter was one of the four Indian wives of Castine.

[4] Jeremiah, son of Joseph Moulton, a sturdy youngster of four and later a colonel, remembered the attack and his escape through the snow.

sion shown in thus giving up these women and children, adding that the English would not have been so "merciful." The Abbé Casgrain wrote that this was due to the influence of the priest, but Williamson says it was done because the English had recently spared some Indian women and children at Pejepscot.[5] The Indians did not forget a kindness.

One single Indian was killed; of the English, one hundred were killed and eighty-four taken says the chief "who counted them."

Mr. Pike wrote: "Jan. 25 Monday, 10 clock in ye morning, the Indians fell upon York, killed about 48 persons (whereof ye Rev. m^{r} Dummer was one) & Carried Captive 73."

Captain Floyd and his Company "lay in pay at Pascataq," whence he with fifteen from the Great Island and some from the Point hurried off, "but we feare" says a letter from Hooke and Fryer "all will be to Little purpos if God in mercy, doe not devirt them." Floyd's own letter dated January 27[6] says that he made the greatest haste he could for the relief of the people, though he hardly expected that any were left. He found Alcock's and Preble's garrisons standing, but the greatest part of the town had been burned and robbed, "the Heathen had killed & caried captive about 140; 48 of which are killed & 3 or 4 wounded & the rest caried away. Mr. Dum^{r} . . . is barbarously murthered, stript naked, cut & mangled by these sons of Beliall, his wife & family Caried Captive so that there is not only a famine of bread among them by reason of the indians carring away so much of their provision but also a famine of hearing the word of God . . . I have caused all the inhabitants to be in there garisons, 2 at Yorke & the other at Scotland,[7] I have left 12 men there; w^{c} is more than they

[5] "Hist. Maine," I, 629. [6] Arch. 37, 257.

[7] Scotland, still so called, was the second parish of York. Joseph, or "Handkerchief Moody" being its first minister. It was settled by some Scotch royalists, sent over as prisoners after the battle of Dunbar. They were put out to service in different places. The garrison was probably that built by Alexander Maxwell, one of these Scotchmen, and later owned by Micum McIntire.

can provide for one week: for there is a hundred souls in Capt Alcoks house that have their whole dependance upon him for bread & likewise at Leuit Prebles for the houses are all burned & rifled except half a dozen or thereabout." He adds that they have carried away all the powder, the leads from the windows as well as pewter and other lead for their supply of shot. A captive boy who ran away the first night reported about a hundred Indians and no French. He says about seventeen or eighteen houses were burned and advises that men be quickly sent in pursuit to "Amaroscoggin," where "they might happily give them a great blow, but they must have rackets for the snow is very deep. . . . The Indians Incamped that night they went away at Cape Nuttick pond about 5 miles from the town of Yorke & left 30 of their choisest men for their rearguard that night: the snow being so deep we could not follow them."

On the same day a letter was sent to the governor signed by five men of Wells.[8] Its beautiful handwriting is probably that of the Rev. George Burroughs, he who was executed seven months later for witchcraft. It describes "ye insultations of ye heathen enemy, shouting, shooting, hacking (not haveing regard to ye earnest supplications of men women or Children.)." Jeremiah is quoted to prove that "God is still manifesting his displeasure against the Land, he who formerly hath set to his hand to help us, doth even write bitter things against us." They ask for "strength to keep Garrison . . . and also to issue out upon & pursue ye enemy to their discouragement if not destruction. . . . This day two Indians came into Wells with a flagg of truce & said; if ye English will come to Saccadehoc (in a fortnight time three weeks ye outside) they may redeem their captives . . . Signed:

Geo. Burrough
John Littlefield
Jona^n^ Hammond
Joseph Storer
John Hill."

[8] Arch. 37, 259.

Lieutenant Storer asked if some might not be redeemed then and there. The Indians answered: "noe, for they are all gone as far as blew-poynt."[9]

Before dividing their plunder the savage "Christians" sang a Te Deum for their victory, and on the homeward march they chanted their matins and vesper service, as the priests had charged them not to omit the sacred offices if they would be successful in war.

The captives were distributed in the villages where the old men, women and children were astonished by the rich spoils.

In mid-February Captains Alden and Converse are sent "to negotiate the affair [of redemption] the well management whereof is of great concernment." They are to "represent the baseness treachery and barbarities" which are "contrary to the methods of Christian nations . . . having alwaies declined a fair pitched battle, acting like bears and wolves." The Indians are to understand the Regard their Majesties of England have for their territory & good subjects here and to boast of the ships and supplies coming from England; to learn everything possible about the captives; and if they "find any wanting especially of those lately carried from Yorke: Examin that matter strictly and urge it upon them that they have offered foule play unto them and be not gulled by them in their reserve of persons of the best account. Insinuate unto them that we doubt not by the blessing of God to oblige them to deliver our captives without makeing Terms for them; But the severity[s] of the weather are such at this time that the fears of their being exposed by cold and hunger (consisting mostly of women and children) induceth us out of meer pity and compassion unto them to treat in this way for their Redemption, not that we intend the practice thereof for the future.

You are to Insist upon the delivery of all the Captives both formerly and lately fal'n into their hands, especially all those lately carried from York . . . urgeing upon them their promiss

9 Letter from Francis Hooke, Kittery Point.

that they should all be there to be ransomed; But if finally you cannot obtain the whole then agree for all that shall be at the place on the Easyest Terms you can And oblige them by writing under their hands with further Security of hostages or else to return all the Rest at an appointed time and place and for a certain sum."[10]

A week after these orders were given William Vaughan of Portsmouth sent to Boston information brought in by Mr. Francis Tucker, a magistrate of the Great Island, who had been captured at York. He had been taken to Sagadahock, but had escaped on a fishing shallop after Alden and Converse had reached the place.[11] He reported that "after a day or two's capitulation," the Indians agreed upon the ransom of all the prisoners.[12] The commissioners had already received on their sloop thirty-six captives; the rest were dispersed but were being brought in daily. Tucker did not know how much was paid. "Their masters carried them on board, received their pay & Soe march't off," he said. The three principal sagamores were "Maduckawando, Edgeremit & Moxis." With them were about two hundred able fighting men "who have been long abroad." He reported that some Sandy Beach captives had told the Indians that Boston was sending out men with snowshoes, designing a considerable army, and the Indians, seeking but not finding this army in the woods, fell upon York, which does not agree with other statements. He said also that they had sent two captives to Canada "to Satisfie ye French wth ye truth of this Exploit, they formerly not beleiving the Ind^ns^ report of service they doe ag^st^ us."

In a *Mémoire* for 1692, when the services of the Christian Abenakis were recounted, a request was made that the Sillery Indians be included in the rewards granted by the King.[13] In August of the same year Madockawando went to Quebec, taking with him five English prisoners. He saw Governor Frontenac and received a reward.[14]

[10] Arch. 37, 305. [11] Arch. 37, 308.

[12] The appeal for money sent out to all the congregations may be found in Chapter IV. [13] Que. Docs., II, 88. [14] See Nelson, Chapter VIII.

In these reports mention has been made of seven captives sent to Canada. Records of eight who there became Roman Catholics have been found.

In the list of garrison-houses made in November, 1711,[15] we find in York "21 houses, 89 families, 109 men, 30 soldiers and 548 souls." Owners' names of all but two are given; these being at Cape Naddick and Scotland. They held from two to ten families each; Ensign Bragdon's having the largest number. Abraham Prebble, Esq., has the store-house; Moulton's guards the harbor; Richard Milbury has liberty to Garison Mr. Dummer's house; a new one is to be erected between Cape Naddick and the town and liberty is given to two other builders.

Captives

1691/2. Alcock, Mrs. Elizabeth.
Atkinson, Theodore.
    His wife.
Moulton, Joseph, Jr.
    Jeremiah.
Bane, Joseph.
Austin, Mary.
Cooper, Mary.
Dummer, Mrs. Lydia.
    Her son.
Heard, Anne (of Dover).
Milberry, Dorothy.
Moore, William.
    Mary.
Paine, Bethiah.
    Samuel(?).
Parker, Mary.
    Mehitable.

15 Arch. 71, 871-6.

Parsons, John.
Mercy.
Ruth or Richard.
Plaisted, Mrs. Mary.
Sayward, Mary.
Esther.
Tucker, Francis.
Young, Rowland.

1692 } Bragdon, Mrs. Sarah.
1703 } Abiall.

1693. Trafton, Charles.
1697. Moulton, Abel.
1703. Parsons, Hannah and "young daughter." See Wells.
1705. Stover, Joseph.
1710. Harmon, Johnson (taken at Winter Harbor).
? Weber, Barsheba (Marie?).

Cary redeemed the following of York.

Henry Simpson, b. 1670, s. of Henry and Abigail (Moulton). He was killed by Indians at Wells, 5 July, 1697.

Mary Tibs.

Mag[d] Adams, dau. of Mainwaring and Mary (Moulton) Hilton, and wife of Nathaniel, and twice again married.

Left behind in 1695 were

Rob[t] Clark, boy, and

Abiall Masterson, who had "gon to Penacook" when in 1698/9 others returned on the Province Galley. She was the daughter of Nathaniel and must have come back from Penacook because in 1703 she signed a deed with her sister Sarah (Masterson) Bragdon.

On the roll of 1710/11 (of York) are

Jabeth Simpson and

Obediah and Benjamin Preble, sons of Nathaniel, who was killed, and of Priscilla (Maine) who was probably captured. She was absent when her husband's estate was settled in 1692. After her return she mar. —— Carroll.

James Frethy, called of Kittery, was of York, probably son of James and Mary (Milberry). No further reference.

ALCOCK, MRS. ELIZABETH.
ATKINSON, THEODORE.
HIS WIFE.
BANE, JOSEPH, "and many others."

Joseph Bane told the story forty-five years later (1736) in a deposition concerning Madockawando.[16] He said "that in 1691, he was with Theodore Atkinson, late of Newcastle, in N. Hampshire, Esq., said Atkinson's wife, and Mrs. Elizabeth Alcock of Portsmouth, widow, and many others at the house of Joseph Moulton of York . . . when they were taken captive by a large number of Indians."

As Moulton's house is not known to have been a tavern this suggests a party. Moulton was probably killed, although the inventory of "Mr. Joseph Moulton's" estate is dated 12 Oct., 1692, and he was "lately deceased." The few articles "left in a Chest at Lieut. Preble's Garrison" may show how little was needed in the communal life. There was "one Cotton Coverlid, one Vallin, one shawl and some old Pewter."

Two of his sons seem to be among the "many others." The terror experienced by the four-year-old Jeremiah before the Indians released him helped to make the fighting Colonel Jeremiah. "Joseph Moulton of York" is on the list of 1710/11, already a long captivity if it began in this assault.

Alcock, Mrs. Elizabeth, of Portsmouth was probably Elizabeth (Chadbourne), b. 1667, widow of Capt. Samuel.

Atkinson, Theodore (b. 1669, d. 1719), was perhaps the most important of the group.

Madockawando kept him as his own and commanded him to write to the Governor of Massachusetts that a vessel might be sent to Sagadahock with goods to redeem the captives. This was done and Atkinson, his wife and forty more were released.

[16] Drake's "Book of Indians," III, 108.

"*Bean, Joseph*, of York, a young man" was "yett in the Indians Hands" in 1698.

In 1736 he related that he had been sold to an Amaroscoggen Indian and had lived with him until redeemed in 1699.

He learned their language and gained their confidence which made him later a valuable interpreter. Ten years after his redemption when Lieutenant Littlefield sent from Sagadahock for a messenger the Indians asked for Joseph Bane, adding that they would have no other man if he were living.

In 1702 when a lieutenant at Fort Mary, Saco, his hand was "Broke into peeces" by the "spliting of a Gun," The Great and General Court allowed him £20 to pay his colonel for curing the wound, for which he is "humbly thankful," but he had to pay also £4, 10s. "for vittles and Lodging and Attendances" and he begs their "Honnors" to take his sad circumstances into their consideration for he was "but of Late Released from Eight years Captivety with ye indians etc."[17]

Getting what he asked, the next year, "Imboldened by your good nature And many singuller vertues," he entreats the governor "to augment Something to my monthly weages, it being but thirty-six shillings pr month, which is very little considering the trouble that I meets with all, being exposed sometimes to weary and teadius journeys in the woods, viz, formerly to speak with the Indians to come to your Excellency In order for peace, & since that two weary and teadius Journeys &c."[18] This time he is paid £13, and is exempted from his Poll the rest of his life. In 1743 "in his advanced age" he asks for an increase in his pay as interpreter and it was then made £8, 10s., instead of £6.

AUSTIN, MARY.

Dau. of Matthew and Mary (Littlefield).

In 1695 Mary Astin remained still, and in 1710/11 Mary Osten is still there. In the summer of 1708 Lieut. Josiah Littlefield wrote from Montreal that "Mary Austin of York is well."

[17] Arch. 70, 578. [18] Arch. 70, 650.

On the 7 Jan., 1710, Etienne Gibau, twenty-three years old, son of Gabriel Gibau of the parish of La Valterre, and of Suzanne Duvand, living now in this parish, married Marie Elizabeth haustein, daughter of Mathiew haustein and of Marie Littlefield his wife, of the town of York in New England, in the presence of Etienne's brother; Jaques la Selle, his brother-in-law; the Sieur de Senneville and of several other relatives and friends.

Etienne could not write his name but Mary could. Among the witnesses was Marie Françoise (Freedom) French of Deerfield.

Etienne was a carpenter.

On the Notre-Dame register are baptismal records of nine children.

1711, M. Elizabeth, whose godmother was Marie-Joseph Sayer, the only name of a N. E. friend appearing as sponsor. In 1735 M. Elizabeth m. André Langlois in Montreal.
1712, Etienne was baptized; and died 1722.
1714, Jean-Baptiste.
1716, Geneviève, died in 1722.
1718, Marie-Thérèse — the mother's name given as hasting — she m. 1744 Pierre Dubois. Maddox of old England was a witness.
1720, Jacques-Joseph, died 1722.
1722, Jean-François.
1724, Charlotte, m. 1742 Alexis Dubois, and d. 1748.
1725, Antoine, died 1733.

Oct. 4, 1755, Marie Elizabeth Hastin, wife of Etienne Gibau, joiner, was buried in the cemetery near the church (Notre-Dame of Montreal) having died the preceding day about 8 o'clock A. M. and about 68 years old. Present Reverend Amplement and Durumer, priests.

Cooper, Mary.

Dau. of Philip and Anne (Ingalls).

Mary Cooper of York was redeemed by Matthew Cary (1695). Here is her baptismal record.

"The 25th March 1693 was baptized by me, François Dollier, curé de quebec, Marie françoise, English girl, aged twelve years, daughter of philippe coupart (coupard in margin) and Anne ingells his wife: the godmother was marie bari wife of françois sauvin citizen of quebec." May not her father's name — Coupard — have been thus given back to her, for on York records, he is called "Philip Cooper ye Walloone?"

DUMMER, LYDIA (Alcock).

Wife of Rev. Shubael Dummer.

Mrs. Dummer's parentage has been misstated. She has usually been called a Rishworth, but Col. Charles E. Banks has many proofs that she was a daughter of John Alcock of York.

Mr. Dummer was the first ordained minister in Maine, John Wheelwright having been settled, not installed. He, "their godly learned pastor was shot dead off his horse as is supposed"[19] in front of his house "near the sea-side, on a neck of land near what is called Roaring Rock." To Francis Tooke his death did "bespeak Gods dreadfull displeasure agaynst us, the first minister kild in all our warrs."

The grief of the captives was "aggravated" when one of the Indians, dressed in Mr. Dummer's coat, in an insulting manner pretended to preach.

The French letter, already quoted, says "the life and liberty of his [Mr. Dummer's] wife was spared like that of the old women, but that she, having returned twice to demand her son [about twelve years old] who was among the prisoners, they told her that since she wished it, she could increase their number. She no sooner arrived in an Abenaki village than she died of grief." Mr. Vaughan's letter says that she "died in ab[t]: 10 dayes after she was taken."

The careful editors of Sewall's Diary believed that she had no children, but contemporaneous accounts say that "the family was captivated."

19 Sewall "Letter-Book," I, 129.

HEARD, ANNE (of Dover).

Daughter of Benjamin and Elizabeth (Roberts).

"Hannah Heard York" is on the list of 1710/11. The little girl may have been visiting in York at the time of the massacre. At Montreal on "April 10th 1694, *Monseigneur L'illustrissime et Reverendissime* the Bishop of Quebec gave the sacrament of baptism and immediately that of confirmation, to a little English girl named Ann Herd, born at Chistho[20] near Douvres, in New England, of the marriage of Benjamin Herd, shoemaker and of Elisabet Roberts in the year 1681, having been captured by the Mohawks Jan. 25, 1692, living in the service of Pierre Prudhomme master-armorer. Her name of Anne was kept. Her godfather was Monsieur Jean Martinet, called Toublanche. Her godmother Anne Châlet, wife of the said Sr Prudhomme.

Jean frémont Curé."

Perhaps she did not always live with her godparents or they may have died before her marriage, which they did not witness.

"On Monday, Oct. 19, 1705, after one publication of the banns Monsieur de Belmont, Grand Vicar of Monseigneur the Bishop of Quebec having granted the dispensation of the other two, and having found no impediment, I, the undersigned Priest of the Seminary of Villemarie, with the permission of the said Grand Vicar after having received the mutual consent, verbally expressed, of Sebastien Cholet, aged twenty-six years, son of the late Sebastien Cholet, wheat merchant and of Perrine Hilaire, his wife, native of Aubigné in Anjou of one part and of Anne Herd, aged twenty-four years, daughter of Benjamin Herd and of Elizabeth Robberts, his wife, native of Chitcho, near Douvre in New England, of the other part, have married them and given them the nuptial blessing, according to the rites of our Holy Mother Church, in presence of Philippe Robitaille, relative of the bride,[21] of Sieur Nicolas Janvrin Dufrèsne, Merchant, of Jean La Croix, of Jean Hevé and other friends of the bride and groom, who have

20 Cocheco. 21 Husband of Grizel Otis.

all, with the exception of Sieur de Frèsne declared they could not sign, inquiry having been made according to law." Their children were:

Marie-Anne, 1706.

Jean-Baptiste, 1707, m. M. A. Fancher.

M. Marthe, 1709 (Martha French of Deerfield, only thirteen herself, was godmother).

M. Joseph, 1711.

Joseph-Sébastien, 1713.

M. Joseph, 1714; the family living at Pointe Claire.

Sébastien, 1715.

Louis-Sébastien, 1717, at Bout-de l'Isle.

"Anne herd, Englishwoman, married to Sébastien Cholet, called la violette, weaver, established at Villemarie," was naturalized in 1710.

MILBERRY, DOROTHY.

Henry Milberry wrote in 1695: "Unto my Deer Daughter in Captivity with the Indians Dorothy Millbury I will and give the summ of five pounds. In Case she return by Gods good Providence from Captivity but if [partly erased] not till then to be paid; which Legacy I intend not payable by my son at all if she never return." Dorothy Milbury of Yorke was brought home in the Province Galley in January, 1698/9.

MOORE OR MORE, WILLIAM.

MARY.

Children of William and Dorothy (Dixon). William, Sr., died in 1691. By his will William, Jr., and Mary were given "five shillings in good pay." When the estate of the "Widow More of York" was divided at a court held in Kittery in January, 1693/4, it was ordered that: "Whereas William More is uncertain, his portion is to be paid out of the rest that have their parts appointed by the Judge provided said William be alive & demand it." His name is on the list of 1710/11, so he had not demanded before that date. The Division also says: "And if Mary More doo not return from captivity, then her redemption money and her portion to be equally devided among the rest of her brethren and sisters." No other mention of Mary's captivity is found.

PAINE, BETHIA.

Dau. of Thomas and —— Milberry.

Her father, who lived on the eastern side of York River may have been killed in the attack. She was brought home in the *Province Galley* 1698/9. Henry Milberry left ten shillings to his grandchild Bethiah Paine, but does not mention her captivity. She was unmarried in 1711 when she sold land that had belonged to her father.

Samuel Paine has been mentioned as a possible captive.

PARKER, MARY, b. 1676.
MEHITABLE, b. 1684.

Daughters of John and Sarah (Green).

Mary was yet a captive in January, 1698/9, when her sister was redeemed. In 1707 at York, Mehitable married John Harmon.

PARSONS, JOHN.
MERCY.
RUTH OR RICHARD.

Children of John and Elizabeth ——.

John and Mercy can be identified. "Ruth or Richard" must be counted a lost captive. The York town records, destroyed in 1692, were again begun in 1695, but several earlier dates have been entered. Among them is that of the birth of John, eldest child of John Parsons and Elizabeth ——, born 31 July, 1677; a marginal note says "baptized in Canada 20 April 1693." Here is the record: "The 20th April 1693, was baptized by me François Dupré, *curé de Québec*, Jean, aged sixteen years, English son of

Jean persan and elizabeth pansan his wife. His godfather was Louis Sainson, called beauieu who signed . . .

John Pasons Louis Sainson, Dubreuil

François Dupré"

"Jn° Parsons Boy, Dover" is on the list of those remaining in 1695, as is "Rich Persons boy." On a list given at the peace of Casco in 1698/9 are the names of Ruth and John. We may be sure that these are all York names. It is known that there was a Ruth of York, but Richard's name is not found there. Colonel Banks says that a Rachel was born about 1685. Mercy was the seventh and youngest child of John Parsons. The day but not the year of her birth is recorded. She, "Marcy Parsons" of York, was a captive still in 1710/11.

Plaisted, Mary (Rishworth | White | Sayward | Hull), b. 1660.

Mary was the daughter of Edward Rishworth or Rushworth of Exeter, Wells and York and of Susannah Wheelwright whose father was the Rev. John of Boston, Exeter and Wells.

James Plaisted was Mary's fourth husband, she having had the marrying habit.

Her grandfather Wheelwright in his will of 1679 names "my grandchild, Mary White, daughter of ye said Rishworth." The identity of White is not discovered; possibly he was the William whose name is found with Edward Rishworth's.

Before 1681 she had married John Sayward. He died in 1689 and in February of the next year she is Mrs. Mary Hull when she takes her oath upon the inventory of her father's estate. Hull was Phineas of Saco and York, but he soon died leaving an estate of £39, 0s., 6d., and at the time of the massacre, when only thirty-two years old, she was the wife of James Plaisted.

Taken with her were two Sayward daughters — Mary and Esther, aged respectively eleven and seven.

Cotton Mather, the unreliable, gives her a third captive child,[22]

[22] As does family tradition. She was taken from the Rishworth home on the north bank of what is now Cider Hill Creek.

a baby boy of three weeks, and describes the great suffering of the mother on her journey because of her lack of strength and food. He says her master finally killed the baby and threw its little body into a river; then he told the poor woman that now, eased of her burden, she must walk faster than before.

In the very next paragraph,[23] Mather tells a similar story of Mary Plaisted's sister-in-law, Mehitable(Plaisted)Goodwin. Was the tale true of both women or did he repeat it because of similarity of name?

James Plaisted who wrote the "Bearths of His children" in the old book of town records did not name this one, who would have been his eldest, or possibly the posthumous child of Mary's third husband. He wrote the names of four Saywards, thus adopting them, and two Plaisteds, born after his wife's redemption.

The Indians must have soon sold Mrs. Plaisted to the French for in Montreal, "On 8th December, 1693, was baptized *sous condition* an English woman from New England, named in her country Marie, who born at York 8th January O. S. 1660, of the marriage of Edouard Rishworth and Suzanne Willwright both Protestants of Lincoln in old England and married last to Jacques Pleisted, Protestant of New England, was captured the 25th January O. S. of the year 1692 with two of her children, Marie Genevieve Sayer[24] born the 4th April O. S. 1681 and Marie Joseph Sayer born 9 March O. S. 1685, by the savages of Acadia, and now lives in the service of Damoiselle Catherine Gauchet, widow of M. Jean Batiste Migeon, appointed by the King first lieutenant-general of the bailiwick established by his Majesty in Villemarie. Her name of Marie has been kept, to which was added that of Madeleine. She had for godfather Monsieur Jean Batiste Juchereau,

[23] Magnalia, II, 599.

[24] Sayward, Sawyer, Sayer are used indiscriminately. In the register the names of girls are interlined and it is written that "The two Demoiselles Sayer were baptized the same day as their mother." As they are not therein recorded it is probable that the act was in the convent chapel of which no records were kept.

lieutenant-general of the Royal bailiwick of Monreal, and for godmother, Damoiselle Madeleine Louise Juchereau." Signed by Marie Madeleine Pleistead, her godparents and Jean Frémont curé.

"Mrs. Mary Plasted York" was redeemed by Carey in 1695.

Was it because she could not turn again quickly to her old faith after her redemption that she was in 1696 presented at the Court "for not attending ye public worship of God upon ye Lords Day"? James, appearing for her, paid a fine of 4s., 6d. Mary was admonished, but she "an aged widow" was on the church list of 1754.

Happy though James must have been at his wife's return, the first child born to them was named for his first wife Lydia, and the next for his mother, Olife.

Father Meriel, never forgetting the converts, sent her his "commendations" in a letter to Johnson Harmon.

She settled the estate of John Sayward, her second husband, making her first account in 1715. It is interesting to note that the "mourning clothes" were the largest item, but "Drink" for the funeral cost four times as much as the coffin and the grave.

In the account are costs for "bringing up the children." For "Easther," then "at Canada," seven pounds annually for three years was charged. She was four when her father died. Mary was nearly eight and no charge stands against her name. This is explained by the decision of the probate judges that children of seven were self-supporting; that is, masters could be found willing to assume the charge of the upbringing, anticipating returns out of their labor before they reached their majority.

In the divison of real property John, only son, has his double portion; and the share of each girl is £19, 2s., 11⅓d. In the record of a controversy between Mary Plaisted and her son John Sayward it is stated that "ye shares of Esther & Mary Sayward, now in Canada, remains to them if demanded."[25] Did they demand?

The Plaisted home was about three miles inland from the har-

[25] York County Court Records.

bor. Mrs. Mary was living there in 1722/3 as she was, doubtless a little later, when her daughter Esther came to New England.

SAYWARD, MARY.
ESTHER.

On the list of "Thos remaining" in 1695 are "Mary Sayard girll Dover and Ester Swayard Do." In 1710 they are called Mary Sawyerd and Herster Saywerd from York.

Mary, baptized Marie Geneviève, was taught by the Sisters of the Congregation, and about 1699 gave up her baptismal name to take her vows in their Order as *Soeur Marie-des-Anges*. Probably Marguerite Bourgeoys was present at the ceremony. *Marie-des-Anges* was sent to the Mission at Sault-au-Recollet as Superior of the few Sisters who were on duty there, and she must have been very kind to her fellow-captives, the little English pupils, one of whom was Abigail Nims of Deerfield.

"*Angloise*" written in the margin of a Quebec register leads to the following: "The 28th March, 1717, was buried in the Parish Church[26] Sister *Marie-des-Anges*, a mission sister of the Congregation, who died the same day, aged about 36 years. The burial was made by me, the undersigned priest, Vicar of the Parish, Canon of the Cathedral, in presence of M. Glandelet, Dean and M. Des Maizerets, precentor of said Cathedral."

She died in the convent which was in the Lower Town. "The choice of *Soeur-des-Anges* for residence in Quebec proves the great esteem with which this dear sister was regarded by the Superior, for there were sent to the Episcopal city only those Sisters distinguished by the virtues of courage and prudence." So writes a nun of the Order to Miss Baker in 1896. She adds: "I am proud to tell you that this honor was shared by Lydia Longley,[27] called Ste. Madeleine and the Sisters Raizenne and Sabourin, daughters and granddaughters of Abigail Nims and Sara Hanson,[28] who all worked successfully in Quebec and adjacent places."

[26] In the chapel dedicated to Notre-Dame de Pitié.

[27] See Groton, Chapter X. [28] See Chapters XVI and XVIII.

Esther Sayward,

Known in Canada as Marie-Joseph Sayer, probably educated by the nuns, was naturalized in May, 1710, and in Montreal on "January 5, 1712 after having obtained the dispensation of the three banns I, undersigned curate of the parish of Villemarie, having received the mutual consent of Sieur Pierre de Lestage, Merchant of this town and of Damoiselle Marie Joseph Sayeres English woman, have married them in the presence of Jaques Le Ber, *Ecuyer*, Sieur de Senneville and Estienne Rocbert, Keeper of the King's stores in this town, of francois Bere, *Ecuyer*, Ensign in the troops of this country, Estienne Veron, Sieur de Grand Mesnil and of several other relatives and friends of the parties." The bride signs: "Marie Joseph Sayer." Their first child, Marie Joseph, was born Oct. 1, 1712. Its godmother, Marie hardin, "could not sign the record, on account of her great age." In the baptismal record of the second, Jacques-Pierre, the father, is called "*Marchand Bourgeois* of this city and treasurer for the King." In 1718 he bought the seigniory of Berthier — opposite Sorel — "with the adjacent islands and islets." He built there a house for himself, a stone church and a sawmill. Six years later the mill and much wood, both cut and standing, were destroyed by fire; but not "his zeal." On the contrary, to encourage the coming of *habitants*, he built a grist mill, rebuilt the sawmill and asked for further grants and privileges from Governor Beauharnois, which were given because "he was worthy of it."

We hear of him in 1725 as living at Longueuil. Mr. Atkinson, one of the commissioners coming to Montreal, writes that they were entertained there at "Mr. Laphashs" on account of Captain Jordan having married his wife's sister (Capt. Samuel Jordan, interpreter, had married Olive Plaisted, half-sister to Esther Sayward).

While in Montreal Atkinson wrote: 7 March, "Sabath This Day nothing remarkable, visited Mons Lestage at night."

Evidently Samuel Jordan asked Esther to go home with him

for Atkinson says that putting down the river on April 20th they camped early for some of the company was behind, and "about Sun down Mad^{m} L Stage over tooke us a Mircht wife bound for N:E: to See here relatives She being an English Wo: Daughter to Mr Plaisted of York." Did he refer to her again and perhaps to her friend Mary (Storer) Gaultier, who was doubtless with her in this confused entry of May first? "We left Mad^{m} Cono [canoe, this being the spelling of the "honorable gentleman"] And passed on with our Lougage one half at a time being too heavy and being all absent. Mad^{m} had ord^{d} a fire to Day her tent was ticken & while we were absent it fired & burnt almost up." That night they "got down to Sarritogue about Sun Set."

The route of the commissioners may be found in "Redemptions." Probably the women went down the Hudson and by water to Rhode Island.

Did Esther go first to the Jordan home on the banks of the Saco and there see her half-sister for the first time?

Surely we may picture her visiting what is now called "the Barrell house" on York River at its junction with the mill pond, where her people used to grind their neighbors' grists? That house, built by Jeremiah Moulton, was bought in 1720 by Esther's cousin, Henry Sayward, whose descendants own it. And how long did Esther tarry in her mother's inland home? Her own country must have seemed very strange to her. Did she and her mother have a common language and did she demand her share?

If she returned to Canada with Mary (Storer) Gaultier, as is probable, her visit was short.

In 1743 Esther's husband died. His burial is recorded in the Register of Notre-Dame. "The twenty-second December, 1743 was brought into this church the body of S^{r} pierre lestage, merchant, aged about sixty-two years deceased the day preceding at eight o'clock in the morning, for whom was a solemn service and the body was then taken to the church of the Rev. recollet fathers there to be buried." Priest, ecclesiastic and "all the clergy" were present and signed. To be buried in that church was a mark of distinction. *"Pierre de Lestages, Sieur Desperons, Seigneur de St. Pierre les Becquets et autres lieux,"* divided his fortune between his wife, sister and nephew; the last two living in his old home of Bayonne, France.

Their children died young (Tanguay's Dictionary names also *Pierre René* of La Prairie as their son, but the date of birth, given by Tanguay, the father's will and other facts disprove it).

Mme. de Lestage, now alone, turned to her beloved nuns. Buying a house on Saint-Jean-Baptiste Street, next to their convent, she was allowed to cut a door between the two buildings. She adopted two little orphans who were educated by the Sisters and who afterwards joined the Order. They remembered how as children they used to be led through the connecting door into the recreation-hall of the Sisters.

From the foundation of the convent until 1848 the nuns received at the Mother House as "permanent boarders" maiden ladies and widows, who not having any religious vocation loved to live retired from the world that they might serve God more easily. Marguerite Bourgeoys found these *"Soeurs associées,"* or perpetual boarders, "very inconvenient," and asked Monseigneur if he insisted upon their remaining to please make the same rules that were in other Orders.

For more than twenty years Mme. de Lestage was of the Sisters' household. They called her their "Illustrious benefactress." She bought for their chapel twelve fine, tall, silver candlesticks. She gave to them her household furniture, of which the few remnants left by fire are still used; and she freely bestowed her money, saving but a small income for herself. The contract of a gift made in 1769 is in their archives.

The Annals of the Ursulines of Quebec, too, record that she never tired in generosity or in showing her affection for her cousin, *La Mère de l'Enfant Jésus* (Esther Wheelwright).

In 1750 she transferred her rights in the Seigniory of Berthier

Notre-Dame de la Congrégation

to the Bayonne nephew, keeping an annuity of fifteen hundred livres ($250). Major Nath. Wheelwright lodged at Berthier in 1754 on his way from Quebec to Montreal, and "Mons. Courthian," brother of the Bayonne nephew, accompanied him along the fine road by the river to Montreal. A month later, Wheelwright wrote in his Journal: "Apr. 21, Sunday morning, parted with Madam Lestage, from whom I not only received many civilitys, but many distinguished marks of her affection."[29] She died Jan. 17, 1770, in the convent and was buried in the Chapel of Sainte-Anne in the parish church of Notre-Dame. In the city's growth the dead of this church have been twice moved; their last resting place being the cemetery at the *Côte des Neiges.*

It is interesting to note that after her marriage, she writes her name "esther sayer" and "esther marie joseph Sayer Lestage."

TUCKER, "MR." FRANCIS.

Merchant and magistrate of New Castle; b. abt. 1651.

Was he, perhaps, one of "the others" taken with Atkinson from Joseph Moulton's house? His escape from Sagadahock has been mentioned.

He was a Selectman in 1693.

YOUNG, ROWLAND.

Although "Roland Young boy Dover" is on the list of "thos Remaining" in 1695 it is an error. He was of York, the son of Job and Sarah (Austin). He returned, married Hannah Preble and had a large family.

1692-1703.

BRAGDON, SARAH (Masterson), wife of Captain Arthur and mother of Abiall, Arthur's "eldest daughter."

Mrs. Sarah Bragdon was daughter of Nathaniel Masterson and Elizabeth (Coggswell).

She was captured in 1692 and as "Sarah Braginton of Yorcke" was "yett in the Indians Hands in January 1698/9."

29 MS. in Mass. Hist. Soc.

Ann Jenkins[30] testified in 1695 that Sarah Bragginton had been bought by the Indian minister Prince Waxaway (whoever he may have been) and was thus freed from "hard usage." That princely Indian could not have kept her long for she was at home and was killed in 1703 when her daughter

Abiall was captured. From Pike's Journal we learn that on Oct. 13, 1703,[31] "about sun-set the Indians stole in upon Arthur Bragdon's house at York, (hard by the gar:) killed his wife and two children Carried his eldest daughter Captive."

Penhallow says: "Another Company of Indians, commanded by Sampson fell on York, where they slew Arthur Brandon's wife and five Children,[32] carried Captive with them the Widow Parsons and her Dau."[33] Abiall is on the 1710/11 list. Her fate is unknown.

There were several Arthur Bragdons. This one was a weaver and lived near Cider Hill; therefore the garrison "hard by" must have been that of Samuel Came. Others "hard by" were built later.

1693, *May*.

TRAFTON, CHARLES.

Son of Thomas and Elizabeth (Moore).

"Charles Trafton—York, boy" was of "thos Remaining" in 1695 and also in 1710/11. "On Sunday, Sept. 12th 1694 was solemnly baptized a young Englishman named in his own country Charles, who born at York, near Boston in New England, in the month of May of the year 1681, of the marriage of Thomas Trafton and Elizabeth Moore, both Protestants, having been taken in the beginning of May of the year 1693 by the Abenakis has lived since that time in the service of the High and Mighty Seigneur Louis de Buade de Frontenac, Chevalier, Comte de Pallieau Councillor of the King in his Councils Governor and Lieutenant General for the King in Canada, Acadia the Island of New-

[30] See Oyster River, Chapter X. [31] Hist. Wells gives 26 Sept.

[32] Pike's number is thought correct. [33] See Wells, Chapter XIV.

foundland and other countries of France Septentrionale. The name of Charles, which this young Englishman bore was changed at baptism to Louis Marie. His godfather was the same Seigneur Comte de Frontenac, his godmother Dame Marie Madeleine Chaspoux wife of Messire Jean Bochat de Champigny N (illegible) and other places. King's Councillor, Intendant of justice, police and finance in New France, who all signed.

Frontenac
Marie Louis Trafton

M. Caille, vicaire."

Louis Marie Strafton, gunsmith, petitions for naturalization in 1706. That same year his brother Benjamin "intending A vige to sea," makes his will and does not mention Charles; but he is named in the division of his father's estate in 1707 as follows: "wee appoint the fulling mill to Charles Trafton for which he is to pay six pounds of the Debts and if said Charles do not retorne from Captivity his part or portion is to remaine in the hands of the administrator (Josiah Mayne) till the rent thereof pay the said six pounds"

And Charles returned, induced perhaps by that "double share in his father's estate" for which he gave his brother Zaccheus a receipt in 1716.[34] He is not among those to whom Letters of Naturalization were given in 1710. This may have been an error of omission, or he may have left Canada, although the date of the receipt suggests a later return. He married Sarah (Linscott) Dill, widow of John. His name is found on many deeds. In 1721 he made a will which was not proved until 1748; in it he names wife, brothers and sisters, but no children.

1697, *May* 20.
MOULTON, ABEL.

On this day Pike wrote: "Young Moulton taken by the Indians at York." Is not this the son of Jeremiah and nephew of

[34] From 1693 to 1806, in the Province of Maine, the eldest son of an intestate had two shares, a double portion of the whole estate.

Joseph, and probably the "Able Morton drowned" on the 1698/9 list? Jeremiah's Abel was born about 1678 and nothing is known about him.

1705, *October* 20.
STOVER, JOSEPH.

Son of John and Abigail (Alcock).

"Ye Widow Elizabh Stover late of Cape Neddick" after her husband's death "maintained her fort . . . She was very redy and forword to supplye Soldiers with beefe and other provisions upon their march . . . but she was neglected." Her neighbors left her and her sons removed; so in 1691 Elizabeth went away.[35]

Perhaps the "neglected" fort encouraged the attack upon the house of John Stover, who was Elizabeth's son, and who lived "near the garrison at Cape Neddick." The account in the "Boston News-Letter" says: "On Saturday the 20th Currant, about 20 Indians appeared at Cape Nidduck, and Carried away 4 Sons of John Stover, who were at a little distance from the Garison; several others that were out of the Garison retired to it with all speed; on which the Enemy fired about an hour, then drew up the Children in sight of the Garison and marched off." It says further that "Capt. Browne at Wells hearing of the unhappy Enterprize in Carrying away the 4 Children from 3 to 12 years of Age" hurried to their rescue. There were two crossings on the little river near Saco so he divided his company. He overtook, wounded and killed some of the enemy, but did not recover the children; Penhallow,[36] after describing the attack which he says was on the fifteenth, adds "The youngest, not able to travel was knockt in the head; the other three were carried captive, but being attacked by Lieut. James March, and losing one of their company they killed a second child in way of revenge." The fate of the third is unknown, but Joseph, the fourth, reached Canada; if he returned is not known.

"On Thursday, 24 Feb. 1707, was baptized *sous condition* by

[35] Arch. III, 381. [36] "Indian Wars," 41.

me, the priest undersigned Joseph Stover, son of Jean Stover inhabitant of Cape Nadick between York and Wells in New England and of Abigail —— his wife, both Protestants, who was born —— 1690, having been captured in the spring (sic) of last year and ransomed by Françoise Domitille, Abenakise living among the French, has been sent by her to Monreal. The godfather was Gilbert Maillet, Master Mason. The godmother, Jeanne Dumonthel, wife of Pierre Biron, who have declared they do not know how to sign, inquiry as to this having been made according to law Meriel Priest."

The Abenakise, evidently a kindly convert, may have married a Frenchman.

Joseph Stover was naturalized in 1710.

One of his name, married, was living in York in 1730.

The year after the children were captured Governor Dudley demanded their release. He sent a ship to Port Royal in April, 1706, with prisoners to be exchanged and orders to "acquaint M. Bonaventure [temporarily in command of Acadia, after the death of the governor] that there are three little boys caryed away last summer supposed at Penobscot; I desire him to Demand them of the Indians and let me have them. The boys are sons of John Stover."

1710, *October* 8. *At Winter Harbor.*

HARMON, JOHNSON.

B. 1680; son of John of Saco and York and Deborah (Johnson) Foxwell).

He was not averse to fishing on the Lord's Day for at Winter Harbor on Sunday, Sept. 21, 1707, he was one of those who repulsed "fifty canoos" of Indians.[37] "The men warc all Good and Valliant that ware thair Lieu^{t} Astin of York & Johnson Harmon, dacon of the church of York. The Indians pursued our men fore miles to see," so said another account.

Three years later he was captured at Winter Harbor.

[37] Arch. 71, 429.

Major Livingstone saw a captive at the Island of Lett[38] who told him that there were about a hundred and fifty soldiers in the attacking party, that three men were killed and he, the informant, was one of six who were taken. Later, in Quebec, the major wrote: "Dec. 11, This day Johnson Harmon, an English prisoner came to see me."

Vaudreuil wrote to Dudley June 16, 1711, that Harmon, having represented that he had sufficient influence to effect an exchange of the "Sr de beaumeny" for himself, has been allowed to go to New England to beg for that exchange, and has given a note and his word of honor that he will return immediately if Dudley does not send back the Frenchman.

Vaudreuil used the opportunity to send back Major Livingstone's servant, who had been detained by illness, and that no accident should befall on their journey three Frenchmen went with them as far as Orange, as is told in "Redemptions." Vaudreuil believes that his own honest behavior—ignoring the true reason of the Frenchmen's visit—will make Dudley act as honorably and he is sure that if the "S^r^ de beaumeny" is not sent back that the said "Johnson harmon" will be immediately.

The S^r^ de beaumeny was Ensign Beauvenire de Verchères, taken at Haverhill in 1708, but he was not sent back immediately nor did Harmon return.

While Harmon was at Chambly on his way home he received a long letter from Father Meriel, written in English.[39] Dated 25 July, 1711, it recounts the success of the King's armies and the great superiority of the army of Flanders over that of Marlborough. He mentions vessels that are expected from France; the dissolution of the English Parliament, the efforts made to redeem Eunice Williams, and sends messages to former captives and friends.

Arrived in New England Harmon presented the following to the Governor and Court: "Y^r^ Petitioner being about his Lawful

[38] See p. 88. [39] Arch. 51, 212-213, which Miss Baker printed in "True Stories."

Occasions at Winter Harbour on the 8th day of October last, was taken Captive by a party of Penobscot & Kennebeck Indians & by them Carried to Quebecq in Canada, where he continued A Prisoner untill the 22d day of may following, Having Borrowed some money of Majr Levingston & other friends, by it prevailed on Maj Parotte to come home to see his family & settle his affairs, Providence favouring this good humor of Monsr De Vaudrieull, and his Excellency's Goodness to Return A prisoner from here in his Room (which favour is for Ever to be Acknowledged) But now he is Comanded Away in the present Expedition (wherein he hopes & designs to do Some Signall Service) But his misfortunes are such by this Imprisonmt & his affairs are Such that all that is dear & good to him lies at Stake & his family Suffer Extreamly for want of his being at home &c Therefore he humbly prays this Honble assembly to Consider the Great fateigue & Expence he hath been at & the poor Circumstances of his family and affairs, & to afford them Some Support & help to fit himself out in his Station this Expedition as in yor Wisdom Shall seem meet"—It is dated July 24, 1711. Twenty pounds from the treasury of the province was given him.

"Boveney" had been a prisoner two years when Dudley sent him from Boston with letters to Vaudreuil concerning the exchange of prisoners—there were forty-three in Massachusetts—but he was detained by the "Gentlemen at Albany," who did not consider it expedient to let him proceed, and they said "the Roads are such at present as he could not possibly wade through." Albany begs Massachusetts to give her notice of all such as are to be sent that way. There were frequent clashings between the two governments. Dudley describes his young prisoner as "a poor Country Boy," for whom he had received "Captain Harmon, a very Good Officer," whom he will be obliged to return if the boy is not allowed to go home. A bill of charges for his "keeping" for "13 or 14 Months" shows that roads grew dry and wet again

[40] Arch. 71, 819.

ere they let him go; but Johnson Harmon was not sent back. He stayed to serve his country as is shown by his Memorial of 1727 in which he asks for a grant of two hundred acres because of his many services in divers capacities and offices in the wars against the Indians. Among these was the expedition against Norridgewock, of which Captain Westbrook, writing from Falmouth Aug. 18, 1724, says: "Capt Harmon arrived this day with the Fryars and Twenty Six scalps more from Norridgewock and brought Bombazeens Squaw and three more Indian Captives, retook three English boys; he Informed a great number of Indians are comeing on our front . . . God has now been pleasd to Crown your Honours unwearied Endeavours with success, which I desire to rejoyce at. I hope yr Honour will smile on Captn Harmon and favour him with a Commission for a feild officer."[41] He was made a lieutenant-colonel.

Harmon's wife was Mary, daughter of Jeremiah Moulton. They had seven children. Their house was just below Sewall's Bridge, on the left bank of the river. It, or another on its site, is still occupied. The family later lived in Harpswell.

WEBER, BARSHEBA,
MARIE. } ?

The daughter of Samuel and Deborah? Deborah Webber of York, "being old and weak and infirm'd in Body but of perfect mind and Memory" gives to each of her seven children five shillings, and one of the seven is: "(Barsheba who is now in Canada)." The will was proved 23 April, 1737. Was not the testator Deborah (Littlefield), widow of Samuel who was son of Thomas?

Samuel, b. 1658 at Falmouth, lived there until driven off by Indians in the second war. The family seems to have first gone to Gloucester and later to Cape Neddick where in 1691 they were living in a garrison-house. His will, proved in 1716, does not name Barsheba.

[41] Arch. 52, 34.

In 1716 Samuel and Deborah (she making her mark) deeded about forty acres of land on Cape Neddick River to their sons Thomas and Benjamin, keeping one half acre at the old sawmill.

Is not Deborah's "Barsheba, now in Canada," the English girl of the following record? On "17 February 1714" was baptized in Quebec "an English girl named Wabert aged twelve years, to whom was given the name of Marie. Her godfather was le Sieur Louis Guerain and her godmother Dame Héléne Lemieux who have declared they did not know how to sign," and is not Barsheba now the Marie, "daughter of Samuel," who marries on "March 11, 1720 Mgr. of Quebec having granted by a *billet* of the preceding day the dispensation of the time prohibited and the publication of the three banns of marriage between Joseph Saleur, son of Claude Saleur and of Marie Magd. henri, his father and mother, parish of St. Martin, town and diocese —— of one part and marie Wabert daughter of Samuel Wabert and of —— her father and mother of New England of the other part; having discovered no impediment to the marriage, we, the undersigned curé and official of Quebec have married them according to the form prescribed by the Holy Church in presence of the relatives and the undersigned." Marie Waber signed.

The children of Joseph Saleur (bourgeois), son of Claude and M. Magd. Henry of St. Martin ville de Metz, were:

M. Joseph, b. 1720.
M. Jacques, b. and d. 1723.
Jos.-Louis, b. and d. 1724.
Joseph, b. and d. 1726.
M. Françoise, b. 1728.
J. Bapt.-Joseph, b. and d. 1730.

CHAPTER X

Oyster River and Groton

I

Oyster River (Durham)

1689 — 1694 — 1705 — 1707

1689. Huckins, Sarah (Burnham).
"The daughter of one Willis."
Willey, Abigail (w. of Stephen), and daughters, perhaps
Abigail.
Judy.
Elizabeth.

1694. Adams, Mercy.
Davis, "Two daughters" of John.
Sarah?
Mary Ann?
Dean, John's wife and child.
Denbow, Peter.
Derry, John.
Deliverance.
John or Joseph.
Drew, Thomas.
Tamsen.
Edgerly, Thomas, Sen.
Joseph.
"A daughter."
Some children of Thomas, Jr.
Emerson, Judah (Davis).
Jenkins, Ann.
Three children.

Rand, Samuel.
Remembrance.
Watson, Mrs. Hannah.
Joseph.
1707. Drew, Lydia (Marie-Anne).
Lomax, Elizabeth.

Other Oyster River names are on the lists of 1695 and 1710/11. Three of these are: Eliz^h Smart, Sara Whitt, not identified, and Joseph Thomas; Stackpole says he was s. of James and Mary (Smith), that he m. Abigail Jones and lived until about 1795. If these dates are correct and if he were the 1710 captive he must have been taken when very young.

James, Thomas and Mary Huckins on the 1710/11 list are not identified.

Until 1732 Oyster River was within the township of Dover. It suffered from Indian attacks between 1675 and 1725. In August, 1689, not long after the massacre at Dover, the garrison-house of Lieut. James Huggins (Huckins) was attacked by Indians who had watched the eighteen men who lived in it go out to their fields. These they killed or captured. Three women and two boys, one of whom was lame, bravely defended the house. Only when the roof was burning did they yield; only then because of the Indians' promise to spare all their lives; yet some they killed and the rest they carried away.[1] The next September Captain Church sent a letter to Governor Hinckley of Plymouth[2] saying that at Fort Androscoggin (Laurel Hill, Auburn) "We found a prety deal of corn in barnes under ground and destroyed it, also guns and amunition a prety deal with beaver, and we took 5 English Captives viz: Lieut. Robert [probably mistaken for James] Hookins his widow of Oyster River, Benjamin Barnards wife of Salmon Falls, Ann Heard of Cochecho, one Willises daughter of Oyster River and a boy of Exeter."

The Huckins widow must have been Sarah (Burnham) whose

1 "Maine Hist. Coll.," IX, 57. 2 Dexter's Ed. "Church's Wars," II, 72.

husband was James and who married in October, 1700, Capt. John Woodman. She died before 1705 for he did not name her in his will.

The daughter of one Willis is not identified. Others of the name, Willis or Willey, are found in Canada.

1689.

WILLEY-WILLIS.

The New England and Canadian records of those named Willey or Willis (pronounced alike in French) are confusing. To add to the perplexity there were at the same time in Canada some of the name from Old England.

On the Canadian registers we find Marie Louise Pitman, who was Stephen Willey's wife, and her two daughters, Marie Magdeleine and Marie; these baptismal names alone being given. We find also Marie Magdeleine Thérèse confirmed in 1693; Marie Magdeleine, married to one named Vildaigre, *garde-port* of Quebec, who was naturalized in 1710; and in Dec., 1697, Madeleine Ouëlli—plainly the same name—was received by the Ursulines of Quebec as a *pensionnaire perpetuelle.*[3] She was to pay fifty *écus* for her board and to give her trousseau upon entering. M. Montigny, the Superior, opposed her coming, but the Sisters received her out of charity for a poor stranger who was besides very virtuous.[4] She surely must have come from England for no young girl from New England could have been possessed of money and a trousseau! The Oyster River captives are:

ABIGAIL, wife of Stephen and dau. of William Pitman of Dover and Barbara (Evans) and either two or three daughters.

Among those remaining in 1695 are "Abig^{ll}, Judy and Eliz^{h} Willey."

Abigail probably was redeemed for her father named her in his "deed of gift" later quoted. Are not the Marie Magdeleine and

[3] See Sayward-Lestage, Chapter IX.

[4] *"Ursulines de Québec,"* I, 457.

Marie of New France the Judy and Eliz^h of New England?[5]

Stephen Willey, son of Thomas, lived at Oyster River Point. He was such a painful consort that captivity—even before it gave her a new and doubtless kindlier husband—must have held charms for the wife of his youth and abuse.

At this period all persons were not equal before the law: "a gentleman could not be punished with stripes," nor by common law could a man beat his wife with a stick bigger than his thumb. Stephen Willey exceeded his legal privilege. Abigail, his wife, presenting to the "Much Honored" Sessions of the Court at Portsmouth on Sept. 27, 1683, the story of her "deplorable and distressed condition" says: I, "Humbly showing the great grief of my heart, the unquiet and uncomfortable life I have for several years past lived and spent . . . with Stephen Willy my husband, often suffering much by sore and heavy blows received from his hand, too much for any weak woman to bear, as also by frequent threatening to take away my life by the evil disposition of his own mind, seeing that neither his own relations, neither my own natural brothers dare countenance in any way of natural friendship, but that I must become the suffering subject of his insatial jealousy; all which I hope will fully appear to the honored authority. When you have considered his drawing me before Judge Edgerly and at his own request procured of said judge the Shameful sentence of ten Stripes to be laid upon me at a post which sentence was, by much persuasion, reversed by Judge Edgerly and twenty shillings in money taken by him in place thereof; and afterward I, giving a visit to one of my own sisters at Kittery said judge sent after me as a runaway to be procured; the second time to be dealt with according to law. I hope his own conscience convincing him was not quiet at first, For relief in the premises I humbly implore your honored authorities' clemency and favor."[6] John Willey testified that he saw his brother throw his wife down, heave a hoe at her,

[5] Stackpole in "Hist. of Durham" names only Thomas, b. 1671, Abigail and Marie Magdeleine, which last is from the Canadian record.

[6] "Coll. N. H. Hist. Soc.," VIII, 147, doubtless corrected spelling.

and that he saved her life by taking an axe from his threatening hands. Captivity must have spelled freedom for this poor woman, however great was "the clemency" of the "honored authorities" of New Hampshire.

The service of Messire Hector de Callières must have been pleasanter than that of Stephen, the "insatial jealous" one; and she probably found comfort in her new Church.

"On Tuesday 8th Dec. 1693, was baptized an English woman of New England, called in her country Abigail. She was born at Peskatoüe, 15 Nov. O. S. of the year 1657, of the marriage of William Pitman and Barbe [Barbara Evans] both Protestants of old England; married to Etienne Willis, Protestant of New England, was taken by the Indians in October 1689, and lives now in the service of Messire Hector de Callières, Chevalier, Governor for the King in the Island of Monréal and adjacent places. She was named in the baptism Marie Louise & had for her godfather the same seigneur Chevalier de Calieres and for godmother, Damoiselle Marguerite Renée Denis widow of Monsieur la Nauguière[7] in his lifetime Captain of the Guards of Monsieur the Count of Frontenac, Governor General of New France. Signed by

Le Sr de Calliere

Marguerite renée denis

Jean fremone curé."

Before her capture she received three shillings by the will of her father, William Pitman, blacksmith. After her capture, her husband believing her dead or forever lost, or perhaps more jealous than before, ignored her in the deed of gift he made in 1696 when he, "bound to Sea on a voyage in shipp Unity . . . for Barbadoes" said "I do if death should Seize me or in case of my never Returne to new England Give Grant and Bequeath unto my Sonn Thomas Willy" the dwelling-house 50 acres of land "two Oxen, one Cow, one Calfe and all my Sheep wherever they may be

[7] Sometimes Naudière de la Perade.

found"; and to his daughter "Abigall" land he had bought of Bernard Squire at little Bay, "Together with one Cow and a Calfe and Two Sheep for ever (my owne mortality as above Exprest and Excepted)."[8] This was recorded in 1700, so Stephen had then died.

Abigail, now "Marie Louise Pilman, widow of Estienne Willis living at Quebec" received naturalization in 1710. That year she married in Quebec.

"Oct. 6th 1710 after the Publication of the three Banns of marriage between Edoüard de Flecheur, son of Jaques de flecheur and of Marie Hannesson citizen of the town of Narez in old England of one part and Marie Louise Pittement Wellis widow of the late Etienne Wellis of the other part and having found no impediment to the said marriage, I, P. Pocquet curé of this town of Quebec have married them according to the form prescribed by my mother the Holy Church in presence of sieur Jean de la Lande interpreter of the King for the English, of sieur Claude Cliche, citizen of this town, Christophe Dubois, Englishman, of (illeg.) Alliot also English, who have signed; the bride and bridegroom having declared they could not sign.

Claude Cliche

Jean de la Lande
Christophe Dubois
(illeg.) Elliott. Pocquet."

Although the identity of "Judy and Eliz[h] Willey" cannot be proven, here are the two daughters of the family whom they may be — Marie Magdeleine, a *tourière* and a wife, and Marie, three times married.

Marie Magdeleine.

On "June 23, 1692, was bap. *sous condition* Marie Magd Willis[9] English, daughter of Etienne Willis, Englishman and of gabrielle picman[10] his wife also English, the said Marie Magde-

[8] N. H. Hist. Soc. Mixed Records, 5, 405; and printed N. H. Prob. Rec., I, 420.

[9] The surname, in Père Meriel's handwriting, is inserted.

[10] Abigail is frequently changed to Gabrielle in these records.

lenne aged 16 years, having been born 16 June 1676[11] living in the service of the Sisters of St. Joseph, Villemarie, as their *tourière*.[12] Her godfather was the high and mighty Seigneur Messire Louis de Buade de Frontenac, comte de paleau[13] *conseiller du Roi en ses conseils*, Governor and lieutenant-general for the King in Canada, Acadia, Newfoundland and other places of France *septentrionale;* her godmother, Madame Marie Magdaleine Chaspoux wife of Messire Jean Bochart chevalier, Seigneur de Champigny, Noray and other places, Intendant of justice police and finance of New France, who have signed.

Louis de Buade Frontenac

M. M. Chaspoux

E. Guyotte, Curé."

Before 1698 Marie-Magdeleine opened the door for herself, and ceasing to be a *tourière* became in Quebec the bride of Jean Leconte. "The 29th Sept. 1698, after the publication of the three banns made the 14th, 21st and 28th of the present month and at the —— between Jean le Conte, son of Vincent le Conte *laboureur* (four illegible words)[14] and of Marie Gombault, his father and mother of one part, and of Marie Magdeleine Willis daughter of Etienne Willis, inhabitant of New England and of Marie Louise Pitman, her father and mother of the other part, finding no obstacle, I, François Dupré curé de Québec married them and gave them the nuptial benediction according to the form prescribed by our Mother, the Holy Church in presence of monsieur Fred ——, monsieur Dupuis, *lieutenant particulier*, monsieur Du-

11 Added to original record.

12 This was at Hôtel-Dieu. Her duties were to open the door, receive messages, etc. Before the nineteenth century the *tourières* did not make vows.

13 Palluau.

14 M. Tanguay says he was coachman of the intendant whose wife was Marie's godmother.

plessis [and other illegibles] who have signed with the bridegroom and bride.

Le Conte J. Dupuis
M. M. Willis Regnard Duplessis
F. Dupré."

Their first child, Jeanne Thérèse, b. 1699, m. Jos. Rouillard.

Etienne, for whom his forgiving(?) grandmother, now "Marie Louise Willis," was sponsor, was b. in 1700, the year Stephen Willis d. in Oyster River. Etienne d. in 1746.

Louis, b. 1702, d. 1709.

When he was six months old his mother "The wife of Jean Leconte [here called] Marie-Louise Wellis, English woman was buried the 1st February 1703," and Jean, her husband, took a new wife at the end of three months.

Here is another daughter of Gabrielle (Abigail) Willis.

"The 27 Oct. 1702, after the publication of the three banns made the 8th, 10th and 17th of September of this year, between Charles Arnault, son of René Arnault and the late Marie Mignier, his father and mother of this parish and bishopric, of one part and of Marie Ouellis, daughter of —— ouelis and of Gabrielle ouelis English also, her father and mother of this parish and bishopric, and having discovered no obstacle, I, François Dupré, curé de Québec married them and gave them the *bénédiction nuptiale* in presence of André Spennard, brother-in-law of Mr. André, of monsieur de Champigny . . . all of whom have signed, also the bride, the bridegroom declared he could not.

Marie Willis André spennert
Andre. D. Baufort
H. André François Dupré."

She must have been soon a widow for on "May 31, 1704 after one publication of the banns, and having obtained the dispensation of the other two from Monsieur de la Colombière, *Vicaire Général de Mgr et reverend evesque de Québec,* between Pierre Perot, widower of the late anne Jourdain of one part and of Marie

Magdeleine Wellis, widow of late Charles regnau [corrected in margin] of this parish and bishopric of the other part, and having discovered no obstacle, I, François Dupré Curé de Québec, married them according to the form prescribed by our mother, the Holy Church in presence of Joseph Delestre Michot, of Pierre Mailloux, Vincent Lepine and Marguerite Perot sister of the groom all of whom signed"—the husband could not. She signs "Marie Willis" in a good round handwriting.

A record of only one child was found. Martin, b. 1712, who died two years later. There may be more.

Although the husband could not sign his name in 1704, in 1722 he is called "Pierre Perrot, Sieur Derizy, merchant" when he sends a petition for his wife's naturalization. Perhaps he fears danger for her as New England is at war with the Maine Indians. He calls her Marie Willis, native of the town of Esteval—not very like Oyster River—where she was captured at the age of eight by the savages and brought to Quebec. She had become a Catholic and desires to end her days in New France.[15] Marie must have had charms for in 1741 she takes a third husband, seven years younger than herself. He can write his name and this time no banns are required.

It was the 13 Nov., 1741, when Barthelemy Cotton, aged about fifty, son of the late Barthelemy and Jeanne Le Rouge and Marie Willis, widow of Pierre Drezy, were married. There were fewer witnesses—and Marie still signs as Willis, and as Marie Wellis she is buried Sept. 17, 1776, aged ninety-six years. Barthelemy Cotton lived until May, 1780, when he was said to be eighty years old. They were buried in the Chapelle Sainte-Famille of Notre-Dame, Quebec.

1694. *Wednesday*, 18 *July*.

A few months after the burning of York a hundred Abenakis went to Naxouat, a fort newly built on the St. John river, to demand their reward. They were not disappointed for much more was expected of them. They were flattered and feasted by Ville-

[15] Que. Docs., III, 73.

bon, the governor, who adopted as his brother Taxous—one of the most hostile—to whom he gave the cleanest coat he had.[16] He opened for his guests a barrel of wine which they drank in a quarter of an hour.[17] After many speeches, war-dances and gifts, couriers were sent out to sing the war-song in all the villages while the Abbé Thury and Père Bigot unceasingly urged to war the tribes on the Kennebec and Penobscot.[18] But all the great plans they made failed and the ardor of the Indians weakened. In August, 1693, at Pemaquid a "perpetual peace" was promised between the Massachusetts Commissioners and thirteen chiefs who pretended to represent all the tribes from the Merrimac to the Saint-Croix.[19] Possibly the promise would have been kept—for some of the Indians wished to reopen their trade with the English— had the French not been so eager to increase their disaffection.

Louis XIV was told that the Canadians had every reason to dread Indian negotiations with the English as they "supply them with goods at a low rate, and the fort of Pemquit has its foot on their necks. Considerable presents[20] and an open trade to supply their wants will alone prevent them seeking what they require from the English."

In the meantime Sieur de Villieu, the newly appointed commander of the Indian allies, set out to put an end to their parleyings with the English. It was difficult to keep the Indians at the fighting point, but Villieu's zeal and that of the two missionaries did not lessen. Thury was all the more eager because he had heard that *un ministre* had come to Pemaquid "to teach the little savages to read and write."[21] Finally, at the end of June, 1694, commander and missionary, with their Indians and an interpreter, began the long canoe voyage from the Penobscot; Bigot's Indians

16 Hutchinson says "Toxus has been the name of a Norridgewock chief for divers successions, perhaps as the Pharaohs and Ptolemys were kept in respect for those who first bore their names."

17 Parkman MSS. 18 Villieu's "*Relation.*" Que. Docs., II, 135.

19 Magnalia, II, 625. 20 See Chapter III. 21 Que. Docs., II, 138.

joining them the number was doubled. Opinions differed about the place to attack. Some wished to strike above, some below Boston.

After many delays there were murmurings because of the far-away aim when an enemy was distant but a day's journey.

The governor, Villebon, vexed because Villieu had superseded his brother, had refused him proper support of men and supplies, yet warned him that he could not subsist without them! Now food being gone "Those who were dying of hunger, of whom Villieu was one," asked that scouts be sent to find the nearest settlement, and on July 18 they "fell suddenly & unexpectedly upon Oyster-River about break of Day . . . killed & Carried away 94 persons, & burnt 13 houses—this was the fr. act of hostility Committed by y^m^ after ye peace Concluded at Pemmaqd,"[22] which was in August, 1693.

In the small village was a church, a mill, and scattered along the river-banks were farms and twelve garrison-houses. The people, not dreaming of danger, slept in their own homes and a loose watch was kept. The Indians separated into bands to attack different points. Seven of the garrison-houses were successfully defended. By Villieu's statement one hundred and four persons were killed and from the sixty houses that were burned and pillaged twenty-four captives were taken. Four men only of the enemy were killed. Ann Jenkins gives a different number. She testified that she with her three children and the rest of her "neighbors whose Lives were spared" were at first forty-nine, but "in one miles goeing" three children were killed; and from her we learn that after the first night "the Company parted & the Captives were distributed."

The priests celebrated mass—the first in New Hampshire—on a hilltop near the Woodman garrison. The report sent by Redford, deputy-secretary to Governor Phips, says: "There is two Fryars[23] among the Indians who after Victory said Mass twice, the

22 Pike's "Journal." 23 Doubtless Pères Bigot and Thury.

Indians did spred 6 or 7 miles and engaged all at once. Oyster River in a manner Ruined, only ab^{t} 20 houses left." He asks for men that the place may not be deserted, which would "give the enemy an inlett in to the whole Countrey; for their Majest^{s} Service, he wants 100 men with Ammunition & Provision; its Judged Eighty psons killed & taken, abundance of Cattle killed."[24]

One of the friars wrote with chalk sentences in an unknown language upon the wall of the meeting-house. Miss Mary Thompson[25] says in the "Catholic World" of Nov., 1890, that it may have been a clause of the *Credo*, or perhaps a prayer left to greet the sad eyes of the surviving colonists when they next ventured to assemble to mingle their tears and to try to "justify the ways of God to men." A Protestant writer (Drake) thinks that the writing may have been "a warning to all heretics to beware how they provoked the just anger of heaven in the future." Miss Thompson believes that the priests accompanied the savages "to soften their ferocity and to watch over the captive women and children, many of whom were spared and finally redeemed through their intervention." She may be right, but we have proof that before this expedition Villieu and Père Thury instructed their savages to give no quarter,[26] and after the attack the governor wrote that the blow was of great advantage to Canada because it put at end all propositions of peace between the Indians and English, and the latter were in despair because the Indians had killed even infants in the cradle.[27]

One of the leaders at Oyster River and Groton was Bomazeen. Cotton Mather described him and his companions "as loving as bears and as harmless as tygres." These loving, harmless Indians were seized by Captain March at Pemaquid in 1694 after they had asked for a parley under a flag of truce.

The justice of this was not questioned nor was March censured, but he apparently felt the need of justifying himself as follows:

[24] Arch. 3, 482. [25] Author of "Landmarks of Ancient Dover."

[26] "*Mémoire du Sieur de Villebon,*" July 7, 1694. Que. Docs., II, 157.

[27] Que. Docs., II, 158.

"November 19 Bomazeen with ten or a dozen Indians called over the barbican & by setting up a white flag in time of peace, declared themselves enemies. We did not put up ours for an hour or 2, reminding them of the treaty, which Bomazeen himself had signed. We resolved to seize him & made no other promise than to treat him kindly & do him no hurt. After taking him we said we must know who had done the mischief at Oyster River & Groton of which they made themselves ignorant & why & by whom the peace had been broken. We thought it not unlawful . . . to apprehend such perfidious villains & traitors (tho' under a white rag.)"[28] All the Indians were sent to Boston, but Bomazeen alone was held. After four years in prison he was released. His petition and the manner of his release may be found in "Redemptions."

While Bomazeen was in prison in Boston several redeemed captives testified to his cruelties. In the postscript to the deposition of Grace Higiman[29] is the following description of his elegant appearance:

"Further I add that when I saw Bomazeen at Canada, after the time that Oyster River was destroyed, he had on a pair of red plush breeches, a clos-bodyed Coat of Searge, and a cane with a Silver head and in a boasting manner, related to me . . . that he brought in Ten Scalps and two English Prisoners, and was greatly caressed and treated kindly by the French Governour." He was released and allowed to live — in his red plush breeches — to fight another day. This two-sided Indian had a fondness for finery. In July, 1703, he and a companion brought news to Boston of the arrival of a French ship at Mount Desert and they were "rewarded for their Duty with a good Coat, Shirt, Neck Cloth & Hat each of them."[30] In 1722 he was killed at Norridgewock and his squaw was brought a prisoner to Boston by Captain Moulton.

28 Letter from John Pike to governor and council; Pemaquid 7 Jan., 1694, quoted in Hutchinson's "Hist. of Mass.," II, 81.

29 See Pemaquid, Chapter VII.

30 "Coun. Rec.," VII, 404.

Adams, Mercy, dau. of Charles and Rebecca (Smith).

The garrison-house of Charles Adams was burned. He, his wife and twelve more persons were killed. Mercy was taken to Canada and was among "Thos remaining in 1695." "On Holy Saturday, April 6, 1697 was solemnly baptized *sous condition* an English girl named in her own country mercy, who born at oyster River, province of hampshire in new England of the marriage of Charles Adams, *habitant* and of Rebecca Smith both protestants the 3rd (old style or 13th new style) of March, 1674, having been captured 29th July[31] 1694, has lived for five or six months in the island of monreal. Her godfather was monsieur pierre Lamoureux de St. germain merchant. Her godmother damoiselle marguerite seigneuret, wife of Monsieur Bourdon, merchant, who named this English girl Ursule, the godfather and godmother signed. The English girl declared she did not know how to sign, inquiry as to this having been made according to law.

R. C. de Breslay."

On the parish register of Saint-François-du-Lac is: "The 3 August 1704 I, Jacques Bigot of the Company of Jesus acting as curate in the parish of St. François after two publications of the banns, dispensation being given for the third, having found no impediment, have married Charles du bois, son of the late Pierre Dubois and the late Anne Dumont with Marie Ursule baptized in her infancy in this parish and adopted by Mr. de Plagnol. The witnesses were Claude Pinard, Labonte Losière." Charles is sometimes Dubois, sometimes Brisebois, the names being interchangeable; his father was Pierre René, his mother Anne-Juliene. Mr. de Plagnol was an officer — Planiolle — who fought against the Iroquois and who lived in Montreal and Saint-François-du-Lac, perhaps in garrison. He had to do with the Abenaki grant at the latter place.

Mercy's name is variously written. Is Meystrey a guess for Mercy as perhaps is Mistrot?

[31] New Style.

In 1710 "Marie Ursule Mistrot, married to Charles Brisebois, living at sainct francois" is naturalized.

Their children were:

M. Catherine, m. at Saint-François-du-Lac in 1724 François Lonier. Her parents, Charles and Marie Ursule Elie, were of the parish of Saint-Michel d'Yamaska.

M. Ursule, bap. 1708 by Jean Loyard, Jesuit at St. Francis. Tanguay gives her marriage in 1734 to Alexis Lefebre.

Marguerite Joseph, aged seventeen, was buried in the cemetery of Notre-Dame, Montreal, 19 Dec., 1727. She is dau. of "Charles dubois and Marie Ursule Mestré," who were at the burial.

Appoline francoise dubois, aged about fifteen, was buried 15 April, 1728, in the same place, having died the day before. Her parents, written as above, of the parish of St. Francis.

M. Françoise Brisebois, b. 15 Aug., 1716, was bap. *sous condition* 21 July at St. Francis. Charles Dubois, *habitant* of Yamaska, and Marie Ursule, parents. Godparents, two members of the Hertel family. In 1734 she married at Saint-Michel d'Yamaska Jean François Comparet, merchant.

Catherine Brisebois, dau. of Charles and Marie Ursule, was bap. *sous condition* 24 June, 1718, having been born fifteen days before. Her godfather "le Sr. Chabiely" could not sign. In 1748 in the parish of Saint Michel she m. Joseph Lavallé. Her mother (dead many years) is "Ursule native of England."

François Regis Brisebois, "son of Charles and Matie . . . English woman," bap. at Saint-François 10 Apr., 1720, Marguerite Hertel godmother. Died in September. Tanguay gives another François bap. 1723.

Joseph-Marie, bap. at St. Francis 1726, and there, as son of Charles and Ursule Mestrée, of the parish of St. Michel d'Yamaska, in 1750 he mar. Catherine Renoux.

Mercy died and on Sept. 29, 1732, Charles, widower of the late Marie Ursule, Englishwoman, married Marie Anne Soucy, widow of Robert Gautin. It was the *prêtre-curé* of the parish of Saint-François-de-Sales on the Ile Jésus who married them. The island is made by the two branches of the Ottawa, north of the Island of Montreal.

But it was in the parish of Saint-Michel that Charles died Jan. 9, 1747, aged seventy. Marianne, his widow and much older, lived eight years longer and the record says she was "about ninety years old."

DAVIS. "Two Daughters" of John and —— Burnham. They were perhaps SARAH, b. 1687 (?), and MARY ANN.

Many members of the Davis family were killed. Of this branch the parents and "several" children were massacred and two daughters were carried away.

Dr. Quint, annotating Pike's Journal,[32] writes of the two; "one of whom returned, the other remained in a nunnery." It was Sarah who returned, and she, on Oct. 14, 1702, when "aged about fifteen or thereabout" desired that her uncle Jeremiah Burnham who was administering her father's estate be made her guardian.[33] She married Peter Mason and was living in 1771. The captive lists are confusing—"Sara Davis (gerll) Cascow" was remaining in 1695. On the roll of 1710/11 are several unidentified Davises of Casco and a Sarah of Oyster River, but she cannot be Sarah, daughter of John.

"*The other* who remained in a nunnery." To identify her is difficult for we have Marie-Anne Davis an Ursuline and Marie-Anne Davis a Hospitalière, and we have not only lost the names of their parents but probably of their parent-given names. Marie-Anne doubtless being the names of baptism.

Our only sources of information concerning these two of the nunnery are the Community Narratives. Miss Thompson writes: "There is not the slightest doubt" that the Ursuline is the Oyster River captive. There would seem, however, to be some doubt.

32 "Mass. Hist. Soc. Pro.," 1875.

33 "Probate Records," Concord, Vol. 4, p. 250.

The annalist of the Ursulines says that the child was hardly six years old when in 1686 she saw her parents massacred and was herself captured at Salem, although she later accepts Miss Thompson's statement of Oyster River as her home. To be sure, there was no massacre at Salem, and in 1686 the colonies were not at war, but if she were taken at Oyster River, aged five, could she have fulfilled her history as it is written in the "History of the Ursulines of Quebec" and in "Glimpses of the Monastery"?[34] In both narratives we are told that the little girl was adopted by an Abenaki chief; was much cherished by his family and quickly forgot her home and people. When about fifteen — which if Miss Thompson's theory is correct should be about 1703 — she was instructed and baptized conditionally by Père Rale; so she was probably then living with the Kennebec Indians. Two or three years later the priest took her from the Indians and found for her some French friends with whom she learned the habits and language of civilization. When she came as a boarding pupil to the Convent she was "transported with joy," crying: "This is the House of Jesus, here will I live and die." From the classes she entered her novitiate in 1699, which proves conclusively that she must have been born before 1689. She made her profession in 1701 and was the first nun of English descent in the Convent.

Several generous persons helped to pay her *dot*,[35] but the larger part was given by the Community because of her vocation and because she sacrificed her country for her faith.

She became Marie-Anne Davis de Saint-Benoit and served her Community faithfully for nearly half a century, dying March 2, 1749. It seems impossible that she was that daughter of John of Oyster River who "remained in a nunnery." Is it not more likely that Mother Marie-Anne Davis de Saint-Benoist was one of our lost captives? But here is

[34] By Sr. Saint-Croix — M. J. Holmes of Vermont — a convert of the nineteenth century.

[35] Twenty years after this the *dot* was fixed at a minimum of 5000 livres.

Marie-Anne Davis of Hôtel-Dieu.

Her story is told in the Abbé Casgrain's "History of the Hôtel-Dieu of Quebec." He relates that the child being "thrown by a violent shock from the arms of heresy into the arms of the Church, her vocation causes us to admire the *suavité* and power of God in the salvation of souls." A party of Abenakis brought her, with other prisoners, to their village of Saint-François-du-Lac. She was five or six years old, named Marie-Anne Davis, and had been carried half-dead with terror from the carnage in which her family had disappeared. Father Vincent Bigot placed her in an Abenaki family and himself taught her French and "the elements of the sciences." The little girl is described as loving solitude and liking to wander by the lakeside gathering iris, water-lilies and violets to place upon the steps of the altar where the father would find her praying in ecstasy. For fourteen years she led this life "without a wish to break her captive bonds." Father Bigot was in the habit of talking of her "angelic virtues" to the Sisters of the Hôtel-Dieu, and when he had secured for her a small *dot* he carried her to their Superior at whose feet Marie-Anne begged to enter the Convent. Their historian says: "It was a pleasure to see this fair daughter of England in her picturesque costume with hair falling over her shoulders, wrapped in a white blanket and shod in moccasins ornamented with beads."

After two years of preparation she received the white veil of the novice, and as Sister Davis de Sainte-Cécile was always grateful for having been snatched from the terrors of heresy and led in such a wonderful way into the paradise of the religious life; which "paradise" continued fifty-one years. It began in January, 1710, when she was twenty-two years old. It ended after fifteen years of invalidism on June 13, 1761.

Was not she the daughter of John Davis and —— Burnham of Oyster River?

Dean, John's wife and daughter.

John, "whose house stood by the sawmill at the Falls," was

shot; his wife and daughter were carried about two miles up the river and left in charge of an old Indian. He had a pain and asked for a remedy, she answered "occapee" (rum), knowing that he had already drunk some; a large dose put him to sleep when she and her child escaped.

DENBOW (DENMORE, DINSMORE), PETER.

"Petter Denbow of Oyester River" was "yett in the Indians hands" in 1698/9.

He was the son of Salathiel and —— Roberts. His fate was sad. In 1751 he was "let out" for £27; that being the amount paid by the town for his support for one year.

DERRY, JOHN.

DELIVERANCE, his wife.

"One child" Joseph? John?

John, Sr., died in captivity according to his wife's petition.

A John Derry of Oyster River was received on board the *Province Galley* in 1698/9. This could not have been John above for his wife, already redeemed, had become Deliverance Pitman. It may have been the "one Child" who is elsewhere called Joseph.

"The humble petition" dated Nov. 17, 1697, "of Deliverence Pittman; formerly the wife of John Derry; and now the wife of Nathaniel Pittman" sheweth: That in 1694, the House was burnt, Cattle Killed "as alsoe most of our children; my husband, one Child, and y^r^ Petition^r^ taken Captives; in wch Captivitye my husband dyed; none but your Petition^r^ Returned; hopeing to enjoy what Estate was Left by y^r^ Petition^rs^ husband; in due method of Law." But her bondsmen objected. They allowed a division of the "movebely" (moveables) but maintained that "The Lands being in contryversy we thought it not convenent to coseren [concern?] ourselves aboutet." Letters of Administration, however, were given to Deliverance, but in January, 1698, she sends another petition to inform the Court that the "Securityes Seized upon y^r^ Pet. Cows; and Estate; the whole Amounting to Ninety

Pounds, forty-five of wch are in Lands; all there Pretence being for soe doeing; that it is for the Good of my Children, which I had to my first husband; Derry; But in truth yor $Petition^{r}$ Knows of noe: Such Children; being now Liveing: and if yor $Petition^{r}$ have not the Cows; & Land againe; she & family must needs perish." The Governor and Council are asked "Seriously to Inspect into the illegall method of the said bondsmen etc." Signed: Nath: Pitman, on behalfe of his wife Deliverence.[36] Soon after she sent this petition she must have learned that "one child" was living, for it was in that month that "John"—or Joseph—returned on the *Province Galley*, justifying the judgment of her bondsmen. She was living in 1728 when she conveyed property to her son, Derry Pitman, whose wife was a kinswoman of Sir William Pepperell.

Drew, Thomas, son of Francis.
Tamsen, his wife.

The Drew garrison-house, still standing on Back River, was built by William Dam and is pictured in the local history.

Francis Drew surrendered with promise of quarter, but they killed him. His estate was not administered until 1696 when Thomas who was the eldest son had returned.[37]

There were fifteen in the Drew family. John was put out of a window and escaped, probably to be killed by Indians a few years later. Benjamin, who was about nine years old, was made to run the gauntlet—"at Winnipeseogie"—until cut down.[38] Thomas and Tamsen, "newly married," were captured. He was taken to Canada and redeemed in 1695. She to Norridgewock and was gone four years during which time she "endured everything but death." Her child, born "in the open air and in a violent snowstorm," was killed because she could not care for it. Other hardships, which may be traditionary, are described by Belknap. Ann

36 "Probate Records," I, 428, N. H. State Papers.

37 "New Hampshire Wills." 38 "Hist. of Durham," I, 94.

Jenkins says that "Thomasand drue," bought by Prince Waxaway at Pemaquid, was thereby "freed from hard usage."

"Damson" Drew's own deposition proving that "Bombazeen the Indian" (then in Boston prison) had been at Oyster River is printed elsewhere.[39] She had a long life with her husband until she was eighty-nine and he ninety-three years—then dying within two days of each other they were buried in one grave.[40] Fourteen children were born to them.

The following records were made by the Rev. Hugh Adams.[41] Aug. 12, 1722, baptized "Thomas Drew and Tamsen Drew, his wife, they both being so (but profanely and idolatrously) baptized by a Popish Priest or Friar in their captivity, for which I had the warrant of Acts 19, 3-5." The "Popish Priest" made his second baptism *sous condition*, but not this Puritan divine.[42]

In "1727/8 Lord's Day Adar 22, i.e. March 3, Thomas Drew of the Little bay & his wife Tamzen Drew admitted to the Church." The next month seven of their children were baptized.

EDGERLY, THOMAS.
JOSEPH.
ELIZABETH.
SUSANNA.

Thomas, "weaver," owned a garrison-house which was destroyed. His captivity seems to have been but a day's length. Dr. Quint says that a daughter, a son, Joseph, and some children of Thomas Edgerly, junior, were taken with him.

Elizabeth and Susannah were brought home on the *Province Galley* in 1698/9. They had, perhaps, been kept in one of the Maine villages. Did they belong to Thomas Junior or Senior?

Joseph is the only one known to have been in Canada. He,

39 Gen. Reg., 18. 40 Belknap, p. 141, but perhaps a tradition. 41 Gen. Reg., 30, 62.

42 However harsh may have been the opinions of Parson Adams the following shows that he was a tender father: "On a fair, sunshiny Lord's day my Infant Daughter . . . was after the name of her father's Godly Mother and her own Grandmother, baptized Avis Adams."

born in 1677, was son of Thomas and Rebecca (Ault | Hallowell).

One can read of him in "The Redeemed Captive"[43] when he was living on the Island of St. Lawrence, as was Zebediah Williams of Deerfield. This was two miles from Château-Richer where the Deerfield minister was held.

Zebediah died in 1706. After his death it was related that he appeared unto Edgerly and told him that he was in torment because he had rejected the true faith and had influenced his friend (Joseph) to stay away from mass. Mr. Williams refused to believe the miraculous tale and was much relieved when he learned from a serious young Newfoundland captive, who lived on the island and knew both the young men, that it was false. The lad said that one day when "Egerly came in I spake to him before the whole family (in the French tongue, for he could not speak much English) and asked him of this story. He answered 'It is a great falsehood' . . . and that he had never been at the mass since Zebediah's death."

Which shows that in Joseph's twelve years' captivity he did not become a convert and that he almost lost his mother-tongue.

In that year (1706) he came home on the brigantine *Hope*, landing in Boston on November 21. He married Mary Green.

EMERSON, JUDAH (DAVIS).

Wife of Capt. Samuel; eleventh and youngest child of Ensign John Davis of Haverhill and Oyster River and Jane Peasley (Haverhill). "Juda Emmerson" was still in the Indians' Hands in January, 1698/9, but she must have been redeemed soon after. Mr. Stackpole says she was ransomed by "a Mr. Morrill" for two shirts, one of which he took off his back.[44] Captain Samuel believing her dead went to Portsmouth to arrange his second marriage. He met there a friend who told him of the return of some captives and offered to "bet a double drink of grog yr wife is in town" and thereupon took him into his wife's presence.[45]

[43] Edi. of 1853, pp. 84-86. [44] Was it Peter of Casco Bay?

[45] "Hist. Durham," I, 99.

JENKINS, ANN, wife of Stephen.
AZARIAH, her son?

Ann was Stephen's second wife; the first having "wilfully destroyed herself by casting herself into the water." Ann's "Mark" was "W."

Stephen, his grandmother and one child were killed. Anne and three children were carried away. From her "written testimony" dated 11 June, 1695,[46] concerning the attack and Bomazeen's part in it we learn that "about the dawning of the day my husband being up, went out of the dore, & presently returning cried to me & our children to run for our lives, for the Indians had beset the town; where upon my husband and myself fled with our children into our corne field & at our entrance into the field Bomazeen whome I have seen since I came out of captivity in the prison Came towards us & about tenn Indians more & the *sd* Bomazeen then shot at my husband & struck him three blows on the head with a hatchet." She describes the murder of the grandmother and child and the route followed by the Indians, saying that she "with nine captives more were Carried up to penecook & were Left with three Indians, & that party went to Groaten & Bomazeen being their Commander." After the Groton party came back they went all together "with their Cannoes sometimes a float & sometimes Carried untill that we came to Norridgewocke, which took us fifteen dayes, & staied about two months there; then dispersed into the woods twoe or three families in a place & kept Removeing toe and froe, staeing about aweek in a place untill they brought uss down to pemaquid & delivered uss to Capt March. Bomazeen was my Master, his wife my Mistress untill about two months before I was brought Down to pemaquid, for then the Indian Minister called Prince Waxaway bought me when I was brought to great weekness . . . by thir Bad usage & shewed me great kindness by whose meanes under god my Life was pre-

46 Printed in Gen. Reg., 18.

served. My mistress was very cruel to me & I was cruelly whipt seaven times."

Jabez Jenkins, administrator of his brother's estate, gave a bond of a hundred pounds in "behalfe of the several Small Children" Stephen had left. Perhaps it was believed that Ann had died, but she makes her mark on Oct. 22, 1695, acknowledging that Jabez had paid to her "all the womans part for his labour & care in saving and transporting the moveables and rest due to the widow 15 pounds."[47] Ann married David Kincaid of Oyster River, but she did not find relief from anxiety for

"On Sept. 18, 1708," says Pike, "David Kinked of Oyster River was assaulted by 3 Indians at his house some Considerable distance from Woodmans Gar: Three guns were fired at him & his Lad, but (thro Mercy) both escaped well." After David died Ann took for a third husband Thomas Potts.

Azariah. This name is on the roll of prisoners in 1710/11. He may have been one of Stephen's and Ann's children.

RAND, SAMUELL.
REMEMBRANCE.

"Sam[ll] Rand (boy)" was a captive in 1695 and Remembrance is named in 1710/11. They were children or possibly grandchildren of John and Remembrance (Ault) who were probably killed.

In 1672 John Alt and his wife Remembrance made a deed of gift — to become effective after the death of both — to John and Remembrance Rand and their children.

WATSON, HANNAH, widow of Robert.
JOSEPH, their son.

Among those killed were: "Robert Watson and family, except his wife — yet I think that one son escaped;" so wrote Dr. Quint, annotating Pike's Journal. One son did escape to marry and die in Canada.

47 Prob. Papers in N. H. Hist. Soc., Concord.

Mrs. Hannah was a woman of many names. New England writers call her a Beard and a Kent. Canada writes: Austin, Sterman and Anne hesemenne. The will of Thomas Beard—made in 1678—names Elizabeth Watson as his daughter. He was a carpenter of Dover. But whatever her name she was not long a captive or a widow. In 1702/3, as the wife of John Amblar, weaver, she signed the inventory of the estate of Robert Watson; administration having been granted to her after her redemption. To the inventory, over her mark, is added the following:

"Sir, I have hear given an Invitary of my Estate that now Remaineth, but I must further aquaint you that I have Laid out for

my Ransom	20^{ll}-00^{s}-00^{d}
to a french man who promised to redeem my son there-with	02^{ll}-10^{s}-00^{d}
to bro Kent for his administeration and Care	05^{ll}-00^{s}-00^{d}
for Rates Laid while I was in Captivity	01^{ll}-01^{s}-00^{d}
	28^{ll}-11^{s}--00^{d}

besides Cloathing myself when I Came naked out of Captivity & besides Repairing and fencing the hous and Lands, this was dispursed out of the Estate by me."[48] On "Ap. 8, 1706, Sister Amblar (formerly Captive with the Indians) deceased suddenly after Long Illness with a Consumptive Cough."[49] Seven months later her sorrowing husband married Elizabeth Trickey.

Joseph.

In the parish register at Three Rivers is the following:

"In the year 1697, the eighth of April, was baptized *sous condition* by me, undersigned, an Englisman named Joseph Houatsan, who has kept his name of Joseph, aged seventeen years. His godfather was Monsieur Estienne Veron sieur de Grandmesnil;

48 "N. H. Wills," 416.

49 Pike's "Journal."

his godmother Marie-Joseph Jutra, who have signed as do I.

Marie Joseph Jutrat
Grandmesnil
Fr. Maxime Brache Recolé
faisant les fonctions curiales."

The Recollets were the parish priests of Three Rivers.

In this Montreal record the names are strangely changed. "The 15th November 1711 after the publication of three banns without opposition, I, undersigned Priest, Vicar of the Parish of Villemarie having received the mutual consent by word of mouth of Joseph Robert, English by nation, aged about twenty-eight years son of Jean Robert and of hanna oisten, his father and mother, inhabitants of Piscatoué in new England of one part, and Marie Madelene Demers, aged seventeen years, daughter of charles Demers and the late Elizabeth papin his wife, her father and mother of this Parish of the other part, have married them according to the rites of our mother holy Church in presence of the said charles Demers, Father of the Bride, of Robert Demers, her paternal uncle, of Pierre Pibaran, surgeon of this Town, of René Colet, *voiageur* to the 8ta8ak, and of several other relatives and friends of the said parties and of marien Taillandier, master surgeon of Boucherville. The bridegroom and said Charles Demers have declared they do not know how to sign, inquiry as to this having been made according to the law.

Magdeleine demers Robert demers
puibaran
Tailhandier Ursule demers
Catherine demers
Priat Vicaire"

Their first child, Madeleine, baptized in 1712, married Joseph Marcheteau, and died in 1730.

At Boucherville in June, 1715, was baptized Marie-Josef Robert Ouetsin, daughter of Joseph and Marie de Mers. The wife of the royal notary, Magdaleine Beaudry, was her godmother.

She married (1738) 1, Jean-Baptiste Joliet-Baillargé and (1752) 2, Joseph Lamoreux.

Marie Demers dies and another marriage is recorded at Boucherville on April 11, 1717, between Joseph Robert Ouatsenne, Englishman, about thirty-three years old, son of Robert Ouatsenne and of Anne hesemenne,[50] an Englishman of the village of Pectaoüé, with Angelique Benard Carignan, aged about 21 years, daughter of Joseph Benard Carignan and of Margueritte Faille of this parish of Boucherville. Angélique (1718) their first-born, alone lived beyond childhood. She mar. Joseph Baby. In 1719 Joseph Jaques Robert was baptized in Montreal, and in 1721 a third child was born and its mother died. But it was not until July 14, 1749, that Joseph-Robert, son of John and Anna Austin of Piscatoué, N. E., was buried.

1707.
DREW, LYDIA (Marie-Anne).
LOMAX, ELIZABETH.

May 22, 1707: "Two young girls were carried away by the Indians from Bunkers Garrison[51] at Oyster River, viz: the Daughter of Tho: Drew (near 13 years old) & Daughter of Nathl Laimos (much younger). This was the first mischief done by y^{m} in ye year 1707."[52]

At Qubec:

"On the 20th October 1709 was baptized by me, the undersigned priest marie anne Dreux daughter of Thomas Dreux cooper, inhabitant of oister-river and of Marie Bunker his wife, who born at —— in New England in 1696 in the spring, was taken by the Abenaquis in the month of June 1707, lives with M. Dumoutin, *serviteur* of Messire philippe de rigaud, Marquis de Vaudreuil, chevalier of the order of St. Louis, Governor General

50 Tanguay gives Sterman.

51 The Garrison of James Bunker, Lydia's grandfather, is pictured in the "History of Durham."

52 Pike's "Journal."

of New France. Her godfather was M. Charles guillemin, *Marchand Bourgeois* of Quebec. Her godmother d[lle] marianne Rivard Wife of the said S[r] dumoutin who have signed.

marie anne rivard
guillemin Meriel priest."

Duplicate copies—with some variations—were made of the registers. In one record of this baptism the name Lidia is added, which identifies this daughter of Thomas even though she was not born "in 1696 in the spring," but in the "10th mo. of 1697," as says the home record.

In 1713 Marie Anne Drew, living near Quebec, is naturalized, in spite of which she seems to have been redeemed and probably again a Protestant to have married Francis Mathes of Oyster River the 28 November, 1720.

Lydia Mathes was appointed administrator of her husband's estate, there called Junior on May 26, 1742.[53]

Lomax, Elizabeth, daughter of Nathaniel and Deliverance (Clark).

Elizabeth, four years younger than her fellow-captive, was baptized two years earlier by the zealous Father Meriel.

"On Sunday, 11th Sept. 1707, was solemnly baptized by me, Priest undersigned, a young English girl, called in her country Elizabeth, who was born the —— May, 1698, of the marriage of Nathaniel Lamax, inhabitant of Oister River New England and of Delivrance Clark, both Protestants; having been taken at the said place the first of June of the present year, and carried by the Abenakis to Canada, living there at Villemarie with M. Etienne Rocbert, Keeper of the King's Stores in this town. Her godfather was Monsieur Charles de Ramezay *Ecuyer,* Sieur de La Gesse, son of Messire Claude de Ramezay, Chevalier of the military order of St. Louis and Governor of the Island of Monreal and other dependent places; her godmother was Damoiselle Marie Elizabeth Rocbert, daughter of said Sieur Rocbert, Keeper of the Stores, who has added the name of Marie to that of Eliza-

[53] "Pro. Rec. Rockingham Co.," 15, 174. N. H. Hist. Soc., Concord.

beth, which the little English girl bore, the godfather and godmother have signed. Meriel priest."

In 1710, when twelve years old, she was naturalized and on

"The 25th November, 1721, after the publication of the three banns, I, undersigned priest Vicar of The parish of Villemarie, have received the mutual consent in spoken words of Joseph parent aged twenty-three years, son of the late Michel parent and of marie benoist, his wife of this parish, of one part and of Elizabeth La maxe aged twenty-three years, daughter of Nataniel La maxe and of Eliverance Clerck of Esteriver, his wife of new England of the other part, have married them, presence of monsieur Estienne Rocbert, Keeper of the King's Stores in this Town, of mr Loüis Rocbert his son. Of the said marie Benoist, mother of the bridegroom, of Jean Batiste parent, his brother, of Pierre Le Vasseur *maître-sculpteur*, and of several other relatives and friends. The bridegroom and The bride and The said Benoist declared they could not sign as required.

J. B. Parent rocbert rocbert
De Lamorendiere Levasseur
françois petit

Priat vicaire."

Of this marriage there are recorded in the Notre-Dame register the baptisms of four daughters. Geneviève (1722), Elizabeth (1723), Angélique (1725), Catherine (1726).

Joseph Parent dies and

"On June 6th, 1735, after the publication of the three banns, meeting neither hindrance nor opposition, I, undersigned priest of the Seminary of St. Sulpice acting curate in the parish of villemarie, having received the mutual consent by word of mouth of Jean Baptiste Jetté, aged thirty-one years, son of the late nicolas Jetté and of Catherine giard, his father and mother of this parish of one part, and also present Marie elisabeth La Masce aged thirty-six years, widow of Joseph parent, daughter of nacsanial La Masce and of Levreune sclac her father and Mother Of aistrever in new england of the other part, have Married them according to the rules and Customs observed in the holy church in presence of nicolas and of pierre Jetté, brothers of the bridegroom, of Joseph goyer and of pierre goyer who have all declared they could not sign this register. have signed

bourisse Lauson Michel barré

Deat vic."

No births are recorded; and on "April 5th, 1737, was buried in the cemetery of Ville marie by me Jean Bouffandeau, priest of the seminary of Montreal the body of Elizabet La Maxe, originally of new England wife of Jean B. Jetté, formerly widow of Josef parent, aged about thirty-eight years, deceased yesterday, after having received the sacraments of penitence, of Eucharist and of extreme unction, was present at her burial, Mr. Breuil, priest of said seminary and Jean B. parant.

Breuil J. B. Parant

Bouffandeau priest."

"Originally of New England," but seemingly wholly of New France. The Rocberts, perhaps assuming the kindly relation of foster-parents, made her a French citizen and, perhaps, did not seek for the child any New England friendships, for not at her baptism, marriages or burial was there a single English witness. Was the J. B. Parent at her burial her son, or perhaps the brother of her first husband?

II

Groton

1694 — 1697 — 1704 — 1706 — 1707

Friday, July 27, 1694.

A friendly Indian called Hector or Hezekiah Miles, having been taken at Salmon Falls in 1691, was held as "servant" at Naxouat above Norridgewock. After his release he testified in Boston against Bomazeen, and stated that the chiefs before leaving Norridgewock, "Discoursed of faling on Oyster River and Groton;" but from the French *"Relation"* it would seem that the decision was made later.[54]

In that account we read that two days after the Oyster River massacre the war-party with some of the captives arrived at the place where they had left their canoes, in which most of them embarked.

The Indians of Pentagoet, however, not having as many prisoners nor as much booty as those of the Kennebec were dissatisfied and fifty of them, led by Taxous and joined by some of the Kennebec braves, left "to go above Boston to knock people in the head."[55] *(Casses des testes à la surprise)* Ann Jenkins, who calls Bomazeen the commander of the Groton expedition, says they returned to Penacook in nine days and brought back twelve captives. Sewall and Pike say about twenty were killed and thirteen "captivated." "They were pursued by about 100 Horse, but they returned without finding them."[56]

Dr. Samuel Abbott Green collected and printed everything he could find about Groton. I quote the following New England statements from his "Groton in the Indian Wars" and "Three Historical Addresses." He says perhaps all those carried away were children. Captives having a market value, children were the most valuable, because they were more easily guarded and kept for ransom.

The families that suffered most lived near the site of the first meeting-house. He gives as an incomplete and partly conjectural list the following:

Captives

1694. Hobart, Gershom, Jr.
Longley, Children of John,
Betty.
John.
Lydia.

[54] See Oyster River. [55] Que. Docs., II, 142.

[56] "Diary of Lawrence Hammond," Mass. Hist. Soc. Pro., 1892.

Parker, Phinehas.
Rouse, Thomasin.
Shepley, John.
1697. Holden, Stephen.
John.
Stephen, Jr.
1704. Butterfield, Samuel.
Farnsworth, Mathias.
1706. Seager, Henry.
1707. Tarbell, Sarah.
John.
Zechariah.

HOBART, GERSHOM, JR.

"Mr. Gershom Hobart, the minister of the Place with part of his Family, was Remarkably preserved from falling into their Hands, when they made themselves the Masters of his House; though they Took Two of his Children, whereof the one was Killed and the other some time after happily Rescued out of his Captivity."[57] Gershom, Jr., was the captive. Judge Sewall wrote May 1, 1695: "Mr. Hobart's son Gershom is well at a new Fort a days Journey above Nerigawag," (Norridgewock) Dr. Green thinks he was rescued soon after this date.

LONGLEY, BETTY.
JOHN.
LYDIA.

William Longley and Deliverance (Crisp), with eight children, were living on a small farm in a house of hewn logs, the site of which has been marked by the town.

Tradition says that early in the morning the Indians turned Longley's cattle out of the barnyard into the cornfield and when he hurried out to drive them back he, his wife and five children were killed and the other three were captured. Little Betty soon

[57] Magnalia, VII, 86.

perished; perhaps before they reached Penacook, for Ann Jenkins said only twelve arrived.

John.

He was twelve years old. It is said that after going some distance he told his captors that his father's sheep were shut up in the barn and would starve unless he were allowed to go back and let them out, promising to return. They consented and the lad kept his word. The Indians called him John Augary.

Later in life, when he was "Deacon John," he testified that he was in captivity more than four years (part of the time in Canada says Dr. Green), the last half of which he was servant to Madockawando.

It is said that he was ransomed against his will, being so reluctant to give up his savage life that "those who brought him away were obliged to use force."

About the time of his return Grandmother Crispe died and gave unto her "three Grand Children y^t are in Captivity if they returne, Vizdt: three books one of y^m a bible another a Sermon booke treating of faith and the other a psalme book." John, the only one who returned, had the comfort of all three.

He married 1, Sarah Prescott; 2, Deborah Houghton, and died in 1750.

Lydia.

"Lidey Langly gerl Dover" is remaining in 1695, and on the roll of 1710 she is said to be of Groton. Taken by the Indians to Montreal she was soon ransomed, probably by Jacques Le Ber, and

"On Tuesday April 24, 1696, was baptized a young English girl named Lydie Langley, who was born at Grotten, ten or twelve leagues from Boston in New England of the marriage of William Longley and of Delivrance Crisp, both Protestants, the 2nd of April, old style or 12th of the same month new style of the year 1674[58] taken in the month of July of the year 1694, by the Abena-

[58] This date was written at a later time over an erasure.

kis, and living for about one month in the house of the sisters of the Congregation of Notre Dame. Her godfather was Monsieur Jacques le ber, Merchant. Her godmother, Dame Marie Madelaine Dupont, wife of Monsieur de Maricour, *Ecuyer, Capitaine d'une compagnie de la Marine.* She named this English girl Lydie Madelaine. The said ceremony was performed in the Chapel of the said Congregation and that by special permission of Messire François dolie *Grand Vicaire de Monseigneur l'Illustrissime et Reverendissime* Bishop of Quebec for certain reasons. Signed:

lydia magdalen longley Le Ber
M. Mg. Dupont

M. Caille faisant les fonctions curiales"

Probably Marguerite Bourgeoys was present at the baptism of this promising convert. The "special permission" for "certain reasons" was doubtless given, says a nun of the Order, because Jeanne Le Ber, daughter of Jacques, had already immured herself in the cell behind the altar of their chapel which was close to the Mother House; because Lydia had been a member of her father's family, Jeanne was especially interested in the ceremony.

When Lydia Longley became a nun is not known, but on April 17, 1733, she was living at the Convent of the Holy Family on the Island of Orleans (near Quebec) and was probably its Superior. She was that day godmother to a child of Judge Prémont. Now, a nun could accept this responsibility only by the permission of her bishop. Then, in the early days of the Order, their vows were less solemn and restricted. Marguerite Bourgeoys herself was both godmother and a marriage witness.

After many years of religious life Lydia Longley died in Montreal and on "July 21, 1758, was buried in the chapel of the infant Jesus in the parish church the body of lidie longlé de Ste. magdalene, English woman, Sister of the Congrégation de Notre Dame, deceased yesterday, aged eighty-four years. There were present M. Vallières and poncin priests."

PARKER, PHINEAS, son of James, Jr.

Josiah Parker of Cambridge petitioned the General Court on 31 May, 1699, saying: "James Parker Junr Brother to yor humble Pet^nr: was killed, with his Wife, severall of his Children also were then Carryed away Captive.[59]

One, named Phineas, something less than a year ago was by the Master of an Ipswich vessel redeemed for about six pounds, which said master has been reimbursed by the Pet^or."

The boy's uncle desired humbly that the Court would consider the "poor Orphan, now about twelve years old, and is like wise lame of one of his Leggs occasioned by ye cruelty of ye salvages and it is very questionable whether even he will be Cured & has little or nothing left him of his Fathers estate for his support."[60] After three years Josiah Parker received the amount paid for the child's ransom.

ROUSE, THOMASIN.

Probably child of Alexander, who, with his wife, was killed.

Among the "minutes of remarkable things" collected by one of the Commissioners sent with the *Province Galley* and written at "Mares-Point in Casco-Bay, Jan. 14, 1698-9,"[61] is the following: "Assacombuit sent Thomasin Rouse, a child of about ten years old, unto the water-side to carry something. The child cried: he took a stick and struck her down: she lay for dead: he took her up, and threw her into the water: some Indians not far off ran in and fetch'd her out. This child we have now brought home with us. This Assacombuit hath killed and taken this war (they tell me,) an hundred and fifty men, women and children. A bloody devil."

SHEPLEY, JOHN.

The inscription on the monument says that "the Indians massacred all the Sheples in Groton save a John Sheple, 16 years old, who the(y) carried captive to Canada and kept him 4 years after

59 Dr. Green gives three, but adds that the number is conjectural.

60 Arch. 70, 401. 61 "A Taste" given in Magnalia, II, 643.

which he returned to Groton and from him descended all the Sheples or Shepleys in this Vicinity."

On the list of those remaining in 1695 he is "Jn° Shipley boy oy^{r} River." But he had returned to Groton in 1704 when his petition[62] of Oct. 25, 1704, shows that he "and Thirteen men more being some reaping & ye rest Warding in a ffeild" about twenty Indians came upon them and he with Samuel Butterfield[63] killed "one lusty stout Indian with a holland shirt on" and both were allowed four pounds for the scalp. It may easily be believed that he was "a willing recruit" in this war after the captivity of his youth. He lived until Sept. 14, 1736.

1697.

HOLDEN, STEPHEN, with his sons John and Stephen.

"John Houlding of Grotten" was redeemed at Casco, January, 1698/9. Stephen and Stephen, Jr., were "yett in the Indians Hands." In July, 1699, Stephen wrote that "myselfe & my two biggest sons thô small" had been with the "Esterne enemy" nearly two years. In his petition[64] he says that he and one son being very desirous to gitt home before the English vessels came, he had promised "his Indian Pilotes" three pounds and twelve shillings, paid to them at Dickman's Island, which was repaid to him "out of Publiq stock."

1704.

In August, 1704, the Indians "fell on Lancaster and Groaton where they did some Spoil, but not what they expected, for that these Towns were seasonably strengthened."[65] Strengthened as we have seen by John Shepley and by

BUTTERFIELD, SAMUEL, of Chelmsford, s. of Nathaniel and Deborah (Underwood).

He "assisted" at the killing of that lusty Indian for whose scalp he, too, received four pounds,[66] but Butterfield did not sign

62 Arch. 30, 496. 63 See Butterfield. 64 Archives 70, 400.

65 Penhallow's "Indian Wars." 66 See John Shepley.

the petition in October of the same year because he, less fortunate, was in captivity as is shown by another dated April 10, 1706,[67] in which he says that: "when the Enemy came upon Nashoway & Groton" he was sent to assist Colonel Taylor and "being ordered out with some others to guard a Man who was going to work in the field, the Enemy came upon them, killed, one man, and took yo[r] Petitioner and one other Prisoners, tho' yo[r] Petitioner made all the resistance possible, killed one, and knockt down two more after they had seized him, for which yo[r] Petitioner was cruelly used by them afterwards & threatened to be burnt, several times." He adds that he was well accoutred "and was stript of all and was between fourteen and fifteen months a Captive exposed to great hardships and has sustained great Loss and damage;" and five pounds were allowed.

Penhallow gives an interesting account of his escape from death. "Being overpowered by strength [he] was forced to yield; and it hapning that the slain Indian was a fr Sagamore it caused matter of Lamentation among 'em for some time being highly Esteemed for his dexterity in wars which enrag[d] y[m] to such degree that they studyed the utmost revenges. Some were for whipping him to death, others for burning him alive; but differing in their opinions it was afterwards determined to submit the issue unto the Squaw-widow, concluding that she would resolve on something very Execrable, but her spirits were so moderate as to make no other reply than fortune Leguare, saying however If by killing him you think you can bring my husband to Life again, put him to what death you will. Otherways let him alone and suffer him to be my servant which he accordingly was during his captivity and he had much favour shown him."[68] Butterfield was by trade a tailor. He married Rachel Spalding in 1703. They had a family of nine children and he died in 1737.[69]

67 Arch. 71, 195.

68 MS. Penhallow's "Indian Wars."

69 Gen. Reg., 44.

1704.

FARNSWORTH, MATHIAS.

"On Sunday, 10 January 1706 the rites of baptism were administered by me, the Priest undersigned, to Mathias Farneth, who, born at Boston [Groton] in New England the —— of the year *mil six cens quatre vingt*[70] — of the marriage of the late Mathias Farneth, Weaver,[71] and of Sara Nutting, having been taken the —— of August 1704 and brought to Canada, is living at the Mission of N. D. de Lorette on the Island of Montréal.[72] His godfather was Messire Claude de Ramezay, knight of the order of Saint Louis, Seigneur de la Geste, Boisfleurant and Governor of the Island of Montreal and other places, who has given him the name of Claude; And his godmother was Dame Elisabeth Souärt, wife of Charles le Moine, Knight of the order of Saint-Louis, Baron de Longueil and Captain *d'une compagnie du Détachement de la Marine*, who have signed:

De Ramezay
Elisabeth Souart
+
Mark of Mathias
Claude Farneth — Meriel Priest."

His godmother was niece of the Abbé Souärt, first priest of Ville-Marie. The name of "Mathias Claude farmont" is one of many on the Letter of Naturalization of 1710, and by accident or intent in March, 1714, Louis the King in this seventy-first year of his reign gave a special and individual letter to "Claude Mathias fanef, established at Montreal." In the margin he is given the dignity of "*Le Sr*" but that may be an error. In two and a half pages of elegant phrasing the Groton-born lad is "recognized, held, accounted and considered" as if he were a "true and native-born subject" of the great King.

70 "Mathias, son of Mathias & Sarah ffarnsworth born Aug: et 6th 1690." Middlesex Records.

71 The captive was the third Mathias, his grandfather, also a weaver, was one of the earliest settlers of Groton. 72 At Sault au Recollet.

The Gentlemen of the Seminary[73] not only looked after the spiritual welfare of their seigniory but developed it by granting concessions of land, thereby helping themselves and the colonists. A small annual rent was paid and the land had to be cleared.[74] The banks of the Rivière des Prairies were dangerous until a wooden fort was built at Pointe-aux-Trembles. That made this river-route less inviting to the Iroquois enemy who had often chosen it in descending in order to avoid the rapids.

It was on that river near the Sault-au-Recollet Mission that a homestead was granted to Farnsworth. On 19 July, 1711, "in one of the rooms of the Seminary," most probably in the old stone building[75] next the parish church, was written this concession, signed by M. de Belmont for the Sulpitians and by Robert Le Gay, priest of the Mission, for Mathias.

It states that he was living in the service of the Gentlemen of the Mission having been bought out of the hands of the savages who held him as a slave; that the priests, wishing to give him "an advantageous establishment" since he so desired, granted to him a domain three arpents front and twenty arpents deep on condition that he live on it in a Christian like manner.[76] His annual rent — paid on Martinmas day — was thirty sous and about six bushels of wheat. Among those who had received earlier concessions from the Seminary was Jean Charpentier, whose land was near that now granted to the New Englander. The next time Mathias went to a notary's office Jean Charpentier, his wife and daughter Catherine, with many of their kin, went with him. This time it was to sign a marriage-contract. The lad of Groton now writes his name C. M. Fanef.

Jean and his wife, Françoise Henaut — in presence of Claude de Ramezay, Governor of Montreal and godfather of Mathias; François Vachon de Belmont; Pierre Breyé, bourgeois; and Daniel Madox, cooper — for their daughter, promise to give Mathias

[73] See Chapter II. [74] See Note 76 (below). [75] See Chapter II.

[76] For the obligations required of feudal tenants see Joseph Fry, Kittery, Chapter XIII.

on his wedding-day two bulls of eighteen months, one cow of four years, a pig of eighteen months and two goats (age not specified). They give to Catherine in gratitude for the considerable labor and services she has rendered them two arpents of land outright, which is not to prejudice her rights at their death to an equal share of the estate with her brothers and sisters. Mathias and Catherine declared that they understood and agreed to the contract and her brother and brother-in-law, uncle and cousin consented to the marriage.

The only records we find of their family are the baptism of one daughter and marriage of another.

On the 15 Dec., 1715, was baptized Marie-Josette, daughter of Claude-Mathias Fanef, Englishman, and of Catherine Charpentier. The godfather was Louis Dicker, English,[77] a servant of the Mission.

In 1750 Marie-Anne Phanef was married to Louis Renaud; nine children were born of this marriage. M. Cuoq wrote: "This Fanef is sometimes spelled farnet and again phaneuf. The Missionaries of that time did not know the English language, and it can be easily understood that they could mutilate the proper names of that language."

1706.

SEAGER, HENRY, JR.

Henry Seager of Newton had "Two Sons prest out into ye Country's Service" at Groton. One was killed and one captured "summer before last," says his petition, dated Nov., 1707.[78] He received 40 shillings because "they both of them Lost their Arms wch I think were Justly valuable at five pounds and four Powder horns, half a Pound of Powder, twenty bullets & a snapsack." The captive was held fourteen months until John Sheldon redeemed him in September, 1707, at cost to the father of "ten pounds currant at Cannaday, beside the loss of time while he was absent & now he is come home, he is caled upon to do douty both

77 Of Old England. 78 Arch. 71, 419 and 637.

in military & publick as much as those y[t] weare never captivated." In John Sheldon's account we find "Pd for Diet for Henry Segur, captive 41 livres. More paid for sd Segur for stockins & shoes 9 livres 10 sous. Pd. to a man for fetching sd Segur from the Indian town to Mont Roy'[l] 3 livres."

This from the "Boston News-Letter" of July 22-29, 1706, may be the account of his capture. It is fourteen months prior to his release.

"At Groton on the Lords Day the 21st Current 3 Souldiers going to the place of Publick Worship over a Fence passing through a Field of Corn some of the Sculking Indian Enemy being hid in the Field, shot at them, kill'd two and Captivated the third."

Pike, writing of the same occurrence, says: "July 21, 1706 Sab: 2 souldiers slain & one carried away by the enemy at Groton. They were all new-Cambridge men & were returned from one Bloods house who had invited y[m] to Dinner."

1707, 20 *June*.

TARBELL, SARAH, b. 29 Sept., 1693.
JOHN, b. July, 1695.
ZECHARIAH, b. 27 Jan., 1700.

Children of Thomas and Elizabeth (Wood). Different stories are told of their capture. The following is the tradition accepted by Dr. Green. The children were picking cherries in the early evening and were caught before they could get down from the tree. Dr. Green carefully explains that by new style June 20 would be July 1 when cherries are ripe in Groton.

In 1713/14 their brother Thomas went with Stoddard and Williams to Canada hoping to effect their release. Stoddard wrote: "June 8th we sent Thomas Tarball and one English prisoner (with a letter to Governor Dudley) to return by way of Albany."[79]

In June, 1715, he petitioned for "Consideration & Allowance for his Time and Expences," and although nothing was "due," he having gone as a volunteer, the House allowed him ten pounds.

[79] Gen. Reg., V, 35.

Their father, making his will in 1715, left, after certain bequests, "all the rest and residue of his Reall Estate to be Equally divided" between the captives upon their return "or In Proportion unto any of them that shall return etc." Not one of the three did return.

"Zech[a] John and Sarah Tarbal" are on the Roll of 1710/11. The boys were kept by the Indians. Sarah was taken by the French and

"On Monday, 23 July 1708 was baptized by me the undersigned priest, Sara Tarbel, born at Groton in New England the (29 Sept) ninth day of October of the year 1693, of the marriage of Thomas Tarbel and of Elizabeth Woods, and there baptized by the minister soon after her birth; having been taken by the savages Monday June 20, 1707 and brought to Canada has since been ransomed and is living with the Sisters of the Congregation, established at La Chine where she made abjuration on May 1st. Her godfather was Monsieur Jacques Urbain Rocbert de la Moraudière, secretary of Monsieur L'intendant, and her godmother Damoiselle Marguerite Bouat, wife of Monsieur Antoine Pacaud, deputy-treasurer of the customs of the king in this country. Her name of Sara was changed to that of Marguerite. They all signed according to the ordinance

Mg[te] Bouat
Pascaud
Lamoraudiere
Meriel Prêtre."

"Marguerite Tarbel" is on the naturalization list of 1710, and here Sara-Marguerite disappears.

John and Zechariah lived at Caughnawaga and at St. Regis. They were Indianized and married Indian women.

"No personal trace" of them can be found because the early records were destroyed, but by careful study of later registers, Mr. Forbes[80] is sure that the son of one of them was a chief and founder of the later Mission at St. Regis.[81] This was Pierre or

80 M. J. Guillaume L. Forbes, former priest at the Mission. 81 See Chapter II.

Tier Karekohe who married the daughter of the chief of the clan of "the little Turtles." In the baptismal records of one of their thirteen children is the name of the paternal grandmother, Marie Madeleine Kanerote.

She was buried at Caughnawaga in 1779 and the record says: "She saw her fourth generation," which seems to show that Tarbell generations followed each other with great rapidity. Twenty-five years after Thomas's futile journey to Canada John and Zechariah visited Groton. How and why they came is not known, but in April, 1739, a bill for the costs of their journey made out against their brothers Thomas and Samuel and payable to William Rogers, Jr., an interpreter, was paid by the General Court upon Thomas's promise of reimbursement. The charges included Biskett, Pork and 1½ Galls Brandy, 8 blanketts Strouds,[82] Lodging, Victul, horse Hire and "To my Trouble for bringing your Brothers from Canada to Albany & here from ye 10th febry to April 27th is 77 days at 20/."

On 20 April, 1739, Governor Belcher sent the following communication to the Council and House: "There are lately come from Canada some Persons that were taken by the Indians from Groton above thirty Years ago who (its believed) may be induced to settle into this Province, on your giving them some proper Encouragement. If this Matter might be effected, I should think it would be not only an Act of Compassion in order to release them from the Errors and Delusions of the Romish Faith; but their living among us might, in Time to come, be of great Advantage to the Province." Four days later it was ordered that "Forty pounds New tenor bills," be allowed to Mr Eph Kellogg Esqr for the Use of these two Captives in the following Manner: one third "to be laid out at their discretion as a present to their Wives in the purchase of such things as they are desirous of," a like sum to be "at their own disposall, And the remainder . . . to bear their Charges homewards." The government also offered them land

82 Coarse blankets used by Indians.

in some new township and to pay them "as Soldiers at Ft. Dummer during Life;[83] to give them bread for their Families without being obliged to the duty of the Garrison only behaving themselves peaceably and Orderly Among us;" and also if they returned to stay their brothers should be paid the sum of William Rogers' account.[84] Although they could not be "induced" the government apparently did pay Rogers' charges.[85] Hutchinson says:[86] "I met at Albany two or three men in 1744, who came in with the Indians to trade, and who had been taken at Groton . . . one of them —— Tarbell was said to be one of the wealthiest of the Cagnawaga tribe. He made a visit in his Indian dress and with his Indian complexion (for by means of grease and paints but little difference could be discerned) to his relations at Groton but had no inclination to remain there."

Dr. Hough[87] says that their wives were the daughters of Sakonentsi and Atawenta and that both families went to the new mission at St. Regis, but when the Rev. Sylvanus Ripley went to Caughnawaga in 1722 for pupils for the "Charity School at Hanover" he saw one of the Tarbell captives whom he described as "a hearty and active man and the eldest chief and chief speaker of the tribe. He expressed affection for his relatives in N. E. and desired they might be informed that he had a grandson in the school." The boy was about eight years old.

Dr. Hough tells interesting and romantic tales of later Tarbells, especially of Joseph Torakaron who as a chief was taken by a Frenchman named Fovel to Paris and Rome, receiving gifts from Charles X and the Pope. The latter gave him a second and private audience. When they reached New York on their return Fovel ran away with all the gifts except a valuable rosary and three paintings—two of which are at St. Regis and one at Caugh-

83 Ontosaga and two other Caughnawaga chiefs had already been given commissions in that garrison, which, however, did not make for loyalty.

84 Prov. Laws, XII, 560.

85 Shown by the Act of Jan. 8th, 1746/7.

86 Vol. 2, 139.

87 St. Regis in "History of St. Lawrence and Franklin Counties of New York."

nawaga. The poor chief had to receive charity to get home. At St. Regis Dr. Green learned from the priest that the Tarbells were prominent people in the parish and that many still bear the name. Louis Tarbell was a soldier in our War of the Revolution.

The province took better care of its people in 1711 than in 1690 as is shown by the two lists of garrison-houses. In the latter year Groton had eighteen, sheltering from one to twelve families, Mr. Hubbard's having the largest number. Fifty-eight families were there, having ninety-three men; three hundred and seventy-eight souls, protected by seventeen soldiers.

CHAPTER XI

The Massachusetts Frontier

Squackig — Billerica — Lancaster — Worcester — Pascomuck — Marlborough — Dunstable — Brookfield — Northampton

Captives

Squackig.

1695. Wannannemim, Jeanne.

Billerica.

1695. Dunkin, Hannah.
Levistone, Sarah.
Rogers, Daniel.
Marcy.
Shed, Zechariah.
Toothaker, Margaret.

Lancaster.

1692. Howe, Elizabeth (of Marlborough).
1697. Fairbanks, Mary.
Glasher, Mary.
Hudson, Elizabeth.
Joanna.
Roper, Ephraim, Jr.
Rugg, Hannah.
Skait, John's Son.
Wheeler, Tabitha.
1705. Sawyer, Thomas.
Elias.
Bigelow, John (of Marlborough).

Worcester.

1703/4.

Sergeant, Mary.
Martha.
John.
Thomas.
Mary.
Daniel.

1709. Ward, Elisha.

Pascomuck.

1704. Jones, Esther.
Huggins, Margaret.
Searle, Elisha.

Marlborough-Westborough.

1704. Rice, Asher.
Adonijah.
Silas.
Timothy.

Dunstable.

1706. Galucia, Daniel.
Cummings, Etienne?

1709. Whiting, Samuel.

Brookfield.

1708. Woolcot, John.

Northampton.

1711. Strong, Samuel.

SQUACKIG (NORTHFIELD)

1695.

WANNANNEMIM, JEANNE.

"The same Thursday, May 1st 1698 was baptized *sous condition* an Indian woman, about fifty years old, named Jeanne Wannannemim, born in the village of *Loups* [Mohegans] called

Natick belonging to the English, near Medfield; having been brought up and married there, *en premières noces* to Jean Mamusko, having afterwards lived in the woods near the coast and elsewhere, was taken near Deerfields at a place called Squackig by Sowati, an Indian of the Saut, in November 1695, and is now living in this town. Her godfather was Monsieur Francois Hardouin, merchant. Her godmother Marthe Mills, English woman, widow of Christophe Grant, who have signed." The baptism was administered in the Chapel of Notre-Dame de Bon Secours by the special permission of M. Francois Dollier de Casson, Priest, Grand Vicar of *Monseigneur L'illustrissime et Reverendissime* Bishop of Quebec.

Much may be read between the lines of this record of a New England Indian captive. It shows that the same interest was taken in a savage as in a white convert; a French merchant being one sponsor and Martha (Mills) Grant of Salmon Falls the other.

Jane belonged to Eliot's Indians who, alas! because of the distrust felt towards all of their race during Philip's war, were taken from their home in Natick and sent from a place called "The Pines" on Charles River (where now is the Arsenal at Watertown) to Deer Island in the bay. Dr. Ellis says it was "after a comforting prayer by Eliot" that they went at midnight by the serving tide down the river into the bay. "Patiently, humbly and piously" they went, wrote Eliot, "without murmuring or complaining against the English."

Some "Praying Indians" did go back to the wilds. Jane and her husband *en premières noces* were probably of them; but if this be true of some let us not forget that other village converts put on again their war-paint and feathers in order to fight with the English, their "dubious benefactors."[1]

In August, 1695, there was trouble between "our Indians" who were hunting above Deerfield and "many canoes of enemy Indians."[2] Perhaps Jane was taken at that time, the scribe erring in

[1] "Mem. Hist. of Boston," I, 273. [2] "Hist. Northfield," 126.

the month, or some wandering Indians of the Sault may have found her as stated in November.

Half a century later when some New England Indian captives had been sold as slaves in Montreal Phips told the Council that Massachusetts must do something about it for they were Freemen and Subjects of his Majesty.[3] Negroes, on the contrary, being of less account were slaves wherever they happened to be. Jonquière in 1750 says that it was the English who first took this ground.[4]

Billerica

1695. *August 5.*

The town clerk wrote: "This day received that awful stroke by the enemy of fifteen persons slain & taken."

It began at the house of John Rogers in that part of the town which is now Tewksbury. Because the Indians were on horses, contrary to custom, they were not recognized as they approached the little settlement at high noon on this hot day.[5]

The Rev. John Cotton of Plymouth Church wrote to his son Rowland of Ipswich about the attack, telling him that "Indians had beset Billerica . . . a Garrison there about 2 or 3 of the clock P: M: when they were at dinner, the gates open, killed & carried away 15 or 16 men woemen & children (Mr. Brattle writes so to me also) the enemy Judged to be about 40; Rogers (whose Garrison it was) & his son were killed, & Goodwife Toothacre (once accused for a witch) & severall more; one maide was pursued into the Garrett where she hid herselfe behind a birch basket & soe was not found, but when the garrison & house were on fire, she was forct to Jump out at a window which was very high (its a great wonder she brake not her neck) & had noe hurt; one of the garrison that was wounded escaped & is likely to doe well; severall men went after them & it is judged they certainly overtook them,

[3] Arch. 108, 352. [4] N. Y. Docs., X, 210.

[5] The local accounts in Hazen's "History" and Nason's "Centennial Oration" seem to have been based upon Farmer's "Historical Memoir."

for they were soe neere as to heare them give fifteen cohoops."[6]

Governor Stoughton, writing from Boston August 24 to Governor Fletcher of New York, gives a different version: "A party of Indians about a Fortnight since, came over Merrimack River neer unto Bilrica a Town not above ffourteen or ffifteen miles distant from this place, and sheltring themselves in a great swamp watched their opportunity, surprized a man at worke in his Field, kil'd him and then made up to his house, which was somewhat remote from the body of the Town, but a good Fortification about it, the men belonging to it being all abroad, the Indians got in, burn'd the house, kil'd and carried away nine or Ten women and Children; also entred another house neerby & kil'd a man lying upon his Bed."[7]

DUNKIN, HANNAH, b. 1683.

The daughter of John and Johanna (Jefts).

John died of smallpox (his inventory is dated 1690), leaving seven children. His widow married Benjamin Dutton. She and two children were killed in 1692.

Hannah Dongan is on the list of those remaining in 1695 so she was soon in Canada. In that list she is of Oyster River, but mistakes of domicile are frequent. In 1706 Catherine Denkyin witnesses the marriage of Elizabeth (Price) Stevens in Montreal; so she has already become a convert and been renamed, and that year she asks to be naturalized. She marries in Quebec.

"The 19th of the 9th month, 1709, after the publication of two Banns of the marriage between Claude Cliche, son of the late Nicolas Cliche and of the late magdeleine Peltier, father and mother, of this parish and Bishopric of quebec of one part and Catherine danquin, daughter of jean Danquin and of jeanne d'aphuis her father and mother of Belriquey in New England, of the other part, after having had the dispensation of the third Ban & of those of the place where they have just previously lived, from Mre Charles glandelet, vicar general of this diocese and having

[6] "Cotton Papers," Mass. Hist. Soc. [7] Arch. 2, 406.

found no impediment, I, undersigned, curé of this parish have married and given them the nuptial benediction according to the form prescribed by our mother holy Church in presence of . . . the brother of the bridegroom and several friends

Pacquet."

On the first day of the seventh month of 1710 Claude Cliche was baptized *(ondoyé)* by the midwife at home because of danger. He lived seventy years!

Tanguay gives the births of other children:

Marie-Catherine, 1712; m. Joseph Caron; d. 1733.
Marie-Thérèse, b. and d. 1714.
Jean, b. 1716, d. 1717.
Marie-Elisabeth-Geneviève; m. Dominique Dasilva; d. 1746.

On "the 4th October, 1727, was buried in the cemetery of this place[8] Magdaleine Catherine Dunkin, wife of Claude Cliche, carpenter of this town, deceased the preceding day, after having received the last sacraments, aged about 45 years." Two priests were present.

The next year Claude took a new wife and became the father of ten more children.

LEVISTONE, SARAH, b. 1684.

Eldest daughter of John and Margaret (Ross).

This was the family that suffered most. Five young children and their maternal grandmother from Cambridge were killed. The wife and eldest son escaped. Sarah was still a captive in 1710/11, but may have been later redeemed as a Sarah Levistone m. in 1722 Jonathan Dutton.

ROGERS, DANIEL, b. 1683.
MARCY, b. 1685.

Children of John and Mary (Shed).

Here, where the attack began, the father was killed by an arrow which pierced his neck as he was taking his noon-day rest.

[8] Quebec.

Nothing is known of the two captives except that they were in the French and Indians' hands in 1710/11.

SHED, ZECHARIAH, b. 21 April, 1685.

Son of Zechariah and Mrs. Ann (—— | Bray), who was killed in August, 1692.

His name is among those held by the French and Indians in Canada in 1710/11. The "Shed Genealogy" says that he was a soldier in the French and Indian wars of 1710 and died in captivity, but gives no authority. Is it not more probable that he was taken with the others in 1695 with whose names his stands in the list?

TOOTHAKER, MARGARET, b. 1682/3.

Youngest daughter of Dr. Roger and Mary (Allen).

Mrs. Mary was arrested as a witch with her sister Mrs. Martha Carrier; the latter was hanged.

LANCASTER

No "out-town" suffered more in the early wars, nor is any narrative of Indian captivity better known than that of Mrs. Rowlandson, wife of its minister. She was carried away in 1676 when fifteen hundred of Philip's men did their cruel work. Her husband was spared because he was "in the Bay" seeking help.

From 1680 to 1720 little is known of Lancaster's history.

The early people seem to have been too much crushed, and too unmindful of the interest of those to come after to leave any memorials. In the list of garrison-houses in 1711[9] we find in Lancaster twenty-seven houses (Preist's the largest) holding from one to six families; the number of families given is eighty-three — one hundred and eleven men, four hundred and fifty souls and twenty-one soldiers.

[9] Arch. 71, 871-6.

1692, *July* 18.

HOWE, ELIZABETH, of Marlborough.

Born 16 July, 1675, the daughter of John and Elizabeth (Ward).

Her father was killed at Sudbury in April, 1676, and her mother soon married in Charlestown, Captain Kerley. Marlborough was at that time untenable, but the family returned later and there was Elizabeth's home.

Her sister Sarah was the wife of Peter Joslin of Lancaster and Elizabeth was carried away from their house.

Perhaps Joslin told the story to Mr. Harrington, and perhaps he was in the meeting-house and heard the parson repeat it in his "Century Sermon" of 1753, for he outlived four wives, dying in 1759.

It was "on the 18th of July, 1692 that the Indians assaulted the House of Mr. Peter Joslin, who was at his Labour in the Field and knew nothing of it till entring the House found his Wife and three Children and a Woman [the widow Whitcomb] that liv'd in his Family barbarously butcher'd by their Hatchets and weltring in their Gore. His Wife's Sister with one of the Children were carried into Captivity, she return'd; but that child was murder'd in the wilderness. Thus was he stript naked and call'd to bitter Weeping and Lamentation."[10] The child Peter, aged six, probably soon became a burden. Mrs. Bigelow in her "Reminiscences of Marlborough" says that Mrs. Joslin with a two-year-old child was taken and that she so wearied the Indians by asking for release that they, gathering all together, pushed her naked into their midst, danced around her "in their hellish manner," knocked her and the child on the head and burnt their bodies, threatening others with similar punishment. But this is a much later story than Harrington's. She says also that Elizabeth Howe had so sweet a voice that the Indians spared her life that she might "give sweet sounds," and when she complained of

10 "Hist. of Worcester Co.," Whitney.

the delay in her redemption (which was in 1696, according to Nourse, who says also that she was carried to Canada) that she was answered that had it been a question of bartering for furs it would have been sooner accomplished. It is said that she kept certain Indian habits, such as sitting on the floor, and that she never recovered from the terror and shock, and that one can easily believe. When captured—at seventeen—she was "about to be married" to Thomas Keyes. He, believing her dead, took a solemn vow never to marry, which vow he gladly broke when Elizabeth came back, but not immediately if the given dates are correct—the marriage in Marlborough being January 23, 1698/9. They had a family of five children; she living to be eighty-nine years old.

On 17 April, 1701, the House voted that three pounds and eighteen shillings be paid "to Mr Thomas Howe, he having Paid so much for the Redemption of Elizabeth Howe, who was Captive to an Indian."[11] Thomas probably was Elizabeth's uncle.

1697, *September* 11.

And again in King William's war the Indians came. Lieutenant-Governor Stoughton, writing three days later to the Governor of Connecticut, says: "Upon ye 11th instant twelve o'clock forty Indians surprised and killed twenty-six persons, burnt two Garrison houses and two barns, the Garrisons having been left open and ye inhabitants surprised in their fields."[12] One of the victims was the minister, John Whiting. It is said that the Indians "offer'd him Quarter, but he chose rather to fight to the last than resign himself to those whose tender Mercies are Cruelty."

It was with sympathy and understanding that Mr. Harrington used these words, for before he began his long service in the Lancaster Church he and his people had been driven from their homes in Lower Ashuelot.

We have the names of only eight captives and of them we know little.

[11] Arch. 70, 518. [12] Arch. 2, 256.

FAIRBANKS, MARY (Howard).

Jonathan Fairbanks and two of his little children were killed. His wife, who was of Concord, is said to have been carried to Canada, but as she was one of those captives at Casco Bay who reported the "remarkable things" quoted by Mather[13] and as she returned — according to the list — on the *Province Galley* in 1698/9, it would seem to be an error.

In the inventory of her husband's estate is "a smity, anvill, blows & other tools belonging," all valued at five pounds, so he must have been a blacksmith. "Weomans wearing cloathes," too, are listed, for his wife's apparel, of course, belonged to him. It is pleasant to know that they were saved, and in the account made three months after her return they are "allowed" to her; four pounds and five shillings being their value. She was given also four pounds "for Mourning Apparell."

GLASHER, MARY (sometimes Glasser).

She was probably daughter of John and Elizabeth and had a short captivity, returning on the *Province Galley*. The widow "Mary ffarbankes" doubtless was kind to her.

John Glasher (so he signed his will in 1691) gave certain land rights to his wife, but "if she sees cause to marry" then she is to have only her thirds. He names three daughters, Mary being one, and each is to receive five pounds upon her marriage. Was it this Mary who married Robert Powers in 1733?

HUDSON, JOANNA.
ELIZABETH.

Daughters of Daniell Huttson — so he signed his will — and Johannah. He was a brickmaker and bricklayer.

There were at least five sons and as many daughters in the family. It is said that some were killed. Little seems to be known of the two named, who were respectively thirty-seven and thirty-nine years old, but their surviving brothers and sisters (for whom

[13] Magnalia, II, 643.

the husbands signed) made an agreement in December, 1697, in which was written "for our sisters wearing cloathes we mutualy agree to Leave them undevided at present . . . hoping that one of them namely: either Johanah or Elizabeth may be yet alive . . . & also in case that either of our said sisters shall by Gods goodness be againe Reduced from captivity that then we do farther oblidge our selves as aforesaid to allow & pay unto either of them that so Returne her portion double or two shares through all that would of Right have appertained to either of them had they now been Resident & present to Receive their part, all which wee oblidge our selves & heirs . . . to performe."[14] Did either survive to wear her dresses and to receive "her portion double?" The author of "The Shed Family" says the women were killed in captivity, but does not give his authority.

ROPER, EPHRAIM, JR. (about twelve).

Son of Ephraim and Hannah (Goble). Ephraim, Sr., was the only man who escaped from the burning Rowlandson house in 1676. His wife was killed then, but he took a new one who with him and a daughter were killed in this attack. Ephraim, Jr., was "yett in the Indians hands" when the *Province Galley* brought home two of his friends, but he returned later.

RUGG, HANNAH, dau. of Joseph.

Joseph Rugg, son of John and Martha (Prescott), his wife and three children were killed, one child only escaping death. Mr. Harrington says "Joseph Rugg's Son" was captured, but it is "Hannah Rugg of Lancaster" who, on the list of 1698, had "gon to Albanie." No further record is found.

SKAIT (or Scate), John's son.

A John, b. 1659, and his wife were killed. This John may have been son of John Skeath "cordwainer from Boston" and Sarah (Walters). Were these the forbears of the nameless son?

14 Middlesex Probate.

WHEELER, TABITHA.

She was the widow of Abraham, who had been killed in 1695.

1705, *October* 15.

In the summer of 1704 the town was furiously attacked, but the people were better prepared and although some were killed, the meeting-house and other buildings burned, and much live stock destroyed, no captives were taken. In November of that year their humility, real or conventional, is shown in this sentence of their petition which says they are "destressed . . . under ye Awfull Rebukes of Gods hand In ye Manifest Tokens of his Displeasure against us In pe^r^ mitting those Barbarous Heathen to be such a Scourge to us."[15]

The next year on 15 October Sewall wrote: "Three men are carried away from Lancaster from Mr. Sawyer's Sawmill." They were

SAWYER, THOMAS, b. 1649, d. 1736, son of Thomas and Mary (Prescott).

ELIAS, his son (Hannah, a second w. was his mother), b. abt. 1689, d. 1752.

BIGELOW, JOHN, of Marlborough.

Sawyer was a blacksmith; Bigelow a carpenter.

The mill, named by Sewall, was on Dean's, later called Goodridge's, Brook.

Whitney, whose "History of Worcester County" was published in 1793, says that the men "were captivated at Mr. Sawyer's garrisoned house about the dawn of day," and that Sawyer's youngest son escaped through a back window.

The Indians treated Mr. Sawyer cruelly on the journey, but, as the narrator casually remarks, at Montreal he "observed to the French Governor that on the River Chamblee was a fine site for mills and that he would build a sawmill for him, provided he would procure a ransom for himself, his son and Bigelow. The Governor readily closed with the proposal as at that time there

[15] Arch. 113, 364.

was no sawmill in all Canada, nor artificer capable of building one."

The Indians quickly sold Elias and John Bigelow to the French, "but no sum would purchase Mr. Sawyer's redemption: Him (being distinguished for his bravery which had proved fatal to a number of their brethren) they were determined to immolate." He was actually tied to a stake and surrounded with material for firing when "on a sudden a Friar appeared, and with great solemnity held forth what he declared to be the key to the gates of Purgatory; and told them unless they immediately released their prisoner, he would instantly unlock those gates and send them headlong thereinto." So their victim was delivered from the perils of death and built the governor's sawmill!

In the census of 1719 there are nineteen sawmills in Canada, which proves that Thomas Sawyer's model was appreciated. In 1754 Major Wheelwright counted twelve between Three Rivers and Quebec built, he says, "the same as in New England. An Englishman built the first, who was taken prisoner . . . and this he did to purchase his Liberty."[16] Sawyer's mill was finished in a year and the two older men were released, but Elias was kept another twelve-month to teach the French how to use it, then he was "amply rewarded" and sent home.

An old plate of crude color in the museum of the Lancaster Library tells the story of a Canadian romance: "This plate was brought to Lancaster by Elias Sawyer about 1708 or 1710 from his captivity among the Indians of Lower Canada. Tradition asserts that it was the gift to him of an Indian Maiden whom he promised to return and marry. Its warped appearance was caused by his carrying it in his bosom on his long march homeward. His family persuaded him not to return, and about 1726 he married Beatrice Houghton and had a numerous family. On his deathbed he regretted his broken faith with the Indian maid [Let us hope that Beatrice had gone before] and directed that her

16 MS. Journal Mass. Hist. Soc.

love-token should be carefully preserved by his descendants."

In 1894, at the death of an old man who left no children, it was given to the library.

John Bigelow, the son of Samuel of Watertown and Mary (Flagg), was born 9 May, 1675.

A letter which he wrote to his wife Jerusha (Garfield) in January, 1706, did not reach her until August. She answered sixteen days later in part as follows: "Marlbury August 22, 1706. Dear and loving Husband. In much grief and tender affection, greatly lamenting your miserable condition, hoping in the mercy of God who has prospered you and kept you alive" and that He will in "His own due time work your deliverance . . . And I do most Humbly and importunately petition the Governour to have pity and compassion on yourself and me." She hopes he is well as she and the children are; quotes from "Lamentations" and then in a postscript she adds that "brother Samuel and Thomas are well, and the rest of our relations."[17] Before he received the letter he had been very ill, as we learn from Mr. John Williams.[18] "The last summer [1706] one Biggilow from Marlborough, a captive at Montreal, was very sick in the hospital and in the judgment of all, with a sickness to death. Then the priest and others gave out that he was turned to be of their religion and taken into their communion. But, contrary to their expectation, he was brought back from the gates of death, and would comply with none of their rites; saying that whilst he had the use of his reason, he never spake any thing in favor of their religion; and that he never disowned the Protestant faith." We must remember that Mr. Williams was a prejudiced person.

Bigelow and Jerusha Garfield were married in 1696 and had a large family. A daughter b. in 1707 was named Comfort. The

[17] "Hist. Rem. of Marlborough," 131. Ella A. Bigelow — A careful search has not discovered her petition. Unless this letter is edited she spelled better than her generation.

[18] "The Redeemed Captive," Ed. 1853, p. 83.

next child, b. in 1710 was called Freedom in gratitude for his deliverance.

He lived to be very old.

WORCESTER (ORIGINALLY QUINSIGAMOND)

1703/4. *Winter.*

DIGORY SERGEANT'S FAMILY.

The date of this attack is not known, but as the Indians attacked other places in Massachusetts during this winter the year seems probable.

Digory Sergeant,[19] a carpenter of Sudbury, was of those who began the planting of Worcester.

Having come and having made his home on Sagatabscot hill he was determined to stay. After the outbreak of King William's war he alone kept his family there. When the next war came he was urged to remove to a safer place. Admonitions failing, some soldiers were sent to compel his departure; Captain Howe and twelve men were to fetch the family from their hazardous home.

The night was cold, the snow was falling, and alas! Howe halted his men at a house two miles distant from Sergeant's home. The men made a fire, set a watch and lay down upon the floor to sleep.

The next morning when Howe reached his destination he found the house desolate and its intrepid owner dead upon the floor. Had he only pushed on the night before the story would be different.

Moccasin tracks surrounded the place; tracing them backward they led the Englishmen to their own house of refuge; but it was not until the war was over that they knew how the same roof had covered soldiers and savages on that stormy night. The watch saw no enemy-Indians, for they were safely hidden in the cellar below; their only exit being the trap-door upon which the soldiers were sleeping.

[19] Various spellings are used. In 1685 he wrote Sargent; he signed his will Serjent. Among authorities quoted in the following account are Lincoln's "Worcester" and "Some Descendants of Diggory Sergeant."

Sagamore John and his Indians made a better running in the morning than the New Englanders and had time to finish their horrid work. Sergeant seized his gun before they killed him. His wife and children they carried away. The poor woman, terrified and grief-stricken, faltered and hindered the progress so as they climbed the hill of Tataesset an Indian stepped out from the file as if looking for game and as the fainting woman passed he slew her with a single blow.

She was a second wife. While a widower Sergeant made a will leaving his possessions to his only child Martha. They were so modest as to invite naming: "One flock bed and boulster; with one rugg and two blanketts and two coverlets; six frocs; one broad ax and one falling ax and one handsaw; one frying pan; one shave, one drawing knife; one trunk and a sermon book that is at Mrs. Mary Mason's, widow, at Boston; with one pewter pint pot; one washing tub, one cow and calf; one mare: three iron wedges: two beetle rings . . . There is one gun too."

On the Roll of 1710/11 are "Mary Sargeant, Martha, John, Thomas, Mary Jr. and James [which should be Daniel] from Wooster."

Mrs. Mary's name should not be there for as shown above she was dead. She was supposed to have been the sister of Digory's friend, George Parmenter, but the Canadian record gives her a different name.

When Sargeant's estate was administered in 1707 all the children were said to be living. "Daniel and Mary are still at Canada . . . whither they were carryed captive by the Indians & now are living among the ffrench." This implies that the other children had returned which does not seem to be true. In the distribution John, eldest son, was allowed "double the choise and after him Thomas & then the said daughter Martha & so let the other two lots ligh for Daniel & Mary." In his account of 1715 Parmenter says: "Children Martha and Thomas at Boston, at Canada Jn° Daniel & Mary."

Martha.

Her mother was Constance James of Boston, married to Digory in October, 1692.

She had to carry her little sister during the first two days of their journey, then as the child grew troublesome the Indians took her away and Martha never saw her again; so says Caleb Wall in "Reminiscences of Worcester." After seven years Martha was redeemed. She said she saw many persons burned at the stake, so she must have been part of the time with the Indians.

She married Capt. Daniel Shattuck in Marlborough in April, 1719; had one child, Sarah, and died in 1722.

John.

His story is told in the following petition which he sent in 1738 to the General Court;[20] he, then a lieutenant at the Truck House above Northfield, says: "That about the beginning of Queen Anne wars your Petitioners ffather living then at Worcester had the misfortune with your Petitioners mother & one Brother to be killed by the Indian enemy at which time your Petitioner with five of his Brothers & Sisters [This makes seven children!] were taken & carryed into Captivity where your Petitioner Remained Twelve or thirteen years dureing which time your Petitioner underwent . . . hardships & Difficultys at the end whereof by the good providence of God, he was inclined to Return home and tho' he mett with great opposition as well from the Jesuits as Indians yet he came home and was at the sole cost of his Redemption. That upon his arrivall into his Native Country he was put into ye service under Capt Kellog & so Remains at this time. That he has been three times at Canada In ye service of the province since his Redemption in which he suffered greatly especially in the last Journey." He is grateful for what has been done for him, but wants more, and gets a tract of two hundred acres near "the truck house," Fort Dummer.

One of his three journeys was with Captain Kellogg in 1728.

20 Arch. 72, 470.

Then he fell sick in Canada and never received all his pay. He married in 1727 Abigail Jones of Springfield. Seven children were born to them. In 1748, March 29, "About twelve or fifteen Indians Way-laid the Scout-Path from Fort Dummer to Colerain Lieutenant Sergeant and four more went out in this Path to get some Timber for Oars and Paddles. About a Mile from Fort Dummer they were fired upon; . . . Sergeant, his son and Joshua Wells engaged the Enemy, fighting on a Retreat; Wells was soon killed; Sergeant encouraged his Son; said they should have Help from the Fort; They charged many Times: Sergeant shouted as often as the Enemy did, and called upon them to come out and fight boldly. These two fought on a Retreat half a Mile; but Lieutenant Sergeant was killed, and his Son taken: They could not have any Help from the Fort; there being but a few Men there, and some of them sick with the Measels, and others not having Snow Shoes in Readiness, could not go on the Snow."[21]

A family tradition differs from Doolittle's story. As that goes John, when hunting, clad in furs, was mistaken for an animal and shot by a friendly Indian who after killing him showed his friendship by taking his scalp and presenting it to the family, who long treasured it. The story of Daniel, son of John, may be found in the Third Intercolonial War.

Daniel, son of Digory, was given by the Indians to the governor and,

"On Sunday, 6th Nov. 1707 was baptized by me, undersigned Priest, a little English boy named in his country, Daniel Sergeant born at —— of August 1699 of the marriage of the late Dickery Sergeant, inhabitant of —— and of Marie Oben both Protestants, who having been taken at the said place, the —— has been given by the savages to High and mighty Seigneur Messire Philippe de Rigault Gouverneur General of New France. His name of Daniel

[21] Doolittle's Narrative in "History of Northfield," 378.

was changed to Louis Philippe. His godfather was Robert de Poitier, *Ecuyer,* Sieur de Buisson, clerk in the department of the Navy at Montreal with whom he is now living, and his godmother Damoiselle Françoise Bouthier, daughter of the late m^r^ Guillaume Bouthier, who have signed with me.

anne francoise Bouthier

Dubuisson Meriel Priest"

Daniel is mentioned in a deed given by Thomas in 1728 as "late deceased in Canada."

A brief account of this tragedy was printed in the first volume (1792) of the Massachusetts Historical Society's Collections. The writer says that Digory's wife and two children were killed and that John, Thomas and Mary were carried away, and of them he says: "They did not choose to return to their native country. However in the year 1726, they accompanied Mrs. Williams, who was taken captive from Deerfield on a visit to their friends in Massachusetts." This means Eunice Williams, but she did not come to New England until 1740. In 1726 Governor Dudley's commissioners[22] brought home some captives and with them, to visit their New England kin, were the wives of Pierre de Lestage and Jean Gaulthier (Esther Sayward and Mary Storer). Were the two Sergeants also of the party?

Mary was known to be alive in Canada in 1728.

Thomas was in Boston in 1715 and in service until 1726.

1709. *August.*

WARD, ELISHA, b. 12 Jan., 1686.

Son of William, Sr., and Hannah (Brigham), widow of Gershom Eames.

Ward was killed or captured by the Indians at Worcester when riding post from Marlborough to Hadley.[23] He is named as a prisoner on the Roll of 1710/11.

22 See p. 99.

23 Hudson's "Hist. Marlborough," 108.

Pascomuck

(Now within the village of East Hampton)

Saturday, 13 *May*, 1704.

Lacking snowshoes the men who pursued and tried to rescue the Deerfield captives of February accomplished nothing.

It was the same story of unpreparedness. Fourteen years before, after the attack upon Salmon Falls, Mather wrote in his punning fashion that "through the disadvantages of their *feet* by the *snow*, they could make no *hand* in it." "It" being the pursuit of the enemy. But in March, just after the destruction of Deerfield, the General Court ordered five hundred pairs of snowshoes and moccasins for the frontier.[24]

The twenty-five men who had escaped the Deerfield massacre, being forbidden to forsake the place, were impressed as garrison soldiers, but neither they nor the scouts, who continually ranged the woods, could prevent disaster. It fell first upon the hamlet of Pascomuck, which was northeast of Mt. Tom at its foot just where the Connecticut River sweeps around the point now known as Mt. Nonotuck, four miles from the centre of Northampton. The reason for this attack is given in a letter sent to Versailles on Nov. 17, 1704, by the governor and intendant. They wrote that they were not only obliged to satisfy the Abenakis by sending Hertel de Rouville to Deerfield, but "the Indians of Penaské[25] having likewise sent us word at the same time . . . that the English had killed some of their people, M. de Vaudreuil sent Sieur de Montigny thither, with four or five Frenchmen as well to reassure them in the fear they entertained of the English, *as to engage them to continue the War*. This he effected this spring at the head of some fifty of these Indians, having burnt an English fort and taken twenty-three prisoners. Sieur de Montigny distinguished himself particularly on that occasion."[26]

24 Champlain mentioned snowshoes in 1603.

25 This was perhaps one name of the island in Penobscot River where was Père Thury's mission, now Indian Old Town.

26 N. Y. Docs., IX, 762.

Mr. Williams[27] says: "They were wonderfully lifted up with pride after the return of Captain Montinug from Northampton with news of success."

Here is the local account of this uplifting deed of the Sieur de Montigny as written in the "Recorder's Book for Old Hampshire County."[28]

"May 12 [13] Pascomok Fort taken by ye French and Indians, being about 72. They took, and Captivated ye whole Garrison being about 37 Persons. The English Pursueing of them caused them to nock all the captives on the head, Save 5 or 6. [Pursuit meant death for the captives.] Three they carried to Canada with them, the others escap'd and about 7 of those knocked on the Head Recovered, ye Rest died."

The Rev. Solomon Williams in a sermon of 1815 says that the Indians went first to the Merrimac River but could not attack there; then they aimed for the Westfield, which they found impassible; so being nearly starved they sought Pascomuck, for some who had been to Northampton knew of this new, small settlement. Only five families were living in the pretty place. The Indians put the flax which they found there beside the pickets of the only fortified house, which belonged to Benoni Jones, and soon flax, pickets and house were ablaze.

The meadows were flooded, for the season was very late; indeed the trees were not yet budded and the enemy thought it impossible for any to escape or for any help to come, but Penhallow[29] tells us that an express reached Northampton about break of day and the people learned how "the French and Indians fell on a fortified house where no watch was kept," how they surprised the people in their beds, who resisted as best they could, but when the house was burning the survivors surrendered. This "express" was Benjamin Janes. His four children had been killed, his wife scalped and left for dead soon after the journey began; she was

27 "The Redeemed Captive," Ed. 1853, p. 40.

28 Printed in Gen. Reg., IX.

29 "Wars of New England with the Eastern Indians," 15.

found, carried to Northampton and lived to be more than eighty years old. Benjamin eluded his captors near a ravine, where he must have known a boat was waiting.

Of the survivors: "Three they carried to Canada." They were:

Esther (Ingersoll) Jones.

Margaret Huggins.

Elisha Searle.

Stephen Williams wrote that he saw at Coos, a summer camp of the Indians,[30] "one Mrs. Jones, and Margaret Hugins, her maid, &c. who were taken at Northampton Farms." Let us hope that little Elisha was the "&c."

JONES, MRS. ESTHER (Ingersoll), w. of Benoni.

Mrs. Esther, born Sept. 9, 1665, was of the very large family of John Ingersoll of Hartford and Northampton, by his second wife Abigail (Bascom).

She married 1, William Gurley, who was drowned in 1692, and 2, Benoni Jones, who with their two young children was killed in this attack. She died in Montreal at the Hôtel-Dieu, Dec. 8, 1705.

Stephen Williams described her deathbed conversion in a letter to his father dated January 23, 1705. Parson Williams, unwilling to accept so preposterous a change, calls it the act of "a woman distempered with a very high fever, if not distracted." Trumbull,[31] not naming his authority says, she died in Canada "retaining her faith and hope in the midst of the Jesuits."

At another time Stephen Williams explains that his letter was written by Father Meriel, who required him to copy it. Of Esther Jones he wrote in part: "Mr. Meriel with an Englishwoman went to Esther Jones. She did at first disdain, but a little while after she confessed there were seven sacraments etc." The priest "returned to wait by her all night long, he read and expounded to her some of the Catholic Confession of Faith to her

[30] Between Haverhill, N. H., and Newbury, Vt. [31] "Hist. of Northampton."

satisfaction" and "about Midnight he asked whether she might not confess her sins, and she made unto him fervent confession of all the sins of her whole life." Mrs. Stilson[32] and the Superior of the Nuns were also with her.

The nuns hanged a crucifix "with a pair of beads upon her neck." "After the mass had been said for her" she was buried "in the church-yard next the church" and the zealous father wrote in his clear hand in the church register:

"Wednesday Dec. 9th 1705 was buried in the cemetery of this church, the body of Esther Inghesson deceased the preceding day at the Hospital, aged forty-four years, widow of Benoni Jones, inhabitant of Northampton in New England, who after having been received into the Catholic religion the seventh of this month; in presence of M. Michel Barthelémy Priest, of Louis Trafton[33] gunsmith, and Madeleine Warren[34] wife of Philippe Robitaille, cooper; had received the sacraments of penitence and of extreme unction from the hands of M. Henry Antoine Meriel. Witnesses: M. Meriel and M. Antoine Forget, Priest of the Seminary of Ville Marie." Signed by the three priests.

Huggins, Margaret, b. 1686.

The daughter of John and Experience (Jones) of Stony Brook, Suffield.

She was staying at the home of her uncle, Benoni Jones. Stephen Williams calls her the "maid" of "one Mrs. Jones."

Nine months after her aunt died she was baptized:

"On Sunday, 12th Sept. 1706 was baptized by me, undersigned priest, Marguerite Huggins, born at Stony-Brook in New England the 16th March 1686, of the marriage of Jean Huggins and of Experience Jones and baptized four months later at Springfield, having been taken by the Abenakis at Paskamack near Northampton the (12th) twenty-third May of the year 1703, and brought to St. François, has been since bought by Monsieur le

32 See Pemaquid, Chapter VII. 33 Of York. 34 Of Dover.

Marquis de Crisafy Governor of Three Rivers and for six weeks, has lived at Villemarie. She had for godfather, Monsieur Etienne Rocbert, *Garde-Magazin* of the King, and for godmother, Damoiselle Marguerite Boüat wife of Monsieur Pascaud, Merchant, who have all signed with me according to the law.

M H.

rocbert mgte Boüat Pascaud

Meriel Prêtre."

Trumbull says she returned to New England.

SEARLS, ELISHA, aged nine.

Son of John and Abigail (Pomeroy).

John Searles and three children younger than Elisha were killed. Mrs. Abigail was carried a short distance "to a place called ——'s Island in Broad brook" where the Indians, thinking her unfit to travel because of her condition, tomahawked and left her for dead—but she recovered!

Elisha's grandson retold the tales his grandfather told him: How one of the captives escaped, and the Indians, fearing an alarm and pursuit, killed most of the others and concealed themselves. Elisha, "the one boy" not massacred, picked up a pack and ran forward to show his captors that he could be useful.

Captain Taylor who led the pursuing party was killed, after which the men "returned in sadness."[35]

Little Elisha was the first convert of the three captives carried from Pascomuck.

"On Tuesday, Sept. 29th 1705, was baptized by me, undersigned Priest, an English child named in his country Elisée, son of the late Jean Searls and of Abigail Pommerey, his wife who was born at Northampton in New England the —— having been

[35] His wife asked for aid because Captain Taylor had always been "Redy and willing to Jeopard his Life" (Arch. 71, 124), adding that his horse had been killed. The General Court allowed her forty shillings for the animal and ten pounds for the support of herself and eleven children, and her name was Thankful! There was surely no waste in pensions.

taken the 11th March 1704 and brought to Canada, is living at the home of Messire Jean-Baptiste Céloron, *Ecuyer*, Sieur de Blainville, *Capitaine d'une Compagnie du Détachment de la Marine*. His godfather was the said Sieur de Blainville who gave to him the name of Michel, and his godmother was Dame Marie Anne Le Moyne, Wife of Messire Jean Bouillet Sieur de la Chassaigne Captain of a Company of the same Regiment, who have signed with me.

De Blainville le Moyne la Chassaigne
Meriel Priest"

While with the Indians he went to the Mississippi River.

In 1722 he came with an Indian companion to Northampton, seeking his portion of his father's estate. Having lost his English speech tradition says that he made himself known "by walking on a pair of stilts he had been fond of using when a boy."

He was of course attached to his new mode of life and wished to return, but his people "to engage him to abide here & not return to Canada" separated him from his companions who after a few months went back alone. The House of Representatives voted him ten pounds and desired his Excellency "to retain him in the publick service as a Sergeant at the Garrison of Deerfield or Northfield."[36] The next year Colonel Stoddard wrote to Lieutenant-Governor Dummer that "Capt. Kellogg tells me Dwight [Lieut. Timothy, commanding at Fort Dummer] is desirous that Elisha Searle be with him . . . He is at present a sergeant under Capt. Kellogg was put in by request of the Assembly at his return from Canada where he has long been a prisoner, he seems to be a discreet and careful man."

It was said that he had promised to marry a French girl whose "name was Katreen as he pronounced it." He did marry Rebecca Danks and named a daughter after his Canadian love. He took again the religion of his fathers.[37]

[36] 17 Aug., 1722, Prov. Laws, X, 216.

[37] The Reminiscences are printed by Trumbull from the Judd manuscripts.

MARLBOROUGH — WESTBOROUGH

8 *August*, 1704.

RICE.

The Rev. Ebenezer Parkman, minister of the Westborough church, writing to Governor Hutchinson in 1769 described this attack as follows:

"At the South west part of Marlboro' then called Chauncy, now Westboro', as several persons were busy in spreading Flax, on a plain about 80 Rods from the House of Mr Thomas Rice[38] . . . and a number of Boys were with them, of w^c two were sons of ye said Mr Thomas Rice and three more, sons of Mr Edmund Rice, Ten (some say seven) Indians suddenly rushed down a woody Hill close by, and knocking ye least of ye Boys . . . in ye Head, they seized Two of Mr Thos Rice's Sons [Asher and Adonijah] the oldest of about 10, the other about 8 years; and the two other of Mr Edmund Rice's of ab^t 9 & 7; their names Silas & Timothy; and carried them away to Canada."

The persons who were spreading the flax escaped to Thomas Rice's garrison-house. (This house, by a division of land, later fell within Westborough lines.)

Asher, b. 6 July, 1694.

Son of Thomas and Anna (Rice).

He returned in about four years redeemed by his father through the kind mediation of the Rev. Mr Lydius of Albany.

In 1735 when Ontasaga, the Caughnawaga chief who had conferred with Governor Belcher at Deerfield, passed through Westborough Asher recognized him as one of his captors. Asher's wife's name was Tabitha. Their home was in Spencer and they had ten children.

Mrs. Forbes[39] says his mind was affected by his capture and that he never recovered from his dread of Indians; building fortifications for protection long after they had ceased their raids.

38 First settler of Westborough.

39 Harriette M. Forbes in "Two Indian Chiefs."

Adonijah, b. 11 Aug., 1696.

Brother of Asher. Little is known of him. His Indian name is written by New Englanders Asaundugooton. He must have been ransomed from the Indians because Mr. Parkman wrote he "marryd first a french, afterwards a dutch woman, and settled in Husbandry [evidently an occupation, not a location] on some good Land, a little way off from Montreal, on the North side of the great River; has hed a good Farm there for many years (as we have been certifyd)."

Silas, b. 1695.

Son of Edmund and Ruth (Parker of Roxbury) lived, as did his brother Timothy, at Caughnawaga.

He was Jacques Tannhahorens (he splits the door) and his wife Marie Tsiakohawi, alias Tsionnakwannen. Their children were

(1) Marie Joseph Kaniaronkwas (she gathers snakes).

(2) Atonwa (Thomas). Aronhiowonen (great sky). His daughter married Eunice Williams's grandson Thomas. Atonwa was a chief and d. in 1779 aged 40.

(3) Ignace Sonawenhese (alias Sohninon).

(4) Marie Madeleine Tekanonnens (alias Ohnioron).

(5) Catherine Skawennioha (alias Atienni).

Silas died 16 May, 1779, aged 84. His wife, said to be of an advanced age, dying two days earlier.

Mr. Forbes—who sent these records and who was then (1900) curé of the parish, and is now Bishop of Joliette—said that the living descendants of Silas numbered thirteen hundred and fifty; a large proportion of all the Iroquois in Canada and the United States, which in his Almanac for that year he numbered sixteen thousand, two hundred and fifty.

Timothy, b. 1697.

Brother of Silas, became a "*grand chef*." He died 25 Sept., 1777, aged 86 (an error), and three priests officiated at his burial.

His Christian and Indian names were Jacques or Sak Oserokohton. He married Catherine Osennenhawe (she bears a name!).

Mr. Forbes finds the baptismal record of only one child—Pierre (1741)—and of him nothing more.

Mr. Parkman learned much about Timothy from "ye late Sachem Hendrich and Mrs. Kellogg" (who must have been Joanna of Deerfield and Caughnawaga) when they were in Massachusetts.

Timothy was third of the clan chiefs at Caughnawaga,[40] inheriting the honor from his master or foster-father, but given to him especially for "his own Super^{r} Talents" and "warlike Spirit for which he was much celebrated." His name, says the parson, is "Oughtzorongoughton," which "awfully spelled name is nothing else but Oseronkohton (he passes through the year)" corrects the priest.

Mr. Parkman's diary gives us further information. He says that Mr. Rice went to Boston in 1739 to confer with two men (Tarbells) "upon the Affair of his Brethren's Coming down from Canada," and the next summer Colonel Lydius sent word from Albany that "ye Rices of Canada desire one of their Brethren of New England would go up to Albany and meet them on Sept. 6 next in Order to their making a Visit hither," and on "Sept. 15 (1740) This Day arriv^{d} Mr Eliezer Rice from Albany with his brother Ozorongoughton and Mr Tarbell for a Companion & Interpreter." The next day Mr. Parkman saw Timothy when "Tow^{ds} Ev^{g} ye Captive came to view ye old House where M^{r}. Rice used to dwell," and with old Mr. Rice went to view "ye Place whence he was carry'd away, of both w^{c} he retained a clear Remembrance; as he did likewise of Several elderly persons who were then living; tho he had forgot our Language."

The parson wrote to Governor Belcher—so says the Council Record of Sept. 19, 1740—that he thought it would be of service to have Henry Rice, one of the principle men of the Cagnawagas

40 See p. 21.

go to Boston and "receive some civilities from the Government," and the Secretary was directed to send for him.

Henry Rice and John Tarbell[41] (now captives of the Cagnawaga Indians) had conferences with the Governor through an interpreter, received presents and took their leave. On their way back "They visited also Tarbell's Relations at Groton, then return'd to us in their way back to Albany & Canada."

Perhaps the Government "civilities" were too luxurious for the Indianized guest, for on his return the diarist wrote, "Oct. 5, The Chief Rice not well," but the next day: "Charles Rice and other Mrs Dind with ye Captive w^o^ was grown better . . . Several Neighbours at Eve." This was the minister's party. On the ninth "The Captives went off desiring Pray^rs^ in o^r^ Congregation for y^m^ (NB Capt. Tarbell of Groton returned home)."

In 1744 (July 5) Mr. Parkman was a guest at breakfast with the Four Mohawks[42] at Mr. Josiah Quincy's house and learned that "Timothy Rice has been out of health; and y^t^ his son has returned from his Warring with the Flatt Heads." Colonel Lydius "said this Rice was the Chief who made the speech to Gen Gage (w^c^ had in our public prints) in behalf of the Cagnawagas soon after the Reduction of Montreal in 1755. This last may be further enquired into."

Eleazer and Seth Rice of Westboro sent in a petition dated 26 June, 1747/8, shewing that they have expended several sums of money for getting out of the Hands of the Indians two Brothers that are now in Captivity and they were given fifteen pounds.

Many years before—in 1726—Edmund Rice wrote in his will: "And it is my will and pleasure that if Almighty Power should work that Deliverance for my two sons Silas and Timothy out of their captivity, which we indeed of ourselves can have little prospect of, and bring them home, they shall receive five pounds each."

41 See Groton.

42 The "News-Letter" notes the departure of the Indian delegates and the Commissioners on Saturday, July 7.

Deacon Edmund must have seen his children in their Indian homes for he went to Canada with John Sheldon in 1707.[43]

Dunstable

1706, *July* 3.

Galucia (Galusha), Daniel, b. abt. 1652.

Early this summer a warning came from Albany that two hundred and seventy Indians were marching to attack Piscataqua. Penhallow says their first descent was at Dunstable. There is confusion in the accounts, but apparently the Indians went to two garrison-houses in the night, and "at same time another party beset Daniel Galucia's hous who held y^m play for sometime till the old man's courage and strength faild him who surrendering himself informed them of the state of the garrison; how that one man was killed and only two men and a boy within, which caused them to rally anew and with greater courage than before. Upon which one and the boy got out on the backside leaving Jacob to fight alone," which he did until obliged to quit and escape as best he could. "Upon this they burnt the house."

The "two men and a boy" were probably his sons, Jacob, Daniel and Nathaniel. It was after his daughter Rachel had been killed that Daniel, Sr., surrendered.

The house where the family had lived about ten years was on Salmon Brook, some two miles distant from the other places attacked.

Pike, after describing the night attacks, continues: "Near abo^t the same time or soon after, they assaulted another house belonging to one Jacob Guletia a Dutchman. The house was burnt, some persons were kil^d, and some escaped."

The town records do not mention the disaster, only naming those persons who "dyed on July 3rd at night," and Rachel Galusha, who did not "dye at night."

[43] Some authorities are Whitney's "Hist. of Worcester Co."; Mr. Parkman's "Diary," in Mass. Hist. Soc.; Mrs. Forbes' "Two Indian Chiefs"; local histories, and Caughnawaga Records kindly given by the Rev. M. Forbes.

Other records are misleading, wherein Daniel Galusha's wife (Hannah Gould of Braintree, daughter of Francis and Rose) is called widow in 1696.

Pike calls Galucia a Dutchman. Family tradition places his ancestors in Wales. The following record in Montreal places him in the Isle of Jersey and gives the date of his death, which was unknown to the writer of "Thirty Dunstable Families."

"On Tuesday 16 Nov. 1706 was buried in the cemetery of this Church, Daniel Galuccia, native of the Island of Jersey and Inhabitant of Dunstable in New England, who having been taken the 14th of July last and brought to Canada died at the Hotel dieu of this town at the age of fifty-four years, after having abjured the Independent religion the 15th October last, which abjuration he renewed the 10th of the present month and after having received the sacrament of penitence. Witnesses. Messire Pierre Renis, former Curé of La Chine and Henry Antoine Meriel Priest, of the Seminary of Villemarie who have signed

Remy priest Priat, priest Meriel Priest."

The name has been spelled in many ways. A correspondent of the Boston Transcript believes it to have been originally Galichon, he having learned that an old Jersey family is so called.

Cummings (Camane-Etienne)?

And at Dunstable on the same day: "At Sunset Mr. Cummings and his wife went out to milk their cows and left the gate open. The Indians who had advanced undiscovered shot Mrs. Cummings dead upon the spot and wounded her husband who escaped."[44] The town record says: "Goody Cummings died July 3, 1706, at night."

They were Sergeant John and Elizabeth, daughter of Samuel and Hannah (Brackett) Kinsley of Braintree. Is it too wild a guess to say that "Etienne Camane" of Quebec may have been their little boy? A mutilated record of the register of Notre-Dame in Quebec is dated April 11, 1723. "Mgr. de Quebec hav-

[44] Farmer and Moor Coll., II, 303-4.

ing dispensed with one or more publications of bans of marriage between Etienne Camane, English . . . of New England brought up since the age of four years . . . this parish of one part and Catrine Rancin, daughter of . . . Darle Rancin and Angélique HeDeuin her father and mother . . . this parish of the other part were married, and the record was signed by Etienne and Catherine with three or four French witnesses and the priest."[45]

Catharine, who was born in 1702, died in 1728 after giving birth to four children.

1709, *June* 2.

Where taken?

WHITING, SAMUEL, of Dunstable, b. 19 Jan., 1662/3.

He was son of Samuel, the first minister of Billerica, and of Dorcas (Chester).

The son became one of the first proprietors of Dunstable through a grant which had been given to his great-uncle, who was Mayor of Boston, England. The mayor gave fifty pounds to the Massachusetts Colony and in return received a grant of five hundred acres.

Samuel was an ensign in Captain Ting's company.

In November, 1709, Vaudreuil, writing to Versailles, anticipates a bloody war, and his dread is confirmed by the examination of "an English prisoner 46 years old" who had been brought to him by the Abenaki Indians on June twenty-sixth. He calls him "a man of character" and says he has sent him down to Quebec that the intendant and his son might better understand conditions and be put upon their guard. He also sends orders to Three Rivers that the farmers may place their more valuable property in safety, and that every man may be ready with his gun to go to Quebec when the enemy's ships arrive.[46]

The examination of Samuel Whiting, this "man of character," is printed in the same volume. Whether or not it was wholly

[45] Made from a copy deposited in Quebec archives the following March.

[46] N. Y. Docs., IX, 829 and 835.

true it sounds boastful. Mehuman Hinsdale of Deerfield having just before "avoided" giving information was after this put into a dungeon, probably for contempt. Vaudreuil, in a letter to Massachusetts dated Quebec, 7 Oct., 1712,[47] wrote: "According to my last of 5th Septemr I send you Mr Whiting and the two Prisonrs I promist to returne you with him, I make use of the same oppertunity to send Mr Pidgeon, Fox, Sterling, Jolin Mussey, Isaac Parker, & Winn Mr. Pidgeon & Fox being ye Queen's officers have given me their word of honour to returne to this Countrey when I shall demand them, & till then not to bear armes against his most Christian Majesty. I was willing to doe 'em the pleasure of letting 'em goe on their parole that soe they might take care of their affaires themselves etc." He makes Mr. Leguille (who was probably Priscilla's Storer's husband, written also Dagueil) the bearer, Pidgeon having "after a fashion, obliged himself to reimburse" the governor, including the bearer's charges from Albany to Boston. The postscript of the letter is interesting: "As it appears to me by my letters Sr that peace is ready to be made between France and England if you have any news of it, you will doe me a pleasure in letting me know it & making use of Mr. Pidgeon for it, who has acquired the esteem of every body here

Vaudreuil."

The next June "To Samuel Whiting of Dunstable late returned from Captivity in Canada the sum of Ten pounds in consideration of his being obliged by Law to continue in a Frontier Town & of the great indisposition of body he has contracted by reason of his being taken" and by his wounds and sufferings being "uncapable of Labour."[48] His wife's name was Elizabeth and his house, garrisoned in 1710, was "the last refuge in case of extremity."

On March 8, 1714/15, he died of smallpox in Cambridge whither he had gone to the General Court, which was there in session.

47 Arch. 2, 626.

48 Council Rec., VI, 55; and IX, 283.

Major Lloyd wrote that in 1709 "Mrs. Whiten from Dunstable was sick at Quebec," doubtless meaning Samuel.

The report of Dunstable's protection in 1711 seems to be incomplete.[49] There were seven fortified houses, holding from one to three families, of which the number is thirteen and nineteen soldiers, a larger proportion than in most.

Brookfield

1708, *October* 13.

Woolcot, John, son of John.

"Early one morning, John Woolcot, a lad about twelve or fourteen years old, was riding in search of the cows, when the Indians fired at him killed his horse from under him and took him prisoner."[50]

An alarm brought out men in pursuit; one of whom was killed and two wounded.

John was kept with Canadian Indians (probably at Sault Saint-Louis) six or seven years and "became so naturalized to the savages as to be unwilling for a while to return."

Joseph Bartlett, taken from Haverhill in November, 1708, pictures the boy as longing for deliverance. Bartlett's story is printed in the Appendix of Coffin's "Newburyport." He says: I went from Sadrohelly (Sault-au-Recollet) "to another fort, about eighteen miles distant. While I was there, the Indians brought an English lad whom they had taken at Quabog,[51] whose name was John Willet. He was very glad to see me, and I tarried with him about a fortnight . . . The poor boy was sensibly affected at my departure and was very loth to part with me, but I spake as comfortably to him as I could and told him that he should trust in God for deliverance, for he was able to keep us and return us again to our homes. I bade him farewell and told him I hoped we should see each other in happiness in another world."

[49] Arch. 71, 871-6. [50] Whitney's "History of Worcester Co.," 71.

[51] Brookfield was Quabog until made a town in 1673.

The time and way of John's redemption is not known. He came back to Brookfield and married. The Rev. Nathan Fiske[52] describes the manner of his death in 1728, in days of peace, and possibly by the hands of his Indian friends. He with a companion hunter was paddling down the Connecticut, bringing home their skins, when they were hailed by some Indians. Unwilling to go to them they aimed for the other bank. The Indians followed, shots were exchanged and Woolcot was killed.

Northampton

1711, *August* 10.

Strong, Samuel, b. 5 Aug., 1652.

A twin son of Elder John of Northampton and of Abigail (Ford).

He and his son Samuel, Jr., who was twenty-four years old, were on their way to the South Meadows for a load of grain when they were attacked. The people who lived on South Street heard three shots. When they reached the place the son was dead, the father gone and the team was patiently waiting.

While Mr. Strong was in Canada he wrote the following letter to his wife, Ruth (Sheldon | Wright), whom he had married in 1698, shortly after the death of his first wife.[53]

"Dear and loving Wife after my kind love to you and all our Childrn having an oppertunity to wright un to you I was not willing to let it slip k(n)owing that it would be acceptable to you hoping it find you in good health as i am at present blessed be god for it Dear Wife it hath Pleased god to remove me a grate distance from you but tho we are absent in boddy yet I hope present in mind that do not forget each others welfare but dayly apply ourselves to the throne of grace in the behalf of each other Dear wife it hath Pleased god to make us see sad changes since we parted my condition is such as calls for pity [p]ray I say he did

[52] "Hist. No. Brookfield," 173.

[53] The original letter has been given by Mrs. Mary T. Gridley of Orange to the P. V. M. A., which has kindly allowed it to be copied.

pity me O my friends for the hand of god hath touched me I am bereaved of my pleasant things both civil and sacred I am a man that have seen affliction by the rod of gods wrath but why does A living man complain a man for the punishment of his sins When they killed my son they Wounded me in my left Shoulder I had a hard journey of it and the more tedious because of the dificult circumstances I was under by reason of my wound I have not the use of my arm as formerly and I fear I never shall get I can use it to do many things I have greate occation also to blees god for delivering me out of the hands of the indians i was taken from them the next day after I was taken [illeg.] came in because they sought for me & could have killd me as it was said but god has spared my life notwithstanding the many dangers I have ben in blessed & forever blessed be his holy name the lord help me that I may spend it to his praise & the everlasting comfort of my ouwn soul from thence I was removed to the hospital & was thence six weeks untill my wound was thourly cured & since I have been with colonel longuele[54] & they carry it verry kindly to me and likewise to all the english captives with me which were taken from the eastward Dear wife I long to see you & all our children but whether this ever will be god only knows but I would leave this with our children whatever they do to make sure of that one thing needful & to Chuse that better Part which cannot be taken from them We see by sad Experience that our Dearest [illeg.] herein this world may suddenly be taken from us or we from them Therefore let us not set our affections on things here below but seek first the Kingdom of heavn

Give my service to mr stodard and madam & Desire an Intrest on their Prayers I desire allso that thanks may be returned to God in the congregation for his Goodness to me in sparing my life When in such Eminent danger and prayers also that God would santify this Auful bereavem[ent] to us & our Children that both Mer-

[54] Probably M. Charles Le Moyne, Baron of Longueuil, Governor of Montreal, who died in 1729. He was kind to other English captives.

cies & Aflictions might work to gether for the good of our souls Remember my love to all my brothers & sisters as if named & to all my friend and Relations & I hope they will not be wanting in their prays to god for me that he would be pleased to work for my return and Deliverance Desiring Prayres also that God would enable me by his Grace to withstand all Temptation to sin No more at Present but leaving you to the Protection of Almighty God Praing that he would not only Correct me but teach me out of his laws I remain your loveing Husband

Samuel Strong A poor Afflicted
Captive 1710 11

Northamton
Mitte Egleston of Westfield
Massachusetts"

The superscription seems to show that the letter was sent by way of Westfield, the usual way eastward from Albany, to one named Submit Egleston. Sixty years later another "Mitte Egleston" was in Westfield and she was descended from Elder John Strong. Trumbull[55] says that the captive "returned on a Lecture Day and entered the Meeting-house to the surprise of the congregation who received him as one risen from the dead."

55 "Hist. of Northampton," 510.

CHAPTER XII

The Lower Merrimac and Exeter

Haverhill, Salisbury, Jemaico (West Amesbury), Amesbury, Exeter and Kingston

Captives

Haverhill.

1691. Whitticer, Abraham.
1696. Haynes, Jonathan.
 Mary.
 Thomas.
 Jonathan, Jr.
 Joseph.
1696/7. Dustin, Mrs. Hannah.
 Neff, Mrs. Mary (and with them
 Samuel Lennerson of Quinsigamond).
 Bradley, Daniel.
 Cod, Philip (not identified).
 Emerson, Mary (?) "gon to Penacook" in 1698.
 Kimball, Abigail.
 Wood, Susannah.
1697/8. Haynes, Thomas (2d captivity).
 Ladd, Daniel.
1703/4. Bradley, Hannah (2d captivity).
 Eastman, Hannah.
 Avery, Daniel (mentioned by S. Williams, not found in Haverhill).
 Ordway, Joanna, of Newbury.
1708. Silver, Mary.
 Bartlett, Joseph (of Newbury).

Salisbury.

1697. Gill, Samuel (named in petition with him are

Ann White, 1692, from Amesbury and John or Joseph Goodrich from Newbury).

Jemaico (West Amesbury).

1704. Davis, Helen? dau. of John.

Amesbury.

1706. Prowt, Barnes.
1712. Quimby, Benjamin.

Exter.

1697. Wells, Luke.
1704. Taylor, Mrs. Rebecca.
William.
1706. Hall, Edward.
Mighell, Samuel.
"A Melatto."
1709. Moody, William.
Stevens, Samuel.
Gilman, Jeremiah.
Gilman, Andrew.
1710. Dolloff, Sarah.
Margaret.
Abigail.
Wedgwood, John.
Hilton, Dudley.
Lougee, John.

Kingston.

1710. Gilman, Jacob.
Huntoon, Philip.

Exeter captives in Three Years' War are:

1723. The Rollins or Rawlins Family.
1724. Colcord, Peter.
Severns, Ephraim.
Stevens, Two children.

HAVERHILL

1691 — 1696 — 1696/7 — 1697/8 — 1703/4 — 1708

From the little village of Haverhill on the Merrimac River to the far-away villages on the St. Lawrence was the silence of the great forest.

The townsfolk of Haverhill took some measures for defence during Philip's War, but it was not until 1689 that serious danger menaced them. In that year theirs was one of four towns named as headquarters for Colonial troops.[1] Bands of Indians were always hovering near; the people were always anxious. At the March meeting of 1690, after the massacre at Salmon Falls, they considered whether "to send for help abroad or to draw off," but the Government did not allow the inhabitants "to draw off" from frontier towns.

The records show that scarcely a year passed between 1689 and 1708 in which some Haverhill people were not killed or captured. In 1690 a few soldiers were in each of the six garrison-houses.

Whittier describes these in "The Boy Captives."

1691, *August.*

WHITTICER, ABRAHAM, b. 20 May, 1863, "agged 8 or nine" when captured.

He was the son of Abraham, Jr., and Hannah (Beane). She was killed in 1692. We have no further knowledge of the boy, his name occurring only in the petition of 1701.

This family had hard experiences. Several of the name suffered in Indian attacks. It is interesting to note that Thomas Whittier, of similar name, Friend, and ancestor of the poet, refused to take refuge at night in the garrison-house near his home, trusting to his peace principles, and while frequently visited by Indians he was never molested.

[1] Groton, Haverhill, Newichawannock and Casco.

The following shows conditions as seen by Col. N. Saltonstall.

"To Rowland Cotton Haverhill, July 31:94
at Sandwich

Dear Son & Daughter Cotton

. . . We ar so surrounded wth newes of Depredations & losse of lives & estates at Oyster River & ye Bank & since y^t at Groton by ye hands of the publique Enime y^t ye people of this place are gitting wth speed into Garisons on w^c acc^t our place or garison is stowed full wth Lodgers It was in my heart to give you a visit but as my now circumstances are it must unavoidably be deferred." Writing again in October he said: "We are still in garrison crowds;[2] & more than a little also $busi^e$ ab^t Cyd^{er} & Winter apples. N.S."[3]

1696, *August* 15.

HAYNES, JONATHAN, and his four children — three of whom were taken to Canada, the earliest known taken from Haverhill.

Jonathan, b. in England, was son of William and Sarah (Ingersoll of Salem). He married Mary Moulton of Hampton and six months after her death, Sarah, her sister, who was the mother of the children. They lived in the West Parish near Hawk's Meadow Brook. The children were:

Mary, b. 1677.
Thomas, b. 1680.
Jonathan, Jr., b. 1684.
Joseph, b. Aug. 4, 1689.

When surprised by the Indians he was reaping and the children were gathering beans near him.

At Penacook the party divided. Jonathan and his eldest son were taken to an Indian village in Maine, whence they soon escaped, but the man's strength failed as they wandered in the wilderness, and the boy leaving him followed the whirring sound of a sawmill, which led him to Saco where he found help for his father.

2 Not now did he need "annimadeversions," see attack of March, 1696/7.

3 MS. in Mass. Hist. Soc.

A year and a half later the elder was killed and the younger again captured.

Tradition says that the second party tarried until winter near Penacook, then carrying Mary on a sled they went to Canada where they sold her and her brothers to the French.

Mary was redeemed, says tradition, with a hundred pounds of tobacco, carried north on a hand-sled. She afterwards married John Preston of Andover.

Jonathan, Jr., and *Joseph* never came back. On the Naturalization paper of 1710 are the names of "Joseph hins living at Cap St. Ignace, another Joseph hins, his brother, living at Beaupré." Both places are near Quebec.

Their identification cannot be positive.

M. Tanguay names the two Josephs. The first: Joseph, b. 1685, son of Jean and Angelique Holkne (far away from Sarah Moulton!) of Heurel, near Boston, married at St. Thomas, Oct. 3, 1712, Marie Posé (1694-1781), and their children were:

Joseph, 1714, m. 1, Geneviève Vaillancour; 2, M. Louise Charlotte Damours; 3, Marie Gaumont.

Jean, 1716, m. Geneviève Dufresne.

Alexandre-Noël, 1718, m. M. Joseph Barde.

Augustine, 1720, d. 1749.

Marie-Joseph, 1723, m. Joseph Geudron.

Marie-Madeleine, 1725, m. Charles François Langlois.

Angélique, 1726, d. 1727.

François-Marie, 1729, m. Françoise Clément.

Marie-Louise, 1731, m. 1, Pierre Brisson; 2, Jos. Lefebre.

Clément, 1734, m. M. Joseph Pron.

Joseph seems always to have lived at Saint-Thomas-de-Montmagny, where he died. His widow died at Beloil in June, 1781.

The second Joseph mentioned by Tanguay, b. in 1689, was, he says, a carpenter from England; so, although this is the very year that Joseph of Haverhill was born, this one may not be a New

England captive. Whoever he was he had four wives and twenty-one children, and was buried in Quebec in 1756.

Chase[4] quotes a story concerning three Haynes brothers who went to Canada in 1757 and who found Jonathan and Joseph. They had forgotten how to speak English and could not be persuaded to return to New England, which was quite natural, they being about seventy years of age, and the much-married one, according to M. Tanguay, already buried in Quebec.

Thomas again was captured (February, 1697/8) and again escaped. In 1703 he married Hannah Harriman and he died in 1771.

1696/7, *March* 15.

There was no general attack upon Haverhill until this year when "about 7 in the morning," on March 15, some thirty Indians came upon the town like a whirlwind, killing twenty-seven persons—more than half being children—and capturing thirteen. On the Council Records is a criticism of Colonel Saltonstall for neglect of duty because he "Did not (as he ought): when he had notice of ye enemies approach take Care to Draw them into Garrison; nor incourage the persute of them when persons offered." An inquiry was asked for that there might be "Due animadeversions."

This was the attack made memorable by Mrs. Hannah (Emerson) Dustin. Her story does not belong here, but how can so remarkable a captive be omitted?

The best account of the tragedy was written by Cotton Mather who heard it from her own lips.

Thomas, her husband, unable to save her seized a gun and kept between the enemy and his escaping children, firing and being fired upon until their slow steps took them to safety. They were seven, and their ages ranged from two to seventeen. Mrs. Dustin, with her new-born child, and Mrs. Mary (Corliss) Neff, the

4 "Hist. of Haverhill."

neighbor who was caring for her, were taken. The baby was killed immediately.

Slowly the Indians and captives moved northward. With them was a boy-captive, Samuel Lenorson, taken two years before from his father's farm near Lake Quinsigamond — now part of Lake Park in Worcester. After travelling a hundred and fifty miles they reached the island at the junction of the Merrimac and Contoocook Rivers, which has since been called Dustin Island.

Here, on April 29, the two women, maddened by what had happened and terrified by what was threatened,[5] killed, with the help of the boy, ten savages — six of them children! From their hands "only one Squaw escaped sorely wounded," and a boy whom they spared, meaning to take him with them.

As soon as possible after their return to Haverhill the three captives, with Thomas Dustin, went to Boston, carrying the ten scalps, the tomahawk and the gun. Judge Sewall wrote May first "Hannah Dustan came to see us . . . She saith her Master, whom she kil'd, did formerly live with Mr. Rowlandson at Lancaster: He told her, that when he pray'd the English way, he thought that was good: but now he found the French way was better." The women had been surprised that the Indians prayed "Thrice every Day."

The reward for Indians, dead or live, had been cancelled, but because of this "extraordinary Action of his wife (with one Mary Neff) and because of losing his Estate in the Calamity wherein his wife was carryed into her captivity," Thomas petitioned "for what consideracon the publick Bounty shall judge proper"[6] and he, in behalf of his wife, received twenty-five pounds, while half that amount was given to each of her companions "as a reward for their service in slaying divers of those barbarous salvages."

In 1738 Mary Neff's son sought further reward — in a grant of land — because his mother had killed "divers Indians."

[5] They were told that arriving in Canada they would be forced to run the gauntlet, but no record has been found of this torture being offered to any woman.

[6] Arch. 70, 350.

Little is known of other captives of 1697. Some are named in the following petition[7] dated Haverhill, April 17, 1701, addressed to the "leftant gouerner And councel," reminding these gentlemen that they had been pleased "to pass an act for the Redeaming of poor Captives" and begging that the said act be put "in execution as speedey as may be." It was signed

onezepherus Mash[8]
Stephen Dow
Sarah haines widow
Abraham whitticer

Then follow the names "of such as are yet wanting
daniel bradley taken march: 15: 1697: agged seven yeers
Jonathan: and Joseph hains taken August 15 1696: Jonathan agged twelve and Joseph seven yers
Abigall Kimball taken march 15: 1697 agged eight yers
Abraham Whitticer taken August: 1691 agged 8 or nine yeres
Philip Cod taken March 15: 1697: aged about six yeres" (not identified).

Marsh, perhaps, signed in his official capacity; Stephen Dow in the interest of his little nephew "Daniell Bradley carried to Canada 7 yrs ould."

Bradley, Daniel, b. 28 Oct., 1690.

Son of Daniel, Jr., and Hannah (Dow).

His parents and two or three of their children were killed. Nothing more is known of him.

Kimball, Abigail, b. 7 April, 1689.

Daughter of Henry & Hannah (Mash — Marsh).

Abigail had one brother, who was killed in this attack, and six sisters, all of whom married. She is not found unless with a new name and religion she is Marie Louise Kembell who became a citizen of New France in 1710.

7 Arch. 70, 522.

8 Marsh was town constable.

WOOD, SUSANNAH, b. 1673, wife of Thomas; daughter of Philip Eastman.

Her father's house was burned and his family scattered. He was taken but escaped.

Susannah's husband and only child were killed. She was captured and returned on the *Province Galley* in 1698/9.

"The Eastman Family" says she was twice a captive, but gives no details. In 1699 she married John Swan and later removed to Stonington, Connecticut. There were seven Swan children.

A correspondent of the Genealogical Register (July, 1875) says that "their house was attacked in 1708 or 1709 and they killed one Indian as he was forcing an entrance." They were living in Connecticut in April, 1709, when their fourth child was born. Susannah lived to be very old.[9]

1697/8.

On February 22, nearly a year after the general attack, as some Indians were returning from Andover — where they had killed Capt. Pasco Chubb — "by Haverhill they met with Jonath: Hains and Sam: Ladd, with y[r] elder sons. The two fathers were slain & the sons Carried away, but young Hains soon after Returned, which was his second escape from the enemy in less than two years time."[10] Chase[11] says that the men had teams of oxen and horses and were going after hay that had been stacked in London Meadow. Near World's End pond fourteen Indians sprang upon them (Pike doubles the number), killed the men and took one boy, while the other escaped on his horse. When asked why they killed Mr. Haynes they said he was "so old he no go with us;" the historian adding that he was "quite aged." If his parents believed in infant baptism this "aged person" was fifty years old, for he was baptized in 1648.

9 "Eastman Family in America."

10 Pike's "Journal."

11 "Hist. Haverhill," 202.

LADD, DANIEL, b. 19 Nov., 1676.

Son of Samuel and Martha (Corliss).

He was carried to Penacook and almost escaped while his Indian captors were sleeping, but realizing his need for a hatchet he went back to the wigwam and an ailing, wakeful squaw saw him and gave the alarm. They then bound him and tied him by the leg to a tree for fourteen nights. They tortured and gashed his face filling the wounds with powder, which made him until his death "a marked man." Later he did escape and came home on the *Province Galley* in January, 1698/9. He married Susannah Hartshorn in 1701 and died fifty years later.

1697—1703/4.

BRADLEY, HANNAH (Heath), twice a captive.

She was the wife of Joseph, son of Daniel. One account says that two of their children were killed in 1697. Chase[12] names Joseph, Martha and Sarah.

We find some details of the first captivity in Mrs. Bradley's friendly endorsement of Mary Neff's son's petition. She testified that about forty years before, she and widow Mary Neff were carried together into captivity and above "penny cook" she was forced to travel farther than the rest of the captives, and the next night but one there came one Squaw who said that Hannah Duston and Mary Neff "assisted in killing the Indians of her wigwam except herself and a boy." Perhaps the squaw had not been as "sorely wounded" as Mrs. Dustin had represented. Mrs. Bradley was taken to Casco and sent home on the *Province Galley*, January first, 1698/9, to be again captured in the raid of 1703/4.

Bradley owned one of the six garrison-houses.[13]

The savages came southward more frequently in summer than in winter, which may explain the open gate and absent sentinel on the afternoon of Feb. 8, 1703/4, when six Indians attacked the

12 "History of Haverhill."

13 The supposed site is Heath Place, North Broadway.

house. Penhallow, who wrote the name Bradberry,[14] says that the Indians seeing "none on the scentury, violently rushed and became Masters thereof . . . " The earliest account of the sufferings of "this Vertuous Woman" is doubtless that in the tract entitled "A Memorial of the Present Deplorable State of New England," probably written by Cotton Mather as an attack upon the Dudleys, and in its answer, "A Modest Inquiry" into the "Grounds and Occasions" of the Pamphlet.[15]

Mrs. Bradley, with her sister, some children and a man were together, and talking about Indians, when "behold, one of the Fierce Tawnies looked in with a Gun ready to Fire." The man pulled him in, got him down and Mrs. Bradley poured "a good quantity of scalding Soap (which was then boyling over the Fire) upon him whereby he was kill'd immediately." Another who followed "stabb'd the English man to the Heart. Unto him she dispensed also a quantity of her Sope which, not killing him, she with the other Women and Children ran into the Chamber." The house was fired "and Mrs. Bradly with her Companions found it necessary to retire behind" it, Mrs. Bradley and her sister each protecting a child. Her sister was seen and ordered to come forth, but Mrs. Bradley "generously bid her sit still," and "thereby her obliged Sister and the Child with her were preserved;" but the Savages "employ'd a Head-breaker on the Child" that was with its mother. She, with her captors travelled rapidly, meeting incredible hardships and famine. "A Mooses Hide, as tough as you may Suppose it, was the best and most of her Diet." In three weeks they reached "their Headquarters" where they tarried two weeks more. Here they took away her snowshoes, "and yet she must go every step above the Knee in Snow." At another resting-place, with "the Snow under her and the Heaven over her, in a misty and rainy season" she gave birth to her fourth child. A woman with her "got a little Hemlock to lay about her, and with a few sticks made shift to blow up a little Fire." The poor woman sent "unto a

[14] MS. in Congressional Library. [15] Sewall's Diary, Vol. II.

French priest that he would speak unto her Squa Mistress, who without condescending to look upon her, allow'd her a little Birch-Rind to cover her Head from the Injuries of the Weather, and a little bit of dried Moose, which being boiled, she drunk the Broth, and gave it unto the Child." Continuing the journey she lived upon "Ground-nuts and Wild-onions and Lilly-roots" until they reached "Cowesick" where they planted their corn. Mrs. Bradley was put to hard work and the baby suffered. "The Salvages would sometimes also please themselves with casting hot Embers into the Mouth of the Child . . . so that it Starv'd and Dy'd." Mirick quotes a tradition that the Indians promised to let the baby live if she would allow them to baptize it in their manner, and she in her terror permitting, they gashed the child's forehead with their knives.

Stephen Williams, at Cowass with his master, wrote: "There was in Company now one Mrs Bradley of Haverhill and one hannah eastman one Daniel Avery[16] of Haverhill." Stephen reached Chambly in August, probably Mrs. Bradley was not then in company, for "some of our French-Indians" attacked her captors who "fled for Canada" after several had been killed "and they never saw their Corn-field any more. But they made a Forty-Days Ramble of it, before they reach'd thither, in which, if at any time, her Heart began to faint, her Mistress would be ready to strike the Mortal Hatchet into her Head."

Arriving in Canada she was kept a year or more in a squalid wigwam, foul with fever and smallpox. Her mistress died and she herself was ill. At last a priest whom she had known in her first captivity at Norridgewock made her new mistress sell her for eighty livres to a French family who treated her kindly. Now she lived more comfortably.

Tradition makes a romance of her redemption. The story is told that in March, 1705, her husband alone with a dog that drew a small sled travelled through the woods to Canada and immedi-

16 The name is not found in Haverhill records.

ately secured her release. On the sled was a bag of snuff, a gift from the governor of this province to that of Canada. From our Archives we know that Joseph Bradley went to Canada with John Sheldon. They left in January, 1705/6; three New Englanders, two French prisoners, a dog, and perhaps the snuff! They arrived in Montreal early in March.

Among the forty-four captives who came back with them to Boston on August second was Hannah Bradley. In Mr. Sheldon's bill of expenses is "8 livres and 13 sous for a shirt for Jos. Bradley," and Bradley, above what he had in fitting out, received twenty pounds for his "extraordinary Difficulties, Hazzards and Hardships" and "forty shillings beside snow Shoes & pumps which Cost him thirteen shillings and a Dog (!) 15s and Beside there was a Gun hired for the Voyage valued at 50s, which s^d^ Gun was broken accidentally in ye discharging."[17]

In the middle of a summer night that same year another small party of Indians came to the Bradley garrison seeking, as she believed, the twice-redeemed captive. She fired a shot which killed the first who entered. The rest ran away. She declared she would rather die than be taken again. In 1738 widow Hannah Bradley asked for a grant of land in consideration of her sufferings and "present low circumstances," and received two hundred and fifty acres in the town of Methuen. In November, 1761, she died. One of her eleven children was (probably) killed in the raid of 1704.

Eastman, Hannah, w. of Jonathan; dau. of Peter Grenn.

In 1752, Amos, her son.[18]

The various branches of the family suffered much during the Indian wars.

Jonathan's father, Thomas, was killed in 1688 and his mother Deborah (Corliss), who was sister of Mrs. Neff, was captured. In 1697 his sister Sarah was killed. In 1704 Jonathan and Hannah were living in the Bradley garrison. Just a week before the

[17] Arch. 71, 236. [18] See Chapter XXI.

attack her second child was born. After the Indians had secured their prisoners below stairs they climbed the ladder to her bedroom and dashing out the baby's brains against the doorpost, forced her to leave her bed and dress to follow them.

Her captors lingered until spring at Lake Ossipee, then moved on to the "Ox Bow" in Newbury, Vermont. Here they planted their corn, but when it was "in the second hoeing" they were warned of an approaching scouting-party and hastily left for Canada. On their way they tarried for a little near Cowass where Stephen Williams saw them.[19] The "Eastman Family of America," from which I quote, says that the tribe was encamped at Three Rivers. This proves that they were St. Francis Indians and probably lived in their own village near Three Rivers.

A kind French woman "often gave her salt to season her food" and finally helped her to escape. Perhaps she had been bought from the Indians, although the author says she had to remain hidden from them. After about three years Jonathan found her. As the story goes, she, sitting at her chamber window, saw him pass the house. Six feet, four inches high, he was strong and splendid; and although dressed as were the Canadians he could be no other. "Jonathan, Jonathan" she cried. He stopped, looked, and saw no one; she called again but he did not hear. She sent a child flying after him, who lacking his speech pulled him back by his coat, and then at first sight he did not know his wife!

Her ransom paid, together they made the journey homeward walking all the way—and, says tradition, being so much impressed with the beauty of New Hampshire that they later chose it for their home. This was at Concord on land now owned by St. Paul's School, and then called "Eastman's Fort."

Nine children were born after life began again for them.

ORDWAY, JOANNA, of Newbury.

Dau. of Edward and Mary (Wood).

Mr. Pike wrote of the attack of 1703/4: "13 persons were killed

19 See Chapter XVI.

& 5 carried away, whereof one returned." One who probably never returned was Joanna Ordway.

In the spring of 1707 a party of Deerfield men were scouting near Lake Champlain. One of them believing they were discovered fired a shot. Approaching to scalp the dead person he was "startled" to find "it" a white woman who spoke to him. From his description she was thought to be "an Eastern captive Johannah Ardaway."[20]

If it were she, she made a good recovery for

"On Sunday 22 June 1710, was baptized by me, undersigned Priest, a little girl, born six months ago in the woods. that an English girl, named Jeanne Owardway, taken at Haverhill in New England in the winter of 1704 by the Abenakis of the river of Bequancour, has had by an Abenaki savage.[21] The godmother of the child was Dame Marguerite Philippe de Muis, wife of M. René Robineau *Ecuyer*, Sieur de Portneuf. *Lieutenant d'une Compagnie de Detachement de la marine* who named her Marguerite, and has signed according to the law." The mother declared she did not know how to sign.

Marguerite Demuy portneuf

Meriel Priest.

The birth was indexed "Marguerite, Abenaki," the child taking the father's station.

Two weeks later:

"On Sunday, 3 July 1710, the ceremony of baptism was by me, the priest undersigned, administered to an English girl named Jeanne Oardaway, who born at Newbury in New England in January 1687[22] of the marriage of Edouard Oardaway and Marie Wood and taken at Haverhill in March 1704 by the Abenaki savages of the river of Becancour belongs to Bernard Suetaregonstet. She had for godfather Monsieur Francois Le Verrier *Capi-*

20 Sheldon's "Hist. Deerfield," I, 362.

21 *"Neé il y a six mois, dans les bois qu'a eue d'un sauvage Abnakis une Angloise nommée Jeane Owardway, etc."*

22 Newbury records give 28 Nov., 1685, as birth.

taine d'une Compagnie du Detachement de La Marine and for godmother Dame Marguerite Renée Denys, Wife of Monsieur Jacques Alexis de Fleury Deschambauds *Ecuyer, Conseiller de Roi et son Lieutenant General au Siège ordinaire* of the royal jurisdiction of Monreal, who have signed. The English girl, to whom the name of Francoise has been added to that of Jeanne, made her mark."

Jeanne Wardaway was naturalized in 1713 and had perhaps given up her life in the woods. She was living within the precincts of Montreal.

1708.

In June, 1708, Vaudreuil wrote to the home government that he thinks the English will make no move this year; that the French have promised the Iroquois not to strike a blow in Orange — a sort of truce having existed since 1703 — but "as for Boston I will give it no rest."[23] To execute this threat he called together at Montreal a grand council of Indians from the Missions, and although, as he wrote, it needed the patience of an angel to conciliate them he succeeded in soothing "their mutual jealousies and persuaded them to go upon a war-party." His report[24] says that with the Indians there were a hundred Frenchmen (soldiers and *habitants*) led by Saint-Ours, Seigneur d'Eschaillons, Hertel de Rouville and Enseigne de la Perrière. One party set forth by the St. Francis River; another by Lake Champlain. They were to meet at Lake Nikisipique (Winnepesaukee) where they expected Norridgewocks, Penacooks and other eastern Indians to join them.[25]

From the beginning ill-luck followed them. An accident was a bad omen and that caused defections before they reached the St. Francis. A sickness which they pretended was infectious caused more to turn back. The Caughnawagas were half-hearted. Perhaps some of them knew that Peter Schuyler had been told of the plan and had warned New England of their coming.[26] The east-

[23] Que. Docs., II, 495. [24] Parkman Manuscripts. [25] Hutchinson, II, 157.

[26] "Fifty Years of Conflict," I, 92. Parkman.

ern Indians did not join them, but Vaudreuil sent orders to his officers that they must go on.

They dared not attack a strong place so they changed their aim from Portsmouth to Haverhill or "heureïl" as they spelled it. At this time there were here about thirty small houses, six garrisons and four houses of refuge.

Charlevoix says the French leaders knew that soldiers had been sent to some of the frontier towns and that they could not be sure of a surprise. They spent Saturday night in the woods near the village. De Rouville exhorted all his men — French and savage — to reconcile their differences and to embrace; then ranged in battle array the "Abenakis fell on their knees at the foot of the trees," fervently prayed, and half an hour before dawn on Sunday, August 29, "with no thought of booty" they marched to the attack of the fort!

Fighting beside the French commander was Naskanbis8it, or Assacambuit, once sachem of the Pigwacket or Saco Indians, who killed many persons with a sword presented to him by Louis XIV.[27] When the Weekly Journal announced his death in 1727 it said he always carried a club on which were ninety-eight notches, that being the number of Englishmen he had killed. (Cotton Mather's count, in the story of Thomasine Rouse, was higher in 1690.) Forty soldiers had been sent to Haverhill, but they were scattered among the houses, which caused delay in the defence; nevertheless at sunrise the Canadians were being driven northward.

Three miles from the village they threw away their packs and a medicine-box. At the edge of the forest Captain Ayer overtook them and recovered some of the prisoners.

Pike says thirty-three were "killed & carried away." It was in that skirmish that Louis de Verchères and Hertel de Chambly, brother of Hertel de Rouville, were killed and Beauvenire de Verchères was taken.

Chase says that the little army suffered so much in its retreat

[27] Mauràult "*Hist. des Abenakis,*" 330. For his visit to court see p. 57.

from loss of their packs that some Frenchmen returned to surrender, and a few prisoners were dismissed with the message that if further pursuit were made the others would be put to death.[28]

Charlevoix was in Montreal when the party arrived in mid-September. He said some prisoners escaped, but "all the others praised the kind treatment of their captors," and he relates the special kindness shown to Mary Silver.

Printed in the Calendar of State Papers[29] is a letter from Governor Dudley to the Council for Trade and Plantations. Dated March 1, 1709, he says: "I have had but one inroad this summer from Canada. Mr. Vaudreuil, the Governour [of] Quebeck, being in June last at Montreal, gave out his warrant for the raising 1000 men for a descent upon me, of which I had soon notice from my Indian scouts always [lying in] his country, and near him, but not knowing where they intended to light upon me, I was for [ced] to equip 2000 men, 10 troops of horse and the rest ffoot, and lay them about 150 in every village from Deerfield to Wells, 200 miles in length. But it so happ [ened that] Mr. Vaudreuil being then 300 miles from Quebeck, where the most of his troops were to be raised, the people made a great pretence of sickness and disorder amongst them, so that he fell in his demands to 500, and when they mustered they prooved but 300 [and] after 3 days march, half of them, being most Indians weary of the war, deserted and fled so that at 40 days they fell in upon Haverhill, an open village of about 200 ffamilies, where as in other villages there was a troop of horse and 100 men quartered, who soon beat [them out] of town, killed them 20 men, and they carryed away as many wounds and we lost here 3 [ffam] ilys of the poor people, who without that care must 1000 of them have perished in a few hours [time] I have now abroad a force of 200 men upon their snowshoes, ranging all the old [settlem] ents of the Indians at 200 miles distance where I have kept them from their planting and [reside]nce these 6 years, and resolve by the help of God to

28 "Hist. Haverhill," 225. 29 Colonial Papers, 1708-9, No. 391.

keep them from thence till they desert the [Fren] ch service and return to their duty and allegiance."

These boastful, exaggerated statements differ from those told here. The 1000 persons that would have been sacrificed had it not been for Dudley's care could hardly have been housed in the little village!

In the Parkman manuscripts[30] is a copy of the letter sent by Vaudreuil to Versailles in November, 1708, less than three months after the attack, saying that he had told the unwilling Indians—from the Sault-Saint-Louis, Sault-au-Recollet and the Mountain—that since they liked peace they could remain quiet upon their mats; as for him, he preferred war without them. They made many excuses, and said sickness sent them back. Several offered to return; he told them they could if they liked, but what about provisions and munitions? He had none to give them, but secretly he sent Indian corn and powder through their missionary, who made them believe that he gave them of his own generosity. And so, mortified and moved by the scorn of the governor, warriors from the Missions and Abenakis from near the sea again set out. Vaudreuil explains that they have gone in separate parties to attack different places in the Government of Boston, which after the blow of Deschaillons and Hertel will surely create general consternation, and as he has told Monseigneur before, big parties which are not always successful do harm to only one place, but a good many little ones destroy the country and ruin the inhabitants.[31]

The first house attacked on this Sunday morning, August 30, was that of the Rev. Benjamin Rolfe, garrisoned by two cowardly soldiers. Mr. Rolfe, his wife and their youngest child were killed. Hagar, the slave, saved two little girls by hiding them under tubs in the cellar.

30 Mass. Hist. Soc.

31 In 1711 there were here twenty-five garrison-houses, with from one to seven families, Ensign Hutchings, being the largest; the list giving for the place 97 families, 129 men, 17 soldiers and 540 souls—Arch. 71, 871-6.

Silver, Mary, b. March, 1694.

Dau. of Thomas of Newbury and Mary (Williams).

Garneau,[32] writing of this attack, bids us remember the humane deeds of these cruel wars and cites the following: "Among the prisoners was the daughter of the principal inhabitant of Haverhill. Unable to bear the fatigues of a long march, she would have succumbed, had it not been for a young volunteer, M. Dupuy of Quebec, who carried her a good part of the way and so preserved her life."

Simon Wainwright, captain of the town militia, must have been this "principal inhabitant" and Mary Silver "the daughter," for he had married her mother, Mrs. Mary, widow of Thomas Silver.

The Wainwright house was of brick and defended by five men. One account of the attack says that the captain was killed immediately and that Mrs. Wainwright, to the surprise of the others, unbarred the door, spoke kindly to the enemy and offered to get for them what they needed. They demanded money and she, "promising to get it, fled from the house with all of her children except one daughter who was taken captive, and who was not afterward discovered."

Let us imagine that kind M. Dupuy did not leave little Mary among the Indians but took her at once to the Sisters, although nearly eighteen months pass before we "discover" her there, then:

"On Sunday 2 Feb. 1710, the rite of baptism was administered by me, undersigned priest to an English girl, named Marie Silver, who born at Haverhill in N. E. Wednesday 10 March 1694 [28 Feb. 1693/4] of the marriage of Thomas Silver, deceased and Dame Marie Williams widow by her second marriage, of Monsieur Simon Wainwright, Judge, Captain and Commandant of the said place; which girl having been captured Sunday, 9 Sept. 1708 by Monsieur Contrecoeur *Ecuyer*, officer in the troops of Canada, and brought to this country, lives as a pupil in the house of the Sisters of the Congregation of Notre-Dame, at Villemarie. Her

32 "*Hist. du Canada,*" II, 212.

godfather was the High and Mighty Seigneur Messire Philippe de Rigaud, Marquis de Vaudreuil, Chevalier of the military order of Saint-Louis, and Governor General of New France; her godmother, Dame Charlotte Denis, wife of Messire Claude de Ramezay, Chevalier of the order of Saint-Louis, Seigneur de Lageste, Bois-fleurant, and Governor of the Island of Monreal and its dependencies,—all of whom signed with me according to the law."

Her "High and Mighty" sponsors did not give her a name at baptism. That must have been done later for she was confirmed as Adelaide Silver. In 1710 as Mary she is naturalized.

Tidings of her baptism may have reached New England for two months later the anxious Puritan mother addressed a petition to the General Court in which she says: "Whereas my Daughter hath been for a long time in Captivity with ye French in Canada and I have late reason to fear that her soul is in great Dainger if not all redy captivated and she brought to their ways theirefore I would humbly Intreat your Excelency that some care may be taken for her Redemption before Canada be so Endeared to her that I shall never have my Daughter any more; Some are ready to say that there are so few captives in Canada that it is not worth while to poot ye Cuntry to ye charges to send for them, but I hoope your Excelency no [r] No other Judichous men will thinck so for St. James hath Instructed us as you may see Chap. 5 v. 20 . . . this is all I can do at presents."

Mary Wainwright Widow.[33]

Before the close of the year Adelaide Silver was a Hospital Nun of St. Joseph, one of the Sisters usually known as *Soeurs de l'Hôtel-Dieu*, showing by this choice her preference for nursing. After the peace of Utrecht her mother entreated her to return, sending money and also an urgent appeal to the Governor of Canada to send her home. "But," says the Annalist of the Hôtel-Dieu, "the generous girl . . . replied to the governor: 'Monsieur, I tenderly love my dear mother, but before everything, I

[33] Arch. 105, 59.

am bound to obey God, and I declare to you that I am resolved to live in the holy religion which I have embraced, and to die a nun of Saint-Joseph,'" adding that her dearest wish is to see her mother embrace the holy Catholic faith.

Our nun-correspondent wishing to show that Mary had congenial associates says that of the sixty-three Hospital nuns of her time twenty-three were of noble families and the rest of the "*haute bourgeoisie.*" Father Meriel,[34] chaplain of Hôtel-Dieu, was doubtless the strongest influence of her life. At his death, with fervent and untiring zeal, she took his place as catechist and apostle to the captives.

It was after she had taken her vows that Vaudreuil wrote to Dudley (16 June, 1711) that "Mdlle Silve" and generally all the men and women prisoners were as free to return as he had said Esther Wheelwright was,[35] but he would not oblige any to go back who preferred to remain.

After thirty years of convent life Mary (Adelaide) Silver died at Hôtel-Dieu on August 2, 1740. She was buried in the old Convent church, then standing at the corner of St. Paul and St. Sulpice streets in Montreal.[36]

BARTLETT, JOSEPH, of Newbury, b. 1686.

Son of Richard and Hannah.

He was a shoemaker pressed into service and on duty at the Wainwright house; one of the "four houses of refuge." His account of the attack and of his captivity, first printed in pamphlet, may be found in the appendix to Coffin's Newburyport.

He says the family "were all reposing in sleep" and Mrs. Wainwright came to wake him. He put on his small clothes, put his "gun on the window very still," and shot some of the enemy who were lying on the ground with guns pointed toward the windows. He was sure that the house could have been defended.

His narrative shows how male captives were treated and proves

34 See p. 40. 35 See Chapter XIV.

36 Miss Baker printed the story of Mary Silver in "True Stories."

that women and children were more desirable because more easily guarded, whether their market value was greater or less.

He said that at night they tied him down with stakes and cords and "laid each side" of him "upon the strings." In the morning, with arms tied behind and "with another squaw-line" about his neck, he was led by an Indian who had a hatchet in one hand and a pistol in his girdle. They travelled hard for three days with little food, for the Indians had only horse-meat.

From Lake Winnepesaukee the French went northward, the Indians westward. The latter separated as was their custom into smaller parties and he with about fifteen crossed to Lake Champlain and so on to Chambly where he saw Littlefield (a captive from Wells). The Indians shaved half his head and painted his face.

At Montreal the governor asked him many questions and then he was taken to the "Indian fort called by the French Sadrohelly" (Sault-au-Recollet). On the way they allowed one squaw to cut off a finger and another to strike him severely. At the fort his hand was bound with plantain leaves and they gave him "roasted pompkin." All night the Indians sang and danced round the fires in the wigwam, which was about forty feet long. They dragged him up to dance also. The next day they came together again and presented the scalps to the squaws. An Indian took him by the hand and after a long speech gave him to an old squaw who, adopting him as her son, took him to another wigwam, washed off the grease and paint and gave him new "Indian stockings and blanket." "An English woman who belonged to one of the French nuns" told him not to fear "but she being a papist" he "placed little reliance on her assertions."[37] Martin Kellogg of Deerfield in his second captivity lived in the same wigwam. Both the young men suffered from cold and lack of food. In the winter Bartlett was taken (doubtless sold) to "a rich captain with

[37] Perhaps Mary Sayward of York, now Soeur des Anges.

gout, M. Delude," whom he "attended" in Montreal for fifteen months. "At times of leisure" he "wrought at shoemaking."

He said that the French priest, Mr. Meriel, brought him an English Bible and used to sit beside him while he worked and asked him, he says, "whether I had been to their meetings."

Bartlett's language is certainly quaint if not irreverent when he writes that the priest "wished to have me come and witness their carryings on." He went to mass and said: "They were very civil to me not compelling me to kneel." He told Father Meriel "that it seemed strange," and the priest answered, "this was generally the case at first."

Bartlett was at the burial of William Taylor of Exeter in January, 1712, and at the marriage of Elizabeth Hurst of Deerfield in October.

A few days later, being redeemed, he left (Sunday, Oct. 5) for Chambly, Albany, Springfield and Boston.

The General Court allowed him £20, 15s for expenses "to obtain his liberty," for his support during the four years and for the loss of his arms.[38] He died in 1754.

Salisbury

1697, *June* 10.

The little villages along the river banks between Haverhill and the sea suffered from raids. We have the names of captive children from Amesbury, Salisbury and Newbury. Mrs. Joanna Cotton, wife of Rev. John Cotton 2^d^, writing from "Salsbury" March 10, 1697, to her brother-in-law Increase Mather[39] describes conditions which must have been common to the frontier towns. She sends the "dreadfull newes from Haverhill" and adds that "all the rest of the towns are in eminent danger of destruction without the lord doth wonderfully appeare beyound all expectation." She says the people are starving, never did she "heare such a cry for bread some families have bin days weaks and months without one bit of

[38] Arch. 5, 31.

[39] Joanna was born Rossiter. Her daughter Elizabeth married two Salisbury ministers — Mr. Alling and Caleb Cushing.

bread . . . and the rates are so dreadfull hevy that multitudes say they cannot pay if it weare to save their lives with out the constable will take there lands . . . many souldiers have bin prest out of this poor towne & are forsed to leave there one families to be a prey to the heathen this town hath bin and is yet very willing to uphold religion and the ministry but these great rattes scarsety of bread and war . . . that they are afraid to setle a man least thay starve him." Lacking meat, drink and cloth "some begin to steale at exseter from the mils." She says: "my intent in writing these dolefull lines to yourself is to stir up your prayers," and those of "couzen cotton and other of your choys" Christian ministers.[40]

GILL, SAMUEL, June 10.

It was three months later that Mr. Pike wrote: "John Young of Exiter slain by ye Indians, his son wounded, Luke Wells[41] (& a lad at Salsbury) the same day Carried away."

The lad was Samuel, son of Sergeant Samuel Gill and Sarah (Worth). He was b. Sept. 16, 1687, and his identity is proved by the following petition[42] dated May 29, 1700. "That about three yeares since your Petitioners Son named Samuel Gill was taken Captive by the Indians, and carried Captive to Canada, where he hath ever since remained in the hands of ye Indians. And that, besides your Petitioners son befor named there are several other English Captives at Canada aforesd in the hands of the French and Indians which Captives were taken in the Towns of Haverhill, Amesbury & other places within the Province abovesd and all or most of them are destitute of Father, Mother or other Friends able to procure their redemption whereby they are likely to be kept forever from their native Countrey & Friends, and to be deprived of the means of being instructed in the true Protestant Religion" and "in behalfe of his sd Son as of all others that are Captives with the French or Indians," he humbly prays the Court to assist in their redemption.

[40] Arch. 57, 67. [41] See Exeter. [42] Arch. 70, 469.

The Court not assisting, on May 29, 1701, another "humble pettition[43] of samuel gill of Salsbery and of beniemin hutchins of the town of citterie sheweth: that whereas it pleased the honourable the great and generall assembly in May 1700 to grant that ther should be means uessed to recover the captives from the french and Indins at Canida and left it with your honouers to be put in execution: we humbly intreat that it may be put in execution with all speed which will much oblidg your poor pettioners." Then follows: "an account of captives tacken from Salsbery newbery Amesbery Kittery Yorck which are not returned.

Samuell gill taken from Salsbery jun 10th 1697 agged nine yeres

John (or Joseph) goodaridg taken from newbery about october in .92 aboute eight yeeres old

ann whit takene from Amsbery at the same time

Jonathan hutchins taken from Kettery May 9th 1698 agged about fifteen yeres

Charles Traffton taken from York About May About 1695 agged about 15 yeres

and one Robert winchester about July in :96 agged about 14 years

and Joseph Frey of Kettery taken about 1695 agged about 15 or 16 yeres."

Samuel Gill was taken to St. Francis (Saint-François-du-Lac) where he always lived and became the head of a large family.

The late Judge Charles Gill of Montreal printed some family "Notes" from which much that follows is quoted, freely translated.

The *naïveté* of one of the printed papers reminds one of the friendly simplicity of the *habitant* of today. Dated February, 1768, it begins: "We, Joseph Louis, François, Joseph Piche, Robert, Magdélaine, Josephte and Marie" have come together to choose one among us to seek the relatives of our late father, a native of New England. We have never known exactly where he was taken, only that he was brought 80 years ago by the Indians

43 Arch. 70, 525.

to St. Francis. His name was Same Gille, We know also that our grandfather, Sagen Gill, sent twice to seek him, but he, having been taken so young, had become attached to the nation and never wished to leave; "and as we should be greatly pleased to know our relatives, we beg the gentlemen who may know this family to introduce our brother . . . to any of our connections." They also respectfully supplicated the Governors and Generals to protect and aid in this search for the relatives of their father and also of their mother who was taken, they said, at Quenibanc[44] some time after the capture of their father, near a mill, when all the family was brought to Canada except the father and mother who were killed on the spot.

This paper was endorsed by the missionary and the chosen one was "recommended" by Guy Carleton at the Castle of St. Louis, Quebec, to all "that can assist him to find out his relations near Boston."

If the seeker came he certainly did not find their father's home. For that the family waited many years until Miss Baker sent to Judge Gill the petition of Sergeant Samuel of Salisbury. We have no record of the captive's baptism or marriage, the early registers having been destroyed by Rogers, but we know that he was renamed Joseph and that his wife was Rosalie.

The Abenakis use only the Christian name, and although family tradition calls her a James and her father a minister (the story of the mill notwithstanding) she cannot be identified.

The Indians could not agree upon a marrying plan for their two young captives (Samuel-Joseph was twenty-eight!) whether to marry each to a savage or whether to keep a family of pure white blood, so the priest, probably Père Aubéry, settled the question by quickly marrying them saying that he had received an inspiration from the Great Spirit.

They lived like Indians, but Samuel never forgot his native tongue, and was interpreter for the village. They were married about 1715 and their children were:

44 Kennebunk?

Joseph-Louis, whose first wife was Janne, dau. of the *grand chef;* and second, Suzanne Gamelin-Chateauvieux.

François, who mar. Marie-Anne Couturier, great granddaughter of Jean Crevier, seigneur of St. Francis.

Robert, m. Louis Chenevet.

Joseph-Piche, whose two wives were Indians.

One daughter m. a half-breed (German) and the other two pure blood Abenakis.

Mrs. Johnson,[45] who was bought for some blankets by Samuel Gill's eldest son, Joseph-Louis, does not mention Samuel in her "Narrative." He may have died in 1738. She wrote that Joseph-Louis "kept a store of goods and lived in a style far above the majority of his tribe." She milked his cows.

His unmarried sisters worked with wampum and beads.

Samuel's sons were important men of the village, although the Indian name of Joseph-Louis suggests suspicion. They called him "the comrade of the Iroquois," and the Iroquois were their enemies, friends of the English. Once they made an ambush for his destruction. Before his death, however, he had become *grand chef de prière,* assisting the priest in the service. His Indian wife was killed in the Rogers' raid and he took a French woman as second.

Three of the four boys who went from the village to the Hanover School were Samuel Gill's grandsons. The priest approved of their going, but Joseph's French wife and her family opposed it, fearing that her boy might become a heretic, but the chief, with broader outlook, said: "God will preserve the children and lead them in the right Way and when they are instructed in both the Papist and Protestant Religions, they will be capable of choosing that which is best."

Whatever happened to Joseph-Louis' son's religious belief, he was not educated out of the savage life, for he married "the homeliest squaw of the village." The Hanoverian missionary,

45 See Chapter XXI.

when writing of the St. Francis boys, said that their mothers bade them "farewell with g^{t} Tenderness and Affection but without any appearance of Sorrow or Regret." The fathers went in their canoes to the mouth of the river and then took leave of their sons. Many are the descendants of "the lad" of Salisbury. The Abbé Mauraul[46] counted nine hundred and fifty-two persons of white and mixed blood.

Jemaico (West Amesbury)

1704, *August* 9.

Davis.

"The wife, son & daughter of John Davis of Jemaico taken by ye Indians in y^{r} house or in y^{r} field."[47] Of the three we trace only the daughter,

Helen.

At Quebec "On 7th April 1708 was baptized *sous condition* in the Chapel of the Ursulines with permission of the Vicar General by Mr. Du Buisson, Chanoine, Marie Françoise English girl, taken by a war-party named in English helene Darvass in the village of Jameeker aged seventeen years. Godfather Robert Drouard, inhabitant of this town. Godmother Marie Jeanne W—— (illeg.) wife of Pierre Pilotte." As helenne Dauis she is naturalized in 1710, and on "The 31 August 1710 was buried in the cemetery of the Hopital by the clergy of this parish heleine Da Wass, an English girl of the village of Jameeker aged 19 years, named in her baptism Marie Françoise. Her burial was made by me, undersigned curate of Quebec in presence of [names illeg.]

Pacquet priest"

A John Davis married Elizabeth Cilley, who had seven children, and died. Was "helenne Darvass" one of them? His second wife to whom he was married in 1702 was Bethia Ash, and if this is the family it was she of whom Pike writes; but she must have soon died for John had a third wife before much time had passed.

46 *"Histoire des Abenaquis,"* written in 1866. 47 Pike's "Journal."

Amesbury

1706, *July* 4.

Prowt or Prowse, Barnes; perhaps not a Canadian captivity.

Son of John and Hannah (Barnes), b. in 1672, he was in 1707 called their eldest son. In March, 1701/2, he married Deborah Kimball and they had two daughters. Hoyt[48] quotes a letter written on the day. "Hast to Cap. True Sr About one of the clock the Indians killd . . . barnes prouce missing we fear killd all att one time as neer as wee Judg

Yours

John Wadleigh capt."

Pike wrote: "A party of the enemy fell upon the out parts of Amesbury about High-noon. Kill'd & carried away 9 or 10 persons . . . Barnes Prowt Carried away."

Nothing more is known. His estate was not administered until 1715.

About 1712.

Quinby or Quimby, Benjamin.

Is this he? Son of Robert and Mary, b. 10 January, 1689, and married in 1722 to Judith Gould?[49] In the House Journal of 1716, Nov. 8, Benjamin asks that there be paid out of the public treasury thirty pounds, "Which he prevail'd with Capt. Gyles to pay to Redeem him out of the hands of the Indians with whom he had been a Captive four Years being taken when in the Service under Cpt. Lane in the last War." Seventy pounds was allowed.[50] This suggests a Maine wilderness rather than a Canadian captivity.

Exeter

This frontier town suffered of course from Indian raids, but not from a general attack. The year after the massacre at Dover eight or nine men who were working in a field near Lamprey

48 "Old Families of Salisbury and Amesbury," 25.

49 "Old Families of Salisbury and Amesbury," Hoyt, I, 296.

50 Prov. Laws, IX, 495.

River were killed and a lad of unknown name was carried away. The first known Canadian captive was taken in

1697, *June* 9.

WELLS, LUKE, b. 1674.

Probably son of the Rev. Thomas Wells, first minister of Amesbury, and Mary (Perkins).

On this day of June some women and children went to the woods without a guard to gather strawberries. Perhaps it was to frighten and to make them more careful that a gun was fired. That shot probably saved many lives, but it may have cost the man with the gun a fine of five shillings for, said the law: "whoever shall shoot of a gun except at an Indian or wolf shall forfeit five shillings."

It saved the strawberry pickers, it called out men for a rescue and it frightened away some Indians who, intending to attack the next day, were hidden at a place now called Fort Rock, but alas! three men suffered.

Pike wrote: "John Young of Exiter slain by ye Indians, his son wounded, Luke Wells (& a lad at Salsbury)[51] the same day carried away." Young had been impressed into the Exeter garrison the year before and Luke Wells may have been serving there.

1704, *April* 26.

TAYLOR, REBECCA, wife of Edward.

WILLIAM, their son.

"Edward Taylor was slain by ye Indians at Lamper-Eel River, his wife & one of his children carried away."[52] Their home was "nere a sawmill" in what is now Newmarket.

Penhallow repeats the story that Rebeckah Taylor told him.[53] When on the "bank of Mount royall River Sampson who was her cruel master with out any provocation given resolved to hang her, who for want of a rope made use of his girdle, which when he had

[51] Samuel Gill. [52] Pike's "Journal."

[53] Quoted from Manuscript of "Indian Wars."

fastened about her neck begun to pull her up on the limb of a tree that hung in the Nature of a gibbet but in hoisting her up the weight of her body broke it in two, which so exasperated him that he made a second attempt resolving that if he failed in that to knock her in the head; but before he had power to effect it, Bomazeen came along, who seeing the tragedy that was on foot did so interpose as to prevent the fatall stroke."

It is pleasant to read of one good act of Bomazeen!

When she was redeemed is not known, but she came back and had a second husband, appearing on June 8, 1720, as "Rebecr dudley" when asking that her son-in-law "Aren Rolen" be appointed executor.[54]

William was taken to Montreal, made a Catholic and died in the faith.

"On Tuesday, 25 May 1706 was solemnly baptized by me Priest undersigned, William (or Guillaume) Taylor son of the late Edward Taylor, master ship carpenter, living at Exceter in New England and of Rebecca —— his wife, who born at Saumonfall in New England the —— was taken at Exceter and is living in the service of Messire Claude de Ramezay, *Chevalier de l'ordre de Saint Louis,* Seigneur de la Gesse Boisfleurant, Governor of the Island of Monreal and other places. His godfather was Messire Francois Clairambaut Daigremont *commissaire de la marine et subdelegue de Monsieur L'Intendant,* who has added the name François to that of Guillaume, and his godmother was Damoiselle Catherine de Ramezay daughter of the said Governor, who signed, except the newly baptized Englishman, who declared he could not sign inquiry as to this having been made, according to law.

Daigremont Catherine de Ramezay

Meriel Pretre."

"On Monday 11 January 1712, was buried in the cemetery, the body of Guillaume François Taylor, Shoemaker, son of the late

[54] Probate Records, N. H. Hist. Soc.

—— Taylor and of Rebecca his wife, who born at Nitchiwanack in New England in 1691 and taken at Exeter the —— 1704, having been by M. Meriel baptized at Ville Marie (not having been in his country) the 25 March 1706[55] died yesterday in the hospital after having received by the ministry of the said Henri Antoine Meriel priest of the Seminary of Montreal, the Sacrements of Penitence, Eucharist and Extreme Unction.

Witnesses

M. Charles de la Gondalie, priest of the same Seminary of Montreal

M. Meriel

Jacob Gilman

John Wedgewood, Englishmen now in Montreal, who have signed with Joseph Bartlett."

"Guillaume Tailor living at villemarie," is on the Naturalization list of 1710.

1706, *July* 23, *Tuesday*.

HALL, EDWARD.

MIGHELL,[56] SAMUEL.

"A MELATTO."[57]

Of the attack Pike wrote "About Twenty of the enemy fell upon ten Exiter-men as y^y were mowing in a field betwixt Exiter & Lampril-River . . . Three Carried Captive." The News-Letter said they "were insulted by about forty Indians."

The place was near where the New-Market meeting-house was built. There had been depredations at Dunstable, Amesbury and Kingston and Colonel Hilton had marched away from Exeter to intercept the enemy which he did not do. Then the Indians lurked about his house, hoping to kill him. On this day after the men had gone out early to the field, they crept between them and

55 The register gives May.

56 As he spelled it. Bell wrote Mighill; Penhallow Myalls; Farmer and Moor Miles.

57 Perhaps "the negro boy" owned by Maj. John Gilman mentioned in Town Papers, XI, 651.

the guns which had been laid aside. Two escaped, one was wounded, four killed, and the three named above they carried away. Capt. Edward Hall was a nephew of Colonel Winthrop Hilton. He was well treated by the French because he built a sawmill for them — following the lead of Sawyer from Worcester, captured nine months before. For this reason he and Mighell were allowed to go a-hunting, sometimes unattended, and one day "they resolved to hunt for home, and made the best of their way to an English settlement."[58] They had three suffering weeks in the forest, living on "lily roots and the rind of trees till Mighell was so exhausted that he lay down to die. Hall made all possible provision for his comfort, says the narrator, and left to seek the nearest settlement. He soon reached Deerfield and sent a party to rescue his friend. They brought him to the fort, he recovered and the two went home."[59] Edward Hall's estate was administered in 1770. Mighell, dying in 1736, left his wife Sarah sole executor, and as she refused to give bonds, an inventory was made. In the family were two sons and four daughters.[60]

The "Melatto" must have been ransomed by John Sheldon in 1708. The last item of his account rendered in November of that year is: "To pa for the Redemption of a molatto Captive taken from Exeter 40 pieces of 8s 8d. at 17d weight which he is to pay me."

A portion of John Sheldon's payment for services on this, his second journey to Canada, was "a Muletto," valued at thirteen pounds and twelve shillings. Surely not the redeemed one!

1709, *May* 6, *Friday*.
MOODY, WILLIAM.
STEVENS, SAMUEL.
GILMAN, JEREMIAH.
GILMAN, ANDREW.

58 Farmer and Moore N. H. Hist. Coll., I, 247.

59 Bell's "Exeter," 222.

60 MS. Will. N. H. Hist. Soc.

"William Moodey, Samuel Stephens, & 2 Gilmans (all of Ex:) were surprised by ye Ind^{ns} at a Mill . . . William Moodey was Retaken by ye Deerfield men about 16 days after neer Shamblees, but fell again into ye enemies hand, and tis feared he & another English man were Roasted to Death."[61]

It was at Pickpocket Mill in what is now Brentwood. Mr. Bell[62] says the name is probably a corruption of an Indian word. Moody's fate is described in detail in the report of "the Deerfield men,"[63] but it was taken from "lips of the survivors" twenty years after the event!

The Scout was returning, having been as far north as Chambly. One morning when on French River they saw a canoe "with four Indians in it and a Captive-man" taken at Exeter. They fired, killed two Indians, wounded the third and the fourth swam for the opposite shore. Captain Wright called to the captive to paddle the canoe to the shore; the wounded Indian prevented. They bade Moody knock him in the head, but the two "skuffled . . . turned over the Canoe and parted in the water." The Englishman, very weak, cried out that he was drowning, Lieutenant Wells was pulling him to shore when they were fired upon from behind. Wells was killed, and, says the narrator, "we being then in such a fright every one took to his heals, But moody . . . was not able to follow." Being left alone he "hallowed" to the Indians on the other shore — there were nineteen of them in five canoes — "to fetch him over & one came & after they had got him over they Burnt him on the Spot."

This narrative says that after the Indians reached Canada "they Burnt one more of these captives Andrew Gilman by name"— but Andrew came home!

Andrew, b. 1690, and Jeremiah Gilman were sons of Jeremiah and Mary (Wiggin). They were separated in captivity. Andrew returned, had two wives, Joanna Thing and Bridget Hilton, a

61 Pike's "Journal." 62 "History of Exeter."

63 "Hist. Deerfield," I, 369.

family of nine children and a home in Brentwood. Jeremiah never came back.

Three stories are told about him. In one he was killed and eaten, so they told Andrew his brother. In another he escaped after a tedious captivity, followed the Connecticut River to its mouth and there made a home and founded a family. The third story is in a document in the Public Record Office at London.[64] This is a list of the "Names and conditions of all English prisoners taken this year" and dated Quebec, Oct. 3, 1709, and was written by Maj. Thomas Lloyd, sometime commander at Fort St. John (Newfoundland). He had been imprisoned in Canada and in France and it was from France — in spite of the dating — that this was sent to the Council for Trade and Plantations in London.

"One Moudy taken from Exeter with his brother and Jeremiah Killman and Saml. Stevens. Moudy was burnt by the Indians near Willmarie who suffered manfully all the torments that the barbarous heathens could inflict upon him. Sir Kilman his fellow martyr was likewise burnt att the same time and did suffer all the torments that those cursed Devills could inflict on him. I have spoken with one Martin Kellog a very credible young man well known to all Northern parts of New England, who buried him." Martin Kellogg was probably at the Sault Saint-Louis Mission at this time.

Samuel Stevens came back. His wife was Patience; their children were seven, and Samuel died in 1738 as is shown by Probate Records in Concord.

1710, *July* 22 (?).

DOLLOFF. Three children of Richard and Catharine (Bean).

SARAH, b. 1702.

MARGARET, b. 1704.

ABIGAIL, b. 1706.

WEDGWOOD, JOHN.

Penhallow says: "After this, the enemy appeared very bold and

[64] Calendar of State Papers. Colonial Papers, 1710-11, p. 75, as printed.

insolent in the town in open streets where they carried captive four children as they were at play. They then took John Wedgewood whom they carried to Canada."[65] The name of the fourth child is lost. Tradition says they were going "from school to the strong house in what is known as the garrison pasture." In 1715 —April 26—"Richard Dollar of Exeter" petitioning to the Assembly of the Province:

"Most humbly sheweth, That yor Poor Petitioner went some time last summer to Canada by land to redeem three children I had made Captive by ye Ind^{ns}, but could get but one of them, for which I paid £12; 17; 0, to ye Indian captor at Canada, & w^{n} I came to port Albany I paid him twelve pounds mor, for wch I gave my bond to Maj^{r} Skyler, wch your Petitioner . . . cannot possibly discharge (being very poor) my afores^{d} Journey having been vey chargeable . . . & yor Poor Petitioner intending to go again to Canada this Summer to get my other two children, a French gentl^{n} having promist me to redeem them from ye Ind^{ns}: Humbly implores relief etc."

He was given ten pounds in May, 1717, and a like amount the next year.[66] The historian of Exeter quotes further traditions; that the father brought back two girls after peace was established, and that the other who had married an Indian (they were all very young when taken) also came back to Exeter with her husband, but feeling slighted because of him she returned to Canada with him. Richard's will, made in 1744 and proved in 1750, mentions dau. Margaret (Bean), Ann and five sons.

WEDGWOOD, JOHN.

He was taken to Montreal where on January 11, 1712, he was present at the burial of William Taylor. Did he come home soon after? A John Wedgwood witnessed a deed in Exeter in June of that year.

In 1717/18 he made one of those curious deeds of gift of house,

[65] Indian Wars, 64. [66] Town Papers, 11, 647.

lands and belongings generally, to a minor son, John, who "when out of his time" or at the age of twenty-one was to give to each sister four pounds out of the estate. This was not recorded for ten years.

1710, *June* 23, is date on a monument.

HILTON, DUDLEY, son of Edward and Ann (Dudley), granddaughter of Governor Thomas.

LOUGEE, JOHN.

Col. Winthrop Hilton, the leading man of the province, was in "the masting business" and went out with seventeen men to strip the bark from large hemlock logs which had been cut for masts the year before. This delay prevents injury from worms. While working fourteen miles from his home, which was a garrison-house in what is now Epping, he and his men were attacked and could make no defence because the day being wet their guns had become unserviceable. Colonel Hilton, who was especially hated by the Indians, and two more men were killed. Dudley, his brother and John Lougee were captured; the rest escaped.

Dudley Hilton, who lived in what is now South New Market was never heard from. His wife was Mercy Kinsley (Hall). They had three daughters.

John Lougee was taken from Canada to England and was again in Exeter in 1716. There he married and left descendants.

KINGSTON

1710, 22 *July* (?).

GILMAN, JACOB.

HUNTOON, PHILIP.

Kingston was a new plantation in 1707. Belknap says these men were taken on the same day that the Dolloff children and John Wedgwood were captured. In Farmer's edition (p. 188) a manuscript letter from Ward Clark to Prince is quoted:

"A company of Indians who had pretended friendship, who the year before had been peaceably conversant with the inhabitants of

Kingston and seemed to be thirsting after the blood of the enemy came into town and ambushing the road, killed Samuel Winslow and Samuel Huntoon they also took Philip Huntoon and Jacob Gilman and carried them to Canada where after some time they purchased their own redemption by building a sawmill for the governor after the English mode." This was five years after Sawyer of Lancaster and Hall of Exeter had built mills. That built by these Kingston men was probably near Montreal, for Gilman was a witness at the marriage of Elizabeth Hurst and the burial of William Taylor in 1712.

CHAPTER XIII

Kittery, Eliot and Berwick

1692-3-4-5-8 — 1705-6-24

HE Piscataqua Plantation included Lower Kittery, in which is Spruce Creek; Middle Parish (now Eliot) in which is Sturgeon Creek; and Upper Kittery or Berwick. The last was known by many names: Newichawannock, Quamphegan (where was Salmon Falls) and Unity Parish. Except for the massacre at Salmon Falls[1] the district escaped a general attack.

During King William's war, like the rest of the frontier, it was in constant danger. There were for its protection in 1690 in the "Lower Part of Kittery 10 garrisons," among them "Wm. Peprills, & Wido Champernoons . . . not one souldier in them all, but Kept & defended by their sd. inhabitants." In "The uper Kittery—or Barwick, 8 garrisons . . . in all which garrisons but six souldrs."

In 1694/5 many persons in this vicinity were killed or captured. In 1697 the selectmen petitioned for abatement of taxes saying that they "are overcome and discouraged by the tediousness of the war," and that "the People are utterly unable to pay it in money . . . we have offered their Goods and Chattels at an outcry,[2] . . . but find none of abilitie to buy . . . Considering the seat of Warr is with us, and ye Burden exceeding heavy as we are a poor Scattering People Nesesitated to Watch, ward, Scout, buld Garrisons and fortifications and one halfe of us to be furnished with Snowshoos and Mogginsons and all at our own Charge. . . . and

[1] See Chapter VIII. [2] Public auction.

at every alarm Driven from our Imployment."[3] Because of their distress the sum of thirty-eight pounds was abated. The same year "the parish of Barwick" asked aid "to maintain the Publiq worship," they not profiting by the shipping and fishing of the town of Kittery; their principal dependence having been upon their mills "w^c^ are all burnt or by the war made Useless." They are so "Closely Confined to the Garrison that they Cannot attend their Ordinary Occasions w^th^out extreme danger," and "had not ye Charitie of their Connecticut-Neighbours prevented," they might have starved for the "Crops of Corn (w^c^ at best are very small because of ye want of safe Land) have Extremely faild," etc. The Council gave them ten pounds for "the year last past" and twenty for the year to come; and it was recommended that contributions be asked from other towns "that Souls may not perish for lack of vision."[4] In 1711 there was better protection. Then sixteen houses (Major Plaisted's the largest) held ninety-seven families of four hundred and twelve souls, of which one hundred and fourteen were men and twenty-three were soldiers.[5]

Captives[6]

1692? Gray, George.
Catter, Mary.
Ferguson, Mary.
Sarah.
Abigail.
1693. Frost, Nicholas.
Mary, his wife.
Two children.
Smith, the Widow.
Nason, Richard.
1694. Sarah.
Neal, Amy.

[3] Arch. 3, 415. [4] Arch. 11, 125, and Council Records.

[5] List of Frontier Garrisons. Arch. 71, 871-6.

[6] I owe much to Mr. Stackpole's "Old Kittery" for genealogical information.

Abt. 1695. Fry, Joseph.
Hammond, Joseph.
1705. Hammons, Patience.
1698. Hutchins, Benjamin.
Samuel.
Jonathan.
1705. Hutchins, Hopewell.
"Three little Sons."
1706. Shapley, Nicholas.
Tucker, Hugh.

1692 *or earlier.*
GRAY, GEORGE, son of George and Sarah.

"George Gray, boy" remained in 1695; he is erroneously said to be "of Cascow," although he may have been captured there.

George Gray (a Scotchman from Ireland), living in Kittery, wrote in his will in 1692—proved in August, 1693—"It is my will that my sone George Gray If iver it shall please god to deliver him out of captivity shall have and enjoy that halfe of my lands given to his mother for the time of her widdowhood or after her death or marriage and if my sone George Gray shall not returne from Captivity then I give the said halfe of my lands to my two sones Alexander Gray & James Gray in equall partnership after the death or marriage of their mother."

In 1702 he was said to be "at Montreal" where he was given sixty livres of the king's money. In 1723 one of the daughters of George, Sr., brought a lawsuit against her brothers in which it is recited that George, the captive, had died leaving no children, but it does not show that he returned to receive his "halfe."

CATTER, MARY (written Hatter on the 1698 list).

She may have been the daughter of John, but plainly she was "of Kettery." Among the Minutes of Remarkable Things reported by one of the commissioners "at Mares-Point in Casco-Bay" on 14 Jan., 1698/9, is this: Some "of the captives told me that one Mary Catter (which person we now brought home with us, belonging to Kittery)" was taken down to Casco-Bay by her master and other Indians, and they seeing some sloops and thinking that the English were coming upon them ran away into the woods and left Mary very sick in the wigwam without any thing at all to eat. They left a fire, but they stayed away many days. "She lay wishing for something to eat, and at length in came a turtle. She eat that, but afterwards began to despair of out-living the famine, which was returned upon her. At length when she was very hungry, in came a partridge; she took a stick and struck it and drest it and eat it." And when she was hungry again her master came to look after her.[7]

FERGUSON, MARY.
SARAH.
ABIGAIL.

Mary and Sarah were daughters of Daniel and Mary. Abigail, doubtless a granddaughter.

Mary, b. 1664, must have been the first redeemed. She m. in July, 1693, James Treworgy. Dying in 1696, she left two children who were cared for by her brother Alexander. Williamson wrote that when captured she was decapitated by an Indian enemy, which seems somewhat exaggerated!

"Sarah and Abig[ll] ffargeson" were redeemed by Carey in 1695. Sarah, b. 1676, married soon after her redemption (19 Dec., 1695) James Ross of Casco Bay, a fellow-captive redeemed at the same time.

1693, *June* 8.
FROST, MARY (Small), wife of Nicholas.
Two children.
SMITH, The widow; and "about the same time,"
FROST, NICHOLAS.

The Frosts lived at Sturgeon Creek where from the garrison-

[7] Magnalia, II, 643.

house the women and children were captured. Colonel and Judge Ichabod Plaisted of Berwick (son of Roger) wrote to his brother John of Saco on June ninth: "As for news we have not any good. This last week we had four carried away by the Indians and one wounded. The place was Storgin Creek. The parties carried away were Nicholas Frost's wife and two children and the widow Smith."[8] They were taken from the garrison-house.

Frost's wife must have been redeemed before 1698 for in that year she was licensed to keep a public house. He, called "the beaver trader," taken about the same time, was according to the testimony of Ann Jenkins (in 1695) freed from the "hard usage" of the Indians by the "Indian Minister, Prince Waxaway."

At the end of the list of captives made at Casco in 1698 is "Nick ffrost drowned."

Nason, Richard, son of Richard, Jr., and Shuah ——, b. 1667 in what is now South Berwick.

In October, 1675, after the second attack on Tozier's house[9] the Indians went southward to Sturgeon Creek where says tradition Richard Nason, Jr., was killed in his own doorway and his son Richard, third of the name, was carried to Canada. This is a very early date for a Canadian captivity. The boy, only seven years old, may have been kept in the Maine woods and taken later to Canada, or the date of the capture may be wrong. His name is among "thos Remaining" in 1695, which implies the later captivity. In 1710 "Richard Naasson of New England living in sainct francois Married to a french woman and having children" is naturalized. The Nason Genealogy says he lived to an advanced age and was much esteemed for his virtues; that he was sold by the Indians to a Frenchman who lived near Montreal, whose daughter he married.

The first Richard Nason owned a large tract on the river. Here in Revolutionary times lived Colonel Hamilton, and here is laid the opening scene of Miss Jewett's "The Tory Lover."

[8] Printed in Portland Press Herald. [9] See Salmon Falls, Chapter VIII.

1694.

NASON, SARAH, dau. of Benjamin and Martha (Kenney).

In 1694 Sarah, who could not have been more than six years old, was taken. Benjamin, her father, was son of the first Richard. In our Archives[10] is the following petition:

Barwick, Sept. 21st 1700

"To the Honourable William Stoughton, Esqr Lieut. Governour Together with the Honour'd Council and Representatives, of His Majties Province of The Massachusetts Bay Convened In Generall Assembly—Benjamin Nason, of Barwick In the County of York humbly Petitioneth

That, Whereas In the year of or Lord 1694 his Daughter Sarah was by The Indian Enemy Captivated and in their hands detained till January 1699 or 1700, At which time, She was Redeemed by one Thomas Hutchings, off whom yor Petitioner was Necessitated to Purchase her by Paying to him the Sum̄ of five pounds, five Shill, & Sixpence, . . . Or Else to forego her, besides his sustaining Other Losses & being wounded to the Disableing of One hand in a great measure, by the Same Enemy." He begs that the charges be allowed "which favour he Understands Others in Like Case have obtained etc." The following list of expenses was sent with the petition:

"for her ransom 10 jan	3=10=0
for 1 blancet	0=07=0
for 1 pair of stockens	0=03=0
for 1 Shoes	0=07=0
for 1 Com (comb?)	0=00=6
for her being abord 3 weeks	0=18=0
	5=05=6"

After eight months delay four pounds only was allowed.

Mr. Stackpole says she may have married William Divers in Portsmouth August 8, 1725.

[10] Vol. 70, 482.

NEAL, AMY, probably dau. of John and Joan.

"Amie Nell of Newichawanick" was "yett in the Indians Hands" in 1698/9.

John Neal was a Quaker of Unity parish.[11]

The date of her capture is unknown, but she had returned in 1699 when she witnessed a deed. In 1706 she became the third wife of Samuel Johnson.

"*About* 1695."

FRY, JOSEPH, son of Adrian and Sarah.

Among the early Kittery names is that of Adrian Fry, Planter. He was here in 1664. In 1690, having become a Quaker, he and his family "were p'sented for not Comeing to Meeting."

Joseph, his son, does not appear in New England except in the petition of Gill and Hutchins,[12] "Joseph Frey of Kittery taken about 1695, agged about 15 or 16 yeres." That is all. For Joseph, no other parentage fits. He must have been a younger son of Adrian and Sarah. The identification of this captive, begun from the Canadian end, was one of Miss Baker's difficult problems.[13] The story, although personal, may be of interest.

Her first paper, "My Hunt for the Captives," was quoted in a Montreal newspaper. In that "Hunt" she had found certain members of the family of Deacon Thomas French of Deerfield. Soon after the Montreal article was printed she received a letter asking why she had omitted the name of André French, son of Thomas, who had married and founded a large family in Canada? This was plainly an error. There was no son of Thomas French unaccounted for. Then who was André French? How could "a large family" be thus deprived of its grandfather?

Miss Baker's correspondent, his great granddaughter, was a nun who became her devoted friend. To prove her claim of de-

[11] Unity Parish and the upper Parish were separated by Great — or Shorey's — Brook. On one side was Shorey's garrison-house, on the other was Neal's.

[12] See Salisbury, Chapter XII.

[13] See "Joseph Fry of Kittery" in Vol. IV, Pro. of the P. V. M. A.

scent from Deacon Thomas she sent some "*Notes sur la Famille French*"[14] by an abbé, the author of writings genealogical and historical. Herein the founder of the family was André Laframboise (raspberry), son of André Laframboise and Marie Fraim, both of Boston, plainly a muddle of names. The variations of the name are perplexing but not too difficult. Plainly Fray anglicized is Fry. Laframboise is explained by a family tradition as follows: André French, a young son of Deacon Thomas French, was playing on the sandy shore by the river near his father's house when he was seized and carried off by the savages. (The deacon's house was on the village street, not very near Deerfield river; Adrian Fry's was on the south shore of Sturgeon Creek, where it enters the Newichawannock.) They treated him with great cruelty, cutting strips of flesh from the fattest part of his body. A squaw, moved by compassion, offered his captors a sheep in exchange for the boy. They gave her the child. She fed him on raspberries and under her care he recovered.

Was the name Laframboise given him because of the tradition or was the tradition made to fit the name? Until recently in Canada nicknames have often supplanted original names.

A year after his marriage, two of his uncles visited him, urging him to go with them to New England. He consented on condition that he might come back to Canada after seeing his relatives and receiving his inheritance. Embarking in a sloop they were not out of hailing distance when André's young wife, standing on the shore and holding their baby aloft in her arms, cried: "André, André, you are abandoning your wife, but can you desert your own child?" The poor fellow threw himself into the water, swam quickly to shore and the uncles continued their voyage alone.

After Miss Baker received this letter she searched New England records for a Fry to fit, and she found him in "Joseph agged 15, taken about 1695."

14 The family is known in Canada because one of its members, Bishop Plessis, was a distinguished prelate.

He is on the list of prisoners of 1710/11, and in that year he asks to be made a citizen of New France. Joseph, the Quaker lad of Kittery, is now André, the Catholic of Canada.

The next find was his marriage-contract made "according to the Custom of Paris followed in Canada."

At the hospitable home of one of André's descendants in a pretty village on the Ottawa River we read this marriage-contract to many members of the French-Fry family who had come together to honor Miss Baker.

The contract (similar, of course, to all made by our captives who married in their new home) was signed on the afternoon of Oct. 12, 1713, at the house of Jacques La Calle, master-carpenter.

André was about thirty-six; his bride about nineteen. She was Marie Louise, daughter of François Bigras of Rochelle, France, and Marie (Brunet) of Montreal.

Their friends and relatives agreed for them and they reciprocally promised that they would take each other for husband and wife under the names and laws of marriage to be solemnized according to the rites of the Holy Mother Church as soon as possible. They agree to hold all their goods and chattels in common. Neither can be held for the debts of the other contracted before marriage. She receives the customary portion of five hundred livres ($83.-33) to be paid at her option without being obliged to sue him for it. Upon the death of either the survivor is to have two hundred livres of their common property. They take each other with all the rights they now have, and which may fall to them by gift or inheritance, and for the affection they bear to each other they make, while yet living, this present reciprocal gift to each other of all and several of their goods and chattels to be enjoyed by the survivor in full ownership, provided always that no children are born of this marriage. And if this marriage be dissolved by the death of said husband, it shall be lawful for the said wife to reject or accept the said community of goods herein agreed upon, and to reclaim and take back freely, without mortgage for the payment of debts, all that she may have brought as her said dowry — such as her household goods, her wearing apparel, her jewels and ornaments, her bed and bedding, and in general all that may have fallen to her by gift or inheritance . . . Thus it is agreed without which agreement the said marriage could not be consummated.

The future bridegroom and bride, her mother and her uncle declared they could not sign the contract. Four days later they were married in the parish of St. Joachim at Pointe-Claire.

The baptisms of twelve children are recorded; the first at Pointe-Claire, others at Ste-Anne-Bout-de l'Isle.

1714. Elizabeth, Marie Brunet was sponsor, signing her maiden name. She m. in 1735 (as Elisabeth Frinche) Antoine Deboust.

1717. André-Lambert, s. of André Piret and M. L. Bigras; m. Françoise Periar.

1719. Marie-Joseph, dau. André Fray, living at Côte Saint-Remi; m. 1748 François Potevin de Poitiers.

1721. Joachim Fraye, m. 1750 M. Joseph Malette (m. as Laframboise).

1722. Charles Freni French, d. 1723.

1724. Marie-Suzanne, d. 1724.

1725. Marie-Louise, m. as M. L. Frange, M. Joseph Pepin, 1745.

1727. Jean-Baptiste Fraye.

1728. Joseph-Marie.

1730. Jacques, m. M. Joseph Renaud in April, 1757.

1732. Vincent.

1733. Angélique, m. 1757 Jean Poisson, a soldier.

There are other spellings — one Tahé dit Laframboise being the most remote.

André, under Canadian feudalism, became a perpetual tenant of the Gentlemen of the Seminary, the Seigneurs of the Island of Montreal.[15]

15 See p. 15.

His first grant at Grande Anse — between Pointe-Claire and La Chine — was given to him in 1716. Two years later it was cancelled and at Saint-Rémy on the southern bank of the St. Lawrence, he received a domain four arpents front by twenty-three arpents deep (720 feet by 4140 feet). From this deed the following interesting features of Canadian feudalism are quoted:

Monsieur François Vachon de Belmont, acting Superior of his order in Ville-Marie, grants to André Freinch, English by nation, now *habitant*, to be enjoyed, improved and laid out on the following conditions: André is to pay every year ten sous and a half minot of the finest, whitest wheat, clean marketable, and lawful weight, for every twenty arpents of the superficial contents of the domain. In grain a half minot equals a little less than a half bushel, therefore this tenant's annual rent was about 50 cents and two and a half bushels of wheat. He is to sow the said land, to build and have a house and home upon it within a year from the date of the grant at the latest; to clear the adjacent wilderness as shall be necessary, to grind his grain at the mill of said Messieurs Seigneurs and nowhere else on pain of confiscation of the said grain, an arbitrary fine, and of payment for the right to transport the grain which he has had ground elsewhere. He is to permit such roads as Messieurs les Seigneurs shall think necessary, and among others a cart-road, which he and his heirs shall make and keep in good order. The Seigneurs shall have the right to take from his land all the timber, which they may need for their buildings and fences; with an *arpent* of standing wood, nearest to the cultivated land, where the woods shall not have been *couru*[16] which wood the Seigneurs shall cut and carry off, whenever they shall see fit without paying anything for it.

In case of failure to keep this agreement the lands revert to the Seigneurs without any legal penalties.

The contract was read and accepted; André declaring that he could not write his name. The annual rents were paid on Martin-

16 Shall not have been tramped over or beaten for game.

mas Day (Nov. 11). One can picture the group of *habitant*-tenants with their many tributes of grain, fruit and poultry. Probably the alien-*habitants* (captives of earlier years) could be easily distinguished by their English faces and stolid manner.[17]

In 1748 André Franche dit Laframboise was living at Pointe-Claire and was one of five boatmen engaged by the Sieur Sauvage, who was allowed to trade with the Indians at the Post of Michipicoton.[18] In 1757, when his son Jacques married, Joseph Fry of Kittery had died.

1695, *July* 6.
HAMMOND, JOSEPH, b. 1646.

Son of William and Benedictus; an "unusually useful man." He lived in what is now Eliot. His garrison-house, near Green Acre, was the "most thorough" of the region; the only one stockaded. Of his capture Mr. Pike wrote: "July 6, 1695 Capt. Hammons taken by the Indians, as he was seeking a Cow in Kittery woods."

Mather says that the canoe bearing Hammond intended to put ashore at Saco, but some of the garrison soldiers fired upon it and "the Indians carried him clear away" to Canada where "he met with extraordinary civilities." Count Frontenac "nobly purchased him of his tawny master."[19] "Capt. Josf Hamands of Piscadawa" was redeemed in 1695. He died in 1709/10.

The Rev. John Cotton of Plymouth, in letters to his son Rowland, says that "Captain Hammond was immediately carried to Kebeck," that he was "very honourably treated" and was "sent home without any ransome."[20]

1705, *May*.
HAMMONS, PATIENCE.

Dau. of Edmund and Jane.

Mr. Pike wrote on May 4, "Many persons surprised by the In-

[17] See "French terms," Appendix.

[18] *Rapport de l'Archiviste de Québec*, 1922-23, 233. No trader could go into the Indian country without a *congé* or license.

[19] Magnalia, II, 631. [20] MS. in Mass. Hist. Soc.

dians at Spruce Creek & York." He names several who were slain and adds: "Rest Carried Captive by 10 or a dozen Indians." Patience was probably one of these as shown in her baptismal record:

"On Monday 13 June 1707, was solemnly baptized by me, the priest undersigned, Patience Hammond, daughter of the late Edouard Hammond and of his wife Jeanne Montesse Protestants, Inhabitants of Kittery in New England, who was born —— of the year 1688 having been captured the (6th O. S.) 17th day of May, 1705 by the Abenakis and carried to Quebec last year, came a short time ago to Monreal there to be instructed and baptized. Her godfather was Monsieur François le Verrier, *Ecuyer*, *Capitaine d'une Compagnie du détachement de la Marine*, and her godmother was Dame Charlotte de Fleury, his wife as representing Damoiselle Louise Bondi[21] wife of M. Pinaud Merchant of Quebec. They have all signed with me. She was named Marie Françoise

Meriel Prêtre."

Having been "instructed and baptized" she may have been sent back to her godmother in Quebec. In 1710 "Marie françoise hammon" became a citizen of New France.

She must have returned with Messrs. Stoddard and Williams, landing in Boston in September, 1714, for the next January Mrs. Joanna Perry was paid four pounds for the entertainment of Patience Hamond and Margaret Otis.[22] (The shop where Joanna sold books was at the west end of the Town-House, but we do not know where she "entertained.")

A little later Patience herself was entertaining in Boston as shown by the old Court files of 1719 and 1720 wherein are suits for board, etc.[23]

She married Daniel Jones and lived in New York where she died on or about the ninth of October, 1731, leaving no children.[24]

21 Douaire de Bondy.

22 See Chapter VI.

23 S. J. C., 14-591.

24 York Deeds, 16, 614.

1698, *May* 9.

HUTCHINS, HUTCHINGS, HUCKINS.

BENJAMIN.

SAMUEL.

JONATHAN.

Sons of Enoch and Mary (Stevenson).

Pike wrote: "May 9, 98 Enoch Hutchins was killed by the Indians at Spruce-Creek as he was at work in his field; & three of his sons Carried away."

Stackpole says that Enoch lived in a garrison-house near the Eastern branch of the creek. A tradition that his wife Mary was also taken is disproved by the fact of her showing her husband's estate to his executors one month after his death.

Samuel was brought home in the Province Galley the next January. He married Hannah —— and died in 1742.

Benjamin was left behind in 1698, but he must have returned soon for in May, 1701, he signed the petition for the release of Jonathan.[25] He married 1, Joanna Ball; 2, Mary Dill, and died about 1721.

Jonathan, "agged about fifteen yeres," was redeemed, married Judith Weeks, lived in Kittery and died about 1746.

Among the "very remarkable things" reported to one of the commissioners at Mares-Point in Casco-Bay in 1698/9 was one about Jonathan. "Mary Fairbanks and Samuel Hutching, and some other captives, told me that Jonathan Hutching, belonging to Spruce-Creek, a lad fourteen years old, they met him crying for want of victuals, for in two or three days he had nothing to eat. Afterward, as he was going to fetch some wood, he felt something hard in his bosom. He put in his hand, and unto his astonishment he found there two great large ears of Indian corn, which were very well roasted. He eat them, and knew not how they came unto him."[26]

[25] Arch. 70, 525. See Gill.

[26] Magnalia, II, 643.

1705, *May* 4.

HUTCHINS, HOPEWELL, wife of Enoch (2), dau. of William Furbish, and
WILLIAM, b. 1694.
THOMAS, 1696.
ENOCH, 1697.

Penhallow wrote that Enoch, Jr., was the greatest sufferer in this attack "in the loss of his wife and children." His sufferings were not long as shown by the account rendered by his brother of the costs of his illness and funeral (including eight gallons of rum). In that "true and perfect Inventory," appraised in April, 1706, is one item: "To his wives gown under coat and 3 caps 1 — 10 — 0." Happily she came home to wear them again, and she came soon for administration papers were given to her in January, 1707.[27]

On the journey the Indians, or one of them, was kind to Mrs. Hopewell and to one of her little sons whom he carried that the child might not be killed for loitering.

At Sorel, in September, 1705, a baby daughter was born and named Mary Catherine, who was of course redeemed with her mother. Sooner or later Thomas and Enoch came. William only was left and probably it was he who in 1710, with a new name, Nicholas, and a new religion, was naturalized in 1710.

In April, 1711, the widow Hopewell married William Wilson.

In October, 1721, long after Enoch's death, orders were given for the division of his estate; one-third to his widow, the remainder (lands) equally to his surviving sons Thomas and Enoch, provided they pay to Mary, the only surviving daughter, what was left. William, absent, was as if dead.

But in 1733 back from Canada came one who said he was William Hutchins! Denied by his brothers, difficulties and law-suits followed.

In the files of the Superior Court are many depositions which

[27] Probate Files, Alfred.

were sworn to in April and May of that year. Naturally the neighbors' stories were similar. Here is that of John Chapman and Rachel (Ingersoll) of Spruce Creek. "John Chipman of Kittery & Rachel his wife testifieth & saith that the last Spring we these Deponents hearing that a Man was come to Town who was thot to be William the son of E Hutchins Dec^{d} who was carried away Captive to Canada many years ago We went to the House of William Wilson who married ye Widow of the s^{d} Enoch Hutchins to see the s^{d} Stranger & enquired of ye s^{d} Hope whether she really thought that that was her Son? She said she did, for, s^{d} She I told him when he came here that if he were my Son he had a Scar in the Calf of his Legg made by a Cutt with an ax and he pulled down his Stocking & I saw the Scar wch I think is the same scar & further I asked him whether he remembred what House he went into when he came to Canada & he s^{d} the Governors House. I asked him what Coat he wore when he came there & he said a Leather Coat. He also told me that he lodgd in the Governors Kitchen the first Night in a Cabbin in ye Corner of the Room all of which I well knew to be true. I further asked him whether he remembred anything of a Boy whom his two Indian Masters would have tied to Two Horses to divide him & a French Man came by & told him they had better sell the Boy & divide the Money He readily answered I the man & so he was & by that I knew him to be my Child and she further told us that She went into the Room where he lay asleep since he came Home & she saw the Picture of his poor Father Enoch in his Countenance & it brot to her Remembrance Things about her Husband Dec^{d} which she had not thot of for many Years and added she I could give my oath before Judge or Jury that he is the first born of my Body."

Another testified that he had known the lad of "Eleven years of age or thereabouts" and "that he had then before he was taken away by the Indians a light Blew eye."

And "Jos. Gunnison's wife" related how William remembered that they two had played together and that "he did beat her in her grandfather's orchard by a Rock & how he fell into a Brook & was like to have been Drown'd" and that she, too, remembered.

The next, unfortunately, shows family differences. To Jos. Weeks, Jun., Hope told the scar story, and he asked why she kept "so much with her new Son She replyed that his Brothers Did not own him and she was affraid to Let him go alone." In York County Files of April, 1734, is more testimony. Joshua Tucker saw him in a tavern in Montreal and saw also the scar. Martha Salter, too, swore that "about seven years ago being in Canedy I heard of an English captive working at the next house to which I lived." She went to see him, learned his name and "Two Indians present told me that they took this same William Hutchins and his mother at Spruce Creek." All this sounds like manufactured evidence. Martha overdid it. James Oneile, too, knew him "in Canady."

There was introduced also, probably to discredit the claim, the copy of a paragraph in the Boston Gazette of January 31, 1732.[28]

But the mother's word prevailed. "Thomas et al" had to pay the costs of the Court (£15, 15s., 0) and William Hutchins, Indian captive, on 28 June, 1733, recovered Judgment for his Title and possession of and in two fifth parts of two thirds of a Certain tract of thirty acres. Was this the double portion due the eldest son?

William married Mary Keen in October, 1734, and lived some time in Kittery.

Thomas married Hannah Hill and had seven children.

Enoch's wife was probably Elizabeth Johnson, who had two sons, and Mary Catherine, of Sorel birth, became the wife of James Grover of York in December, 1727.

1706, *June* 6.

SHAPLEY, NICHOLAS, b. abt. 1674, s. of John and Sarah (Withers).

In the Boston News-Letter of June 3-10, 1706, is the following, "Piscataqua, June 7 . . . yesterday Mr. John Shaplie and

28 See Chapter XXIII.

his Son being Riding on the Road near Kittery, their Horses were found all bloody without their Riders: a Party of the Garrison that went out in Quest of the Sculking Enemy, found Mr. Shaplies Body, and his head cut off, but cannot tell what is become of the Son."

Mr. Pike had more definite information June 6, 1706: "Lt John Shapley of Kittery was slain by the Indians, & his son Nicholas carried away, as they were Returning from y^r^ Mill at Spruce-Creek. This was done by (y^r^ good friends) the Hegans. Nicholas is come home again."

Penhallow[29] says that Nicholas was carried to Canada. If his captivity were short it was certainly painful, for the historian says that the Indians on their march, were so inhumanely cruel that they bit off the tops of their victim's fingers, and then "to stagnate the blood seared them with hot tobacco pipes."

Nicholas married Martha Langdon and lived at Sandy Hill, Eliot.

TUCKER, HUGH, son of Lewis and Sarah (Gunnison).

In 1709 Bridget Tucker of Kittery was complained of for selling liquor while her husband, Hugh, was in captivity.

29 "Wars of N. E. with the Eastern Indians," 42.

CHAPTER XIV

The Tragedy at Wells

1690 — 1703 — 1708

EE, being the front of all the Estern part of the Contrey Remoatly Scituated; for Strength weak; and the Enemie beating upon us; wee Can think no other but that we are faire for Ruine." So wrote nine men of Wells[1] in 1691 to an unresponsive Government—yet Wells was never ruined!

Twenty years later ten garrison-houses protected the forty families. In the largest, Captain Wheelwright's, at the eastern end there were sixty persons, and the "principal" house, Joseph Storer's, held twenty-three. In the whole place there were two hundred and sixty-seven "souls" of whom thirty-four were soldiers.[2]

In King William's War a series of unprovoked attacks were made all along our border under the pretext of protecting the Eastern Indians from encroachments by our settlers. The first was at North Yarmouth where some soldiers, who had been sent to build stockades, were driven away. In 1690 every settlement east of Wells had been destroyed. In May of that year a letter was sent from Wells to Major Frost to tell him of the capture of Casco fort and to beg for help; "for," it said, "we are in a very shattered Condission. Some are for Removing and Som ar for stayinge, Soe that we Stand in great need of your assistance."

Another messenger carried an appeal to Boston: "our Sad Condition puts us upon yo[r] Charity: the Enimy is now Very nere us

[1] Wells, which included Kennebunk, was incorporated in 1653.

[2] Arch. 71, 871-6.

Sacoe is this day on fire; . . . if wee have not Imadiate help We are a lost people," And again: "There are 3 or 400 most women & Children come in from Eastward this week who will perish unless assisted by the charity of others."

The refugees were probably sent on to Massachusetts, but for several years the townsfolk generally dwelt, for safety, within the palisade of the Storer garrison.

The destruction of York was followed by an attack upon Wells in which a few resolute men foiled a formidable band.

In May, 1702, when Queen Anne declared war, the Abenakis were ready on this side to attack.

At Pemaquid, in June, Governor Dudley met the sachems with whom he exchanged pleasant promises of peace, but John Wheelwright, of greater experience, warns him that they will keep their promises only "So Long as it may stand with theire own interest . . . theire teachers Instructing them that theire is no faith to be kept with Hereticks, sutch as they account us to be, themselves allso being naturialey deseaitful."

The next year Dudley, uneasy, again meets the sachems, this time at Casco. He came, he said, "as to friends and brothers to reconcile all differences," and the chiefs answered: "Brother, the clouds fly and darken, yet we still sing the songs of peace. As high as the sun above the earth, so far are our thoughts from war."

Dudley made a boastful speech, saying: "'Twas once very dark here about 20 or 30 years ago," but now the old century must be forgotten, the "New Hundred, new Queen, new Governour now will be all in a new friendship."[3] He asked the Indians to consider it for two hours; "Gave them a good Ox and 20 bushels corn for diñer. They return'd Thanks for their noble diñer and all other kindnesses offer'd to them." And there were more gifts, more feasting and more stones piled upon the mound called "the Two Brothers" to signify their fraternal love — then when a

[3] Abstract of Report in Sewall's Diary, II, 85-7.

grand round was fired, there were bullets in the Indians' guns![4]

While the Governor of New France was holding with experienced hand the restive tribes of the West, who were ready to tear out each other's eyes, he did not forget that he must prevent New England from attracting and holding the Abenakis.

Alas! very soon the promises they had made to the Governor of Massachusetts were forgotten, while the hopes of the Governor of Canada were fulfilled.

Garneau is obliged to acknowledge that this was a *recours extrême*, but adds that the very existence of the French people demanded and justified it. This supreme reason silenced all others; therefore to break the relations established between the English and certain Abenakis the Governor had to send some Indians and Frenchmen toward Boston, and they, led by Beaubassin, ravaged the country from Casco to Wells.

"As the milk-white brows of the grave and ancient had no respect shown, so neither had the mournfull cryes of tender Infants the least pitty, for they triumphed at their misery and applauded such as the skilfullest artists, who were most studious of inventing the greatest torments which was enough to melt ye most stoical apathie into Rivers of mournful sympathy and Compassion. The town of Wells which valiantly stood its great spoile could not escape a new encounter."[5] At almost every door a savage was watching for his prey on that midsummer day, of which Mr. Pike wrote:

"1703, Aug. 10 About 9 or 10 oclock Tuesday morning, the eastern Indians (notwithstanding y^r^ many solemn and newly Repeated protestations of Continuing peace wth the English) did yet join with the French, and in a very perfidious and barbarous manner falling upon the eastern parts from Casco to ye East end of Wells committed many grievous outrages & massacres upon ye poor peo: Killed to the number of 73 Captivated to the number of 95:" Of these Wells counted thirty-nine killed or captured.

[4] Dudley had kept some of the chiefs near him!

[5] Penhallow MS., p. 6.

Captives

1690. Frost, Nathaniel.
Pawling, Matthew.
1691. Smith, Nicholas.
1703. Adams, James.
Catharine (Ford).
Hill, Samuel.
Elizabeth (Austin).
"Some children."
Littlefield, Aaron.
Ruth.
Tabitha.
Joséphine (?).
Parsons, William?
Hannah (Wheelwright).
Hannah.
Perhaps another daughter.
Sayer, (Sawyer) Mary (Fletcher).
Storer, Mary.
Priscilla.
Rachel.
Wheelwright, Esther.
1708. Littlefield, Lieut. Josiah.
1709. Russell, Thomas or Samuel.
1712. Woodbury, Nicholas (of Ipswich).

On the 1710/11 list are Robert Islington (not a Wells name) and Thomas Dean, neither of whom has been found, and Joseph Cloyes, who must have been son of Nathaniel or John. They were the only two of the name in Wells, and they married sisters named Mills.

1690.

Frost, Nathaniel, son of William and Mary (Wakefield).

In May, 1690, Roger Hill wrote from Wells: "The Indians

have killed Goodman Frost . . . and carried away Nathaniel Frost." He may have died in Canada.

1690.
PAWLING, MATTHEW.

1691.
SMITH, NICHOLAS.

On November 10, 1694, these two men were examined by the Governor of New York at Fort William Henry.[6] They said they had been taken in the Province of Wells. Pawling was a soldier at Fort Mary; he had been kept in Canada four and a half years and his companion about three. Now they had been released because the Indians of the Five Nations had returned some French prisoners.

Frontenac gave to eight Englishmen passports and food for twenty-five days. Two of the eight, afraid of Indians and the dangers of travel, remained in Canada; four had gone to their frontier homes and they, Pawling and Smith, had come to acquaint His Excellency with what they knew of the enemy's motion and designs.

They added that having made choice to come overland to Albany the French were so civil as to give a small compass and a draft of the way.

Pawling was of Plymouth in 1682. He had two wives and two daughters.

ADAMS, JAMES, b. 1668.
CATHARINE (Ford), dau. of William of Charlestown.

Bourne says that his house on the Berwick road was burned and "all his family" taken. He says also that "he had but two children . . . Both were too young to travel and as we suppose, were killed." Were they Mary, b. 1700, and James, b. 1701/2?

A longer tale is in the tract "A Memorial of the Present Deplorable State of New England"; Catherine's experiences being

[6] N. Y. Docs., IV, 116.

one of the Memorial Providences.[7] "The Indians came upon the House of one Adams at Wells and Captivated the Man and his Wife, and assassinated the children; whereof one, who had an Hatchet struck into his Skull, and was left for dead was strangely recovered. The Woman had Lain in about Eight Days. They drag'd her out, and tied her to a Post, until the House was rifled. They then loosed her and bid her walk. She could not stir. By the help of a Stick she got half a step forward. She look'd up to God. On the sudden a new Strength entred into her. She travelled that very Day Twenty Miles a Foot: She was up to the Neck in Water six times that very Day in passing of Rivers. At night she fell over head and ears into a Slough in a Swamp and was hardly got out alive. She got not the least Cough nor Cold by all this: She is come home alive unto us." When she came is not known.

James and his wife seem to have been held in Montreal in the house where Mrs. Hannah Sheldon of Deerfield was kept; for John Sheldon, writing to her from Quebec, in April, 1705, sent messages to "Mr. Addams and his wif," and desires "that Mr. Addames and you wod doe al you can with your mistres that my children mite be redemed from the indanes."[8]

M. de Vaudreuil writing to Dudley from Quebec, June 2, 1706, says: "I send back to you two of your prisoners named James Adam and Fletcher, who have been accused here of making counterfeit paper money,[9] and convicted on their own confession. Their trial was begun in this country only to find out how much they had made, and whether they had French accomplices. The trial ended there, and would not have been begun, had it not been indispensable that we should ascertain this. I have acted in this matter with the same spirit and the same moderation which you have shown in the case of two of my people who deserved punishment as yours deserve it."[10] Adams was one of the forty-four ex-

7 Sewall's Diary, II, 59,* and "Good Fetched out of Evil."

8 "Hist. Deerfield," I, 328.

9 See Card-money, Appendix. 10 Que. Docs., II, 454.

changed for those French prisoners who had been returned to Port Royal in December, 1705. They sailed on the bark *Marie* arriving in Boston August 1, 1706.

Clement.

On Sunday, Nov. 9, 1704, Clement, born the day before, was baptized by Father Meriel. His parents formerly of Wells in N. E. were then dwelling in the service of Messire Pierre le Gardeur de Repentigny *Ecuyer* and Captain. The baby's godfather was Messire Jacques le ber and his godmother Damoiselle Agatha de Nere, wife of M. Pierre le Gardeur.

Immediately below was the record of its burial — aged two days. Father Meriel and a pupil of the Seminary witnessed.

The next November (1705) another Clement, son of Jaques Adams, weaver, was baptized. Its sponsors were Robert de Portier *Ecuyer, Sieur du Buisson,* and Damoiselle Marie Elizabeth Rocbert, daughter of the Keeper of the King's Stores. James Addams signs with the others. But this Clement lived only three months and two priests with Samuel Williams, son of M. Jean Williams, Minister of Deerfield, witness its burial.

Evidently the title to the Adams' homestead was questioned for in 1734 Samuel Wheelwright testified at York that Adams lived on a certain piece of land call "ye Gore" for about four years "till ye Indians took him & his Famaly & burnt his House." He had always understood that Adams owned a hundred acres and had heard that the deed was burnt with the House, adding "& I am Realy of opinnion it was so."

1703, *August* 10.

HILL, SAMUEL, s. of Roger and Sarah (Cross).

ELIZABETH, his w., dau. of Samuel Austin.

Children "old enough to travel." Were they Samuel and Elizabeth?

Roger Hill's family — a large one — lived in Saco until they were obliged to take refuge in Wells. John the eldest son was commander of the small Saco garrison and his mother was staying with him when in May, 1690, her husband (Roger) became uneasy and sent for her saying: "I would have our son John hire a boat and bring you home from Saco and some of our things if he possibly can, I fear it is not safe to come by land. John, be as careful as you can of your mother, for it is very dangerous times. The Lord only knows whether we shall ever see one another any more. Your loving husband till death."[11]

The families of three of Roger Hill's children suffered Canadian captivities. Samuel and his family were carried from Wells; Ebenezer, his wife and perhaps a child from Saco, as were the husband and son of Sarah (Hill) Fletcher.

Mary Storer of Wells was a granddaughter.

Samuel was born Dec. 14, 1668. Mr. Bourne says that with him and his wife were taken "some of his children." Those "who were too young to travel were killed." They had been married only four or five years and one gasps at the age of the babies who were spared as old enough to make the journey!

Samuel was captain of a packet which brought provisions to the far-away settlement, and he was greatly missed. Apparently the first tidings of any Wells captive came in a letter from him dated: "Canada, Oct. 7, 1704." In it he says his family is all in health. He blames the Government for its failure to exchange prisoners. "If the Governor of Massachusetts had only sent one man for me, I and all my family would have been restored. Ebenezer and wife desire to be remembered to you."

In April, 1705, after Livingstone and Sheldon had seen the governor in Quebec, Hill, accompanied by two Frenchmen, was sent on parole (his family being sufficient surety) with letters to Dudley. They came "through the woods" down the Kennebec to Casco Bay, thence in a "Packett to his Excellency." The cost from Casco Bay was something over three pounds and the time, stopping at Piscataqua, four days.

11 "Hist. Wells," 201 — doubtless corrected spelling.

Of the tidings which he brought from the captives Penhallow[12] says: "which unexpected news did somewhat raise the dejected spirits of their mournfull friends considering the many deaths that they Escaped in their Captivity."

After delivering his letters Hill went back to Kittery where he wrote to his brother, Captain John, telling him that his Excellency at Boston allowed him to go to Wells to visit his friends; that "brother and sister Storer and brother Hill (Joseph) had come from Wells" and he was to return with them to wait until the messenger, le Sieur de Courtemanche, came from Canada.

It was in the summer that he, with Courtemanche, sailed on Captain Vetch's boat for Quebec where, or near where, he was probably kept.

He finally came home on the *Hope*, which reached Boston Nov. 21, 1706. Eight days later he presented a petition to the General Court which relates that upon the arrival in Canada of Samuel Appleton Esqr. he was sent by M. de Vaudreuil's "Permission up to Mont Royal for the hastening and Dispatching away of the English prisoners." He shows that when he was in Boston with the ffrench men he had no Quarters allowed, but bore his own charges, as he did in going up to Mont Royal: For these expenses and for his fatigues and hardships he asks to be paid. He was given ten pounds "for his service & expences for and towards the returning of the English prison^rs^ from Canada."[13]

From depositions made in 1749 and 1750 by Dependence and David Littlefield concerning land in Wells once owned by Samuel Austin, and later by Samuel and Eliza (Austin) Hill, we learn that the Hills with some of their children returned to the farm.

LITTLEFIELD.

AARON.

TABITHA.

RUTH.

Children of Moses and Martha (Lord) who was of Kittery.

[12] MS., p. 35. [13] Arch. 71, 273.

Joséphine Littlefield, called a captive, who was she?

Edmund Littlefield, a clothier, joined Wheelwright in Exeter in 1637 and went with him later to Wells. His simple home is described in its history as that "of the richest man in the town." Moses was his grandson. The names of Moses' children are given as Peter, Aaron, Ruth and Moses. On the prisoners' roll of 1710/11 Aaron and Ruth are named as of Kittery. Bradbury repeats a tradition concerning Tabitha.

Aaron's fate took him to the home of the priest of Boucherville, where, on "Jan. 27th 1704, Monsieur Meriel Priest of the Seminary of Ville Marie in presence of me, the undersigned Priest, curé of Boucherville, baptized in the Parish church of the Holy Family of Boucherville Pierre Augustin Littlefield aged about 9 years, born at Wels in new England 20 Oct. 1694 of the marriage of Moyse Littlefield and of Marthe Lord his wife, inhabitants of the said new England, which Pierre Augustin is living with me. His godfather was Pierre Boucher, *ecuyer*, Seigneur of Boucherville. His godmother was Madlle Charlotte Denys wife of Mr. Boucherville. They all signed with me.

R. de La Saudraye."

Joseph Bartlett, captured at Haverhill in 1708, saw Aaron for three or four hours at "Ft. Chamblee" as he was taken northward.

"Pierre Augustin Littlefiere" was naturalized in 1710. Four years later, when Williams and Stoddard were arranging an exchange of prisoners, M. de Ramezay, governor of Montreal, sent for Aaron, who said he wanted to go home, and Baker (Captain Thomas) "supplied him with clothing, but before his departure came the priest of Bushervil (with whom he dwells) while Captain Baker was absent, he took off the boy's clothes and prevailed with him to stay"—as he was probably happier to do. Governor de Vaudreuil sent for the boy to come to Quebec where he kept him some time, "but it was then too late; the same priest (who then took the pains to come to Quebec with him) had made too thorough work with his proselyte."[14]

[14] Stoddard's Journal, Gen. Reg., V, 37.

Pierre Augustin Lidfril on Feb. 3, 1717, married at Boucherville Marie Brunel of Varennes, the next parish. The only English witness was Maddox of Old England.

On the Boucherville parish register are the following:

pierre lidfil was bap. 5 Nov. 1717 born the day before about nine o'clock in the evening, and after a life of three days, the priest, M. Saladin wrote a long record of his burial.

Marie-Joseph, bap. 29 March, 1719, lived five months.

Marie-Anne, b. about seven in the afternoon of Christmas, 1720, and baptized the next day, died in 1732. The priest wrote Lettrefilde.

Elizabeth Lidfril, b. at eight in the morning of 19 April, 1723, was bap. the same day.

Marie-Joseph, b. in the morning and bap. in the evening of 24 April, 1725, was doubtless the Marie who m. Nicolas Lagüe in 1744 and died suddenly at Chambly in 1747.

Marie-Françoise Litrefille, bap. the morning of 21 Oct., 1728, mar. 1, Charles Lagû d[t] Sans Cartier of la pointe Olivier—brother of her sister's husband?—and 2, at Chambly in 1773, Basile Pelletier.

François, b. and bap. 12 Oct., 1732, mar. 1, Marie Parent at Chambly in 1753, his father being present. In 1768 François, living in the Parish of the Conception m. Marie Lavoïse; then both his parents were dead. The first wife's people must have approved the second marriage for many of her name were witnesses.

Perhaps Aaron-Pierre and Marie Brunel had an eighth child. Michel Le Vasseur, Recollet, acting curé in the parish of the Conception of the Holy Virgin in Chambly, wrote of the burial on 13 Sept., 1742, of Isabelle Litrefil, twenty-two years old, and her father—not named—was present at the usual ceremony in the cemetery.

There must be many descendants of Aaron in Canada. We have records of five children born to François, and in Chambly there are Lagües.

It is interesting to note the friendships among the families into which our captives married. Several Gaultiers (Mary Storer's people) were sponsors for Littlefields.

In May, 1728, Mary (Storer) Gaultier wrote to her brother Ebenezer in Boston that "aron Litelfielde is well and his famelie he remembers his love to you." Were they playmates in Wells?

Moses Littlefield having died his widow, Martha, married John Abbot of Berwick, and to Berwick came Aaron from Boucherville to see her.

John Abbot died and Martha took Alexander Taylor for a third husband in 1720.

In 1726 she died intestate and after several years — perhaps of hopeful expectation — Aaron, her only son and heir, claimed his inheritance, but it was not until April 4, 1738, that he, husbandman of Montreal, brought suit in the Court of York County against three of his Lord kinsmen — Benjamin, William, and William, Jr. Aaron sued "to recover Possession of one Seventh Part of a Certain Tract or Parcel of Land with ye Edifices & appurtenances in Berwick," which had come to his mother from a nephew. "The Case after a full hearing was Comitted to a Jury who returned their Verdict . . . Specially viz: that if a Papist is by Law Debarr'd from maintaining an action for a Real Estate then Cost for ye Defts but if not the Jury find for the Plt ye Land Sued for & Cost upon wch Verdict the Court having maturely Considered and advised is of opinion that a Papist Cannot by Law maintain an action for ye Recovery of a real Estate It's therefore Considered by the Court that the Defts Shall recover against the Plt Cost of Court."

Aaron appealed and bonds were given on condition that he "prosecute the appeal with Effect at the next Supr Court," in York County.

And: "To the Honourable ye Justices of his Majy Superior Court of Judicature" which was held "at York within & for said County of York on the third Wednesday of June Anno Domini, 1738" he did prosecute "with Effect."

Four papers are in the Early Court Files of Suffolk County.[15] The first recites the claim; the decision of the inferior court; and gives reasons why the decision should be set aside. The defendants had held "the Pet: out to his damage as he saith three hundred Pounds as per ye writ," and the appeal was made:

1. "Because Judgment ought to have been for ye Plt to recover against ye defts ye Premises sued for & Costs.

2. the Plts being a Papist or not a papist was not mentioned in the Issuable Plea & so not proper or Lawfull for the Jury to give a Verdict upon nor Could they lawfully take notice of ye Pleas made in abatement but only ye issuable Pleas.

3. their is no Euidence to proue that ye Plt is a papist nor ought any deposition of any Person be deem'd as sufficient Evidence to prove it and ye Plt ought not to Loose his Inheritance (if there was such a Law) before he be Convict of Papish Recusancy in a Court proper to try the Same for ye Pet is now a Protestant for aught that now appears to the contrary & may settle on ye land himself."

4. This shows that he has proved his descent and rights.

5. "Many of ye Kings Subjects in many parts of his dominion are Papists yet enjoy their estates altho they may not bear any office & there is no Law that does Debarr ye Pet. from maintaining this action if he was a Papist for which reasons with what else may be offered the appell^t^. prays reversion of ye former Judgment the Premises sued for & Cost.

Noah Emery Atto^r^. to appellt.

June 4 1738."

A man testified that when Aaron came to visit his mother in Berwick he told him that his name was Peter; but Samuel and Walter Abbott saith that his mother called him Aaron and he stayed "with hir fore sum time . . . which was about three weeks & this was ab^t^ ten or Eleven years agoe." Before the first trial, Christine (Otis) Baker, living in Dover, deposed: "All that I Can

[15] Number 46571.

Say Concerning Aron Littlefield who where taken by the Indians from Kenibunk" is "that I Very well knew him in Canada and that he was baptized Peter, & that he was a Papist by Profession & his Living & his Marriage Was in a Place Called Boshervell in Canada nine miles from mount Royal and that I See his Sister in the Nunnery in Canaday about fifteen or Sixteen years agoe and this is the whole truth of what I know." Sworn to at Dover April 1, 1738, signed: "Christen Baker."[16] This was perhaps unwelcome testimony to Aaron's attorney, who had the legal imagination when he assumed that his client might *now* be a Protestant, and might choose to settle on that seventh portion of the hundred and twenty-nine acres; a not very probable choice for a man who had left a wife and seven or eight children at Boucherville in the bosom of the Catholic Church! Perhaps for this reason he asked Christine to speak again, and on the reverse of her Dover deposition is this: In Sup[r] Crt. at York, June 23, 1738, Christan Baker declared: "that she was not present nor ever saw Peter Littlefield baptized in Canada nor any Priest ever tell her that he was baptized but she only concluded he was from y[e] Custom of y[e] Papists & that he always went by the name of Peter after she was acquainted with him."

But Noah Emery won the suit for his client and in April, 1739, the sheriff was instructed that Aaron had "recovered Judgment" for the land which had been "unlawfully withheld;" and the costs, which were £16, 3s., 6d., the defendants had to pay.

And here is the last glimpse of Aaron. On Monday, September 8, 1749, the Rev. John Norton wrote: "This morning there came an Englishman to see me; his name is Littlefield. He was taken a lad from Piscataqua & so continued with the French & lived, having a family at Champlain [Chambly]. We had a considerable discourse together."

Mr. Norton says that he was living at Chambly. In 1733, on 11 December, he received a *concession* of two lots of land, of

[16] Printed, with cruder spelling, in Bourne's Hist., 253.

three by forty arpents, in the seigniory of Chambly. G. de Chevremont was the notary, the Brothers hospitaliers making the grant to Pierre Augustin Litrephil.

Ruth? Tabitha, or both?

The only name we are sure of is Angélique. Which was she? Tradition says both were taken. Angélique Lidrefil was a Sister of the Hôtel-Dieu. The story told by Bradbury[17] about Tabitha does not suggest the cloister. Tabitha was supposed to have been killed, but one day when Mrs. Stephen Harding (Abigail Littlefield) was trading with some Indians "a young squaw who was standing near, asked if she did not remember Tabitha Littlefield and immediately darted from the house." Searchings and promisings could not induce the Indians to bring her back. She probably preferred the wild life. The convent record—the Hotel-Dieu of Montreal—says that Sister Angélique was born in 1699, (Ruth's birth was 23 June, 1698) was a nun in 1719 and died on 9 January, 1732, when thirty-three years old.

At Hotel-Dieu there are Choir and Lay Sisters; *Soeurs des Choeurs* and *Soeurs Converses*. Habit, privileges and table are the same. The Choir Sisters repeat the offices four times daily. The Lay Sisters care for the sick in their absence at prayers, and for themselves have only one short period of ten minutes for daily devotion. Angélique, a lay sister, must have known well the choir nun, Mary Silver of Haverhill. Was Angélique Ruth of Wells?

Joséphine Littlefield.

Who was she? The daughter of some other than Moses? A granddaughter of Aaron's mistakenly called of an earlier generation?

In the Museum of the Château de Ramezay, Montreal, is a spinning-wheel which, says the catalogue, belonged to a Mrs. Bourgeois of Saint-Marcel, who "got it from her grandmother,

17 "Hist. of Kennebunkport," 154.

Joséphine Littlefield who was one of the captives brought from New England about 1703, and adopted by a Canadian family who had ransomed her from the Indians. Later she refused to return to her own people." Mme. Bourgeois was Archange Littlefield.

PARSONS, WILLIAM.

HANNAH, his wife; dau. of Samuel and Esther Wheelwright.

HANNAH, dau., aged two.

Perhaps another daughter.

They were of Wells, but were, except perhaps one child, taken from York. Mr. Bourne says that William Parsons lived near Joseph Hill; that his house was burned, two little boys (William five and Samuel eighteen months) were killed and a daughter taken captive; that he, his wife and two other little children escaped to York. Two months later, when the house of Arthur Bragdon was attacked, the "Widow Hannah Parsons & her young daughter" were taken.[18] Perhaps she was not a widow at the time of the attack, but at the time of writing.

Bourne says William, too, was taken at York and soon died. We know he was not living when his "young daughter" was baptized in Montreal in January, 1704.

John Wheelwright was appointed in October, 1705, to administer his estate of £101, 16s., and 9d., but in January, 1706/7, he gives up his power to William's widow, Hannah.

One wonders about the "money laid out to Cloath their daughter £3, 13s, 3d." Was it perhaps laid out in Canada and now repaid?

Mrs. Hannah was a witness at the wedding of Elizabeth Price in Montreal in February, 1706. Probably she came home with John Sheldon, reaching Boston in August, 1706, as she was in New England the next January, as shown above. In the Mather tract "Good Fetched out of Evil" and in another about the Deplorable

[18] See Chapter IX.

State of New England[19] is an account of Barbarities and Memorable Providences one of which is about Hannah, the child: "A Crue of Indians had been three Days without any manner of Sustenance. They took an English Child, and hung it before the Fire to Roast it for their Supper . . . A Cannow arrived at that Instant, with a Dog in it. The lesser Devils of the Crue proposed their taking the Dog instead of the Child; they did and the Child is yet Living. Her name is Hannah Parsons."

Penhallow's version gives a different value to the dog. He says "that within the canoe were 3 dogs which did not a little revive these hungry monsters; the child was instantly offered in Exchange for one, but preferring the dog before the child they refus[d] it, after that a gun was tendred, which they accepted off and by this means the life of the child was wonderfully preserved."[20]

The little girl was carried to the Sault-au-Recollet, where Father Meriel baptized her:

"On Thursday, Jan. 10th 1704, was solemnly baptized by me, priest of the Seminary of St. Sulpice, established at Villemarie, undersigned, a little English girl, born at Wells, in New England the (25 April O.S.) sixth of May of the year 1701, of the marriage of the late Guillaume Parsons and of Anne Wheelwright, who was taken and brought with her mother by the savages the 22nd August[21] of the last year 1703. The name of Hannah, which she had in her country without having been there baptized, has been changed to that of Catherine, to which the savages add the surname of ——. She had for godmother Hélène Tekaeronta of this mission. Meriel priest."

The surname, left in blank in the record, was Tsiosenneco, which, as translated by Père J. A. Cuoq, means "She has a very fine name."

What must have been the feelings of the child's mother, for it was doubtless she who gave the information to the careful priest,

[19] See Sewall's Diary, Vol. II. [20] MS. Cong. Lib.

[21] Pike says captured at York, October 13, Bourne gives September 26.

as she listened to the promises of the Indian godmother who gave her the "very fine name"?

Probably little Hannah-Catherine was not brought up *en sauvage* for Catherine Parsons of Montreal, aged twelve, was made a citizen of New France. As Hannah she was on the New England list of 1710/11.

As the Indians gave her a fine name so did the ensign she married. Here is the contract:

"Claude-Antoine de Berman, *Esquyer, seigneur de la Martinière, Enseigne en pied dans les troupes du detachement de la Marine en ce pays,* son of the late Claude de Berman de la Martinière, who living was first Councillor of the Superior Court of this Country at Quebec and of the late M. Françoise Cailleteau, and Catherine Parsons, daughter of the late S[r]—— Parsons and of Anne Wheelwright her father and mother of Wells, near Boston in New England who is of age, in presence of Pierre de Lestage *marchand bourgeois* of Montreal, seigneur de Berthier and Captain of a Company of the militia of this town, and of Marie-Joseph-Esther Sayer his wife, cousin of the said D[lle] Parsons . . . Made and enacted at the house of the said sieur de Lestage the 17 March 1729. J. C. Raimbault, notary."

Tanguay gives the following list of their children, the first two were born in Montreal, the others in Quebec:

Marie-Catherine, b. 1730.
Claude-Jacques, 1732.
Marie-Louise, 1733.
Gilles-Claude, 1734.
Marie-Charlotte, 1736. She m. Antoine Demellis.
Marie-Anne, 1737.
Marie-Angélique, 1739.
Marie-Joseph, 1741.
Geneviève-Esther, 1743.
Marie-Anne, 1746.

Claude-Antoine Bermand died in Quebec in 1761 aged about sixty-five.

The first born, as Marie-Catherine de Sainte-Joseph, was for thirty-eight years a Sister of the General-Hospital at Quebec, making her profession at sixteen. She died in 1784.

SAYER OR SAWYER, MARY.

Wife of Joseph and dau. of Pendleton and Sarah (Hill) Fletcher.

Bourne, Hoyt[22] and Parkman[23] say that Joseph Sayer and all his family were killed in 1703, but did not Ebenezer Hill refer to Joseph's wife when he wrote from Quebec in March, 1705: "Mary Sayer is well"? She must have been redeemed—perhaps by Captain Vetch and young William Dudley—before 28 April, 1706, when "Mary Sayer, widow," was baptized in the Wells church "upon profession of faith. In the following September she married John Gibson of Boston.[24]

Hoyt, upon the authority of Mr. Appleton, says that a daughter, Mary, was captured. The estate of Joseph, who was son of William, was administered in his widow's absence.

STORER.

MARY.

PRISCILLA.

RACHEL.

The names of Mary, Rachell and Precilla Storer, Kittery, are on the Roll of Prisoners of 1710/11. The same year Naturalization is granted to "Marie Stozer," and to "Marie françoise Stozer, English woman married to Jean Berger painter established at villemarie,"[25] and to "Marie pricille Stozer, English woman."

Josiah Littlefield, captured five years later, saw the girls and wrote from Montreal: "Mary Storrar is well and Rachel Storar and —— Storer is well and Mary Austin of York is well and dasiares to remember their duty to thear father and mother and their

22 Old Salisbury Families. 23 "Half Century of Conflict," I, 41.

24 York Deeds, XIV, 51.

25 He was established in Quebec.

kind love to all thear friends and ralations, hoping in god you are all well."[26]

Mary, b. 12 May, 1685, was one of the nine children of Lieutenant Joseph and Hannah (Hill).

Bourne says that Joseph Storer did more than any other to save the province from desolation. His garrison-house[27] on the Province road was the largest of any. Within its palisade he built several small houses of refuge. He gave up to the people land near the garrison for tillage and pasturage. The wounded were brought to his house; indeed, it was the last refuge in dangerous times for the fleeing inhabitants.

Mary was taken to Boucherville, and "On Feb. 25, 1704 Monsieur Meriel, priest of the Seminary of Ville Marie in presence of me, the undersigned Priest, curé of Boucherville, baptized in the parish church of the Holy Family of Boucherville Marie Storer daughter of Joseph Storer and of Anne Hill his wife, inhabitants of Wells. This girl born at the said place the 22nd of May (new style) of the year 1685 and baptized a few days later by the minister of York. Her Godfather was Mr Niverville son of M. Boucher, Seigneur of Boucherville. Her Godmother was Claire Françoise Chavet wife of Monsieur Montbrun living in this Parish."

In 1707 Judge Sewall sent to Albany a letter from Mary Storer. Was this from captive Mary, bringing information? She was soon more closely bound to Canada when "On the 26th November, 1708 after the publication of the three banns made the 17th, 18th and 20th Nov. 1708 at mass in the Holy Church of the Holy Family of Boucherville, no impediment having been found, M. Meriel Priest of the Seminary of Ville Marie, with my consent and acting for me, undersigned Priest, curé of the said Church of the Holy Family of Boucherville, married Jean Gaultier, aged 26 years, son of Germain Gaultier and of Jeanne Beauchamp his wife inhabitants of Côte Saint-Joseph in this Parish with Marie Storer

[26] "Hist. Wells and Kennebunk," 268. [27] The site is marked.

aged 23 years, daughter of Joseph Storer and Anne hil, his wife inhabitants of Wells in New England, and gave them the nuptial blessing in presence of M. Boucher" &c. (illegible names) "The father and mother of the groom and of several other friends who signed with me according to the ordinance."

The following records of the children of Jean and Mary are in Boucherville and Montreal:

Jean-Baptiste, bap. 1709, and in 1739, June 8, he, "Jean-Baptiste Gauthier, aged 30 years, son of Jean gauthier dit st. Germain, inhabitant of Côte St. Martin and of Marie Storey, his father and mother of this parish . . . and Barbe gervaise 40 years, daughter of Louis Gervaise and of Barbe Pigeon" were married.

The next found is:

Paschal, bap. 1712.

Jacques, 1713 (?); m. 1745 Marie-Joseph Benoit.

Joseph, 9 Apr., 1714, at Montreal, s. Jean gautier and Marie Story. Priscille Story Dagueil godmother.

François, b. 1716. His uncle, françois gautier, godfather. In 1739 his mother wrote that her younger son had died, but Tanguay marries him in 1743 to Madeleine Nadon.

Marie-Louise, 1718, called dau. of Jean gautiere and marie Stauré, m. 1, 1736, Philippe Gervaise (28), brother of Barbe (above); m. 2, 1752, Louis Bélec (25). Here she is "Louise gauthier St. germain (33) . . . dau. of Jean gauthier dit St. germain and the late Marie Storer."

Marie-Anne, 1720, m. in 1749 Paul descarris (Her father spells it de carye).

Joachim, 1722, March; d. in June.

Marie-Angélique, b. and d. October, 1723.

More than one Gaultier family in Canada is surnamed Saint-Germain; even as late as 1848 "Gaultier dit St. Germain" was written in the register.

While in Montreal Mr. Theodore Atkinson[28] wrote: Apr. 5, 1725: "In the afternoon we went about a League Down to see Mr. Storess Daughter who is very well marryed to a french man, a farmer & Lives very Grandly they have 5 Child 3 m. & 2 female." This grand person must have been Mary. Priscilla's husband is called soldier, merchant and town major—never farmer. Perhaps on this very Sunday afternoon Mary decided to go to New England with the commissioners and her friend Esther (Sayward) de Lestage.

They left April 20. Some details of the journey may be found in Atkinson's Diary[29] and in Esther Sayward's story.[30] Probably the women went from Albany to New York by the Hudson, thence by boat to Newport and by the Providence Road to Boston.

Perhaps they went together by boat to Maine. What were the feelings of these daughters of Joseph Storer and John Sayward as they journeyed toward their homes and their mothers?

We have learned that Mary Storer made this short visit to New England by reading a bundle of twenty-four letters, owned by Mrs. David Murray of Brunswick, New Jersey, and now deposited in the library of the Massachusetts Historical Society by Dr. Malcolm Storer. The first, written as she begins her return journey, is "from road Island, new port," dated 26 June, 1725, and addressed to her brother Ebenezer, "shop keeper in boston." The last, written by a scrivener, is from her husband, dated 1754, seven years after her death. Like most letters of the period they are made of pious phrases and tender messages, giving very little information. Of course her family tried to bring her back to their "true faith," and of course she could not be brought; but politely expresses her gratitude and asks for their prayers. She thanks Ebenezer for books he has sent to her and says: "if I can sende one of my Childrine I will." She adds: "my cousin remembers his love to you my deare brother," and one guesses that the "cousin" may be Priscilla's husband, J. B. Dagueil, who was of their escort.

28 See p. 102. 29 See Chapter IV. 30 See Chapter IX.

To her brother Seth, youngest of the family and minister of the church in Watertown, she wrote, after the usual tender messages: "my deare brother I had but a litel time with you who I thought woulde show and teach me more then aney bodey sir but what you have saide to me I will not forgett it and I hope god will in able me in all my aflictions and that it may be for the best and good of my soule deare brother doe not forget me in youre prayers which I hope will be a coumfort to me and what evere paines and troble I have and shall have in all my jorney I take it with pations and I hope god will have mercie on me and helpe me I am sorey that I coulde not stay no longer with my deare father and mother which makes my harte soe heave all most redei to brake and my eyes full of teirs." She must have had less than six weeks with her people. In another letter, regretting that I "had no coumforte to stay longe as I was wiling to doe now I am heare a waighting for the vessell but thee lorde knows when she will come." The "vessell" came and took her to New York where on July 13 she says "I finde the time very longe with strangers and longe to be with my famelie."

In 1727 from "Moriall" she thanks Ebenezer for his "Letter and token;" says that "my son is not willing to goe frome us," and asks him to look up an "inglish man" named "greenhill," to find whether "he is a dead or a live," he has a wife and two sons in Montreal.[31]

Anxiously she addresses one

"For Mis
hannah Storer
living at Wells
with Care

My deare and ever loving and tender mother our kinde duties remembred to you hoping that thies fue liens will findc you in good health as theye lieve me at time blessed be god for it deare mother I recived one letter frome my brother Ebenezer the last

[31] Joseph Greenhill from Worcester, Eng.; mar. a French woman in Montreal in 1711. Some of our captives were his witnesses.

of July and in it the death of my father it is a grate grief to me now I am a poore fatherles Childe [aged forty-eight!] my hart brakes with sithing and my ioys smart with teers now my deare mother I am a fraide now you are very aged to the same news soe sorefull to me concarning you my deare mother my brother ebenezer wright to me that my deare father maide his will that I may be equeal to my sisters you may belive my deare mother whey I am far of frome you and my deare familei I be-lave that is not cappable to kep it frome me in consent that is for me who is youre one child now wee have a governer he will not give any permission to goe in Ingland to our contre deare mother pray siend it to Mister Windel merchant liveing in boston then I shall recive it by his father that lives in Albene my cossen prissila and her husband and children are well they[r] love to you my hus-band and children are well theire duties to you our loves to my brothers and sisters and all our friends I pray to you to concarve your farewell deare mother

Youre dutifull daughter

Mary St germaine

Mary Storer

(In different writing.)

A Montreal

ce 19[e] avril 1733"

In the letter of same date, written to Ebenezer, she shows more anxiety, saying "we are al the same blode you can not denie it."

He answering from Boston, May 24, gives family news and con-tinues: "Concerning what I wrote to you about Fathers will I in-formed you as near as I could in my former letter, but I shall send y[r] letter to mother as soon as may bee so that she may order you what was Designed for you which I know she will do any thing y[t] is proper if it be not against y[e] will of our Father Deceas[d] this is all y[t] others Except my Love so Rest yr Loving

Br[o] Eben: Storer."

Here was trouble; either Ebenezer had blundered or Mary had misunderstood, for their father's will, made in 1721 and proved in February, 1729/30, did not give Mary the "equal" to her sisters. Joseph Storer wrote: "I Give & Bequeath to my beloved Daughter Mary St. Germain Fifty pounds in good Contrey pay upon Condition that She return from under the French Government & Settle in New England Otherwise if She doth not returne Then I Give & bequeath to her the Sum of Tenn Shillings in Contrey pay to be paid by my Executor within Two Years next after my Decease over and above what I have already given her."

So she had written to her people; she had used the St. Germain name and she had received money from her father before 1721. Evidently all this brought unhappiness. For six years no letters pass; then Mary writes to Ebenezer.[32] She says: "I have not heard any knews of mother I dont know weather she is on the Land of the Living which obliges me to adress myself to you to lett me hear from her if you have still any Love for me I hope you will not refuse that comfort . . . we have had the mortification to Loose our younger Son[33] about a year ago. wee have left Two daughters & two sons the Eldest of our daughters was married about three years ago with one Gervais they have two sons the Eldest of our sons was married last spring with a Gervaise woman my son in law sister."

In 1746 the Rev. John Norton wrote in his diary that "Mrs. St. La Germaine" came with her cousin's husband to call upon him in Montreal; that she "was able to discourse in the English tonge," and he regretted that he was not acquainted with her brother, the minister at Watertown, or any of her friends.

In the parish register of Notre-Dame is the record of her burial. "In the year 1747 the 27th day of the month of August was buried in the cemetery the body of marie storir Englishwoman wife of —— st germain, aged About —— In presence of Mr clarimber (?) et faure witnesses

Courtois priest."

[32] In French, but with a translation; neither being in her own hand.

[33] To him Tanguay gives a wife at a later date.

But it was not until March, 1748, that her husband wrote to Ebenezer.

"Monsieur et tres cher frere;

C'est avec beaucoup de douleur que je vous apprens la Mort de ma tres chere femme votre chere Soeur qui est decedé le 25 d'aout 1747 selon notre stil, d'une fievre avec un flux qui l'a emporté en huit jour de temps, elle est morte avec toute la resignation possible a la voluntée de Dieu c'est a dire en parfaite Chretienne et comme elle a vecû Depuis trente neuf ans que nous avons été ensemble nous avons fait un menage D'Ange et navons jamais eu aucune difficulté." Surely a wonderful record! Thirty-nine years of perfect happiness in an angelic household. He says that of the five children God gave him but three remain, Jean, the eldest, and the two daughters, of whom one is a widow with two little boys and the other is unmarried. He seems to have forgotten that he had carried to baptism nine children that God had given him — four probably having died young.

Receiving no reply the bereft husband wrote to another brother in June of the following year, saying it is difficult to believe that Ebenezer had not received the letter because the Governor had promised it should be sent with his own.

In the meantime he has married the last of his daughters to an "*habitant*" of the region.

In April, 1750, another letter is sent to Ebenezer to tell him that his long silence causes many reflections and if he had a Desire to mortify him he had entirely succeeded. He thinks Ebenezer must have been affected by his sister's death and asks if there have been other deaths in the family.

Ebenezer, finally answering, says he has written by every opportunity; that after Mary's death he "answered by commissioners, who went from hence to exchange Prisoners,[34] our aged Mother Storer died in July 1748 almost 2 years agoe."

[34] Did he give his letter to Messrs. Heath and Chandler who did not go to Canada, and did they fail to give it to Stevens who did go?

In April, 1754, Mary Storer's husband profits by the opportunity of sending a letter by "Monsieur Willeraite."

Storer, Priscilla.

Daughter of Jeremiah and Ruth (Masters) was baptized at Wells on May 21, 1702, with other children of Jeremiah, and again

"On Saturday 21 Nov. 1705 was baptized by me, the undersigned priest, Priscille-Storer born at Wells in New England the —— day of August 1684 of the marriage of Jérémie Storer[35] inhabitant of the said place and of the late Ruth Masters which Priscille Storer having been taken 21 Aug. 1703 and brought to Canada lives at the house of Pierre Lanequet. To the name of Priscille which she had in her country, having been baptized there at the age of eight years, has been added that of Marie. Her godfather was the same Pierre Lanequet, *Habitant*, and her godmother Marie Anne le gras, wife of Charles de Launay, who signed with me. The godfather, as well as the girl, having declared that they could not sign etc." (A childish signature of Marie Priscille, however, is added.)

"On May 26, 1711 after the publication of the three banns, with no opposition, I, undersigned Priest, vicar of the Parish of Ville-Marie, having taken the mutual consent of Jean Baptiste Dagueil, Sergeant of the company of mr de La forest aged twenty-six years, son of Pierre Dagueil and of Marie Meudon his father and mother, of the Parish of St. Elay of the City and Diocese of Bourdeaux of one part and of Marie Priscille Storer, native of Wells, daughter of Jérémie Storer, inhabitant of Baston in New England and of the late Ruth Master, his wife, of the other part; have married them according to the rites of our Holy mother Church, in presence of Mr henry meriel Priest of the Seminary of this town, of henry Jules le fouriner, *Ecuyer*, Sieur durivier, Lieutenant of the troops of this country, of Louis hector Le fournier, son of said Sieur Durivier, of francois oger dit La fleur, ser-

35 Brother of Joseph.

geant of said company of la forest of Jean Gautier, Cousin-german of the said bride[36] of Pierre picart, inhabitant of this town, and of marie Storey cousin of the said bride." Among the signatures are Marie prisilla Storer, Marie Storer and Meriel priest.

The first child, Jean Baptiste, was bap. 16 March, 1712; his godfather, Jean Gautier dit St. Germain, living at Côte St. Martin.

Charles, born and d. 1714.

No records were found during the next seven years, then a baby daughter of "Marie prissil Sertori" dies and the sad story goes on. Between 1721 and 1732 five young children are buried "in the cemetery near the church." Surviving, we have the names only of Jean-Baptiste and Marie-Thérèse (1725), but Jean Gautier writing to New England in 1749 says they have three sons and one daughter and that the eldest son was married five years ago.

Dagueil's name had various spelling, once he is "dit Leguide," and we hear of him in that capacity. In 1732 he is "d'Aiguille, merchant of this town." Jean Gautier calls him Léquille and L'Eguille. He seems to have been a person of some importance. In 1712 he was in Albany, doubtless on an official errand, and Schuyler sent by him some letters from Dudley to Vaudreuil.

In May, 1728, Mary Storer, sending a letter, probably by Martin Kellogg, says: "my cossen pressella Storer is well and her Children and remembers there loues to you her husband is now in ould france and he will come this fall."

Mary frequently mentioned her cousin, but only in regard to health and "Kind Duties to her deare father and loves to brothers and sisters." Priscilla wrote to her father in 1732 and getting no answer Mary begs her brother Ebenezer "to mention Prissilla."

In 1746 the Rev. John Norton wrote that he was visited by "the Major of the Town,"[37] married to an English woman named Storer and that one of his sons "was down at the taking of us"—that was at Fort Massachusetts. Let us hope that this soldier-son

[36] Husband of her cousin. [37] See Chapter XVIII.

of a captive was kind to the women and children they carried away.

Jean Gautier wrote to New England in 1754 that the Daguilles were in perfect health.

On 5 July, 1762, was buried in the chapel of Ste. Anne (Notre-Dame, Montreal) Jean Baptiste Dagueil "a merchant of this town, former major of the militia, aged about 85."

"Priscilla Storer widow of St. Jean baptiste Daguille," died May 13, 1768, aged about seventy-six, and was buried in the Chapel of Saint-Amable. Two priests witnessed the burial.

Storer, Rachel.

Daughter of Jeremiah. The Canadian record calls Rus leselfek her mother.

She was bap. in Wells on May 3, 1702. In Canada we hear of her first in "The Redeemed Captive." Mr. Williams, writing always from his standpoint, says that whenever our messengers were sent to the French government everything possible was done to delay the return of the captives and "to gain time to seduce our younger ones to popery. Some were sent away who were judged ungainable and most of the younger sort still kept. Some were still flattered with promises of reward; and great essays were made to get others married among them. One was debauched [lead away from her religion] and then in twenty-four hours of time published, taken into their communion and married; but the poor soul has had time since to lament her sin and folly, with a bitter cry; and asks your prayers that God of his sovereign grace would yet bring her out of the horrible pit she has thrown herself into. Her name was Rachel Storer of Wells."

Mr. Williams was in Quebec or its neighborhood when

"On April 16, 1706, was baptized by me, priest, curé of Quebec, rachel, Englishwoman aged about nineteen, the name of marie françoise was given to her. her godfather was Monsieur Jacques Le Vasseur de Nerey, Knight of the military order of St. (illeg.) Louis, captain and engineer for the king in this country and the godmother was dame Marie françoise achille chaveneau wife of Monsieur Levasseur, who have signed.

François Dupre Priest."

And the next day, after Barbel, the Notary, wrote out their marriage-contract Jean Berger and she were married. In the contract Jean Berger, painter, soldier of the Company of M. Le Vasseur, . . . son of Jean Claude berger & the late Eleonor moncalan, native of Laon, aged 25 years is of one part. The sieur pierre hacmard, merchant living in this town of québec acts for Rachel Stora, Englishwoman (baptized under the name of Marie francoise) daughter of germain Stora & Rus leselfek, native of baston in New England. This impossible name is legibly written.

The marriage record is more detailed.

"The 17th April 1706, having obtained dispensation of the three banns of marriage by Messieur . . . Jean berger, formerly a soldier in the company of Monsieur Le Vasseur, son of Jean Claude Berger and of leonore Montalan, his father and mother of the parish of St. didier, archbishopric of léon (Lyons) of one part, and of marie francoise rachel English woman aged nineteen and having discovered no lawful impediment, I, Francois Dupre, priest of Quebec married them and gave the nuptial blessing according to the rites prescribed by our mother Holy Church in presence of Monsieur Jacques Le Vasseur . . . of hubert houssar, of pierre Tuliot, who have signed"—All but Rachel. Jean Berger wrote especially well. In these three records the name Storer appears but once.

Their child, Marie Françoise, was baptized by Father Meriel 21 Nov., 1707. Rachel's sister, Marie Priscille, was its godmother. The baby died the next year. Another child was born and died in 1708.

Perhaps Rachel died young; Mary Storer never mentioned her in letters to the family, but Jeremiah believed her to be living in 1729 when he, then of Boston, made his will and named her, "Rachel Bargee," his second daughter, to share with two sisters

(Priscilla was not named) and three brothers in equal proportions of all his possessions.[38]

WHEELWRIGHT, ESTHER, b. 1696.

She was one of the eleven children of John and Mary (Snell), and great granddaughter of the Rev. John, of Exeter and Wells,[39] and was one of the five Wheelwright children baptized in 1701, immediately after the Church in Wells was formed.

Before the attack of 1693, when the Indians expected to take many prisoners, they divided their spoils beforehand, and Cotton Mather says that "the worthy councillor," John Wheelwright, was to have been "the servant of such a netop." So now, ten years after that failure, his daughter Esther may have been counted a great prize.

Her father and mother were probably ignorant of her fate for five long years, and there must have been great rejoicing in their home at the Town's end — the easternmost end — when Lieut. Josiah Littlefield's letter came from Montreal. He wrote not long afer his capture in 1708. That very morning he had seen the governor, who promised to redeem him and "Wheelrite's child" if Governor Dudley would send back two Indian prisoners. He adds that a man had been sent to redeem the child, whom he expected every day, and prays "whilrite to be very brief in the matter" that they may come home before winter,[40] but neither came.

Evidently "whilrite" was not "brief" because over four months passed before the following was written on the General Court Record:[40a] "Ordered that Mr Commissary Belcher take Care for the Transportation of an Indian Boy sent from Wells by Mr Wheelwright, to Albany by way of New York, or otherwise in the

38 Suffolk Probate.

39 The Story of Esther Wheelwright is told in Miss Baker's "True Stories" and here repeated, with some additions, because her book is out of print.

40 "Hist. of Wells," 267.

40a Vol. VIII, 393, under date of 25 Oct. Littlefield's letter was written 2 June, 1708.

best Manner he can, to be exchanged for Mr Wheelwright's Daughter now Prisonr at Canada." Why was nothing done?

Père Bigot had found Esther in a wigwam on the Kennebec River, and after much trouble had bought her from the Abenaki, who, either from affection or desire for a larger ransom, was loath to part with her. The priest took her, not to Montreal as Littlefield expected, but to Governor Vaudreuil at Château Saint-Louis in Quebec.

It is said in the "History of the Ursulines"[41] that as soon as Père Bigot found her the Governor-General sent a deputation to New England, but no record of their coming has been noted.

The Marquise de Vaudreuil having been summoned to France,[42] and believing or pretending to believe that it was impossible to restore the little girl to her family,[43] placed her in January, 1709, with her own daughter Louise as a pupil with the Ursulines.

For the English child the Marquise de Vaudreuil "will pay 40 *écus*" (about forty dollars) says their Register, which says also that Esther "had forgotten her childhood speech."

The entry of July 18, 1710, says: "It is the Rev. Superior of the Jesuits who pays this year for the little Esther," and during that year she asks to be made a French citizen.

At the end of her short school-life she wishes to enter the convent but the governor, considering himself pledged to her redemption, would not consent and she returned with Louise de Vaudreuil to the château.

Vaudreuil says in a letter sent to Versailles in 1709 that he has "fed and lodged . . . for more than a year the daughter of the Governor of a small place."[44] This must refer to Esther.

41 Vol. II, 77.

42 The Ursulines were proud of this appointment — that of assistant governess to the royal children, for she, a Canadian, had been their pupil. The vessel on which she embarked was captured by the English, who treated her with respect and sent her on to France. There she stayed five years at Court. Much younger than her husband, she became, says Ferland, "the man of the family."

43 "*Hist. Ursulines de Québec.*"

44 Que. Docs., II, 506.

In refusing his consent the Marquis may have thought that at fourteen or fifteen the girl's judgment was immature.

During the next two years there were many negotiations concerning the exchange of prisoners, and Esther must have been restless.

In June, 1711, Vaudreuil, writing from Montreal to Dudley,[45] said: "Mr. Wheelwright's daughter being no longer considered a prisoner I await only a safe and fit opportunity to send her back, although she does not wish to return.

As her brother speaks French, he can, with a passport from you, come to seek her, and it will not be my fault if he does not take her back. I will give him every possible help, and the change of her religion shall not be a strong enough reason to oblige me to keep her."

Perhaps he was seeking that opportunity when he took her to Montreal where she was a guest at the Hôtel-Dieu, and to Three Rivers where she stayed with the Ursulines.

At Montreal, in October, 1711, she was sponsor for Abigail Stebbins' child, Dorothée de Noyon, and she probably saw there her aunt Hannah Parsons and her Sayward cousins.

According to a Wheelwright tradition one of the governor's sons wished to marry her,[46] but the convent call was imperative, and Vaudreuil yielding, she began her novitiate in October, 1712. The following January she took the white veil.

Père Bigot, like a true father, bore the expense of the occasion, as he did of all those connected with her entrance into the religious life. The *dot* at about this period was thirty-five hundred francs. Urgent letters came from her family — probably brought by John Schuyler in 1713 — "but the voice of grace was louder than that of nature, and she found strength to resist." She begged the bishop to hasten the day of her final vows. Bishop and Governor assenting her term of probation was shortened by nearly a year; the first and perhaps only time that the rules of the Community were thus

[45] "Can. Arch. Cor. Gén.," Vol. 32, 119-123.

[46] Which of the ten children was it, Louis Philippe, Philippe Antonie or Jean?

broken. They may have wished to spare the young novice further temptation for in "the old manuscript" of the convent it is written that: "Some English from Boston having come, they brought letters from her family; . . . [and] in the fear that her relatives might make greater efforts to see her again, it was decided to advance her profession."

On the morning of April 12th, 1714, in the Chapel of the Ursulines, which was decorated as for the greatest festival, in the presence of the Marquis de Vaudreuil and of the *élite* of Quebec, Esther Wheelwright was invested with the black robe and veil of their order by the Sisters of St. Ursula.

Father Bigot's sermon was from the text, "Thy hand shall lead me, and thy right hand shall hold me." He showed Esther "by what marvels of God's goodness" she had been "transplanted from a sterile and ingrate land . . . to one of blessing and promise," and admonished the nuns to be very tender to this young stranger because their Immortal Bridegroom went so far to seek her, and thus "the young New England captive, known thereafter as Sister Esther Marie Joseph of the Infant Jesus, serenely turned her face away forever from her childhood's home and friends."[47] Contrast this day of pomp when John Wheelwright's daughter became "the bride of Jesus" with the wedding day of her eighteen-year-old sister Hannah when she married Elisha Plaisted. It was one month later at their home in Wells. Nearly two hundred Indians were attracted to the place by the merry-making. They stole some horses belonging to the guests and shot the men who went in search of them. The shots made known their presence to the rest of the company. The bridegroom, not backward in his duty, joined in the pursuit, and alas! he was captured with one other, but after a few days he was ransomed at Richmond Island.[48]

[47] True Stories, p. 56.

[48] He took his bride to Portsmouth. Mr. Edmund M. Wheelwright, not giving his authority, says in "A Frontier Family"; "John Plaisted their son, when a lad was captured by Indians and carried to Canada."

Sr Esther m Joseph De L'Enfant Jesus

In 1739 John Wheelwright wrote in his will: "I give and bequeath to my daughter Ester Wheelwright, if living in Canada whom I have not heard of for this many years and hath been absent for more then thirty yeares, if it should please God that She return to this country and settle here, then my will is that my foure sons . . . each of them pay her Twenty Five pounds . . . within six months after her Return and Settlement."

He died in August, 1745. Perhaps his daughter did not know it until two years later. Then she sent the following letter to her mother:[49]

"Madame my dear Mother

I am much obliged to you for the Favour you did me in honouring me with one of your letters, which I received the 23d of this month, and which hath been faithfully interpreted unto me by a Person of Vertue. And as Providence over-rules and governs all things has had a particular regard unto me, and assisted me in all my wayes, this is what ought to lessen your cares and concerns for me in beholding me living in a distant Country. You know my dear Mother that the Lot which I have chosen hath been that of consecrating myself wholly unto the Lord, to whom I belong without reserve, being bound by Obligations which 'tis impossible for me to break . . . Thus you See my lovely Mother the impossibility there is of complying with the desire you have of my return to you. It hath been always an infinite trouble to me to resist a desire which you and my Dear Father have so often repeated in times past, but I hope the Lord to whom I have devoted myself will greatly reward me from his infinite goodness, since he himself assures us in his holy word that he who leaves for his sake, Father, Mother, Brothers and Sisters, shall have an hundred fold in this life, and Life eternal in the next. Methinks I have been for a long time in the possession of this happy reward since I want nothing necessary as to Temporals, and as to Spirituals such con-

[49] Printed here through the courtesy of Mr. George A. Plimpton.

tinual favours do I receive from heaven that are beyond expression.

Oh, what joy, what pleasure, what consolation would it give me, my dear Mother if you had the happiness of knowing this holy religion which a kind providence hath made me embrace since I left you. An established religion which our Forefathers professed for a long time with much need and fervour until the happy Schisme. This moment one comes and tells me he is obliged to depart, wch. obliges me to finish Sooner than I intended. However I cannot forbear saying I am greatly affected with the news of the death of my father, whom I loved so tenderly, and whom I shall never forget, and I shall always share with you in the trouble of so grievous a seperation. Be persuaded that I shall not cease daily to pray to the Lord Jehovah to be himself your strength, your support and your consolation during this Life, and that we shall have one day the happiness of meeting together in a *blessed and glorious Eternity*. This is what I wish from the bottom of my heart . . . Adieu, my dear Mother, until I have an opportunity to write more largely unto you, but before I finish my Epistle permit me to assure you of my tender attachment and Sincere regard to all my relations, especially to my Brethren and Sisters, whom I embrace a thousand times, and you more tenderly than any one, being with all love and possible Respect, Madam, my Dear Mother

Your very humble
and very obedient
daughter and Servant
Esther Wheelwright.
Quebeck 26 Septem^r 1747"

"To Deacon Pierce

Sr.

According to your desire I have translated and Sent you

Mrs. Wheelwright's Letter which she wrote to her Mother, and sent her by the Flag of Truce

I am Sr
Your friend
and very humble
Servt

Wm. Smith."

Both parents ignored their child's irrevocable vows. Her mother made her will in 1750—she died five years later, which "furthermore Provided my beloved Daughter Eesther Wheelwright who has been many years in Canada is yet living and should by the Wonder working Providence of God be returned to her Native Land and tarry & dwell in it I Give & bequeath unto her one fifth Part of my estate which I have already by this Instrument will[d] should be divided to and among my afores[d] Daughters & Grand Daughters to be paid by them in Proportion to their Respective Shares in the above mentioned Division, unto her my s[d] Daughter Esther Wheelwright within one year after my decease. Any thing above written in this Instrument to the Contrary in any wise notwithstanding."

Major Nathaniel Wheelwright of Boston was twice our messenger concerning the exchange of prisoners. In 1754 he saw his aunt within the cloister,[50] for the Bishop "Kindly granted the entrance to the Convent to the said Monsieur Ouilleret hoping that it might result in his conversion."[51]

Of this visit Major Wheelwright wrote in his journal:[52] "Jan. 26. This day with the leave of the Bishop, I had the honour to visit the Convent of the Ursulines, in which is my aunt Esther Wheelwright, who is now called La mère de L'Enfant Jesus. I was very politely received and Genteely entertained with Variety

[50] A visitor in the *parloir* can see the face, but cannot touch the hand of an Ursuline Sister, the double gratings of the *grille* prevent.

[51] "*Les Ursulines de Québec,*" II, 327.

[52] The manuscript was given with the Belknap Papers to the Mass. Hist. Soc. in 1791.

of wines & sweetmeats, the next morning they sent me a very Genteel desart. They are conveniently Lodged, each one hath her separate appartment, with a small bed, a table, & one Chair, nothing but what is necessary, the Church is very handsomly adorned, and their Chapels, in which are very curious embroidery, all of their own work." At a later date he wrote that he went often to visit his aunt, who was of a cheerful disposition, "and as she thought she might confide in me as a friend and near Relation she gave me a particular account of her being detained in Canada after she got out of the hands of the Indians, and the reason why she was not returned according to the desire of her Father and the promise of Mons. La Marquis de Vaudreuille . . . who received her as a present from the Indians." This contradicts the statement that M. de Vaudreuil spent fourteen hundred livres for her ransom and other expenses, and that he was reimbursed by the priest with money sent by "a Lady in France to make a nun," but Esther may have forgotten the facts or Major Wheelwright may have misunderstood her story.

Perhaps it was he who carried to her the miniature of her mother. From "the old manuscript" we learn that he brought a beautiful *couvert* of silver — which bears the family arms — and a cup of the same metal; this is still used in the infirmary. The miniature, changed into a Madonna by the addition of a veil, is reverently preserved in their chapel. This is a common device as a means of preserving a family portrait by one who has entered a convent.

It must have been soon after Major Wheelwright's visits that Mrs. Johnson — of Charlestown — saw Mother Esther, when she went to see the Phips girls who were pupils in the convent. She wrote: "We here found two aged English ladies who had been taken in former wars. One by the name of Wheelwright who had a brother in Boston on whom she requested me to call, if ever I went to that place. I complied with her request afterwards and received many civilities from her brother."

During the siege of Quebec most of the Sisters, together with those of the Hôtel-Dieu and many women and children of the town, took refuge at the General Hospital, a mile beyond the walls.

Esther may have been one of the brave eight who remained in the Convent and who repeated the responses in the service for the dead when Montcalm was buried in front of their altar.

On Dec. 15, 1760, three months after the establishment of English Supremacy in Canada, the first (and last) English Superior of the Ursulines of Quebec was elected.

Mother Esther was worthy of the trust in this difficult time. Letters sent to the Superior at Paris describe the perplexities of new conditions. One of her problems was that of dress.

"We shall very soon be in a condition not to be able to dress ourselves according to the rules. Since the war, we are especially in need of bombazine for our veils. Indeed the need is so pressing, that soon we shall not be able to appear decently, having nothing but rags to cover our heads. We cannot buy these things of the English. They do not yet know how to *coiffer* the nuns. I think, my dear mother, you might send us a few pieces of bombazine by some of our Canadians, who must return to their poor country."

The year after her election Joshua Moody, her sister's son, visited her. By him she sent gifts to her grandniece and namesake and asked that she might be entrusted to her care to be educated, but the suggestion was not accepted by the Puritan parents. By him, too, she sent her own portrait to her family. A few years ago a photograph of this painting was sent back to the Convent through the courtesy of Mr. Edmund M. Wheelwright of Boston.

In 1764 was celebrated her Golden Jubilee, the fiftieth anniversary of her profession. In the chapel, again adorned for a festival, she renewed her vows. It was the Vicar-General who received them, for the Bishop "with all the families and persons of distinction, followed the army to Montreal."[53] During mass "many motets were sung" after which the nuns, each bearing a lighted taper, sang a Te Deum, accompanied by a German flute and violin. There was great happiness "The Community and our priests also were treated magnificently" says their historian.

Writing to their Procurator in Paris[54] concerning their finances Mother Esther says they have only what they earn by their embroideries on birch bark which they sell "at a high price to the English gentlemen" and she wishes to know what will be left after paying their indebtedness to the Government, for they had been living upon rations? "We are not lacking in debts," she wrote, "and some pretty large ones. Nobody but myself, however, knows about them and I am in no hurry to acquaint the Community with the fact, for fear of distressing them." This clearly shows her consideration and self-reliance.

Too constant use of her eyes caused weakness of sight and disease. When she could no longer embroider she mended the underclothing of the Community. She was Superior two successive terms — only two are permitted by their rules — and was again re-elected, when seventy-two years old, in 1769.

On the 28 October, 1780, when nearly eighty-five years of age, "She died as she had lived in continual aspirations towards Heaven, repeating unceasingly some verses of the Psalms." Today we see the buildings very much as Esther Wheelwright saw them. Sister Saint-Croix, who had then passed sixty-one years as an Ursuline, wrote in 1896: "Mother Esther de l'Enfant Jésus . . . saw the present church built. It was begun in 1717, finished in 1723. The other buildings date from 1712/13, parlors etc. along the street; novitiate lengthening the wing Holy Family; in short the Monastery completed as I saw it in 1835."

From the garden "you see the choir or nuns' chapel in which Esther recited the Divine offices, heard Mass and prayed, I am

[53] "Hôpital-Général," 353.

[54] The procurator, who was a Jesuit, looked after their wants, their Mother-Superior in Paris choosing their clothing.

certain, very devoutly. There the venerable mother celebrated the golden jubilee of profession, and there took place her burial service and burial."

1708, *April* 22.

LITTLEFIELD, JOSIAH, s. of Capt. John and Patience.

The road between Wells and York was wooded and full of peril; yet men had to traverse it. Lieutenant Littlefield, who lived at Batcomb in the part of Wells nearest York, while making the journey with Joseph Winn was seized by four Indians. His friend escaped. Littlefield was a millman and engineer and was much needed in the little community. The Indians took him first to Norridgewock, then to Quebec and Montreal, whence on June second he wrote to his "Dear and loving children" and to the Governor asking that two Indian prisoners be sent in exchange for himself and "Wheelrite's Child." In the autumn of 1709 he was released, but trying to make his way home through the wilderness was recaptured by "a canady Indian," who sold him to one of Norridgewock! The latter was "like a father" to him and Littlefield promised "payment for the love he bare" him.

To secure this payment and his own release he sent a letter to his cousin, Thomas Barber,[55] asking for hogsheads of meat, corn and pease; rum, cider and tobacco: blue broadcloth and some of a sad color; cotton, lace for coats, four pairs of shoes with French soles and a good suit of clothes for himself. The Indians wanted Joseph Bane to bring the sloop to "Sacaty Hock," for they would have no other man if he were living, "and if not some other good onest Man." For himself he asked Captain Moody, to whose care the letters were sent, for "an old Cot [coat] and a pair of Stockins, and a little solt, if it be but a pound or two." He asks him to be kind to the Indian messengers for one is his master.

Dudley says that Bane can go to release Littlefield, but after giving the order he learns of the generous list of articles desired by the Indians, which Captain Moody had not mentioned. Then

[55] Arch. 51, 182.

Bane's instructions are changed. Littlefield must be "delivered without any purchase," and Moody is blamed for the suppression, for which he later humbly apologizes to the Governor and Council.

Dudley wrote Feb. 15, 1709/10, that he always pitied a prisoner in Indian hands yet, he says, "no Circumstance of that nature has yet altered my resolution [never to buy a prisoner of an Indian] lest we make a market for our poor women & children in the frontiers."[56]

On Feb. 3, 1709, very detailed "Instructions to Lieut. Joseph Bean" are given: He is "to make sayle in Samuel Hill's sloop [Goodwill] to lay off as Safe as he can, to remain three days going on Shoar every day and if nothing appear to return . . . and discharge the Sloop." If the Indians did appear he was to meet them with a flag of truce and his instructions open in his hand; to demand Littlefield "and receive him kindly in their presence." If they have anything to say let Littlefield write and the sagamores sign it. "Take leave of them Friendly and tell them if they have anything further to say, they may send Safely to Casco Fort, where the Governor's answer shall be as soon as may be." Ask about "that great news they Speak about in their Letter from Canada and tell them if they want news that the French King is Beaten everywhere." Signed: Dudley.[57] In Council, twelve days later, His Excellency repeated his Direction to Captain Moody that he insist upon the delivery of Littlefield without any purchase—that is, if the Indians showed themselves—and "to Tell 'em" that he will report what they desire his Excellency to know from them.[58]

Poor Littlefield must have found all this very discouraging, but at last the Indians did bring him in with no promises given, trusting that the Governor would "do what was right."

Two years later he was killed by Indians who were still lurking

56 Arch. 51, 187. 57 Arch. 71, 741.

58 Arch. 71, 616.

about in the forest; "a Person very much lamented" says Penhallow.

During his captivity the Court appointed a custodian for his children and his property. This caused a controversy after his return, which, leading from one thing to another, was continued by different members of the families involved for fifty years.

Mr. Bourne criticizes his second wife, Elizabeth (Hilton), who may have been unduly tenacious of her own rights, "not having much of that meek, quiet and peaceable spirit which becomes the female sex . . . for it seems she ruled the family without any deference to the teachings of the Bible."

RUSSELL, THOMAS OR SAMUEL?

Thomas Russell's name is on the list of 1710/11. Among the names of some prisoners taken in 1709[59] is: "The last prisoner that was made was brought to Quebec about a week agoe [the letter is dated October 3] he was taken from Wels, Saml Russell by name, but they have misused him much for he being shott into the arme and more than that it was the Lord Intendant that sent them and gave them 600 livres for to take an English prisoner. He is now att the Hospital att Quebec etc."[60]

1712, *April.*

WOODBURY, NICHOLAS, of Ipswich.

Was he the son of Isaac, Jr., and Elizabeth, baptized at Beverly, Aug. 12, 1688? His is an oft-repeated name in the family, but Isaac's Nicholas is the only one to fit.

The first word concerning him seems to be in the draft of a letter to Vaudreuil from Dudley, dated Apr. 15, 1717.[61] It is headed: "Nicholas Woodberry about the 3 Rivers St. Francis Servt to an Old Squaw, taken at Wells." Governor Dudley wrote: "Monsr Since my arrivall to this Government I am informed that not-

59 See Gilman in Exeter, Chapter XII, for Major Lloyd's letter.

60 Calendar of State Papers. Colonial Papers, 1710-11.

61 Arch. 2, 638.

withstanding the mutuall Stipulation for restoring the Captives taken on both Sides in the time of the War & which has been faithfully complyed with on the part of the English, there are yet severall English Captives rem^{g} within ye Government & particularly one Nicholas Woodberry said to be somewhere about the three Rivers or Fort St Francois in the hands & Custody of an old Indian Squaw who hires him out to Work, the Friends of s^{d} Woodberry making their application to me that I would use my Interest to forward his return." And he desires (according to the Justice of the matter) that Vaudreuil give directions to such as have Woodberry in custody that he deliver him "to the person imployed by his friends to go in search of him." The letter brought no immediate result as is shown by the captive's story, dated December, 1720.[62] He certifies that in November, 1711, he was impressed into the service and sent to the Eastward under Captain Hermon. He served until the following April when he was captured "by Indians at Wells & carried to Canada, where he cut his Leg & remains yet very lame & a few Days since after Nine Years Captivity return'd Home, During which time he endured many Hardships & at last was obliged to pay Thirty two pounds for his Ransom. Besides the Charge his Father was at to Hire two Persons to go to Canada to treat about his Freedom, which amounted to about Fifty pounds more."

Sixty pounds was allowed for his expenses and injuries and it was resolved that he "be Recommended and Improved as an Interpreter of the Indian Languages as there may be occasion."[63]

Was he the Nicholas who married Elizabeth Thorn in November, 1722, to whom another Nicholas was born in 1729/30?[64]

62 Prov. Laws, X, 46.

63 House Jour., 1718-1720, p. 316.

64 "Genealogical Sketches" of the family says that the captive was made an interpreter.

Ursuline Convent